THE TRANSFORMATION OF
COASTAL WETLANDS

Exploitation and Management of Marshland Landscapes
in North West Europe during the Roman and Medieval Periods

Reconstruction drawing, by Kelvin Wilson, of an Early Roman 'duiker' (sluice-gate) and dam at Vlaardingen, The Netherlands (reproduced by permission of Jeroen ter Brugge, Rijksdienst voor het Oudheidkundig Bodemonderzoek).

The Transformation of Coastal Wetlands

Exploitation and Management of Marshland Landscapes
in North West Europe during the Roman and Medieval Periods

Stephen Rippon

A British Academy
Postdoctoral Fellowship Monograph

Published for THE BRITISH ACADEMY
by OXFORD UNIVERSITY PRESS

Oxford University Press, Great Clarendon Street, Oxford OX2 6DP

Oxford New York
Athens Auckland Bangkok Bogotá Bombay
Buenos Aires Calcutta Cape Town Dar es Salaam
Delhi Florence Hong Kong Istanbul Karachi
Kuala Lumpur Madras Madrid Melbourne
Mexico City Nairobi Paris Singapore
Taipei Tokyo Toronto Warsaw

and associated companies in
Berlin Ibadan

Published in the United States by
Oxford University Press Inc., New York

British Library Cataloguing in Publication Data
Data available

ISBN 0–19–726229–5

Typeset by Wyvern 21 Ltd, Bristol
Printed in Great Britain
on acid-free paper by
Bookcraft (Bath) Limited
Midsomer Norton, Somerset

Contents

List of Figures

List of Tables

Preface

There are many ways by which human communities can chose to exploit their landscape, depending upon a wide range of variables within the natural and cultural environment. In an earlier study of the Severn Estuary region in South West Britain, the author noted marked spatial and temporal variation in how what were basically the same type of landscape—coastal marshes—were used over the Roman and medieval periods. A British Academy Postdoctoral Research Fellowship gave the opportunity for exploring this theme over a much wider area, to encompass the rest of southern and eastern Britain and the coast of mainland North West Europe. What was revealed is that these wetlands cannot be studied in isolation: human communities living in such environments were part of far wider social, political, and economic systems that had a profound effect upon the decisions as to how such physically very harsh environments should be used. As such, a comparative study of one type of landscape that occurs in a wide range of regions can be used to shed light on issues of far wider significance.

The research which forms the basis of this study was carried out whilst the author was a British Academy Postdoctoral Research Fellow at the Universities of Reading and Exeter, and I am extremely grateful to my friends and colleagues at both places for their inspiration and encouragement. In particular, I would like to thank John Allen, John Coles, and Michael Fulford for their helpful comments on earlier drafts of various chapters. A study of this type inevitably involves the synthesis of a wide range of data, and I am particularly grateful to those scholars from mainland Europe who have assisted in this, notably in Belgium (M. Dewilde, D. Tys), The Netherlands (J. Besteman, T. Bloemers, P. Van den Broeke, J. Bos, J ter Brugge, D. Gerrets, H. Groenendijk, J.-K. Hagers, W. Hessing, H. Van Londen, T. de Ridder, and P. Van Rijn), and Germany (K.-E. Behre, J. Ey, E. Strahl, and H. Zimmermann). Translations have kindly been provided by Terry Green, Melissa Percival, Carlyn Van Ravenstein, and Laetitia de Wijkerslooth. I am also grateful to Stephen Coleman for information regarding the 'saltways' of Bedfordshire, Bob Delderfield for access to his research into the estates of Westminster Abbey in South East Essex, David Hall and Tom Lane for information regarding the English Fenland, Elaine Morris for access to her thoughts on early salt production and Ken Steedman for unpublished data on the Hull area.

SJR, Exeter, August 1999

Acknowledgements

Certain illustrations were reproduced by kind permission of the following: Figures 29 and 37: Robert van Dierendonck (Provincial Archeologisch Centrum Zeeland); Figures 30–4: Tim de Ridder (Vlaardingen Archeologisch Kantoor); Figures 38 and 46: Heleen Van Londen (University of Amsterdam); Figures 38 and 80: Peter Vos (Nederlands Instituut voor Toegepaste Geowetenschappen TNO); Figure 39: Rog Palmer; Figure 40: Stephen Penney (Cheshire County Council Museum Service); Figure 45: Tim Potter (British Museum); Figure 60: Bob Silvester/Norfolk Archaeological Unit; Figure 77: David Strachan (Essex County Council); Figure 79: National Monuments Record/Ministry of Defence.

List of Abbreviations

AD	calendar date after Christ (or calibrated radiocarbon date)
BAR	British Archaeological Reports
BB1	South East Dorset Black Burnished Ware pottery
BC	calendar date before Christ (or calibrated radiocarbon date)
Bede	*A History of the English Church and People* (Sherley-Price 1968)
BP	uncalibrated radiocarbon date 'before present' (1950)
Bristol Charters I	Harding 1930
Bristol Charters II	Cronne 1945
Bristol Trade	Carus-Wilson 1936
BROB	*Berichten van de Rijksdienst voor het Oudheidkundig Bodemonderzoek* (Netherlands State Archaeological Service, Amersfoort)
CBA	Council for British Archaeology
CChR	*Calendar of Charter Rolls* (PRO, London)
CIPM	*Calendar of Inquisitions Post Mortem* (PRO, London)
CPR	*Calendar of Patent Rolls* (PRO, London)
CRR	*Curia Regis Rolls* (PRO, London)
DB Gloucs	Gloucestershire *Domesday Book* (Moore 1982)
ERO	Essex Records Office
FF Essex	*Feet of Fines for Essex*, 4 vols (Kirk 1899–1910; 1913–28; 1929–49; Reaney and Fitch 1964)
FF Kent	*Feet of Fines for Kent* (Churchill *et al.*1956)
HAT	Highest astronomical tide
Hist. Man. Comm.	Historic Manuscripts Commission
MHWST	Mean High Water Spring Tide
Milton 1299	Nichols 1932
Milton 1309	Nichols 1926–8
NMR	National Monuments Record (English Heritage, Swindon)
OE	Old English
OD	Ordnance Datum (a measure of mean sea level in Britain)
ON	Old Norse

PRO	Public Records Office, London
RCHME	Royal Commission on the Historical Monuments of England (now part of English Heritage)
Red Book	*The Great Red Book of Bristol* (Veale 1937)
SMR	Sites and Monuments Record
S.00	Number of Anglo-Saxon charter in Sawyer 1968
St Augustine's	Sabin 1960
WAM	Westminster Abbey Muniments (Westminster Abbey Muniments Room)
WD	Westminster Domesday (Westminster Abbey Muniments Room)
VCH	Victoria County History

CHAPTER 1

Introduction:

taming the wetland wilderness

God created the sea, the Frisians created the land (Larsen 1997: 1)

1.1 Introduction

This is a study of how human communities decided to increase the intensity with which they exploited one particular type of environment—coastal wetlands—during the Roman and medieval periods. Any change in how an environment is exploited entails certain costs, risks, and benefits, making for a complex decision-making process on the part of those human communities. Traditionally, when any two landscapes are used in different ways explanation is sought in terms of the natural environment, but such a physically deterministic approach usually overshadows equally significant, but less obvious, cultural variables. To really understand the 'human factor' we need to minimize variations in the natural landscape, and so this study examines mankind's varying strategies towards the exploitation and management of the same type of environment that occurs in a wide variety of locations. As such, any variations over time and space in how human communities chose to use this landscape type must to a considerable extent be down to socio-economic factors.

There are three broad ways in which human communities can use coastal marshes, each of which involve increasing productivity. The first is simply *exploiting* what was naturally on offer (Figure 1). In their unaltered state these wetlands offer a wide range of resources: coastal saltmarshes can support rich seasonal grazing and offer the opportunity to produce salt, while freshwater backfens further inland can yield building and craft materials (willow, reeds, and rushes), food (fish and wildfowl), and fuel (peat).

The second strategy is to increase the landscape's natural productivity by physically *modifying* it, most notably through the control of water. This can be achieved by locally enhancing drainage by digging ditches, or the construction of low banks that improve conditions during the summer and so lengthening the grazing season. However, such areas remain vulnerable to flooding and, as a result, minor modifications such as these were eventually taken even further through a more dramatic *transformation* of the landscape: the construction of a sea wall to keep out the tides all year round, and the

1. Intertidal mudflats grading into saltmarshes looking south-east from Middlehope towards Worlebury (background), North Somerset (NGR: ST 325 655). Coastal wetlands such as these offer a wide range of natural resources includ-ing seasonal grazing and the opportunity for salt production.

digging of a more complex drainage system to control water levels on the newly protected land (Figure 2). This was a costly and complex undertaking, and this study examines where, when, and why coastal wetlands were exploited, modified, and ultimately transformed, and the wider socio-economic context in which these decisions were made during the Roman and medieval periods.

1.2 Holding back the tides — pushing back the margins?

The transformation of tidal saltmarshes into freshwater agricultural land is traditionally known as 'reclamation' (cf. Allen 1997c prefers 'land claim'): 'the process of physically restructuring the environment ... by simplifying or eliminating existing flora and fauna, as well as by reshaping and contouring the landscape so as to make it more amenable to a human presence' (TeBrake 1985: 22). A simpler definition is to 'bring under cultivation esp. from state of being flooded by sea or marsh' (*The Concise Oxford Dictionary of Current English* 1976). The term can also be used in dryland contexts to imply the creation of new agricultural land, for example, through the clearance of heathland or woodland (e.g. P. W. Cox and Hearne 1991: 8; Hallewas

2. Reclaimed marshland in Brean, Central Somerset, looking north-west across the River Axe (bottom: see Figure 20) (NGR: ST 30 57). Brean Down can be seen extending into the Severn Estuary. The embankment and subsequent drainage of coastal wetlands entail a major transformation of the landscape, with intertidal saltmarshes being replaced by a range of freshwater environments. However, reclamation permits the use of these marshlands for far more intensive cultivation.

1984: 299; Roberts 1996; TeBrake 1985: 12), or the construction of riverside waterfronts (e.g. Milne 1981; 1987).

This study examines the decision to reclaim coastal marshes and the wider context in which this policy was adopted. In recent centuries, marshland landscapes have not been viewed very favourably due to their waterlogged soils and damp air. For example, Hasted (1797–1801) said of Chalk (near Gravesend) on the North Kent coast that 'Its contiguity to so large an extent of marshes, to which its situation is wholly exposed, makes it accounted very unhealthy, and much subject to agues, particularly in Autumn.' Traditionally such landscapes have been regarded as 'marginal': not really suited to settled agriculture and so only exploited at times when conditions such as population pressure on the surrounding areas forced people to settle less desirable land. However, the rather negative view of wetland landscapes described by post-medieval writers contrasts with the evidence we have from earlier periods, illustrated, for example, by fourteenth century land valuations which show that reclaimed marshlands were often as highly valued e.g. Fenland (Darby 1983: fig. 16; Glasscock 1973: fig. 41) or, in some cases, much more highly valued e.g. Somerset (Glasscock 1973: fig. 35; M. Williams 1970: 75–9) than the adjacent dryland areas.

The traditional view of marginality and the 'population resource model' developed by Postan 1972) has had a major impact on the ways in which archaeologists and historians have studied the rural landscape. In recent years the model has been subject to considerable critical analysis (e.g. M. Bailey 1989; Dyer 1990), though it has also been argued that the basic concept is still of some use (e.g. Rippon 1997a; R. Young and Simmonds 1995). However, there is certainly a need to move away from the traditional idea of 'marginality', with all its negative connotations, and think more positively of 'landscape potential' (Table 1). Indeed, a central theme of this study is how human societies decided to exploit the potential of a particular landscape type, with both agricultural and non-agricultural resources being considered alongside physical and cultural facets of that landscape and its hinterland.

Postan envisaged an area as being 'marginal' if physical disadvantages such as poor soils or high altitude led to it only being settled and farmed at times of high population pressure. However, neither the physical landscape nor environmental conditions are constant as both can change over time. Such changes, for example, in climate could also affect different areas in different ways. For example, an increase in rainfall would make cultivation increasingly difficult in regions with very heavy soils, whereas it may be beneficial in areas with light, dry soils. A fall in temperature may make the growing season in upland areas so short as to make cultivation impossible, while in low-lying locations changes in temperature would have been far less significant (though the decreased evapo-transpiration would have had a different impact upon heavy and light soils). The capabilities of soil can also change over time for the better (e.g. desalinification) or the worse (e.g. podsolization or erosion). Many areas that are cultivated today may not have been so readily in the past simply because techniques such as liming, marling, under-drainage, and mechanization have made them more suited to modern agriculture. For example, coastal wetlands in their unreclaimed state are undoubtedly *physically* marginal in terms of agriculture: the soils are saline making them unfavourable to cereal cultivation, the potential growing season is short, and the risk of prolonged flooding is high. However, 'physical marginality' can change, as, for example, following the construction of a sea wall, and the digging of an effective drainage system, the former saltmarsh will quickly lose its salt and become ideal for arable, pasture, or meadow.

Bailey (1989) has shown that there is also a considerable range of *cultural* factors in addition to agrarian technology that determine how the rural resources of any area are exploited. For example, during the majority of the Roman and medieval periods covered by this study there was a market economy, or at least a well-stratified society within which part of a region's surplus agricultural production was taken as tribute or taxation. As a result, the location of an area of land with respect to centres of consumption and the transportation network was of great importance when it came to decisions regarding how that land should be exploited. Thus, in a market economy, areas of fertile soil may not have been cultivated if they lay a long distance from the nearest town, yet an area of poorer soil may have been farmed if it lay close to a potential market (M. Bailey 1989).

Landscape exploitation was not, however, just about market economics as certain *social and political systems* also affected a region's potential. For example, periods of unrest and instability were not conducive to investment in agriculture, although the aftermath of migration, invasion, and conquest often was. Another key issue was who took the initiative in landscape change: were major events such as reclamation and the replanning of settlement patterns and field systems necessarily the work of a powerful lord or landowner, or were local communities capable of such undertakings? Documentary sources from the thirteenth and fourteenth centuries show that villagers were able to collectively manage their landscape (Dyer 1985; 1990; P. Harvey 1989), but there is a great difference between the day-by-day running of an existing system of rural-resource exploitation, and its wholesale replacement with another.

There is also a very considerable difference between the members of one community managing their own affairs, and several communities collaborating with each other in a major piece of engineering such as the construction of a sea wall. Indeed, common rights over certain resources, such as pasture, may have prevented enclosure in certain wetland areas long after economic factors on their own would suggest that improvement should have taken place (e.g. Roffe 1993*a*). The same phenomena is seen in dryland areas as the system of open field agriculture proved very conservative in certain areas, providing relatively few opportunities for individual tenants to experiment or improve their land (which they only held for a year). In contrast, where land was enclosed and held in severalty, there was much greater freedom and encouragement to innovate and invest in agriculture, which proved to be particularly important during periods of economic decline (e.g. M. Bailey 1989).

Another aspect of 'marginality', therefore, is the tenurial context within which resources were exploited and the relationship between common and private rights. When examining changes in how landscapes were used in the past it is important to know who was taking the initiative. In terms of the expansion of settlement into previously unoccupied areas there are three possible scenarios: first, free farmers who may have been able to colonize wilderness or waste areas on their own initiative; second, tenants who colonized land in the context of a lord's estate but without the direct involvement of that lord in shaping the landscape; and third, settlement expansion which occurred as a planned colonization organized by the lord or their agent. The estate structure within which marshlands were exploited is discussed further in Chapters 3 and 11.

Finally, when considering the marginality, or rather landscape potential, of a region we should always consider *non-agricultural resources*. A good example is Dartmoor in South West Britain, an elevated upland whose thin acidic soils are certainly no longer suited to agriculture, though this was not always the case (Fleming 1988: 89). However, the area is rich in mineral resources—notably tin—and during the medieval period communities there were surprisingly wealthy (Kowaleski 1995). Coastal wetlands also offered a range of non-agricultural resources, including the opportunity for producing salt, though this was clearly not compatible with reclamation: the exploitation of a wetland's natural resources and its transformation through reclamation represent mutually exclusive resource utilization strategies.

An appreciation of the physical, environmental, and cultural dimensions to marginality is critical to our understanding of why settlement expanded and contracted in the wetland regions that are the focus of this study. The traditional model argues that physically 'marginal' environments such as wetlands were only settled when communities in adjacent dryland areas were *forced* to do so, for example, due to over-population, soil exhaustion, or climatic change. However, this view, of people only ever being *pushed* into wetlands, represents a very dryland perspective (Louwe Kooijmans 1993: 71; and see Anthony 1990; 1992; 1997; Chapman and Dolukhaov 1992; Chapman and Hamerow 1997). The alternative way of understanding wetlands is to argue that they had enormous *potential* both in terms of their natural resources and agricultural productivity, but that this potential changed over time due to factors both intrinsic to a specific region and, more generally, society as a whole. For example, the relief, soils, and drainage of a particular area are factors that will affect the landscape potential of that specific region: an improvement in soil condition will pull farming communities towards that area, whereas over-exploitation leading to soil exhaustion will push communities elsewhere. Human communities may also have been attracted to an area if urban development led to an increase in demand for agricultural produce, or the nature of land tenure made that area conducive to investment and innovation. However, none of these factors operated in isolation: we need to look at the wider context of both environmental and cultural change. For example, soil exhaustion may have been the result of expanding population and rising grain prices that encouraged over-exploitation: this would affect many areas of the countryside, but certain soils will be more vulnerable than others. Similarly, urban development occurs because of economic expansion over a very wide area, yet it will have its most profound impact upon the immediate hinterland of individual towns. Thus, landscape potential results from the interaction of factors that are intrinsic to specific regions and wider contextual factors that affected a much wider area.

Overall, the decision to reclaim coastal wetlands was a high *cost*, high *risk*, but high *return* endeavour: high cost in terms of the loss of natural resources, the capital investment in flood defences, and the subsequent maintenance they required; high risk in terms of the constant threat of flooding and disease; yet high return in terms of their agricultural yields and connections to market structures through water transport that a coastal location offered. The decision whether or not to reclaim was a complex one and much would depend upon the contemporary view regarding these costs, risks, and benefits, and the imperfect information that existed with which to come to this decision: it was people's perceptions of these factors and other external pressures that was all important. It is also crucial to appreciate that many of these natural and cultural variables can alter over time and that such changes will not affect all areas equally. Market towns can grow and decline, while new transportation systems can emerge as others decay (particularly rivers and estuaries which can silt up). New political and social systems can be introduced which may give particular encouragement to the production of an agricultural surplus, while warfare or political instability may disrupt market structures. The climate can deteriorate or improve, and relative sea level can rise

Table 1. Factors determining landscape potential

	Push/pull factors (intrinsic to a specific region)	Contextual factors (affecting many regions)
Physical	Relief/topography Geology/soils Natural drainage	
Environmental		Sea level Climate Temperature Precipitation Weather/storminess
Cultural	Proximity to centres of consumption i.e. military establishments and urban populations	Demography
	Proximity to centres of trade and exchange	Economy/prices State impositions (tax, military service) Agrarian technology

	Tenurial structure
	    nucleated vs. dispersed estates
	    common vs. private rights
	Non-agricultural resources	

and fall. This is the complex and dynamic background against which people had to decide how best to utilize coastal wetlands.

1.3 Why study wetland landscapes?

Wetlands are an inherently important type of landscape as they cover some 6 per cent of the earth's surface (of which *c.* 0.03 per cent are saltmarshes), and around 25 per cent of the world's population currently live within one metre of mean sea level (Devoy 1990: 17; Pethick 1984: 1; M. Williams 1990: 1). Were the sea walls that protect The Netherlands to fail, 65 per cent of the country would be affected by flooding and 25 per cent would be permanently covered by water (Larsen 1997: 2). Reclaimed wetlands also play a vital part in the hydrology, ecology, and economy of many regions yet they have been largely crafted by man-kind and as such, in order to understand how they should be managed in the future, we must understand how they have evolved in the past (Cook and T. Williamson 1999; M. Williams 1990: 15–38).

Despite the post-medieval view of wetlands as rather unhealthy and unproductive places (see above), in the past they were highly valued and recognized as possessing a distinct identity. For example, Romney Marsh forms a physically very discrete landscape within South East Britain (Figure 3) and was recognized as such from at least the eighth century. For example, in AD 774 there is a reference to 'the region called *Merscware*' (Sawyer 1968: no.111), and during AD 796 the Anglo-Saxon Chronicle records that King Ceolwulf of Mercia ravaged the Kingdom of Kent and reached 'as far

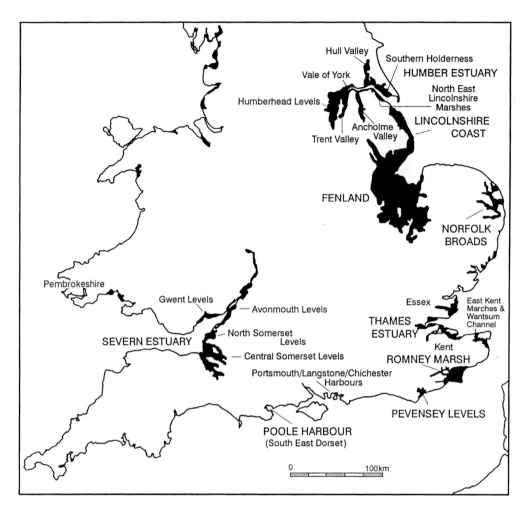

3. Coastal wetlands around Britain considered in this study. (Drawn by Sue Rouillard.)

as the marsh' (Swanton 1996: 57). In AD 838, it is recorded that 'this year alderman Herebryth was slain by the heathens, and many men with him, amongst the Marshlanders' (Swanton 1996: 62). Clearly, Romney Marsh and its occupants were already recognized as being a distinctive and important part of the Kentish landscape.

Wetlands are also important because they can yield a wealth of exceptionally well-preserved information about their past. The excellent preservation of archaeological material and palaeoenvironmental evidence in wetland contexts was recognized as far back as the mid-nineteenth century following the discovery of the Swiss 'lake villages' (see J. Coles 1984). Further spectacular discoveries followed in Britain, including the Glastonbury settlement in Somerset (see J. Coles and Minnitt 1995) and Star Carr in the Vale of Pickering (Yorkshire) (Clark 1954). From the 1930s Fenland became the first area of coastal wetland in Britain to be subjected to a co-ordinated programme of

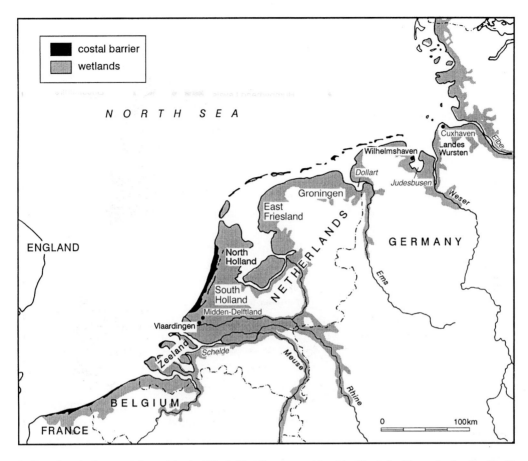

4. Coastal wetlands around the mainland of North West Europe considered in this study. (Drawn by Sue Rouillard.)

archaeological fieldwork and palaeoenvironmental analysis (Phillips 1970), just as systematic programmes of research started in both The Netherlands and Germany (see below). Further advances in British wetland archaeology were made during the 1970s with John and Bryony Coles's pioneering work in the Somerset Levels (B. Coles and J. Coles 1989), which has been followed by major surveys in Fenland (D. Hall and J. Coles 1994; J. Coles and D. Hall 1997), North West England (Howard-Davis *et al.* 1988; Leah *et al.* 1997), around the Humber Estuary (Van de Noort and Davies 1993; Van de Noort and Ellis 1995; 1997; 1998; 1999), and in South East Wales (Bell and Neumann 1995; 1997; Rippon 1996a) (Figure 3). The excellent documentary material that survives for a number of monastic houses that held extensive estates in wetland areas has also led to a number of pioneering studies in landscape history (e.g. Darby 1940a; b; H. Hallam 1954; 1965; J. Sheppard 1958; 1966; R. A. L. Smith 1940; 1943; Williams 1970).

In the north-west of mainland Europe there is an equally long tradition of archaeological and documentary research into wetland areas (Figure 4). During the

1930s fears over the subsidence of coastal areas in northern Germany led to the establishment of the *Niedersächsisches Institut für historische Küstenforschung* (Lower Saxony Institute for Historical Coastal Research) at Wilhelmshaven, which has combined sedimentological, palaeoenvironmental, and archaeological techniques in order to reconstruct the geomorphological and settlement history of the coastal marshlands of North West Germany (Behre 1990*a*). In The Netherlands, until the 1930s, it was assumed that the coastal regions were not settled before the medieval period, though excavations beneath raised *terpen* settlements in East Friesland and Groningen have since revealed their late prehistoric origins (Van Giffen 1936). As in Germany, there then developed a long tradition of interdisciplinary research which has allowed the history of environmental change and human occupation of these wetland landscapes to be reconstructed in considerable detail (e.g. Besteman *et al.* 1999; Henderikx 1986; Vos and Van Heeringen 1997).

Most of the extensive coastal wetlands of North West Europe have now seen major programmes of archaeological and documentary-based research, but what has been lacking is a comparative study covering the Roman and medieval periods to match those that have been produced for the prehistoric period (e.g. B. Coles 1992; J. Coles and Lawson 1987). This study will hopefully start to redress the imbalance.

However, simply because there is a wealth of data in one particular area does not in itself justify studying that region. Indeed, it might also be argued that physically 'marginal' landscapes are so unlike the majority of dryland areas that it is impossible to discover anything other than that which is merely of only local interest. This is not the case. There is, in practice, no such thing as a 'typical' landscape—chalklands differ from claylands which differ from heathlands—and coastal wetlands are simply yet another physically—distinctive landscape that offers a range of potential strategies towards their utilization. As a physically 'marginal' environment, coastal wetlands also represent an ideal landscape-type with which to examine the responses of human communities to changing social, economic, and environmental conditions. Indeed, the impact of these variables may be clearer in such areas, compared with 'core regions' that were permanently settled irrespective of such changing conditions. Wetlands also provide an ideal context in which to study the processes behind the formation of cultural landscapes. Coastal marshes are about as close to a wilderness—'nature untamed as opposed to nature tamed'—as there existed in North West Europe by the first millennium AD (C. D. Smith 1996: 154). Their low-lying position had led to a succession of extensive tidal inundations (transgressions) during the post-glacial period, interspersed with times when freshwater conditions predominated and peat formed (regressions). The periods of inundation led to the formation of mudflats and saltmarshes over earlier cultural landscapes, leaving a 'clean slate' upon which later societies could create new fields, roads, and settlements. Uncluttered by the debris from earlier periods, they provide the ideal context in which to study the evolution of these new cultural landscapes. Finally, marshes occur very widely (around most of the coasts of the southern North Sea) and, as such, can be used to examine how a wide range of cultural factors, such as proximity to towns and the structure of landholding, may have influenced the way in which the same type of physical environment was exploited under different sets of socio-economic conditions.

1.4 Definition of a study area

Rather than adopting the traditional approach to landscape study, which has tended to focus upon discrete administrative units such as a parish or county, the intention here is to examine one distinctive type of landscape that is scattered over a very wide area. On the continent there is a long tradition of studying physically, socially, or economically coherent regions (*pays*), and similar areas with distinct regional identities have been recognized within Britain from at least the sixteenth century (Rackham 1986a: 4–5). However, until quite recently such regions were rarely adopted for the purposes of academic research, with scholars preferring instead to study areas based on medieval or even modern administrative boundaries whose relevance to how the landscape was used in the past is doubtful in the least (e.g. the County of Avon which was only created in 1974 Aston and Iles 1987). Studying *pays* can certainly present logistical problems: a recent examination of the Severn Estuary wetlands straddled five counties,[1] which meant visits to five Sites and Monuments Records and five County Records Offices. The same exercise now would involve eight counties.[2] It would have been much easier to study just one county's landscape in greater depth, but then the remarkable diversity in the history of wetland reclamation in different areas around the Severn Estuary would not have been revealed (Rippon 1997a).

In recent years there has been a greater appreciation in Britain of the value in researching *pays* (e.g. Bailey 1989; Everitt 1986; H. Fox 1989) and this study is another example. The areas considered here are derived from mudflats and saltmarshes which were created under tidal and estuarine conditions and that at varying times have been enclosed by embankments and drained (though the water table remains high and the risk of flooding is ever present). Such areas of coastal marsh represent environments with clearly defined boundaries and, as such, make for well-defined study areas. However, when it comes to understanding how they were utilized in the past, should these marshes be viewed in isolation? From at least the early medieval period, when we first have documentary sources that describe patterns of landholding, it is clear that many coastal wetlands were at least partly exploited from settlements on the fen-edge or even further inland, whose estates encompassed both wetland and dryland areas (Figure 18). Though the pattern of estates in the Roman period is far less clear, concentrations of settlements on the fen-edge suggest that, in some areas at least, a similar approach towards land allotment existed, with estates straddling both wetland and dryland zones (see Chapter 6).

---

[1] South Glamorgan, Gwent, Gloucestershire, Avon, and Somerset.
[2] Cardiff, Newport, Monmouthshire, Gloucestershire, South Gloucestershire, Bristol, North Somerset, and Somerset.

It could be argued, therefore, that any study of a coastal wetland should include all the territory of these fen-edge settlements, since the coastal resources were simply one element in the landscape exploitation strategies of those communities. However, some areas of coastal wetland were part of estates based many miles away, such as portions of the Essex marshes that during the medieval period were owned by St Paul's Cathedral in London, or areas of Romney Marsh that belonged to the Archbishop of Canterbury (see Chapters 8, 9, and 11). Clearly, it would be an enormous task to reconstruct the estates of every landholder who held parts of the Essex and Kent marshes, not least because documentary material will only have survived for a small, biased, sample (the major monastic houses). This study concentrates, therefore, on just one type of landed resource within these estates, coastal marshes, rather than the entire estate within which that resource was found. However, it will hopefully be demonstrated that we cannot understand coastal marshes in isolation: the various strategies towards their exploitation and management were heavily dependent upon their regional hinterlands, and the estate structures within which they occurred.

1.5 Outline of this study

This is a study of landscape which aims to examine how different cultural systems interacted with broadly similar environments, resulting in human responses that show marked variations in both time and space. Before this can be achieved the archaeological and documentary evidence for each area must be drawn together as, although a number of comparative studies have been published relating to prehistoric wetlands (e.g. J. Coles and Lawson 1987), it has never been attempted for the Roman and medieval periods. Since this inevitably involves a certain amount of description and synthesis, an attempt has been made to separate this (e.g. Chapters 4, 8, and 9) from the discussion and analysis (e.g. Chapters 5, 6, 10, and 11).

This is the author's third study of coastal wetlands and, as such, must be seen in the context of the preceding two. The first was a detailed examination of the Gwent Levels, beside the Severn Estuary in South East Wales, which illustrates the methodologies that can be used to reconstruct the evolution of any complex landscape, using a wide range of archaeological and documentary material (Rippon 1996a). Following that careful dissection of one particular landscape, the second study took a broader view of the Severn Estuary wetlands as a whole, highlighting the marked variation in landscape utilization strategies evident within even this one region (Rippon 1997a). The aim of this, the third and final volume, is to look at the southern North Sea basin as a whole, and see whether the trends observed around the Severn are repeated in areas with different political, social, and economic histories.

In an ideal world this study would have examined each and every coastal wetland in North West Europe to the same level of detail. In practice, however, this was not possible as the nature and accessibility of archaeological and documentary research varies enormously over the four counties that have been covered (Britain, Belgium, The

Netherlands, and Germany). Discussion will, therefore, focus on four major study areas that possess particularly good evidence (Romney Marsh, Thames Estuary, and Fenland in Britain, with Holland and Zeeland in the western Netherlands), with other areas discussed where they provide illustrative or comparative material for a particular topic (e.g. Poole Harbour, the Pevensey Levels, and Humber Estuary in Britain; the Belgian and German coastal marshes on the continent: Figures 3–4). The Severn Estuary wetlands are only discussed relatively briefly to avoid simply repeating what has been said elsewhere (Rippon 1996a; 1997a). The more scattered areas of coastal marshland around the coasts of Wales and North West Britain are generally excluded because they have not seen the same detailed archaeological and documentary research that has benefited the coastal wetlands of southern and eastern Britain.

Chapter 2 examines the formation of coastal wetlands, including the role of changing sea level, climate, and the weather. Chapter 3 looks at the potential resources that these landscapes offered human communities and the ways that this potential could be realized. Chapter 4 describes the evidence for the use of coastal wetlands during the Roman period when these areas were extensively settled and utilized in a wide range of ways. These data form the basis of two subsequent discussions. Chapter 5 looks at patterns of natural resource exploitation and especially the production of salt, while Chapter 6 examines the agricultural uses to which coastal marshes were put and, in particular, the instances of drainage and reclamation. The extent of post-Roman flooding and settlement desertion is examined in Chapter 7, providing a context for the subsequent recolonization of the marshes in the early medieval period (Chapter 8). Chapter 9 then describes the continued enclosure and drainage during the twelfth to fourteenth centuries while, finally, Chapters 10 and 11 consider certain themes common to the medieval period as a whole, such as natural resource exploitation and just who was responsible for undertaking reclamation.

CHAPTER 2

The formation of marshland landscapes

2.1 Introduction

Coastal wetlands are a particularly dynamic landform, subject to rapid change due to a divers set of factors including long-term fluctuations in relative sea level, short-term events such as storm surges, and human intervention. This chapter is not intended as a definitive account of the geomorphology of low-lying coastal areas, but is simply concerned with certain key issues that affected their utilization by human communities. The major characteristics of each type of coastal wetland covered in this study are described along with an introduction to their formation processes. The impact on coastal wetlands of changes in fluctuating sea level, storm surges, and the climate are considered with particular reference to the ways in which these factors might have affected how human communities could utilize these landscapes. The impact that human communities themselves had through reclamation is also considered.

2.2 Saltmarsh formation (Figures 5–6)

Saltmarshes may be broadly defined as any area 'vegetated by herbs, grasses or low shrubs, bordering [any] saline water bodies' (Adam 1990: 1), though this study is more specifically concerned with coastal marsh 'covered by halophytic vegetation which is regularly flooded by the sea' (Allen and Pye 1992b: vii). Saltmarshes are built up of fine sediments and are formed through a combination of physical (deposition and erosion) and biological (vegetational) processes. The rate of accretion will vary according to numerous factors, including sediment supply, compaction/subsidence, relative sea level, tide heights, and storminess (Ranwell 1972; Reed 1990: 470–2). Initially, unvegetated mudflats will form in sheltered locations relatively low in the intertidal frame and, as the sediment builds up, these flats are colonized by salt-loving plants leading to the creation of a saltmarsh (Figure 1). Over time, the marsh altitude relative to sea level increases, so the period of inundation and rate of sediment deposition is reduced. Eventually, a mature marsh will develop which is so infrequently flooded that it grows

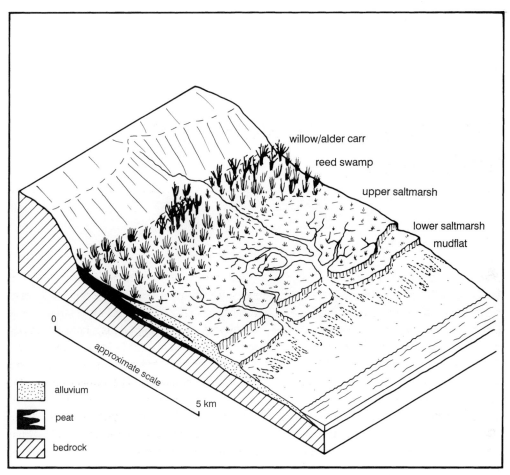

willow/alder carr

reed swamp

upper saltmarsh

lower saltmarsh

mudflat

0

approximate scale

5 km

alluvium

peat

bedrock

5. Schematic cross section through the coastal zone, showing the range of intertidal and freshwater environments (after Silvester 1991: fig. 48; Waller 1994a: fig. 4.1; Wilkinson and Murphy 1995: fig. 2). Note how an episode of erosion has created a small cliff at the edge of the older upper saltmarsh, followed by renewed accretion leading to the creation of a lower marsh.

just a negligible amount but receives sufficient saltwater input to prevent the transition to dryland vegetation. If deposition is the dominant process, then mudflats grade into the saltmarsh (Figure 1). However, periods of deposition are often interrupted by episodes of erosion leading to small cliffs being cut into the edge of the saltmarsh, before deposition of mudflats starts all over again. This leads to the saltmarsh having a stepped profile (Figures 5 and 6).

The coastal saltmarshes are higher than those further inland because, first, they are flooded most often and so see the greatest sediment deposition, and second, because this sediment is also slightly coarser than that laid down further inland since it is transported under higher water-energy conditions. By contrast, the inland parts of the saltmarsh are flooded less often and see finer sediment deposited under lower-energy conditions, with

6. Upper and lower saltmarshes (left) and unvegetated mudflats (right) at Magor Pill, on the Gwent Levels, looking north-east towards the Second Severn Crossing (NGR: ST 440 848).

the result that when a mature saltmarsh is embanked and drained, the lower-lying 'backfen' furthest from the coast will be the most poorly drained area. If this backfen lies beyond the limit of tidal inundation, then freshwater vegetation will develop ranging from reedswamps, through to willow/alder carr woodland.

If relative sea level is rising then the major movement of saltmarshes is upwards, though this is to a certain extent balanced by the consolidation of marsh sediments (Borger 1992; Devoy 1979; Greensmith and Tucker 1971; Haslett *et al.* 1998; Vos, 1999). The greatest compaction is with highly organic deposits such as peat, but even inorganic silty clays are liable to subside over long periods of time. Under intertidal conditions sediment supply to the marsh surface keeps pace or can even outstrip the rate of subsidence, but if sediment supply is disrupted, for example through the migration of a natural barrier along the coast or the construction of a sea wall, then consolidation will become the dominant process leading to a lowering of the marsh surface relative to sea level. If the area of marshland now free from tidal inundation is then drained, then this process of subsidence will be accelerated, especially in peat areas of the backfen.

On an open saltmarsh, tidal creeks and rivers also develop raised 'levee' banks, even as they extend into the lower-lying backfen. At times of marine regression, when tidal influence on the marshes decreases, these creeks will silt up, though the higher energy conditions within them lead to coarser sediment being deposited compared with the surrounding marshes. Over time, the marshes will consolidate though the coarse material filling the creeks will shrink less than the surrounding marsh, especially if the latter contains a high proportion of organic material. Being slightly higher and drier than the surrounding marshes, these creek banks also have a distinctive ecology, and were generally the earliest areas to see human settlement (e.g. Behre 1985).

The result of this wide range of depositional environments is that coastal wetlands comprise a rich ecological mosaic (Figures 5–10; Adam 1990; Hook *et al.* 1988; Waller 1994*a*: 36–8).

- Below mean high water neap tide (MHWNT) there is a zone of unvegetated and highly mobile sand, with unconsolidated mudflats slightly higher in the intertidal frame (Figure 6).
- Above the mudflats lie more consolidated saltmarsh sediments with halophytic vegetation (Figures 6–7). Towards the coast, where tidal inundation is most frequent, the most pioneering flora is characterized by *Salicornia europaea* (and the recent introduction *Spartina townsendii*).
- Further inland, the middle marshes are covered with species such as *Puccinellia maritima*, *Artemisia maritima*, and *Aster tripolium*.
- The highest marshes, which are inundated the least frequently, are characterized by *Triglochin maritima*, *Artemisia maritima*, *Plantago maritima*, *Juncus gerardi*, *Juncus maritimus*, *Agropyron repens*, and *Festuca rubra*.
- In extensive coastal wetlands the low-lying backfens often lie beyond the zone of tidal creeks, and over time a slightly brackish to freshwater reed swamp may develop, dominated by *Phragmites australis* (Figures 5 and 10D, G, J), which may eventually be replaced by wholly freshwater sedge (*Cladium*) fen (Figure 8), and finally willow/alder-carr woodland (Figures 5 and 10I).
- In certain circumstances an oligotrophic *Sphagnum* bog may develop (Figure 10C).

2.3 The occurrence of marshland landscapes (Figure 10)

Saltmarshes occur in a wide range of sheltered locations around the coasts of North West Europe, and these environments can be classified in terms of their physical geomorphology (Allen and Pye 1992*b*: 3; Oele *et al.* 1979; Pethick 1984). However, in the context of this study, a more important set of criteria is the opportunity these landscapes provided for human communities, with a critical distinction being between relatively small areas of marshland that could be exploited from fen-edge settlements, and more extensive areas that supported marshland communities whose territory lay entirely on the coastal wetlands. These marshland landscapes can be divided into four broad types:

1. Extensive areas of coastal marshland, often partly protected behind a natural barrier, that were sufficiently extensive to support wholly marshland communities (e.g. Figure 10C–E)
2. Long narrow belts of marshland, usually along the shores of major estuaries or

18   CHAPTER TWO

7. Surface of a saltmarsh, dissected by tidal creeks (Kingston Seymour, North Somerset) (NGR: ST 383 687).

8. Sedge fen (foreground) and reedswamp (background) (Shapwick Heath, Central Somerset) (NGR: ST 423 407).

9. Porlock Marsh, West Somerset (NGR: SS 876 480). After several years of erosion, the natural shingle barrier was breached in October 1996, leading to the sudden inundation of the marsh it protected. The breach is regarded as unpluggable, and the formerly reclaimed marsh is now flooded at high spring tides, and has reverted to saltmarsh within three years (see Canti *et al.* 1995; Jennings *et al.* 1998).

    occasionally the open coast, which could support wholly marshland communities (Figure 10I–K)

3. Often discontinuous areas of marshland around major estuaries and harbours, that fell within the territories of fen-edge communities (Figure 10L)
4. The minor estuaries of individual river valleys and narrow coastal plains that were exploited from settlements on the dryland margins (Figure 10M)

Most of the extensive coastal wetlands in North West Europe formed when natural barriers of shingle or sand drifted across the mouth of a major estuary, allowing extensive areas of saltmarsh and peat bog to form in the sheltered waters in their lee (e.g. Figures 9 and 10A). The length of coastline can in fact be relatively short compared with the area of marshland that formed in these silted-up estuaries: in the North Somerset Levels, for example, 100 km^2 of marshland have a coastal frontage of just 18 km. These barriers can be an unstable feature of the landscape, and their evolution is often inextricably linked with the character of the marshes behind them. For example, the migration of a natural barrier across an area of coastal marsh will stop tidal flooding, though it will also disrupt the discharge of freshwater run-off from the adjacent dryland areas. In such circumstances, waterlogging on the marshes can increase, especially in the low-lying backfens where raised bog may eventually form (Figure 10C). Subsequent breaches to the tidal barrier may in fact improve the drainage,

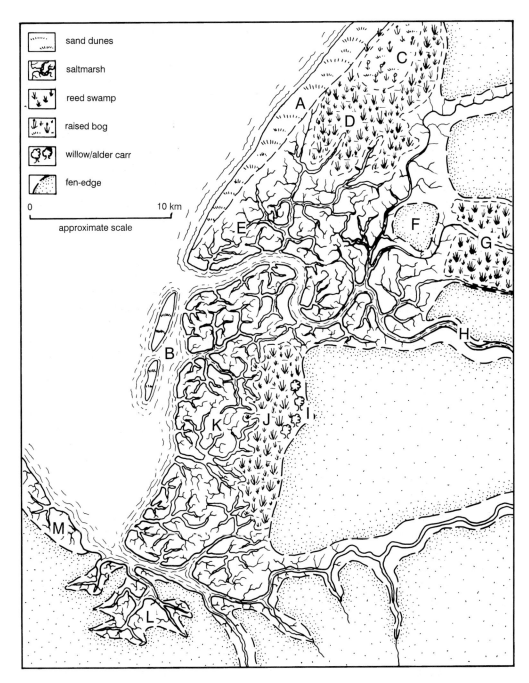

	sand dunes
	saltmarsh
	reed swamp
	raised bog
	willow/alder carr
	fen-edge

0 ———————— 10 km
approximate scale

10. Schematic plan of a lowland coastal zone, showing the range of intertidal and freshwater environments.

and lead to the diversion of rivers to new outfalls (e.g. Romney Marsh: see Chapters 8 and 9, Figure 67).

These extensive wetlands were able to support wholly marshland communities during both the Roman and medieval periods. In Britain they are all of moderate size: the Pevensey Levels in Sussex ($c.$ 70 km^2), the East Kent marshes and Wantsum Channel ($c.$ 80 km^2), the North Somerset Levels ($c.$ 100 km^2), the Norfolk Broads ($c.$ 200 km^2), Romney Marsh ($c.$ 280 km^2), and the Central Somerset Levels ($c.$ 300 km^2). In contrast, some $c.$ 820 km^2 of wetland are protected by natural coastal barriers in northern France, $c.$ 870 km^2 in Belgium, and $c.$ 7,900 km^2 in the western Netherlands (giving a total of around 9,600 km^2 for the mainland of North West Europe).

Areas of continuous coastal marshland without a natural barrier, but which were broad enough to support wholly marshland communities, occur around many major estuaries, and occasionally on open coasts. The coastal frontage of such marshes is usually much longer than they are wide (such as the Gwent Levels beside the Severn Estuary which comprise some 90 km^2 of marsh with a coastal frontage of 65 km; cf. the North Somerset Levels above). Occasionally such areas had a highly intermittent natural barrier which did little to prevent tidal flooding, such as the cheniers along the Essex coast, and sand dunes in Lincolnshire. In the northern Netherlands and Germany some protection is afforded by off-shore islands (e.g. Figure 10B). In Britain these coastal plains are of moderate extent: the Avonmouth ($c.$ 45 km^2) and Gwent Levels ($c.$ 90 km^2) beside the Severn Estuary, the Hull Valley/southern Holderness ($c.$ 181 km^2) and North East Lincolnshire marshes ($c.$ 50 km^2) beside the Humber Estuary, the North Kent ($c.$ 210 km^2) and southern Essex marshes ($c.$ 130 km^2) beside the Thames, the Essex coast between Shoebury and Bradwell ($c.$ 130 km^2), and the Lincolnshire coast between Skegness and Cleethorpes ($c.$ 310 km^2). The largest such area in Britain is the Fenland ($c.$ 4,200 km^2), though even this is smaller than the coastal plain of the northern Netherlands and Germany (which as far east as Cuxhaven at the base of Jutland comprises $c.$ 5,600 km^2).

The third type of coastal wetland landscape is the collectively fairly extensive, but individually small-scale (typically no more than 1 km to 3 km across), areas of marshland scattered around minor estuaries and harbours (Figure 10L). These were not sufficiently extensive to support wholly marshland communities, though the rich grazing and meadowland they afforded would have been a valued resource for those living on the adjacent dryland areas. Examples include Poole Harbour in Dorset, Portsmouth/ Langstone/Chichester Harbours in Hampshire/Sussex, and the Blackwater/Colne Estuaries in Essex.

Finally there are small areas of marshland, typically just 1–2 km across or less, forming around the minor estuaries of individual rivers. These marshes were too small to support wholly marshland communities though, once again, their rich grazing and meadowland would have been an important resource for people living in local, dryland, settlements. Examples in southern and eastern Britain include the valleys of the Exe, Otter, and Axe in Devon, the Arun, Adur, Ouse, Cuckmere and Bulverhythe in Sussex, and the Stour, Orwell, Deben, Alde, Yox, and Blyth in Suffolk.

2.4 **Transgression and regression as landscape events**

In cross-section, coastal wetlands usually comprise a series of alternating layers of minerogenic silty clays (alluvium) deposited as mudflats and saltmarshes, through to organic-rich peats that were laid down under freshwater conditions (Figures 5 and 11). The depth of this sequence varies enormously, though typically it reaches 20–30 m.[3]

In the past, such sequences have been interpreted in terms of fluctuating sea level, with periods when tidal conditions prevailed being associated with rises in sea level (marine transgressions), and periods of freshwater conditions being associated with falls in sea level (marine regressions). However, this is to confuse two very different phenomena: changing depositional environments in coastal wetlands, and the cause of those changes.

A wide range of interconnected variables affect the physical development of coastal wetlands ranging from long-term changes in sea level, through medium-term climatic fluctuations, to short-term changes in the weather (especially storm surges). The supply of sediment to both marshes and coastal barriers is another critical variable, dependent upon the relationship between erosion and deposition over a very wide area, which is itself associated with these environmental factors. The following section will consider the impact of these variables on coastal wetlands during the past two millennia, leading to an attempt to examine whether there is any synchroniety in the transgression/regression events that can be recognised.

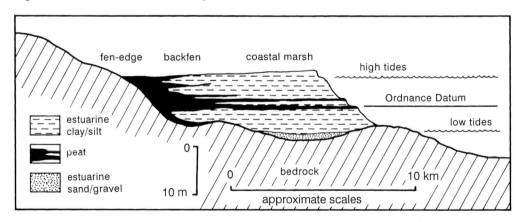

11. Schematic cross-section through intercalated peat/clay sequence on the Gwent Levels, South East Wales, beside the Severn Estuary (after Allen and Fulford 1986).

[3] *Severn Estuary*: Allen 1987; 1990; 1991; Godwin 1943; Hawkins 1967; Heyworth and Kidson 1982; *Pevensey Levels*: Jennings and Smyth 1987; Moffat 1986; *Combe Haven/Bulverhythe, East Sussex*: Smyth and Jennings 1988; *Romney Marsh*: Platter 1992; Plater and Long 1995; Waller *et al.* 1988; *Lyden, East Kent*: Long 1992; *Thames Estuary*: Devoy 1979; Greensmith and Tucker 1973; *Crouch Estuary, Essex*: Wilkinson and Murphy 1955; *Norfolk Broadland*: B. P. L. Coles and Funnell 1981; *Fenland*: Waller 1994a; *Lincolnshire Marshes*: Robinson 1984; Swinnerton 1931; 1932; 1936; *Humber Estuary*: Long *et al.* 1998; Van de Noort and Ellis 1998: 76; *France*: Sommé 1979; Ters 1973; *Belgium*: Denys and Baeteman 1995; Paepe and Baeteman 1979; *Western Netherlands*: Jelgersma *et al.* 1970; 1979; Vos and Van Heeringen 1997; *Northern Netherlands*: Roeleveld 1974; Vos, 1999; *Northwestern Germany*: Behre *et al.* 1979.

2.4.1 **Relative sea level** (Figure 12)

Varying 'sea level' is the product of two factors: the *absolute* amount of water in our oceans (eustasy) and changes in the shape of the earth's crust (isostasy). If the volume of water increases, but an area of land is also rising, then the position of mean sea level *relative* to a fixed point on land may not change, as they both rise together. However, if the volume of water is constant and an area of land is sinking, then relative sea level will rise.

Until fairly recently sea level research was dominated by the quest for a world-wide eustatic curve representing the post-glacial rise in sea level (e.g. Godwin *et al.* 1958), though it is now realized that it may never be possible to isolate just the eustatic

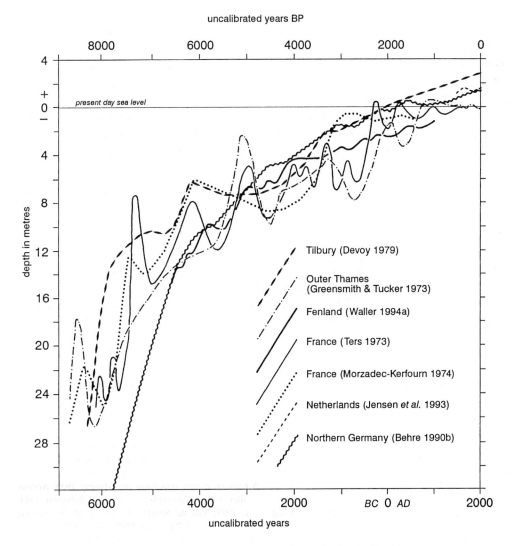

12. Relative sea level curves from around North West Europe. (Drawn by Sue Rouillard.)

component in changing sea level, or anything more than a regional curve for relative sea level. This is because in addition to eustasy and isostasy there are numerous local variables that will have affected sea level change including climate, weather (such as storm surges), alterations to tidal patterns, and human interference (Everard 1980: 1, 15; Long and Roberts 1997). Overall, however, it appears that the area covered by this study has been sinking since the end of the Ice Age (due to the isostatic recovery of northern Europe following the lifting of the ice sheet), and so relative sea level is generally rising (Figure 12).

It is against this background of a general rise in relative sea level that the intercalated sequences of peat and alluvium must be considered (Figures 5 and 11). There is now general agreement that the post-glacial rise in sea level was spasmodic not continuous.[4] The methodological aspects of using these intercalated peats and clays as indicators of past changes in sea level need not concern us here (see Devoy 1982: 70; 1990: 24; Haslett *et al.* 1997; 1998; Waller 1994*a*: 27–34, 39). What is important is the fundamental changes to landscape character that the alternation of estuarine alluvium and freshwater peat represents.

Peat forms after the colonization of a marsh by freshwater plants, and the main context for this is during a period of falling relative sea level. However, the formation of alternate peat and alluvium layers may in certain circumstances have been independent of any change in sea level. For example, the formation of a natural coastal barrier may lead to an area of former saltmarsh being cut off from the sea, resulting in the area's colonization by freshwater vegetation, even though sea level continued to rise. If this coastal barrier was subsequently breached (for example due to a sudden storm surge), the peat would be buried under a saltmarsh and rapid accretion would resume until the marsh surface had caught up with rising sea level (e.g. Figure 9). The result is an intercalated alluvium/peat /alluvium sequence even though sea level had been rising continuously. In some instances it is even possible that freshwater peats may start to form in the backfens of coastal wetlands at the onset of a period of rising sea level, because this disrupted the discharge of freshwater run-off from the adjacent uplands (e.g. Roeleveld 1974: 29; Van de Noort and Davies 1993: 21; Wilkinson and Murphy 1995: 201).

Alternating sedimentological units, therefore, represent changing depositional environments which may or may not have been related to changing sea level. It follows, then, that marine transgression is best thought of simply as a *landscape event* whereby tidal influence increases in a formerly freshwater marsh, and terrestrial sediments are replaced by saltmarshes and mudflats. A marine regression can be regarded as a retreat or removal of tidal influence and the replacement of intertidal environments with freshwater conditions. What is critical in the context of this landscape-based study is that these different environments offered different opportunities for human communities.

---

[4] The literature on this subject is vast but some representative papers include: *Belgium*: Paepe and Baetman 1979; Denys and Baetman 1995; *Britain*: Devoy: 1979; Shennan 1986*a*; *b*; Waller 1994*a*; *Denmark*: Krog 1979; *France*: Sommé 1979; *Germany*: Behre *et al.* 1979; *Netherlands*: de Groot *et al.* 1996; Jelgersma *et al.* 1979; Kiden 1995; Van de Plassche 1982; Vos and Van Heeringen 1997.

2.4.2 Sea level indicators: the interpretation of cultural material in wetland landscapes (Figure 13)

The upper parts of post-glacial alluvial sequences often lack the intercalated peats and clays that are usually used to reconstruct patterns of sea level change, and so most sea level curves stop short of the past two millennia. Where attempts have been made to identify trends in relative sea level during this later period, they are often based simply upon the expansion and contraction of settlement that is assumed to have mirrored regression and transgression. For example, Shennan (1986*a*; *b*) has identified a series of periods which he argues are related to positive and negative sea level tendencies in the Fenland, the 'positive' tendencies being characterized by rising sea level and a landward movement of the coastline ('Wash' periods), and negative tendencies characterized by falling sea level and the seaward movement of the coastline ('Fenland' periods). However, it is quite clear from the dates that Fenland VI (*c.* AD 50–400) and Fenland VII (*c.* AD 800–1000) are based largely upon periods when human communities colonized the Fenland marshes. This assumes that mankind was passively responding to changes in the natural environment yet, as a cultural phenomena, the colonization of coastal marshes may have been related to non-environmental factors such as population increase or other socio-economic conditions, rather than changes in the natural environment.

The interpretation of cultural material intercalated within a sequence of peats and clays, and its use as a sea level indicator, is particularly complex (e.g. Ackeroyd 1972; Allen 1997*a*; Allen *et al.* 1997). The fundamental problem is establishing the type of human activity that this material represents and its relationship to contemporary sea level, since different types of human activity will have occurred at different places in the tidal frame (Figure 13). Sometimes human activity was located relatively low down in the intertidal zone, such as fishing weirs. Higher up, saltmarshes provide good grazing and hurdle trackways were often constructed to aid the passage of livestock across the numerous minor creeks: such trackways are to be expected at around high tide level (Figure 15). Salt production was an activity on coastal marshes that will have occurred just above the limits of summer high tides since the salterns must obviously have had access to tidal waters, yet the tanks, hearths, and ovens would not have been able to withstand regular inundation. Salterns would, therefore, probably, have been located away from the open coast, often on the fen-edge or raised levee-banks beside the marsh creeks within which tidal waters would have been restricted during the summer months (Figure 13A, B, and M). The exception is when most of the coastal marshes were embanked and the salterns had to be located on the narrow strip of saltmarsh left unreclaimed on the seaward side of the sea wall (Figures 13K, 73, and 79).

Salterns were industrial sites and, as such, their use does not imply any form of settlement, though in practice this may have occurred particularly on a seasonal basis (a number of Romano-British salterns around the Thames Estuary, for example, appear to be associated with spreads of domestic refuse and burials: see Chapter 4). The

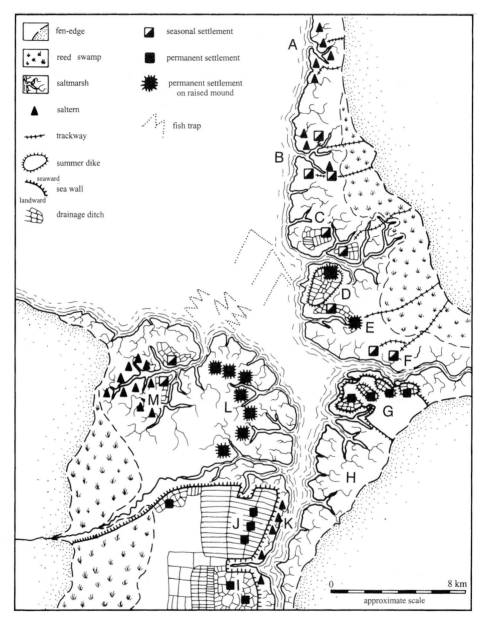

13. Schematic plan of a lowland coastal wetland indicating the range of human activities. A, salt production on the raised banks of a tidal creek tidal creek; B, salt production and seasonal settlement; C, landscape modification (localized enclosure and drainage) on raised banks of tidal creek; D, landscape modification (summer ring-dike); E, settlement on artificial raised mound (*terpen* etc.); F, seasonal settlements; G, area of marsh initially modified with four summer ring-dikes, and later transformed through the construction of a continuous sea wall along the coast; H, open saltmarsh; I, unsystematic reclamation of higher coastal marshes, followed by systematic enclosure of the lower-lying backfens; J, systematic reclamation; K, salt production on the narrow strip of saltmarsh left after medieval reclamation; L, series of artificially raised settlement mounds on higher coastal marshes; M, seasonal settlement associated with localized ditched drainage systems of raised creek banks towards the coast, and salt production further inland.

interpretation of domestic and building debris within an alluvial sequence is particularly problematical. Waddelove and Waddelove (1990: 255) have used the concept of 'minimum occupation level' (the lowest height above contemporary MHWST that occupation will be viable) for relating archaeological material to its contemporary sea level. However, there are problems with this approach since it assumes that archaeological material represents permanent occupation above the limit of even the highest tides, and this need not have been the case. Wetland environments are rich in natural resources and settlements exploiting such areas may well have been seasonal with the occupants prepared to tolerate occasional floods in order to be close to the resources that they were exploiting. For example, stockman's huts could have been located on areas of slightly higher ground such as a creek bank or artificial mound beyond the reaches of normal summer floods, but which were liable to be inundated during the higher winter tides (Figure 13B). Indeed, experimental work on contemporary North German saltmarshes, and palaeoenvironmental work on Roman and early medieval coastal settlements, has shown that even cultivation is possible on high saltmarshes (e.g. Behre and Jacomet 1991; Murphy 1993*b*; Van Zeist 1974). Such marshes may have been protected from unseasonally high tides through the construction of 'summer dikes', representing a simple modification of the natural environment to make it more conducive to human needs (Figure 13D). Clearly, distinguishing seasonal agricultural settlements exploiting a tidal marsh during the summer months, and permanent agricultural settlements occupying a reclaimed marsh all year round (Figure 13I, J), is an important, yet difficult task.

If the character of these various archaeological sites can be established and their relationship to MHWST estimated, then they become useful sea level indicators. However, this is not necessarily the case with archaeological remains found in the freshwater backfens such as the prehistoric trackways of the Somerset Levels which were used in some of the first sea level calculations for South West Britain (e.g. Hawkins 1973: fig. 2; Kidson and Heyworth 1973, 575–6: table I). These trackways were built as a result of rising freshwater-levels in a raised bog well beyond the reaches of marine inundation, and while it is conceivable that rising sea level caused the water-table in these peat bogs to increase, the relationship is indirect and other factors could have been equally important such as increased rainfall due to a climatic change, or increased surface run-off from the surrounding uplands due to human clearance of the forest cover.

Another variable is whether an archaeological site was protected from inundation by natural barriers such as sand-dunes, or anthropogenic features such as sea walls, since this allows activity in areas that would otherwise have been regularly flooded. For example, most coastal wetlands in southern Britain and The Netherlands now lie well below MHWST, yet are extensively settled and normally free from flooding due to the presence of sea walls. However, if future generations of archaeologists excavated these permanently flood-free settlements in a freshwater environment but were unaware of the sea walls they may assume that modern sea level was much lower than it really is.

2.4.3 **Towards a reconstruction of sea level changes in the past two millennia**

The Severn Estuary (Figure 20)

In a seminal paper Allen and Rae (1988; and see Allen 1991) have compared the elevations of a series of Romano-British reclaimed land surfaces and the height of adjacent, still actively accreting, saltmarshes around the Severn Estuary and suggest that these marshes have risen by *c.* 1.2 m since the second century. On the basis of this they suggest that MHWST has risen by *c.* 1.6–1.7 m.

In contrast, Waddelove and Waddelove (1990) suggest that MHWST in the outer Severn Estuary has risen 3.66 m since AD 74 (but just 2.23 m since the late third century) based upon archaeological material stratified within the alluvial sequence at Caerleon, on the River Usk near Newport (Boon 1978; 1980; 1987). The rise of 2.23 m since the Late Roman period is not that dissimilar to Allen and Rae's calculation, bearing in mind that different methods were used. However, the rise in sea level *during* the Roman period of 1.43 m needs very careful examination, as their figures are based upon comparing two separate sea level indicators which would have had very different relationships to MHWST: an Early Roman ground surface with associated timber buildings lying at +5.96 m OD, and the top of a third century quay at +6.56 m OD. The Waddeloves argue that the 'highest astronomical tides' (HAT) must have been 1.83 m below the first century ground surface (+5.96 m minus 1.83 m, giving 4.13 m OD), but just 1.0 m (the freeboard of a boat)[5] below the top of the quay (+6.56 m minus 1.0 m, giving 5.56 m OD), creating the large differential of 1.43 m between the Early and Late Roman periods.

In fact, there is no reason why the highest astronomical tides should have lain so far below the Early Roman ground surface. Firstly, the HAT only occurs every 19 years: it is unlikely that a legionary was stationed by the River Usk for some 20 years in order to establish where the HAT was before construction started. Secondly, the Waddeloves assume that any occupation would have been at a safe 'Minimum Occupation Level' regarded as 1.83 m above HAT, though this figure is derived from a mid-seventeenth century philosopher writing about the Scilly Isles, and whose relevance to Roman military thinking in the first century AD can be questioned.

Overall, therefore, the height of the first century MHWST need not have been so low as 3.66 m below that of today. The actual archaeological sequence, including the intercalation of occupation debris and sterile alluvium (Boon 1978), indicates that MHWST may have risen just *c.* 0.2 m between the late first and late third centuries AD. Indeed, there is other evidence for a continuing gradual rise in sea level during the Roman period from the opposite side of the Estuary. At Portishead, near Bristol, a first/second century occupation horizon is sealed by flood silts which in turn are overlain by third/fourth century buildings (Clevedon-Brown 1965), while at Banwell Moor near Weston-super-Mare, a Late Iron Age saltern was sealed by *c.* 0.3 m of sterile alluvium before a soil formed over the site during the third century (Figures 47–8; Rippon 1997c; forthcoming *a*).

[5] Toft (1992: 249) agrees that the freeboard would have been around 1 m (i.e. 3 Roman *Pes Drusianus*), though Bateman and Milne (1983) suggest a freeboard of 0.5 m.

The Thames Estuary (Figure 22)

Work on reconstructing sea level change around the Thames Estuary has been carried out in two contexts: the Roman waterfront at London in the inner Estuary, and radiocarbon dating intercalated peats and shell ridges within the alluvial sequence around the middle and outer Estuary. Additional data comes from the height of Romano-British salterns found along both banks of the Thames. The results of this research suggest that, in contrast to the Severn Estuary, relative sea level may have fallen during the Roman period.

The position of a late first century AD quay at Pudding Lane in London, along with quarry pits on the foreshore, suggest that mean low water (MLW) was between –0.5 and 0 m OD, and MHWST at *c.* 1.5 m OD (allowing for a *c.* 0.5 m freeboard below the top of the quay at *c.* 2.0 m OD: Bateman and Milne 1983; Milne 1985).[6] During the second century a series of successive quays were constructed further out into the Thames (Brigham 1990; T. Dyson 1986). Because of the sloping foreshore, if Roman MHWST had remained constant at *c.* 1.5 m OD, the quay-fronts should have increased in height to *c.* 3.5–4.0 m. However, as the quays advanced down the Thames foreshore their frontal height remained at 1.5–2.0 m (Brigham 1990: 144). From this structural evidence it appears that MHWST fell some 1.5 m between the late first and mid-third centuries, to *c.* 0 m OD. This somewhat surprising conclusion is supported by palaeo-environmental evidence from the Baynards Castle site where, by the mid-third century, a 0.15 m thick freshwater reed and sedge peat had formed on the formerly intertidal foreshore (Brigham 1990: 145). Therefore, the third century high tide level in the Thames at London barely exceeded the first century low water mark, suggesting a marked period of regression. By the twelfth/thirteenth century, MHWST had recovered to at least *c.* 1.5 m OD, rising to *c.* 3.75 m OD today (Dyson 1986: 71; Milne 1985: 84–5).

At Tilbury, in the middle Thames Estuary (Figure 22), Devoy (1979; 1980) has recognized five transgressions (Thames I–V) and five regressions (Tilbury I–V), based on intercalated peats and clays. The Tilbury V regression, represented by a thin intermittent *Phragmites* peat, is dated to *c.* 1750 BP (*c.* third/early fourth century AD), and lies around 2.5–3.0 m below modern MHWST (*c.* 3.1 m OD: Devoy 1979: fig. 4, table 5; Spurrell 1885; 1889/90: 214–20). Probably the same peat horizon, associated with first to third century Romano-British activity, is also found on the southern (Kent) side of the Estuary (see below).

In the outer Thames Estuary, at Foulness, Greensmith and Tucker (1973; 1980) have identified six episodes of transgression and five regressions in the post-glacial period, though the upper part of the sequence is poorly dated. Transgression IV may have started during the late second millennium BC and ended around the late first century BC/early first century AD, to be followed by a fall in mean sea level (supporting the evidence from Tilbury and London). Transgression V began around the third century AD,

---

[6] Toft (1992: 250) argues that the freeboard would have been 1 m, making the top of the quay *c.* +2.0 m, the 1st century Highest Astronomical Tide +1.0 m, compared with the modern HAT of +4.7 m.

and ended around the early eighth century AD, to be followed by a period of steady or very slightly falling sea level (Greensmith and Tucker 1973: fig. 6; and see Milne 1985: fig. 50).

Early Roman salt production sites can also be used as approximate indicators of the contemporary sea level, probably having been located near or slightly above summer MHWST (see above). At Hullbridge, in the Crouch Estuary (Essex), a red hill appears to have lain on the surface of a marsh at *c.* 0.9 m OD, whereas the modern MHWST is *c.* 2.9 m OD (Grieve 1959: 859; Wilkinson and Murphy 1995: 183). At Leigh Beck, on Canvey Island, the base of a Roman red hill lay at *c.* 0.7 m OD compared with modern MHWST at *c.* 2.8 m OD (Grieve 1959: 859; Wilkinson and Murphy 1995: 184, 220), while Linder (1939; 1941: 51) records several hearths within other red hills on Canvey at *c.* 0.9 m OD. Overall, a rise in relative sea level of *c.* 2 m since the first/second century is indicated. Various heights have been calculated for the Romano-British ground surface and associated peat horizon in the North Kent marshes, ranging from between *c.* –0.5 and +0.5 m OD (Devoy 1979: fig. 21; J. H. Evans 1953: 116), to *c.* 1.4 m OD which is more in keeping with the northern side of the Estuary (A. Firth, pers. comm. 1998). The height of modern saltings at *c.* 2.7–3.4 m OD MHWST is 3.1 m OD (J. H. Evans 1953).

Taken together, this evidence suggests a period of marine transgression in the Thames Estuary during the first millennium BC, followed by a regression underway by the Early and Mid-Roman period marked by falling mean sea level and the development of freshwater peats at various locations. Since the third century marsh surfaces appear to have risen by around 2 m. There is nothing in the geo-archaeological record to comment on whether there was a further period of regression during the medieval period.

2.4.4 Coastal barriers and the impact of storms

Many coastal wetlands around Britain and the North Sea are partly protected by natural barriers of sand or gravel. These barriers form through the process of long-shore drift, whereby eroded sediment from one area is washed along the coast and deposited elsewhere, often at the mouths of tidal rivers. Behind these natural barriers sheltered conditions allow the creation of mudflats and eventually saltmarshes, leading to the creation of substantial areas of marshland (Pethick 1984).

However, what nature giveth nature can taketh away—very quickly. The onset of climatic deteriorations are often marked by increased storminess which can have a profound affect upon coastal barriers, both natural and man-made. In certain circumstances new barriers can be formed as beach material becomes more mobile. For example, parts of the Essex coast between Bradwell and Foulness are fringed by sheets and ridges of shell (known as cheniers) which form an intermittent coastal barrier created under storm conditions during periods of marine transgression (such as that during the mid-first millennium AD (Greensmith and Tucker 1973)). Periods of climatic change can also lead to the migration of shingle barriers across the mouths of tidal rivers and to the inland migration of sand dunes.[7] The importance of these natural coastal barriers in protecting areas of reclaimed marshland was certainly recognized in the past, illustrated, for example, in AD 1283 when the Abbot of St Augustine's and Prior of Christ Church in Canterbury ordered that 'no one of the community of Stonore or Sandwich [in East Kent] should for the future gather or carry away any stone or sea beach, in the walls between Stonore and Clyvesende, nor should take up ballast for their ships' (Hardman and Steebing 1941: 51; Hasted 1797–1801: vol. X: 409).

While increases in storminess can be associated with the formation and migration of coastal barriers, they can also mark periods of erosion. To avoid sea defences being undermined it has been common practice to leave areas of unreclaimed saltmarsh in front of sea walls to act as a buffer zone and dissipate the energy of storm waves. The importance of these saltmarshes, and the vegetation that they supported, is illustrated, for example, by a Commission of Sewers in Kent in AD 1639 which banned the cutting of reeds outside the sea wall before 1st March each year (Bowler 1968: 28).

If natural or man-made barriers that protect low-lying coastal wetlands are breached then the effects can be dramatic (e.g. Figure 9; Jennings *et al.* 1998). A single storm surge, perhaps caused by a combination of high spring tide, low atmospheric pressure (when mean sea level rises *c.* 0.01 m for each millibar atmospheric pressure reduction), and strong on-shore winds, can have a devastating effect, smashing through a sea wall overnight. The impact of sudden storms was graphically illustrated as recently as 1953 when some 300 people were killed in eastern England during floods resulting from one such storm surge (Grieve 1959). In the mid-thirteenth century a series of storms breached coastal barriers along the Sussex coast and washed away the entire town of Winchelsea (Eddison 1998), while in AD 1570 floods killed at least 400,000 people around the North Sea (Lamb 1995: 191). Such tidal flooding was far more serious than a temporary inundation by fresh water. Both kill livestock and crops, and destroy buildings and embankments, but once flooded with salt water the soils of a reclaimed marsh will take several years to recover.

The occurrence of major storms around Britain and the North Sea can only be studied for the medieval period and later, when chroniclers recorded unusual weather conditions (Berendsen and Zagwjn 1984: 226; Bowler 1968; Bailey 1991; Hofstede 1991: 15, fig. 3; Rippon 1997*a*: table 10.1). A number of bad winters are documented between the ninth and twelfth centuries leading to the inundation of coastal areas, though the impression is that these were rather unusual events and, as such, became worthy of documentation. From the 1190s until the end of the thirteenth century the situation is reversed and there are few years without documented storms or floods, with the 1250s and 1280s being particularly bad. The fourteenth century appears to have been even worse and, at times like these, low-lying coastal wetlands would become increasingly unpleasant places to live.

[7] *Axe Valley, Devon*: Parkinson 1985; *Ouse Valley, East Sussex*: Brandon 1971*c*; *Pevensey Levels*: Jennings and Smyth 1985; *Romney Marsh*: Eddison 1983*a*; *Combe Haven Valley, East Sussex*: Smyth and Jennings 1988; *Wantsum Channel, Kent*: Hearne *et al.* 1995; *Orford, Suffolk*: Carr and Baker 1968; *Norfolk Broads*: B. P. L. Coles and Funnel 1981: 127.

2.4.5 **Regression and transgression events around North West Europe**

So, is it possible to generalize about periods of transgression and regression? There was undoubtedly a rapid rise in sea level during the millennia immediately after the end of the last Ice Age, though the rate of sea level increase has certainly slowed in the past three or four thousand years (Figure 12). In continental Europe a complex sequence of peats ('Holland' deposits) and clays ('Calais' and 'Dunkirk deposits) have led to the identification of a series of synchronous transgression and regression events supposedly linked to variations relative sea level, climate, and storm frequencies over the entire Belgian/Dutch coast (e.g. Dunkirk II transgression: AD 300–600, Holland VIII regression AD 650–800, Dunkirk IIIA transgression: AD 800–1000: Jelgersma *et al.* 1970; Louwe Kooijmans 1974; Van de Plassche 1982; Roeleveld 1974; TeBrake 1985). In Britain there has been a tendency to identify similar sequences at a more localized level (e.g. Devoy 1979; Greensmith and Tucker 1973; Shennan 1986*a*; *b*).

There are, however, considerable problems with this simple model of synchronous transgression and regression events linked directly to variations in sea level, as often inconclusive or poorly dated evidence is in danger of being forced into a preconceived straight-jacket, and in The Netherlands recent studies have cast doubt on the Dunkirk/Holland sequence (Berendsen and Zagwijn 1984: 226; Henderikx 1986: 451; Vos and Van Heeringen 1997). For example, it is suggested that there is no extensive body of sediment indicating widespread tidal flooding corresponding to the Late to Post-Roman 'Dunkirk II' transgression, as the Westland and Vlaardingen clays are now dated to the twelfth century. The evidence for a ninth/tenth century Dunkirk IIIA (Carolingian) transgression is also called into question. In the past it was *assumed* that such a transgression existed because this was thought to have been a particularly stormy period with recorded floods, though a closer examination of the documentary record reveals that there was in fact just one great storm (AD 838) and one other major flood (AD 900): there is no lithostratigraphic evidence for a major transgressive event.

Thus, in understanding the evolution of coastal marshes we must move away from the dominance of sea level curves and concentrate instead on transgression and regression as landscape events. Once individual sequences in each region have been established then the possible causes, including changes in sea level, can then be assessed.

Later Iron Age transgression

During the late first millennium BC, saltmarsh and mudflat conditions appear to have predominated in most of the coastal wetlands in North West Europe, though extensive freshwater swamps survived in many of the backfens (*Fenland*: Shennan 1986*b*: Wash VI; Waller 1994*a*: map 10; *Humber Estuary*: Gaunt and Tooley 1974; Van de Noort and Davies 1993: 17–18, 38; Van de Noort and Ellis 1998; *Severn Estuary*: Rippon 1997*a*: 22; *Thames Estuary*: Devoy 1979: Thames IV; Greensmith and Tucker 1973: transgression IV; *Belgium/Netherlands 'Dunkirk I'*: Jelgersma *et al.* 1970; Louwe Kooijmans 1974; Van de Plassche 1982; Roeleveld 1974; TeBrake 1985).

Roman period regression

By the first century AD, and possibly earlier, there is lithostratigraphic evidence for a period of relatively stable or even falling sea level throughout eastern Britain and the western/northern coasts of The Netherlands and Germany (for Fenland see Shennan (1986*b*: Fenland VI) and Waller (1994*a*: 78); the Humber Estuary see Gaunt and Tooley (1974), Van de Noort and Davies (1993: 17–18, 38), and Van de Noort and Ellis (1997; 1998); the Thames Estuary see Devoy (1979: Tilbury V), Greensmith and Tucker (1973: fig. 6); The Netherlands 'Holland VII' see Jelgersma *et al.* (1970), Louwe Kooijmans 1974, Van de Plassche (1982), Roeleveld (1974), and Schoute (1984: 164); and Germany see Behre (1990*a*).

There is some evidence for localized coastal peat formation during the first to third centuries AD notably around the Thames Estuary at Baynards Castle and Southwark in London (Brigham 1990: 144–5), Rainham and Tilbury in Essex (Meddens 1996: 325; Devoy 1979; Spurrell 1885; 1889/90, 214–20), and on some of the North Kent marshes (J. H. Evans 1953; Spurrell 1885: 275). Peats probably of this period have also been recorded on the Essex coast e.g. Langenhoe (Reader 1908: 170) and in the Ancholme Valley by the Humber Estuary (Van de Noort and Davies 1993: 26; Van de Noort and Ellis 1998: 289). The dating of a possible early first millennium AD freshwater peat on the Lincolnshire marshes is unclear (Swinnerton 1932; Van de Noort and Davies 1993: 22–3). In contrast, around the Severn Estuary, there appears to have been a continued rise in relative sea level throughout the Roman period (see above), and organic-rich buried land surfaces recently recorded in a number of places appear to be buried soils formed in the sheltered environment afforded by reclamation (i.e. a cultural process) as opposed to any changes in the natural environment (e.g. Rippon, forthcoming *a*).

Around the second century AD MHWST may have been *c.* 1–1.5 m lower than today in The Netherlands, 1.6–2.2 m around the Severn Estuary, perhaps *c.* 2.4 m around The Wash, and *c.* 2 m around the Thames Estuary.

The Late to Post-Roman transgression

Most Roman-period landscapes in coastal wetlands are buried by estuarine/marine alluvium suggesting there was a period of marine transgression. For Fenland see Shennan (1986*b*: Wash VII) and Waller (1994*a*: 78–9); the Humber Estuary see Gaunt and Tooley (1974), Van de Noort and Davies (1993: 17–18, 38), and Van de Noort and Ellis (1997: 460; 1998: 289); the Severn Estuary see Rippon (1997*a*, 123–7); the Thames Estuary see Devoy (1979: Thames V) and Greensmith and Tucker (1973: transgression V); and The Netherlands see Jelgersma *et al.* (1970), Louwe Kooijmans (1974), Van de Plassche (1982), Roeleveld (1974), and Schoute (1984: 164). This important event is discussed in Chapter 7 in the context of the widespread abandonment of settlements on coastal wetlands during the Late Roman to Early Post-Roman period.

A medieval regression?

There is widespread evidence for the recolonization of most coastal wetlands towards the end of the first millennium AD and this has often been used to argue for a period of marine regression (e.g. *Fenland*: Shennan 1986*b*; *Thames Estuary*: Greensmith and Tucker 1980). However, the expansion of settlement onto an area of marsh may have been due to cultural factors, such as population growth, rather than a period of falling relative sea level and in Britain there is no independent palaeoenvironmental or lithostratigraphical evidence for a fall in relative sea level at this time.

On the continent, the period between *c*. AD 600 and *c*. AD 1250 has also traditionally been regarded as one of regression (Holland VIII and IX), broken briefly by the Carolingian transgression of *c*. AD 800 to *c*. AD 1000 (Dunkirk IIIA: e.g. Roeleveld 1974). The identification of this discrete transgressive period was largely based upon documentary material and can be dismissed (see above). A number of studies have examined sea level trends during the medieval period as a whole, and found little evidence for falling sea level during this period. In Zeeland, around *c*. AD 1000, the higher coastal marshes do appear to have been flooded less often, though it not clear whether this was due to a reduction in storm surges or a fall in relative sea level (Vos and Van Heeringen 1997: 67). Either way, this regressive phase was short lived, and flooding resumed before the end of the eleventh century. Groot *et al.* (1996) have looked at evidence from the Frisian islands and found no evidence for a fall in relative sea level between AD 800 and 1300, while Hofstede (1991) has calculated that Mean High Water off the North German coast rose by *c*. 2.3±9 mm a year between the seventh and thirteenth centuries, with a maximum reached during the climatic optimum around AD 1300 when MHW was about the same as today. Sea level *subsequently* fell, reaching a low point during the seventeenth century *c*. 0.25–0.3 m below that of today (Figure 12; Jensen *et al.* 1993).

2.5 **The impact of climate change**

Changes in relative sea level, and episodes of regression and transgression of whatever cause, can obviously have a profound effect on water levels in coastal marshlands. Climatic change is another factor that could have a major impact upon the environment in a number of ways, with coastal wetlands particularly vulnerable. For example, a global rise in temperature of 1°C will result in a rise in sea level of up to 0.16 m due to thermal expansion in the upper layers of the oceans and the melting of the ice caps (Hofstede 1991: 15).

Climate change affects all landscapes, though in different ways. Archaeologists have often used evidence for climatic change as an explanation for wider cultural trends, for example crop failure resulting in a hungry population seeking new land in adjacent or sometimes distant areas, leading to migration, war, and general upheaval (A. Harding 1982*b*, 2–3). However, human decisions are made within the context of a wide range of variables, both physical and cultural, and the extent to which changes in the natural environment constrained human behaviour in the temperate zone can be questioned. For example, it has been argued that climatic deterioration (notably increased rainfall) was a factor in late medieval settlement desertion in the claylands of the English East

Midlands (e.g. G. Beresford 1975; 1981), although S. Wright (1976) has shown that social and economic factors could have been far more important. Parry (1975) has suggested that while settlement desertion in upland areas sometimes occurred at the same time as climatic deterioration (for example in the late and post-medieval periods), the latter was not necessarily the most important factor: changes in the structure of land-holding, fluctuations in demand for agricultural produce, and deterioration of the soil were more immediate factors.

So what affect might climatic variations have on the marginality of coastal wetlands? Parry (1981: fig. 5) has mapped 'climatically marginal land' in the British Isles, though as this was based largely on temperature it only includes upland areas. In practice a far wider range of factors must be taken into account in determining 'climatically' marginal areas, such as the vulnerability of low-lying heavy soils to waterlogging (making them more difficult to plough, and keep livestock in the fields without the risk of poaching). There is, however, one case where the exploitation of coastal wetlands can benefit from increased rainfall: the cultivation of oats on a high saltmarsh (Bottema et al. 1980: 137). It must also be remembered that climate change is not always for the worse. The direct effect of warmer temperatures on coastal wetlands is beneficial with a longer growing season and greater evaporation leading to less waterlogging and better drainage. At times of drought, the naturally high watertable in wetland areas mean that they suffer less than adjacent 'drylands'.

A wide range of sedimentological, palaeoenvironmental, and documentary data from around Europe has allowed fluctuations in precipitation and temperature to be reconstructed (K. E. Barber 1982; K. E. Barber et al. 1994; Bell and Walker 1992: 16–49; Beug 1982; Briffa and Atkinson 1997; Funnell 1997; Hofstede 1991; Jensen et al. 1993; Lamb 1995; Titow 1960). The first millennium BC saw a major climatic deterioration with a fall in temperatures and increased rainfall and, combined with the widespread evidence for marine transgression during this period, coastal wetlands would not have been a very hospitable place to live. Conditions subsequently improved during the early first millennium AD, with greater warmth and dryness coupled with stable or falling sea level. This would have made the expansion of settlement easier into physically more marginal areas, especially low-lying coastal wetlands with heavy, slowly-draining soils. However, it should be stressed that this climatic change does not in itself explain why such an expansion of settlement should occur: the period also correlates with the Roman occupation of North West Europe, and the socio-economic changes brought about by the closer integration of this region into the Roman world could have been far more important in the decisions of rural communities to intensify their exploitation of the landscape (Chapter 6).

Between the fourth and seventh centuries there appears to have been a return to colder and wetter conditions. This period also corresponds to a marine transgression and the abandonment of many coastal wetlands, though whether there is a causal link is less clear since political, demographic, and economic instability also occurred at this time with the collapse of the Roman Empire (Chapter 7).

There was a climatic improvement from around the eighth century until the late thirteenth century when mean temperatures may have been *c.* 1°C higher than today. The tenth century in particular appears to have been one of drought in The Netherlands and northern Germany, marked by a shift from summer to winter cereals, sand drifting along the coast, and stunted tree growth (Berendsen and Zagwijn 1984; 226; Heidinga 1984). Once again, this period saw a marked expansion of settlement into physically marginal areas such as coastal wetlands, though a causal link once again remains to be established since this was also a period of demographic and economic expansion (Chapters 8 and 11).

2.6 Human impact on the wetland environment

From the examples given above it can be seen that coastal wetlands are highly dynamic landscapes particularly prone to environmental changes, and it is in this context that reclamation must be seen. Reclamation represents a major transformation of the physical and biological environment, with the removal of tidal waters from an area and the replacement of a saltmarsh ecology with a freshwater one. Following reclamation the former saltmarsh will start to dry out and a 'ripening surface' will form through a range of physical (e.g. dehydration), chemical (e.g. oxidation), and biological processes (e.g. root action). The drying of a marsh surface can be increased through seeding plants, whose roots draw water from the subsoil, and the digging of drainage ditches; more recently mole drains and ceramic under-drainage have been used (Pons and Zonneveld 1965; Rijniersce 1982). Eventually, a salt-free soil will develop which, if then subjected to a sustained period of flooding, will appear in the resulting alluvial sequence as a dark horizon (e.g. Figures 47–49).

In these respects a more stable environment was created in which permanent settlement and settled agriculture is possible, though in other ways reclamation could also have a destabilising effect on the environment. One impact is that a reclaimed landsurface will become increasing vulnerable to flooding. Natural saltmarshes grow in keeping with rising relative sea level, though once a sea wall is constructed the sediment supply ceases and the height of the marshes will remain unchanged (or even decrease due to subsidence). If relative sea level continues to rise, then the former marshes will increasingly fall below high tide level. This process will be made worse through the maintenance of a low water table in the reclaimed areas which will increase the consolidation of sediments, especially any peat layers that may underlie the surface alluvium. The embanking of saltmarshes also makes them more vulnerable to storm surges through increasing tidal amplitude in the unreclaimed areas: on an open coast flood waters spread out over the marsh surface and their energy is quickly dissipated, whereas if the marshes are embanked the flood waters are confined to narrow channels and so build up against the sea walls. This squeezing of tidal waters into increasingly narrow estuaries can also have the effect of increasing erosion.

The reclamation of marshes also disrupts tidal flows which can cause the siltation of channels since the remaining body of water is insufficient to flush out any sediment. A good example occurred during the thirteenth century when the Wantsum Channel, that divides the Isle of Thanet from Kent, was silting up. The causes of this were not then known though the marshland innings of the Abbot of St Augustine's were blamed at the time (Hardman and Stebbing 1941: 51; Hasted 1797–1801 Vol. X: 266).

Another impact of drainage is the shrinkage of particularly peat, that makes the reclaimed areas more vulnerable to flooding. In North Holland, for example, around 50 per cent of formerly reclaimed land was flooded in the thirteenth century following peat wastage (Besteman 1990; Van Geel *et al.* 1982/3: 275; Hallewas 1984: 303).

Reclamation could eventually be a victim of its own success, as the balance between arable and pasture was destroyed. For example, in Fenland, areas of newly enclosed backfen were soon put down to arable cultivation which led to a shortage of grazing land as illustrated by an account of the famous invasion of Crowland Abbey's precinct in AD 1189. The chronicler records,

> The men of Holland, who are our neighbours on the northern side, strongly desire to have common of the marsh of Crowland. For since their own marshes have dried up (each village has its own), they have converted them into good and fertile ploughland. Whence it is that they lack common of pasture. (Hallam 1965: 25)

A nineteenth century legend in the Ancholme Valley (beside the Humber Estuary) provides an excellent example of the ecological consequences of wetland reclamation and is also an important insight into how rural communities perceived their environment. 'Tiddy Mun' was a fertility spirit concerned with water levels in the fens, and during times of flood families would call out to Tiddy Mun to make the waters subside. However, large-scale reclamation in the area had some peculiar effects, including the poor condition of livestock, ponies going lame, damage to houses, and sickness in humans. The local populations blamed this on the curse of Tiddy Mun, who was angered because the wetland pools in which he lived had been drained, and families would pour buckets of water into the drainage ditches to try and persuade him that they were not responsible (Horn 1987). There may, in fact, have been some very simple explanations for the problems suffered after reclamation. The poor condition of livestock may be related to the effect of changing soil chemistry on grass, while horses may have gone lame due to the harder ground. Damage to buildings would have been due to subsidence, while sickness in humans was probably due to malaria, which is more of a problem with freshwater mosquitoes compared with those that live in brackish conditions. Land reclamation clearly had some very far-reaching effects.

2.7 Coastal wetlands: a physically marginal environment?

Coastal wetlands are undoubtedly physically marginal landscapes for settled agriculture, which are particularly prone to certain environmental changes. However, some of these environmental conditions can alter over time, and this, along with a wide range of cultural variables, means that the 'marginality' of coastal wetlands is far from constant.

The intercalated sequences of alluvium and peat that make up these wetlands should be thought of as lithostratigraphic units derived from certain landscape events whereby tidal influence increased (transgression) and decreased (regression). Fluctuating relative sea level may have been a factor, alongside changes in the frequency of storm surges and the impact of human intervention into the landscape. Trying for the moment to remove human influences, it is possible to identify certain periods when changes in the natural environment made coastal wetlands more or less attractive for settlement. Though there is clearly considerable regional variation, it seems possible to generalize that the late first millennium BC mainly saw transgressive conditions in coastal areas, though many of the freshwater backfens remained beyond the tidal reaches. There appears to have been a fairly widespread regressive episode during the Early Roman period which may have been related to an actual fall in relative sea level, though this was followed by further widespread transgressions from around the third/fourth century AD. The latter also appears to have been a period of climatic deterioration, with colder and wetter conditions also making the utilization of low-lying wetlands more difficult. Though there was extensive recolonization on most coastal marshes during the early medieval period there is no independent evidence for a phase of marine regression. In fact, on the continent at least, the reverse appears to have been true, though this period does, however, appear to have been one of climatic improvement (with relatively warm and dry conditions) making the cultivation of coastal wetlands a slightly more attractive proposition.

This is the environmental context into which human communities were making their decisions as to how they should exploit, modify, or transform coastal wetlands. Human activity in such areas is heavily constrained by nature—the risk of flooding was always a serious one—but that is not to say that mankind is helpless and the mercy of the elements. Human societies have become very adept at overcoming adversity and this is precisely what the history of wetland exploitation and management shows us.

CHAPTER 3

A wealth of opportunities:

strategies for the utilization of coastal wetlands

3.1 Introduction

Around AD 1150, Hugh the White, a monk at Peterborough Abbey, said of the area around Crowland, in the English Fenland, that 'the marsh is very necessary for men, for there are found wood and twigs for fires, hay for fodder of cattle, thatch for covering houses and many other useful things. It is moreover, productive of birds and fishes' (cited in Page 1906: 102). This statement reflects the divers range of resources offered by the ecological mosaics that coastal wetlands supported before their reclamation and, in this chapter, a brief summary will be given of those natural assets, including the opportunity for salt production, that made wetlands such an attractive environment for human communities. The possibilities for agriculture are then examined, notably the costs, risks, and benefits of reclamation. Finally, there is a brief consideration of the territorial structures within which landscape exploitation, modification, and transformation took place.

3.2 Plant and animal resources

Coastal wetlands are a physically varied landscape which supported an ecological mosaic of high biodiversity (i.e. species richness) and biomass (i.e. productivity) (Dinnin and Van de Noort 1999). Though saltmarshes are by their very nature flooded by the tide with sufficient frequency to prevent the development of freshwater grassland, the vegetation that does grow is nutritious enough to warrant the grazing of livestock and can even be cropped for hay (Adam 1990: 362; Behre 1990*b*: 47). Conditions are particularly ideal for sheep as the salt helps prevent the foot rot and liver fluke that normally exclude them from damp pastures (French 1996: 653; Knol 1983; Stallibrass 1996: 591). Saltmarshes also provide the added bonus that relatively warm sea temperatures mean that the growing season is longer than on dryland areas, while the regular flooding means that the marshes have 'self-regenerating fertility' (Gerrets 1999: 124).

It is not surprising then that coastal marshes have been highly prized for their grazing, and during the medieval period Walter of Henley describes how animals fed on marsh yielded half as much milk again as those grazed on certain other pastures (Witney 1989: 34). The value of saltmarshes is also reflected in a mid-twelfth century grant by the Knights Templar of lands in Dartford (North Kent) including two 'dayworks' of salt meadow (Bowler 1968: 123): one 'daywork' equated to one fortieth of an acre, and that marshes were divided into such tiny parcels of land reflects the contemporary value that must have been placed upon them. However, the grazing of coastal marshes was an inherently seasonal activity due to the severity of winter storms, and this was reinforced in the case of sheep farming as milk and cheese production traditionally occurred between 20 April and Michaelmas (29 September) (Oschinsky 1971: 180).

Coastal marshes are crossed by a network of steep-sided creeks that must be bridged in order to allow the movement of livestock and shepherds. The prehistoric trackways that crossed freshwater peatlands, such as those through the reedswamps and raised bogs of the Somerset Levels, are relatively well known (B. Coles and J. Coles 1986) and recent surveys elsewhere are showing the extent to which similar trackways also crossed coastal saltmarshes (Bell and Neumann 1995; 1997; Meddens 1996; Wilkinson and

14. Remains of a Late Bronze Age trackway across a palaeochannel, in the intertidal zone at Rolls Farm, Tollesbury, in the Blackwater Estuary, Essex (NGR: TL 9418 0809; 2790±80 BP, HAR-7055; Wilkinson and Murphy 1995: 143–6, context 86/191). Scale 1 m.

15. Modern trackway crossing a tidal creek on a high intertidal saltmarsh at Brandy Hole near Hullbridge, Essex (NGR: TQ 832 956).

P. Murphy 1995). Those of cradle construction would have allowed the passage of humans through particularly low-lying areas, but most trackways are of simple hurdle or brushwood construction used to bridge minor creeks or localized areas of soft mud on a saltmarsh or mudflat (Figures 14 and 15). Such structures may have been used by livestock, though they are not really suitable for cattle since such large animals are liable to push their hooves through gaps in the wattles.

The freshwater backfens offer a range of other plant resources such as reeds and rushes that were used in cattle bedding, basketry, and thatch (reed thatch can last up to 75 years whereas wheat-straw thatch needs replacing after *c*. 25 years: Coney 1992: 60). If the succession of vegetation in the backfen is allowed to reach its climax, then eventually willow or alder carr woodland will develop (Figures 5 and 10). The long slender poles of willow withes and pollards can be used for a wide range of purposes, including wattles in timber buildings, and hurdle panels used in fencing and fish traps.

As plants die in the freshwater backfens, the waterlogged conditions inhibit their decomposition and eventually a peat will form which can be used as fuel. The right to cut peat, known as turbary, is well documented during the medieval period, suggesting that at a time when timber resources were increasingly scarce, this alternative source of fuel was highly valued, especially in the salt industry (e.g. Sturman 1984: 54). The earliest evidence for extensive and systematic peat cutting is from the English Fenland and the western Netherlands where several Roman-period turbaries have been recorded (see Chapter 5). Medieval peat cuttings are widely documented though physical evidence is scarce, the most famous examples being in the Norfolk Broads in eastern England, where some 900 million cubic feet of peat was hand-dug during the medieval period (George 1992: 79–98; J. Lambert and Jennings 1960; Williamson 1997*a*: 84–6).

Coastal wetlands support a wide range of fauna that could be hunted and collected by human communities, including birds, fish, and shellfish. In the twelfth century, for example, Thomas of Ely described how in Fenland 'There are numberless Geese, Fiscedulae [?teal], Coots, Dabchicks, Watercrows, Herons and Ducks, of which the number is indeed great. At mid-winter or when the birds moult their quills, I have seen them caught by the hundred, and even by the three hundred, more or less' (cited in D. Hall and J. Coles 1994: 155). Until the post-medieval period, when duck decoys were constructed, wildfowl were generally caught on a small scale in nets and snares (Williamson 1997*a*: 89–90; 1997*b*: 101–2).

Another source of food is freshwater and intertidal fish, which can be caught using a wide range of techniques including portable equipment such as spears, hook/line, and nets, and permanent structures such as fish weirs (Aston 1988*a*; Brinkhuizen 1983). The construction and maintenance of stone or wooden fish weirs clearly represents a significant investment of resources and as such marks an intensification of fish production/consumption, which culminates with the use of off-shore vessels using nets to catch sea-fish on a large scale. This is discussed further in Chapters 5 and 10.

3.3 Salt production

Another vital commodity that could be obtained from coastal marshes was salt, used in the preparation of leather, dyeing of textiles, soldering at the junctions of pipes and gutters, manufacturing distillates from wine, and in medicinal preparations (Bridbury 1955: XV; Keen 1987; Nenquin 1961: 139–54; R. Smith and Christian 1984: 27). The classical writer Pliny describes a wide range of less obvious functions including its use to cure ailments of the skin, maladies of the eyes in cattle, as a purgative upon the bowels, for the removal of corns upon the feet, and for 'bites inflicted by the crocodile'! (Pliny *Natural History* XXXI: 41, 42, 45). However, by far its most important use is as a preservative for a wide range of foodstuffs including fish, red meat, and dairy produce. For example, in the early fourteenth century it is recorded that one pound (0.45 kg) of salt was required for every ten pounds (4.5 kg) of butter or cheese (Bridbury 1955: XV).

There were two main sources of salt in North West Europe during the Roman and medieval periods: the sea and inland brine springs (rock salt was not discovered in the West Midlands of England until the seventh century: Bridbury 1955). The production of salt from coastal waters could be achieved in three ways:
- through directly boiling sea water
- by extracting the salt from peat or sand saturated with sea water
- by retaining tidal waters in large shallow ponds and allowing solar heat to evaporate the water

The latter method has rarely been used in North West Europe due to the unfavourable climate though there were 'sun works' in medieval Hampshire and Lincolnshire (Grady 1998: 81; Rudkin 1975: 37).

3.3.1 Early coastal salt production around the North Sea

Salt production around the coast of mainland Europe started during the Neolithic (Nenquin 1961: 158), while in Britain the first evidence dates from the early second millennium BC (Early to Middle Bronze Age) in the form of distinctive ceramics, known as briquetage, recovered from several sites on the edge of Fenland (Gurney 1980a; F. Pryor 1980). The earliest actual saltern is at Woodham Ferrers (Crouch Estuary in Essex) dating to the Late Bronze Age (Wilkinson and P. Murphy 1995: 157, 219), though coastal saltworks only became widespread in Britain and the mainland of North West Europe during the later Iron Age. Many sites are now either ploughed flat or eroding out of intertidal mudcliffs (e.g. Figure 16), though in Somerset several survive as impressive earthworks (Figure 17).

Though there has been relatively little large-scale excavation to modern standards on early salt production sites (but see Desfossés 1998), a range of excavated and artefactual evidence suggests an evolving method of production was used throughout the later prehistoric and Romano-British periods around Britain and the North Sea coast (see

16. Eroding early Romano-British saltern ('red hill'), including settling tank (foreground) at Leigh Beck on Canvey Island, Essex (NGR: TQ 823 830). Scale 1 m. Looking north-west towards eroding saltmarsh cliff and modern sea wall (background). A blanket of alluvium over many Roman-period landscapes means that intertidal exposures provide an important 'window' into the use of coastal wetlands during the Roman period.

17. Mound of saltern debris ('briquetage mound', 3rd/4th century AD), in the Brue Valley near Burtle, in the central Somerset Levels (NGR: ST 395 444). Height of mound *c.* 0.6 m.

Bradley 1992; Van den Broeke 1995; Fawn *et al.* 1990, 8–28; D. Gurney 1986: 138–45; Riehm 1961; Rodwell 1979; R. A. Smith 1917–18; Swinnerton 1932). Tidal water was fed to the production sites via natural creeks or artificial ditches. The sea water was then placed in large shallow clay-lined tanks cut into the ground surface whose main function was to allow sediment to settle out though, in addition, salinity would naturally be increased on hot sunny days through solar evaporation (Figure 16). In Belgium, wooden tanks probably used for this purpose have been recorded at Zeebrugge and Raversijde (near Oostende) (Thoen 1975: 58–9).

The brine was then transferred to briquetage troughs which were heated so that the remaining water was driven off. During the Late Bronze Age to Middle Iron Age, round-bottomed troughs were placed on pedestals and placed directly over hearths (e.g. May 1976: fig. 72, 147), whereas towards the end of the Iron Age and into the Roman period flat-bottomed pans were used, heated indirectly in oven-like structures (e.g. Desfossés 1998; Gurney 1986: fig. 86; E. Morris, forthcoming; Pryor 1980: 18–19). The use of ceramic (briquetage) vessels continued until the late fourth century AD in a number of places in Britain including Dorset, Fenland, and Somerset, though in the West Midlands there appears to have been a change in technology during the later Roman period, with lead vats used instead of briquetage vessels (Chapter 5, Figure 40; Penney and Shotter 1996; F. H. Thompson 1965).

The final stage in the production of salt was drying and moulding it into cakes. Since this process leaves no sub-soil traces it is archaeologically undetectable, but the saltcakes appear to have been transferred to briquetage vessels for transportation and these have been found on a variety of inland sites (e.g. Cunliffe 1984: 426–30; Morris 1985; Sealey 1995; and see Chapter 5).

Salt production on coastal marshes would have been a seasonal (summer) activity, when advantage could be made of greater solar evaporation and higher water-salinity levels (Bell 1990: 171; Bradley 1975: 22, fig. 10; 1992: 27; Fawn *et al.* 1990: 19). The production sites needed access to tidal waters though they had to be above the level of storm tides. As a result, early salterns appear to have been located away from the open coast on the slightly raised levee banks of the major tidal creeks further inland (Figure 13M). Tide levels are at their lowest around the summer solstice, once again making summer the best time for salt production.

3.3.2 Later coastal salt production around the North Sea

It seems as if the coastal salt industry was in decline during the later Roman period, and as the technology of production was significantly different during the medieval period, a complete discontinuity is possible. During the medieval period the 'open pan' technique used to boil sea water was largely replaced by 'sleeching' which involved extracting salt from intertidal sand or mud that had become naturally saturated with sea water. This sediment was first allowed to dry in order to concentrate the salt crystals, and was then placed in a pit over a layer of rushes, straw, or turves that acted as a filter. Sea water was poured in to wash out the salt, and this concentrated brine was then heated in large lead vats in order to evaporate the water (Grady 1998; Hallam 1960; Keen 1987; Martin 1975: 75; McAvoy 1994; Rudkin and Owen 1960; Sturman 1984). This shift from locally produced ceramic vessels to more expensive lead pans suggests an intensification in salt production with increased investment in the infrastructure and equipment (as was also seen in the fishing industry during the early medieval period (see Chapter 10).

Since these pans could be repaired or recycled, there is far less evidence in the archaeological record for medieval salt production compared with the more primitive briquetage-using technology though, where medieval salterns have been excavated, numerous fragments and droplets of lead, presumably from repairs, have been found (e.g. Bicker Haven, near Boston, Lincolnshire: Healey 1975: 36). The other physical evidence for medieval salt production is the mounds of waste mud and sand which still survive in a number of areas (*Pevensey Levels*: Figures 52 and 65; Dulley 1966; *Romney Marsh*: Vollans 1995; *Essex*: Christy 1925; *Kent*: M. Thompson 1956; *the Lincolnshire coast*: Figures 73 and 79; M. Beresford and St. Joseph 1979, 262–5; Everson and Hayes 1984: fig. 15; Healey 1975; Kirkham 1975; McAvoy 1994; Rudkin 1975). Since sleeching needed ready access to intertidal muds, and because most coastal wetlands were embanked by this period, medieval salterns tended to occur on areas of unreclaimed saltmarsh in front of sea walls (Figure 13K). The routes along which salt was then transported throughout the country can sometimes be identified as 'saltway' road-names (e.g. *Bedfordshire*: F. Gurney 1920; *Lincolnshire*: Figure 73; Grady 1998: fig. 7; Robinson 1970: fig. 1).

Another method of coastal salt production, known as *darinck delven* or *selnering*, was used in The Netherlands and Germany from at least the Carolingian period (eighth century AD). This involved burning peat that had become saturated with salt water and mixing the resulting salty ash with sea water, to produce a concentrated brine which was then boiled in metal vats (Besteman 1974: 171; Bridbury 1955: 10; Borger 1992: 136; Marschalleck 1973). The intertidal peat cuttings have been recorded in a number of places, including near Waarde in Zeeland (Figure 80: Vos and Van Heeringen 1997: fig. 39), and around the Jadebusen in northern Germany (Behre 1990*d*; Zimmermann 1996: 24).

From around the fourteenth century the coastal salt industry in North West Europe went into terminal decline. The climatic deterioration and resulting coastal erosion and flooding must have made production increasingly difficult, though the main reason appears to have been competition from inland brine springs in the English West Midlands, and the Bay of Bourgneuf in southern France, where the more cost effective technique based on solar evaporation could be used (Bridbury 1955; Pelham 1930).

3.4 Landscape modification: the opportunity for agriculture

Saltmarshes that occur at the very highest point in the tidal range are only flooded very occasionally during the winter spring tides, though even this input of salt water is sufficient to prevent the area's colonization by freshwater plants. However, experiments on contemporary saltmarshes have shown that under certain conditions agriculture is possible on high tidal marshes (Behre and Jacomet 1991; Bottema *et al.* 1980; Rhoades *et al.* 1992; Van Zeist 1974; Van Zeist *et al.* 1976), and palaeoenvironmental evidence has shown that agriculture was indeed practised on saltmarshes during the prehistoric, Roman, and early medieval periods (Körber-Grohne 1981; Murphy 1993*b*; Van Zeist 1989). The three important variables determining the success of saltmarsh cultivation are the frequency, timing, and salinity of inundations. Experiments show that flooding during the seedling stage kills nearly all the crops, but when older, some species can withstand submergence for a few hours on several successive days. A wide range of crops can be grown on such marshes of which Camelina (gold-of-pleasure, grown for its oil-bearing seeds) is the most salt-tolerant, followed by four-row barley, flax, oats, and horsebeans, with wheat being the most sensitive.

There are a number of advantages to cultivating a high saltmarsh compared with many dryland areas including a lower risk of drought, and soil erosion, and high naturally-replenished fertility (Guthrie 1985). The high costs of reclamation are also avoided. However, the disadvantages are obvious: the risk of tidal inundation that can destroy an entire crop. A logical step in the progressive intensification of wetland exploitation was, therefore, the construction of initially localized ditched drainage systems and 'seasonal embankments', sufficient to protect the summer crops, but which were never intended to prevent winter storms from flooding the land (Figure 13D). Such 'summer dikes' would have been relatively easy to construct and maintain—an example at Wijnaldum-Tjitsma in the northern Netherlands was just 0.75 m high and 10 m wide (Besteman *et al.*, 1999)—and would represent a fairly short-term investment in the landscape. However, it then became a fairly simple progression from this modification of the natural environment—simply aimed at preventing summer flooding—to the full-scale transformation that is reclamation and year-round flood defence.

3.5 **Landscape transformation: reclamation**

Having improved drainage and reduced the risk of summer flooding at a local scale, the next logical step is to build a continuous embankment along the coast that was designed to prevent inundation all year around, and reduce waterlogging, so improving aeration and allowing the soil to warm up quicker in the spring (Cook 1999: 15–16). This process of reclamation involves dealing with water management at a series of scales. First, the major source of flooding—the tide, and then the freshwater runoff from the adjacent uplands—must be prevented. Second, once the hydrological system was controlled at this regional level, watertables could be lowered locally through the digging of a drainage system.

The detailed accounts of Christ Church Priory's manors of Ebony and Appledore on Romney Marsh clearly illustrate the series of stages through which reclamation had to proceed (R. A. L. Smith 1940: 30–6; 1943: 172–7). Initially, an area of marsh was protected from inundation through the construction of sea walls. These comprised simple earthen embankments built of clay dug from the marsh, but could be strengthened with timber stakes, wattle fences, stones, and straw. The embankments would have been completed within a single summer since half-finished sections were in danger of being washed away by winter storms, though occasionally a timber wall appears to have been built as a temporary measure, such as the late thirteenth century *nova walla* in Appledore (R. A. L. Smith 1943: 180). Where sea walls crossed tidal creeks substantial timber foundations had to be provided, as have been recorded in a fifteenth century example at Shelford, Essex (R. W. Crump 1981).

The dimensions of early sea walls are rarely recorded, though lower sea levels meant that the substantial sea defences of today would not have been required. For example, the excavation of a section through the Westfriese Zeedijk near Enkhuizen in North Holland revealed that the earliest embankment, dating to the eleventh/twelfth century, was just 1.6 m high compared with 6 m today (Van Geel *et al.* 1982/3: 275–6, fig. 2). Early sea walls in Britain were similarly diminutive. In AD 1500, an embankment at Wennington (near Rainham in Essex) was described as just 6 feet (1.8 m) high, 14 feet (4.3 m) wide at the base, and 3½ feet (1.1 m) wide at the top (Grieve 1978: 185). A medieval sea wall survives in Leverington (near Wisbech, Cambridgeshire) and measures 3.5 m wide at the base, 2.7 m wide at the top, and is 2.4 m high (D. Hall 1996: 185), while an excavated example nearby was originally just 1 m high (Silvester 1988, 160). A twelfth or thirteenth century embankment excavated near Sandwich, in East Kent, was just 1.2 m high and 6 m wide, and comprised several layers of marsh clay with individual sods measuring 0.15–0.20 m square and 0.2–0.3 m long (Hearne *et al.* 1995: 268).

The excavation of an eleventh century sea wall at Clenchwarton (near King's Lynn, Norfolk), revealed the stages by which such an early sea wall was constructed (Crowson *et al.* 2000: 225–30). First, a ditch was dug along the edge of the saltmarsh close to the low mud cliff which marked the division between the high marsh and the lower-lying mudflats below. This ditch intercepted any creeks flowing across the marsh, and provided some material for the sea wall. The remaining material used to build the embankment appears to have been scraped up from the intertidal mudflats.

Once a system of sea walls has secured an area of marshland from tidal flooding the problem becomes managing the flow of waters from the adjacent dryland areas. Because of the gradient difference across coastal marshes, rivers flowing off the dryland areas must either be carried in a raised watercourse across the backfen, or in a deeply incised channel across the higher coastal areas. In the Somerset Levels both approaches were adopted, with channels such as the Pilrow Cut being slightly raised, while another artificial river, the Brue, was deeply incised (Rippon 1997*a*: 213–14). Particularly well-preserved examples of raised canalized watercourses are still in use on the Caldicot Level in South East Wales (Mill Reen and Monksditch) (Allen and Rippon 1997*a*; Rippon 1996*a*: 68–71, fig. 5), and in North Somerset (the Congresbury Yeo), though the Rhee Wall on Romney Marsh has long been abandoned (see Chapter 9).

Once the tide has been kept off a marsh it must then be drained through a hierarchical system of gullies and ditches (Cook 1994; Rippon 1996*a*: 7–9, 50–8; 1997*a*: 19–21; Zimmermann 1996: 36). For example, on the Gwent and Somerset Levels, closely spaced furrows were created through ploughing, from where water drained into slightly larger hand-dug trenches ('gripes') which in turn drained into field ditches and finally major rivers that discharged their water under the sea wall through a sluice structure (see below). The larger drainage channels would also have served as field boundaries, marking parcels of landholding and controlling the movement of livestock by acting as 'wet fences'. In the summer these drainage ditches would also be a source of water for the livestock. The antiquity of this system is unclear though the range of features on recently excavated drainage systems around the Severn Estuary suggests that a similar system of gripes and ditches was used from the Roman period (Rippon 1999). Within a few years the salt was washed from the soil, and the land became sufficiently dry to be used for pasture. In order to cultivate for arable, the addition of marl, lime, and manure can be of great benefit (Pals and Dierendonck 1988; Gross and Butcher 1995: 109–10; R. A. L. Smith 1940: 30–6; 1943: 172–7).

Water collected in the drainage system was discharged under the sea wall through a sluice structure, normally constructed from a hollowed tree trunk at the end of which there was a hinged flap. This was pushed open at low tide, allowing fresh water out of the drainage system, but forced shut as the tide rose. Such structures dating from the end of the Late Iron Age/Early Roman period have been excavated in The Netherlands (see Chapter 4; Figures 29–33), while a medieval example has been recorded at Newton (near Wisbech, Cambridgeshire) (D. Hall 1996: 185). The discharge of water in these drainage systems was generally by gravity, though wind-driven pumps were used in The Netherlands from the mid-fifteenth century (Van der Linden 1982: 66), in Fenland from the late sixteenth century (Darby 1983: 48, 107), and in the Norfolk Broadland from the late seventeenth century (Williamson 1997a: 107). Only a single windmill pump is recorded in Somerset, during the early seventeenth century (Kelting 1967/8: 16).

Two broad approaches towards reclamation can be identified: systematic and unsystematic (Figures 13, 19, and 51; Rippon 1996a; 1997a). The generally earlier *unsystematic* approach was simply to enclose and drain as much land within a marsh as was required by a particular community. As population rose, further parcels of marsh were reclaimed, and this gradual, piecemeal approach led to a landscape of very irregular layout. In contrast, if the entire area of marshland had been embanked and then drained as a single action, the layout of fields and roads would generally be carefully planned, resulting in a far more *systematically* laid out landscape.

Reclamation is hugely expensive in terms of particularly manpower but also materials (Rippon 1996a, 50–60, 68–72). The material to build the sea wall had to be dug from the foreshore and nearby marshes, while large amounts of timber for the sluices and bridges had to be felled and transported across a marsh criss-crossed by deep creeks. There is no evidence that stone was used to face sea walls until relatively recently, though large amounts were used in the sluice structures. The system of drainage ditches behind the sea wall was also a major undertaking and, although some use could be made of the natural marsh creeks, a considerable length of new ditches would have been required. While most of the labour came from the local communities, specialist craftsmen, such as carpenters and stone masons, would also have been required. A reclaimed landscape also needs regular maintenance. The sea wall required inspection and repair every year, particularly after winter storms to which the sluice structures would have been particularly vulnerable. The system of drainage ditches would also require regular scouring, though this material could be used to improve soil fertility by spreading it on the surfaces of the fields (Brandon 1971b: 78).

All in all, reclamation was clearly a high cost strategy towards landscape utilization, yet it was also extremely risky due to the constant threat of flooding. For example, in AD 1014, the Anglo-Saxon Chronicle described how, 'In that year, on the eve of St Michael's mass, came the greatest sea flood wide throughout this land, and ran so far up as it never before had done, and washed away many towns, and countless number of people.' In AD 1236, the chronicler Matthew Paris describes in graphic terms the impact of major floods in the Fenland:

> Then on the morrow of saint Martin ... there burst forth suddenly at night extraordinary inundations of the sea, and a very strong wind was heard at the same time as unusually great waves of the sea. Especially in places by the sea, the wind tore up anchors and deprived the ports of their fleets, drowned a multitude of men, wiped out flocks of sheep and herds of cows, ripped out trees by their roots, blew houses down and destroyed the beaches ... an infinity of people perished, so that in one not particularly populous township in one day a hundred bodies were given over to a grevous tomb (quoted Hallam 1965: 127).

In AD 1287, a contemporary chronicler claimed that 50,000 people were killed in the northern Netherlands, while in AD 1421 some twenty villages and perhaps 10,000 people were lost during the St Elizabeth's Day floods that hit Zeeland (A. Lambert 1971: 85, 122–3).

Disease is another problem in coastal marshes, as was recognized by early writers (see Chaper 1), and can be proved through mortality statistics (Dobson 1998a; b). Reclamation often made the situation worse, creating bodies of stagnant water that were breeding grounds for mosquitoes, the carriers of malaria.

If reclamation was such a high cost and high risk strategy towards landscape utilization, then why did anyone bother? The answer is that it offers a high return and represents an investment in the future. For example, the Battle Abbey custumal of AD 1305/6 allows the value of reclaimed land on the Pevensey Levels to be compared with adjacent dryland areas. The best arable was reclaimed saltmarsh rated at 12 pence an acre, whereas the best of the upland fields were valued at 3–6 pence; meadow, however, was worth an even more impressive 18 pence an acre. 'Brookland', land liable to seasonal flooding but generally capable of spring sowing or fit for mowing, was valued at 4 pence though this could rise to 10 pence if properly drained (Brandon 1971b: 70; Dulley 1966: 37; Scargill-Bird 1887: xv–xvii, 17–25).

Reclaimed wetlands were similarly highly valued elsewhere. For example, c. AD 1200 Archbishop Hubert Walter leased a quantity of marshland within the sea wall at Stone-in-Oxney (near Dartford, North Kent) for 12 pence an acre, while marsh outside the sea wall was only worth 2 pence, but with 10 pence to be added should the marsh be enclosed (Neilson 1928: 51–2). In the Darenth Valley nearby, surveys of AD 1255–1307 record that dryland arable was valued at 3 to 5 pence per acre, whereas reclaimed marsh was worth 6 to 8 pence; in Milton (near Gravesend) arable was valued at 4 to 5 pence per acre in contrast to marsh and meadow which was rated at 6 pence (Bowler 1968: 39, 140). Clearly, communities perceived that reclamation was worth the high cost and the ever present risk of flooding.

3.6 Territories, estates, and the exploitation of coastal marshes

Depending on their size, coastal marshes could be exploited in the context of four possible estate structures (Figure 18). First, if the distance was not too great, both the marshland and the sea shore could be exploited by communities living on the *fen-edge* (Figure 18A). Second, if this distance was too great, then a settlement *subsidiary* to an estate centre on the fen-edge might be established on the marshes (usually the higher ground on creek-banks and towards the coast: Figure 18B). In the early medieval period there is certainly evidence for large multiple—or federative—estates which straddled a range of different environments in this way, each containing a series of specialized settlements exploiting the particular resources of that area, with surplus production redistributed through a central estate centre (G. Jones 1979; 1985), and there is no reason why a similar situation did not exist during the Roman period. Such subsidiary

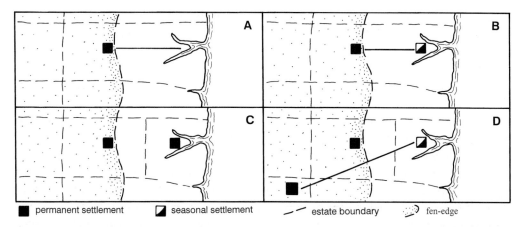

18. Four possible estate structures involving the utilization of coastal marshes. A, marshland exploited directly from a fen-edge estate centre. B, marshland exploited by a seasonal settlement attached to a fen-edge estate centre; C, marshland exploited by wholly marshland, and tenurially independent, community; D, marshland forming a detached part of a distant estate centre.

settlements may initially have been used seasonally, for example by fishermen, salt makers, or by shepherds as part of a transhumant-type economy (though testing this archaeologically is very difficult: e.g. Van Gijn and Waterbolk 1984; cf. Van Gelder-Ottway 1988). The distance over which daily travel from fen-edge settlements became impractical will have varied, though in the Gwent Levels, which vary in width from under 0.1 km to over 5 km, it appears that only when the coastal plain reached around 2 km wide were settlements established on the coastal parts of the marsh (Rippon 1997a: fig. 18).

The third way in which coastal marshes could be exploited was for *independent* settlements to be established on the higher coastal areas (Figure 18C). Such settlements may have emerged from formerly seasonal and subsidiary settlements that gained social and economic independence, or they may have been newly established on previously unoccupied areas of marshland.

In the three scenarios outline above, the area of marsh lay adjacent to the dryland part of the relevant 'nucleated' estate, though this need not have always been the case. The final way in which an area of marshland may have been exploited was for it to be held as a *detached estate* by a settlement some distance away, as part of an estate whose components were dispersed (for examples see Figure 18D, and Figures 57 and 69). For example, during the medieval period, many parcels of coastal marsh, with the opportunity for salt production that they afforded, were granted to monastic houses, while other marshes were used as extensive commons upon which communities many miles inland had rights of pasture. Once these commons were enclosed each community who had previously had rights there received a parcel of marshland which then became a detached part of that parish.

Within these four estate structures, settlement could expand in a number of ways. First, entrepreneurial farmers may have been working independently in colonizing an area of waste ground. Second, settlements may have expanded into an area of marshland due to incentives made by the estate's owner (e.g. low rents), though without the latter's direct involvement in reclamation. Third, an area may have been systematically colonised through the plantation of settlers, a policy often pursued in Europe after military conquest.[8]

3.7 Discussions: models for coastal wetland exploitation and modification (Figure 19)

Coastal wetlands clearly offer a wide range of resources, along with limited opportunities for agriculture including seasonal grazing, and even some arable cultivation on the highest marshes. However, from the start of the first millennium AD, human communities began to change their wetland environment to enable its increasingly intensive exploitation, which eventually led to the impressive reclamation schemes that protect these areas today. There are, however, a number of routes from natural marsh to full-scale reclamation, and this study is an examination of these various strategies towards landscape utilization (Figure 19).

The first strategy is simple landscape *exploitation*, utilizing the rich natural resources of coastal wetlands from settlements located on the adjacent dryland, or perhaps seasonal settlements on the marshes themselves. The second strategy is *modification* through the digging of drainage ditches on those parts of the marsh that were being cultivated in order to improve drainage, perhaps associated with the construction of a low embankment to protect those areas from summer floods. This would have involved only a limited investment of manpower and materials, but would have equally have given only a limited return in terms of increased productivity. This approach towards wetland utilization is most likely to have been associated with settlements, seasonal or permanent, located on elevated areas of the marshes themselves. It is then a simple step from marshland modification to the third strategy, *transformation*, in which tidal influence is removed all year round through the construction of a more substantial sea wall, usually along the entire coast. Once the sea wall was built drainage could proceed in two ways: the gradual and piecemeal enclosure of land as population rose, or the systematic inning of large areas of land in a planned and systematic fashion.

The reclamation of coastal marshes is a high cost, high risk, but high return endeavour: *high cost* in terms of the materials and manpower involved in the initial reclamation and the subsequent maintenance of the drainage and flood defence systems; *high cost* in terms of the rich natural resources that were lost; *high risk* in terms of the constant threat of flooding and disease; but *high return* in terms of the fertile agricultural land that was created. This study examines the decisions taken by human communities whether to exploit, modify, or transform their environment and, in

[8] For example, North East England in the late 11th century (Daniels 1996); South West Wales in the early 12th century (Davies 1991; Kissock 1996; 1997); Frankia in the 12th to 14th centuries (Eigler 1983; Nitz 1983); Transcaucasia in the 18th century (Tiggesbaümber 1983).

particular, the relative importance of changes in the natural environment versus social, economic, and political factors: was mankind bounced around the landscape like balls on a snooker table, or were people to take a more proactive role in shaping their future?

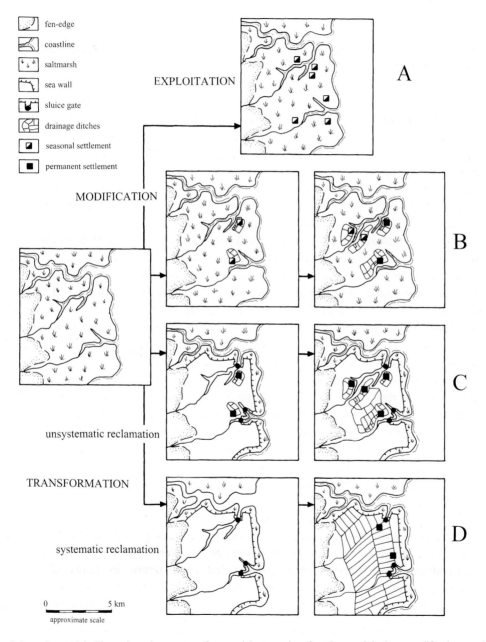

19. Schematic model illustrating the range of potential strategies for the exploitation, modification, and transformation of an area of coastal saltmarsh.

CHAPTER 4

Coastal wetlands in the Roman period

4.1 Introduction

The following chapter describes evidence for Roman-period activity in the coastal wetlands of North West Europe. Fulford and Champion (1997: 217) have commented that, 'Despite the ubiquity of artefacts of Roman date in the intertidal zone, there is little that can be written about the nature of coastal settlement, its inter-relationship with the sea, and the exploitation of marine resources.' Unfortunately, this is also true of the abundant Roman archaeology in coastal wetlands as a whole, and the aim of this chapter is to draw together that evidence for the first time. In this chapter each major area of coastal marshland will be discussed in turn, starting with the Severn Estuary in South West Britain, moving along the south coast, around the Thames Estuary, to Fenland, the Lincolnshire coast, and the Humber Estuary. Attention then turns to Belgium, The Netherlands, and North West Germany. The emphasis will be upon description and synthesis in order to provide background data for more thematic discussions in two subsequent chapters. Chapter 5 examines natural resource exploitation and, in particular, the expansion and subsequent decline of the salt industry. Divergent approaches towards landscape utilization are then given further consideration in Chapter 6 which examines the agricultural use of coastal marshlands, and, in particular, the decision to substantially modify such environments through drainage and reclamation.

4.2 The Severn Estuary (Figure 20)

The extensive coastal wetlands around the Severn Estuary were heavily exploited during the Roman period, though it is only relatively recently that this has been fully appreciated. The evidence has been discussed in detail elsewhere (Rippon 1996a; 1997a) and a short summary must suffice here. The condition of the Somerset Levels during the first to fourth centuries AD has attracted comment in a number of studies (e.g. Cunliffe 1966; Godwin 1943; Hawkins 1973; Lilly and Usher 1972), though these were mostly based upon interpreting unstratified finds of material. Limited fieldwork had revealed an abundance of salt production sites in the Brue Valley (in the central part of the Somerset Levels), but it was only when an extensive Roman drainage system on the

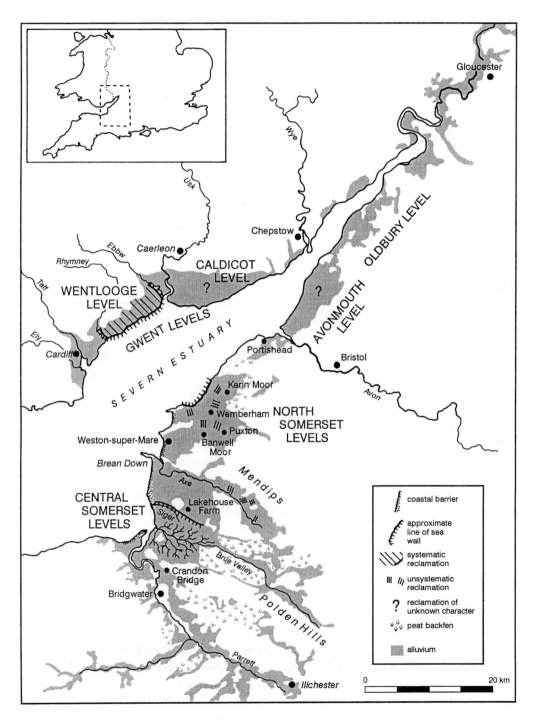

20. Approaches to wetland utilization around the Severn Estuary during the Late Roman period. (Drawn by Sue Rouillard.)

Wentlooge Level was recognized in the 1980s that the scale of the Roman achievement around the Severn Estuary was appreciated (Allen and Fulford 1986; Fulford *et al.* 1994; Rippon 1996*a*; 1997*a*).

The Wentlooge Level (South East Wales) appears to have been embanked and systematically drained, probably in the second century (Fulford *et al.* 1994). This was a major undertaking, since at least *c.* 28 km of sea wall was required to protect at least 31 km^2 of land (the exact figures are unclear as the Roman coastline has been lost to later erosion). A carefully planned system of drainage ditches was created in what was obviously part of a 'grand design' to reclaim the marshes, and the scale of this undertaking (along with an inscription from Goldcliff close by) suggests that the military authorities based in the nearby legionary fortress at Caerleon were responsible. Just one site has been excavated (Rumney Great Wharf, near Cardiff: Fulford *et al.* 1994), and on a very small scale, though the range of material culture and presence of a well suggest domestic occupation of at least a seasonal, if not a permanent, nature. Evidence for arable farming was very limited and the animal bone assemblage showed a relatively high proportion of horse.

Wentlooge appears to be the only example of systematic reclamation carried out on a large scale during the Roman period in the whole of North West Europe. At least part of the adjacent Caldicot Level may also have been embanked, though a number of banks and ditches recently recorded at Goldcliff do not appear to form a coherent rectilinear plan as is the case on Wentlooge, suggesting a less systematic and more localized approach to drainage (Locock 1996; 1997*a*; Locock and Walker 1998). A number of pottery assemblages suggest that the Caldicot Level was occupied between the late first and the fourth centuries AD (Allen and Rippon 1997*a*; Bell 1994; Rippon 1996*a*: 32–5).

Across the Estuary in Somerset, even larger areas were reclaimed: *c.* 55 km^2 between the Rivers Axe and *Siger* in the Central Somerset Levels, and *c.* 100 km^2 in the North Somerset Levels (Rippon 1997*a*: 74–7, 107–10; forthcoming *a*). In these areas there is no evidence for military involvement, and both reclamations are associated with Roman villas (Wemberham in the North Somerset Levels and Lakehouse Farm in the Central Somerset Levels (see Chapter 6)). Unlike on Wentlooge, the very localized field boundary patterns suggest a gradual and piecemeal approach to enclosure and drainage (Figure 19C). The area south of the River *Siger* was left unreclaimed during the Roman period, and was used for salt production; there is no evidence for ditched drainage systems though there have been few excavations in this area (Hollinrake and Hollinrake 1997; Rippon 1995*c*).

Roman-period landscapes over most of the Severn Levels are buried under later alluvium making their investigation extremely difficult, though this is not the case in North Somerset where a recent programme of fieldwork has mapped a number of farm complexes and their associated field systems (Rippon, forthcoming *a*). Each comprises a cluster of small platforms, enclosures, and paddocks, surrounded by slightly larger fields, and although these landscapes show a certain regularity in their individual layouts, there is no evidence for large-scale land allotment as seen on the Wentlooge

Level. The presence of the villa at Wemberham (Reade 1885), along with wide range of flora and fauna from the excavated drainage systems at three other sites (Banwell Moor, Kenn Moor, and Puxton), indicate that during the third and early fourth centuries AD this was a wholly freshwater landscape which must have been protected from tidal inundation by a sea wall. Material culture from these sites suggests that they were of very low status, with an economy based upon mixed agriculture, including the growing of wheat and barley, the keeping of cattle and sheep, along with some metalworking (Rippon 1994*b*; 1995*b*; 1996*c*; 1997*c*; forthcoming *a*). Almost no use was made of local wetland food resources such as fish, shellfish, or wildfowl.

Scatters of pottery on the surface of ploughed fields and eroding into the intertidal zone suggest that settlement was similarly extensive on areas of marshland adjacent to the middle and inner Severn Estuary. Settlement here appears to have begun during the second century, though with the main period of occupation being in the Late Roman period ([third to fourth centuries] Allen 1997*b*; Allen and Fulford 1987; 1990*a*; *b*; 1992; Allen and Rippon 1997*b*).

The only evidence for prehistoric or Romano-British salt production around the Severn Estuary is from the Somerset Levels. The earliest material comes from Brean Down where briquetage has been recovered from a coastal (but dryland) settlement dated to the Middle Bronze Age (Bell 1990), while a number of Late Bronze Age sites on the Avonmouth Level may also be associated with salt production though without using briquetage (Locock *et al.* 1998). There is then a marked hiatus in the evidence for salt production until the Late Iron Age, represented by sites at Badgworth in Central Somerset (Leech 1977*b*) and Banwell, North Somerset (Rippon, forthcoming *a*), both of which must have lain towards the inland margin of the contemporary saltmarsh, close to the fen-edge. From the late first century AD there was a marked expansion of the Central Somerset salt industry and during the second and third centuries AD salterns were spread throughout the Brue Valley, between the Rivers Parrett and *Siger* (Bulleid 1914; Leech 1977*a*: fig. 19; Rippon 1995*c*; 1997*a*: 65–74; Stradling 1850). During the fourth century some of the more coastal locations were abandoned, though salterns further inland continued in use. Despite excavations on a number of contemporary Romano-British settlements elsewhere around the Severn Estuary, there is no other evidence for salt production or even briquetage outside the Central Somerset Levels.

In summary, approaches to wetland exploitation and management around the Severn Estuary during the Roman period show a remarkable diversity. These vary from a major landscape transformation on Wentlooge Level in the form of systematic reclamation, through the more piecemeal drainage behind a sea wall on the North Somerset Levels, to the decision to leave the Brue Valley as a tidal saltmarsh in order to produce salt.

4.3 **Dorset and the south-west coast** (Figure 21)

Two Roman period briquetage-using salterns are known in South East Cornwall, with one site (Trebarveth, near St Keverne) dated to around the second century (Peacock

1969), and the other (Carngoon Bank, on the Lizard) dated to the third and fourth centuries (M. McAvoy *et al.* 1980). Both sites lay in cliff-edge locations and were not associated with areas of coastal wetland.

In Dorset, salt production appears to have been scattered along much of the coast from around the second century BC (Bailey 1962; Brown *et al.* 1995: 76; Cox 1988; Farrar 1975: 14; Woodward 1987*b*), though the Late Iron Age and Romano-British period industry appears to have been restricted to a number of large industrial settlements concentrated around Poole Harbour and Purbeck (Figure 21; Cox and Hearne 1991; Farrar 1962*b*; 1975; Sunter 1987; Woodward 1987*a*). The Kimmeridge salterns were situated on cliff tops and could only have been involved in the final stages of salt production such as drying; evidence for the earlier stages along with the contemporary Roman coastline, has been lost to erosion.

Following a brief period of patronage by the military authorities there appears to have been a decline in these industrial complexes during the late first and early second centuries, though they flourished once again from the Hadrianic period until the fourth century (Anderson 1995; L. Brown *et al.* 1995: 76; Cox and Hearne 1991: 2, 78; Farrar 1973: 87–8; Jarvis 1985*a*; *b*; 1992*a*; *b*; RCHME 1970: 190, 592–3, 603–4; Walkins 1994: 51; Woodward 1987*a*; *b*: 128–9). The production of salt was just one of several industries based upon the rich natural resources of this area which included iron, marble (for mortars and veneers), limestone (for roof tiles and *tesserae*), chalk (also for *tesserae*), shale (for tables, trays, and ornaments), fish, and shellfish (Cox 1988; Sunter 1987; Woodward 1987*a*; *b*). Another important industry was the manufacture of South East Dorset Black Burnished Ware pottery (BB1), which supplied the military establishment in Wales and the North (Allen and Fulford 1996; Farrar 1973; 1976; 1977; 1982; Hearne and Smith 1991; Peacock 1973; D. Williams 1977). The industry appears to have pre-Roman roots and continued through to the fourth century, and while the pottery vessels themselves were clearly important, we have little idea of whether they were also used to transport other local products such as salt and preserved fish.

4.4 **Hampshire and Sussex** (Figure 21)

In Hampshire and West Sussex, a large number of prehistoric and early Romano-British salterns are known along the Solent and Southampton Water, and particularly around Portsmouth/Langstone/Chichester Harbours. Production appears to start around the fifth century BC and ends by the mid-second century AD, though the main period of activity was during the Late Iron Age (Bedwin 1980; Bradley 1975: 23; 1992: 40; Cunliffe 1984: 426–30; C. Fox 1937; E. Morris 1994).

Though less well-known, prehistoric salt production also occurred around the mouths of several Sussex valleys. Iron Age briquetage from the hilltop settlements at Bishopstone and Castle Hill testify to salt production in the Ouse Valley, as do the finds from Mill Hill in Shoreham overlooking the Adur (Bell 1977: 122). A Romano-British saltpan has been recorded at the mouth of the River Cuckmere (Nenquin 1961: 90).

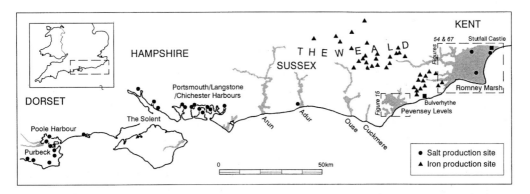

21. Romano-British salt production sites along the English south coast, and centres of the Wealden iron industry (after Bradley 1975: fig. 9; Cunliffe 1988: fig. 6.1; Farrar 1975: fig. 1; Jones and Mattingly 1990: fig. 6.12). (Drawn by Sue Rouillard.)

No pre-medieval salt production sites are known on the Pevensey Levels, though a mound of 'bright orange ferruginous or burnt material' north-west of Boreham Bridge is quite unlike the numerous medieval salterns in the area (Dulley 1966: 28). Bradley (1968) also notes that antiquarian accounts of 'burnt clay cylinders', found in a Romano-British rubbish pit on a hillside above the Willingdon Level, may also represent briquetage. The Pevensey Levels remain a remarkably undisturbed area of coastal wetland, and a potentially thick layer of post-Roman alluvium, along with the lack of modern developments and intensive agriculture, may explain the lack of known Romano-British archaeology.

4.5 **Romney Marsh** (Figures 21 and 67A)

Behind the coastal shingle barrier between Fairlight and Dymchurch lay an extensive area of marshland (Romney Marsh) through which a major river, termed here the 'proto-Rother', flowed discharging its water via a tidal inlet by Hythe (Figure 67A).[9] There is a gradually increasing corpus of Late Iron Age and Roman material from Romney Marsh, though there have been few proper excavations; the state of knowledge is little better than when Godwin (1943), Cunliffe (1966), and Hawkins (1973) were writing about the Somerset Levels.

Several locations on Romney Marsh have produced Late Iron Age material, suggesting fairly widespread but not particularly intense activity, though it is not clear whether this included salt production (R. Green 1968: 27; Kelly 1968: 265; Reeves 1995a: 82; Tooley 1995: 4; Woodcock 1988: 184). The wholly Late Iron Age sites at Snargate and Jesson's Farm (in St Mary's) do not appear to be associated with briquetage (R. Green 1968: 27; Kelly 1968: 265), while the known salterns are all

[9] The alluvial sequence in Romney Marsh and its adjacent valleys has seen particularly intense research. Key papers include: Burrin 1988; Eddison et al. 1983; Lewis 1932; Long and Hughes 1995; Long and Innes 1993; 1995; Long et al. 1998; Spencer 1996; Spencer et al. 1998a; b; Waller 1993; 1994b; Waller et al. 1988; Wass 1995.

wholly Romano-British, with the exception of Dymchurch, which yielded a 'belgic' rim amongst a large Roman assemblage (Issacson 1846), and Scotney Court which may have some pre-Conquest material amongst the otherwise Early Roman assemblage (L. Barber 1998; 89; Philp and Willson 1984; Tooley 1995: 4).

Cunliffe (1988*a*) assumed that the older decalcified alluvium in Romney Marsh, as mapped by R. Green (1968; Figure 55), was dry land in the Roman period, while the younger calcified deposits were thought to be tidal marshes. However, it is now clear that Roman settlement was not restricted to the decalcified alluvium, since Reeves (1995*a*) has found a number of pottery scatters in areas of calcified alluvium in the Newchurch area, while the presence of salt production sites on the decalcified alluvium indicates that the whole of Romney Marsh was in fact a tidal saltmarsh and not dryland (Figure 67A). There cannot have been any reclamation, though the possibility of small-scale drainage on the higher areas of marsh (as occurred in Fenland: see below) cannot be ruled out. Antiquarian speculation that the Dymchurch sea wall and Rhee Wall were built during the Roman period (e.g. Dugdale 1662: 16) can be dismissed: the Dymchurch Wall was built to repair a late medieval breach in the natural shingle barrier (Beck 1995), while the Rhee Wall dates to the twelfth/thirteenth century (see Chapter 9).

The Romano-British sites are often associated with briquetage and other burnt material indicating salt production (Bradshaw 1970: 79; Cunliffe 1988*a*; Isaacson 1846; T. Lewin 1862: ciii; Neilson 1928: 41; Reeves 1995*a*: 81; Woodcock 1988). No saltern has been properly excavated, though observations in the sides of drainage ditches and quarries have revealed mounds of debris of a similar character to the Somerset briquetage mounds such as Dymchurch (Isaacson 1846: 488), Ruckinge (Bradshaw 1970: 179), and Snave (Reeves 1995*a*: 81). There was certainly an expansion of settlement associated with salt production in the first and second centuries AD, although there is almost no material dated to the third and fourth centuries.

As with other coastal wetlands in South East England (e.g. Essex and North Kent: see below) several of the Early Roman sites on Romney Marsh have produced burials (Dymchurch on the shingle barrier, and Ruckinge on the Marsh itself) suggesting communities actually lived in the area, at least during the summer, rather than exploiting its resources from fen-edge settlements. Several locations around the shingle ridges at Lydd have produced evidence for Roman settlement (e.g. I. Jones 1953), along with a handful of fen-edge locations, but overall the scarcity of fen-edge settlement around Romney Marsh, and indeed the low density of settlement, especially villas, in the hinterland as a whole is worthy of note (Ordnance Survey 1978).

4.6 **The Thames Estuary: the Essex and Kent marshes** (Figure 22)

There appears to be relatively little evidence for prehistoric or Romano-British activity on the marshes of eastern Kent though Late Iron Age/Early Roman briquetage has been found at Broadstairs on the Isle of Thanet, at Sarre by the Wantsum Channel, and at Worth and Great Mongham near Deal on the East Kent marshes (Barford 1982; Miles

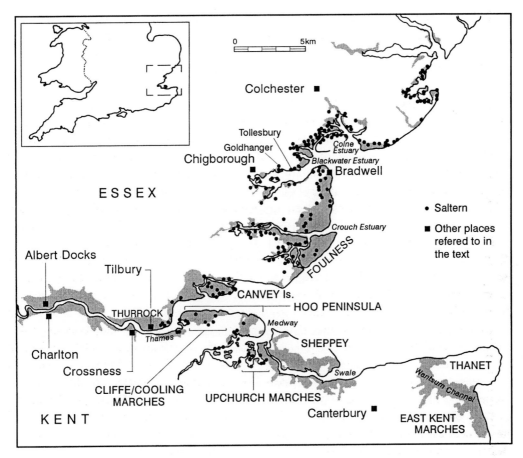

22. Romano-British salt production sites in northern Kent and Essex and places mentioned in the text (after Fawn *et al*. 1990: map 1; Miles 1975: fig. 15). (Drawn by Sue Rouillard.)

1975: 26; Nenquin 1961: 77; Reader 1910: 68). Roman occupation has also been observed stratified within the sand hills that fringe the coast north of Deal (Dowker 1900) and in the intertidal zone at Minnis Bay on Thanet (Powell-Cotton and Pinfield 1939).

In contrast, there is abundant evidence for Romano-British exploitation of the marshes in northern Kent and Essex, most notably associated with salt production (the salterns being known as 'red hills' on account of the thick layers of burn clay and sand). There appear to have been two main foci of activity: around the Blackwater and Colne Estuaries in North East Essex (south of Colchester), and around the Thames and Medway Estuaries in southern Essex and northern Kent; the extent of salt production elsewhere is less clear, largely due to later erosion of the coast (e.g. Andrews and Brooks 1989; Medlycott 1994; K. Walker 1955). These two regions display important differences in the chronology and methods of salt production, and the briquetage used in South East Essex bears a closer resemblance to that from North Kent rather than North East Essex.

The most westerly occurrence of briquetage in Kent is from the fen-edge enclosure at Charlton (Figure 22; Detsicas 1983: 170–1; Elliston-Erwood 1916; 1951: 163; Petrie

1880; Philp 1963). This dryland location cannot have been a primary salt production site and it is not clear from where the briquetage was brought; there are no salterns known on the adjacent marshes. A similar picture is seen in southern Essex, where inland finds of briquetage from the Thurrock area occur much further west than the production sites themselves (Barford 1990*a*; Hull 1963: 30; Sealey 1995; Wilkinson 1988: 22, fig. 30; Wilkinson and P. Murphy 1995: 219).

Though no Late Iron Age salterns have been recorded on the North Kent marshes, briquetage has been recovered from a number of Late Iron Age/Early Roman inland sites in Kent including Canterbury (Barford 1982; 1995). North Kent briquetage has even been found in Late Iron Age contexts at Silchester in northern Hampshire (Timby and Williams 2000: 288–91). Most evidence for salt production in North Kent dates to the Early Roman period with activity concentrated around the Hoo peninsular and the Medway/Swale Estuaries (Blumstein 1956; Detsicas 1983: 156–71; J. H. Evans 1953; Haverfield *et al.* 1932: 132–3, 168, 173; I. Hume 1954; I. Hume and A. Hume 1951; Miles 1975; Philp 1963; Spurrell 1885). Although a site at Cooling appears to have continued into the third century (Miles 1975: 29), there is a notable absence of later Roman material from elsewhere (Blagg 1982: 56–8; Detsicas 1983: 119–39, 171; Miles 1975: 29–30; Monaghan 1982; 1987).

In North Kent a number of sites have also produced evidence for pottery production, notably on the Cliffe/Cooling and Upchurch Marshes (Catherall 1983; Detsicas 1983: 157–61; Monaghan 1982; 1987; Hume 1954; Pollard 1982; 1988). It is curious that these kilns are on the marshland itself, rather than a somewhat more secure location on the fen-edge, as was the case with other coastal wetlands (see Chapter 5). This might suggest that in North Kent potting was an activity which supplemented other seasonal activities that were possible on an un-reclaimed saltmarsh, just as there appears to have been specialized industrial communities around Poole Harbour (see above). The marshland kilns operated from the mid-first century AD with a marked expansion in output during the late first century. The industry flourished during the second century, and though it went into decline from *c.* AD 200 production continued through to the mid-third century (somewhat after salt production had ceased). There is also slight evidence for potting on the northern side of the Thames (see Chapter 5).

In Essex the earliest known salt production site dates back to the Middle Bronze Age (*Woodham Ferrers in the Crouch Estuary*: Wilkinson and Murphy 1995: 157–64), but evidence for production only becomes widespread during the Late Iron Age (Barford 1990*b*; de Brisay and Evans 1975; Fawn *et al.* 1990; Rodwell 1979). Rodwell (1979: 154–7) has argued that the North East Essex industry started around the mid-first century BC and continued into the mid- to late first century AD, whereas Thames-side production started in the mid-first century AD but continued through to the second century. A recent re-assessment of the evidence suggests that this spatial patterning is slightly less clear cut, but as a generalization it still appears to hold true (Fawn *et al.* 190; 35–9; Sealey 1995; Wilkinson and Murphy 1995: 183). The pottery from the red hills suggests production in Essex had ceased by the late second century, though fragments of troughs and firebars have been recovered in sufficient quantities from a dryland site at Chigborough (beside the Blackwater Estuary) to indicate some continued production into the third and even fourth centuries (Wallis and Waughman 1998: 164). However, the scarcity of briquetage finds from other inland sites dating to the third and fourth centuries confirms that the industry that had virtually disappeared by the Late Roman period (Fawn *et al.* 1990: 35–9, 73–80; Sealey 1995: 76); a very small number of fragments from late third to fourth century contexts at Billericay and Great Dunmow appear to be residual (Rudling 1990: 42; Sealey 1995: 78; Wickenden 1988: 53).

As with Romney Marsh (see above), several of the salt production sites in Essex and North Kent are associated with small Early Roman cremation cemeteries,[10] or groups of vessels that presumably came from burial groups.[11] In these cases it would appear that communities were resident on the marshes for at least part of the year, as opposed to living on the fen-edge and travelling to the salterns each day.

The amount of samian pottery, along with occasional amphora sherds, that have been recovered from red hills in both Essex and Kent suggests that these were not impoverished communities (Jefferies and Barford 1990: 74, 77; Kelly 1990: 286; Reader 1908: 193; 1910; W. Rodwell 1976*a*; Spurrell 1885). There are also a number of settlements that have produced significant amounts of domestic refuse and building debris that are quite unlike the other marshland sites alongside the Thames. When the Albert Dock (in East Ham) was constructed Roman pottery, food debris, and tiles were found at a depth of *c.* 2.5 m (Spurrell 1885: 275). Another substantial settlement was destroyed when the Tilbury Docks were constructed. The remains of at least one stone building were observed, along with 'Roman tiles and pottery with bones and food refuse, oyster and snail shells, tiles and flint blocks … in the fine alluvial grey clay … on a mossy and grass-grown surface which could have been unlike the surface of the marsh there at present' (Spurrell 1885: 276; 1889–90: 216; Whitaker 1889: 469).

Three substantial settlements are known further to the east, on Canvey Island. A road running south from Chelmsford as far as Canvey has been suspected since the 1920s (Christy 1920: 219–21), and Roman material has been found at the point where it crosses Benfleet Creek onto the Island (W. Rodwell 1976*a*). A settlement of some status is suggested by the presence of *tegula* and *imbrex* tile, and imported samian and amphora. Briquetage has also been recovered, and the presence of both vessel and hearth fragments would suggest the presence of a saltern nearby (though its date is unclear). Excavations of a site by Thorney Bay, to the south of the Island produced a stratified sequence of Late Iron Age midden debris, sealed by an Early Roman red hill, which was in turn buried by a Late Roman midden. The latter included pieces of tile and building stone, some with mortar still adhering (W. Rodwell 1966: 21; 1976*b*). Occupation appears to have extended into the fourth century. Unstratified collections from the nearby intertidal zone have produced a considerable quantity of decorated and plain samian along with roof and flue tile and a stretch of rubble walling (W. Rodwell

---

[10] *Essex*: Hull 1963: 62; Rodwell 1966; Spurrell 1885: 276–7,
North Kent: Chaplin and Coy 1961; J. Evans 1950; 1951*a*; 1953, 129–31; Hume and Hume 1951: 170; Hutchings 1966; 1987: 376; 1988: 288; Payne 1895; 1902; 1915; Spurrell 1885: 278; Wickham 1876; Wood 1883.
[11] *North Kent*: J. Evans 1951*c*; Kelly 1990: 286; Mason 1994: 447; Payne 1900; 1902; 1905; 1909; Spurrell 1885: 279.

1966: 15–22; 1976*b*). Roman tile has also been found at the nearby Ferndale Crescent red hill (Linder 1939: 152).

A third substantial settlement appears to have lain off Leigh Beck associated with a small cremation cemetery (Going 1996: 103; Hull 1963: 62; Pollitt 1953: 68). Linder (1939: 152) and W. Rodwell (1965*a*; 1966; 1968*a*; *b*; 1971: 16–17) collected large amounts of unstratified material, while later collections confirm a broad date range of Late Iron Age to mid-fourth century AD (Faulkner 1993*a*: 12–14; 1993*b*). A site of some status is indicated by the wealth of the Roman assemblage which includes building debris, an intaglio, large amounts of imported fine ware pottery, including samian, fragments of at least thirty-four pipeclay figurines, numerous brooches, pins, beads, gaming counters, and the finial from a bronze handle (Faulkner 1993*a*: 12–14; Pollitt 1953: 64, 67–8). Such a range of material, and in particular the high proportion of imported pottery, may indicate a small port or landing place.

In North Kent a number of marshland locations have also produced evidence for fairly substantial buildings. At Crossness, a site revealed 'much Roman pottery, mortar, tiles, rubbish and portions of wood' from the upper part of a peat layer (Spurrell 1885: 275). Erosion of the saltmarsh at Black Shore in Cliffe has revealed a settlement associated with pottery, glass, and roof tiles with a 'chalk-gravel floor' dated to the first to third centuries. Several possible substantial buildings also appear to have lain on the Upchurch marshes: a site at Slayhills near Sharfleet Creek has yielded fragments of roof tiles and ragstone (E. Black 1987: no.77; Haverfield *et al.* 1932: 168, 173; Hume 1954: 74; Spurrell 1885: 279), while Milfordhope has produced roof, floor, and 'hypocaust' tiles (Black 1987: no. 76; Hume 1954: 74–6). Roof-tiles, ragstone fragments, and mortar have been found at Funton Marsh in Iwade (A. Miles 1965: 261), while a single fragment of Roman *tegula* has been recovered from a medieval saltern at Falthead Creek on Sheppey (Pratt 1997: 27). The scatter of Roman material, including briquetage, roof tiles, bonding tiles, mortar, and glass found on a second century site near Decoy Farm (High Halstow), is once again indicative of a substantial (permanent?) settlement (Ocock 1969).

A site at St John's Hope in Cliffe has yielded forty late first to second century brooches and over 150 coins, including seventy-nine dating to the fourth century, associated with stone foundations, a rammed chalk floor, and a Roman altar (Hutchings 1987). This may have been a ritual site of some form and, as such, need not have lain in a reclaimed landscape, though its use into the fourth century provides the latest evidence for Romano-British activity on the North Kent marshes.

Clearly, these substantial settlements in both Essex and Kent require further investigation, and may well hold important answers as to the nature of the Thames-side marshes during the later Roman period, though at present it must be stressed that their distribution is limited and none have been subject to proper survey or excavation.

4.7 Norfolk and Suffolk

There is relatively little evidence for Iron Age and Romano-British salt production in

Suffolk and Norfolk, though this is probably due to its cliffed coastline and subsequent erosion. Briquetage has been found at Brantham Hall Farm at the head of the Stour Estuary in Suffolk, associated with early Iron Age pottery (Nenquin 1961: 77). Spreads of briquetage are also recorded from the marshes surrounding the Blyth, Alde, and Orwell Estuaries in Suffolk (Fawn et al. 1990: 43), though the density of these sites appears to have been much less than around the Essex and North Kent coasts. An old land surface associated with briquetage and first century AD Roman pottery has been recorded at Winterton, on the east coast of Norfolk north of Great Yarmouth (Nenquin 1961: 92). A group of seven possible red hills has been recorded at Heacham, on the coast of North West Norfolk, associated with first century Roman pottery (Nenquin 1961: 85), while clay lined tanks associated with briquetage have been recorded at Wolferton north of King's Lynn (R. Clarke 1960: 119).

There is very little evidence for Roman period activity in the Norfolk Broads. Between the first century BC/first century AD and the fourth/fifth century AD there appears to have been a major marine transgression, and a transition within the sediments deposited at this time from estuarine silts through to intertidal sandflats indicates that the Halvergate Marshes were an open, wave-swept tidal embayment during the Roman period. The cessation of tidal influence during the fourth and fifth centuries AD may have been due to the re-establishment of the shingle barrier upon which Great Yarmouth was later built, and by around the fifth century AD tidal waters were restricted to the eastern edge of the Halvergate Marshes (B. P. L. Coles 1977; B. P. L. Coles and Funnell 1981; Funnell 1979; George 1992: 10–20).

4.8 Fenland (Figures 23–5, and 58)

Until the recent expansion of arable cultivation, Fenland had one of the best preserved of all Romano-British landscapes, having been abandoned during the Post-Roman period, then preserved by the encroachment of freshwater peat, and latterly revealed by the desiccation and erosion of that peat; towards the coast extensive areas are still buried under later silts (Phillips 1970: iii–iv). Roman Fenland has also seen particularly intensive research, starting with a series of studies contributing to *The Fenland in Roman Times ...* (Phillips 1970). The systematic plotting of earthworks visible from the air, and the surface collection of material from the sites that had been identified, resulted in a remarkably complete and well-dated plan of the settlements, trackways, and field systems (S. Hallam 1970). During the 1980s and 1990s the re-examination of air photographic coverage, further large-scale fieldwalking, and a programme of palaeoenvironmental analysis as part of the Fenland Project, has further increased our understanding (D. Hall and J. Coles 1994: 105–21). However, this investment of resources in survey has not been matched by large-scale excavation and palaeoenvironmental analysis on marshland sites. While a number of settlements on the fen-edge and southern islands have been investigated (e.g. Gurney 1986; Jackson and Potter 1996; Potter 1981), almost no excavation has been carried out on the marshlands proper. Words written in 1970 still appear to hold true:

> The magnitude and sheer tedium of the examination by excavation of this widespread peasant economy ... must be admitted. ... But if we are to understand these farming groups and the means which made their life possible in this difficult area, a series of carefully considered excavations of the total kind must be undertaken. (Phillips 1970: vi).

The present discussion does not attempt a definitive summary of Roman Fenland (see D. Hall and J. Coles 1994; Potter 1989; Salway 1970), but instead will focus upon those themes which are relevant to this comparative study of how coastal wetlands in North West Europe were exploited and managed during the Roman period. Key topics are the palaeogeography of Roman Fenland, the character of its colonization during the Roman period, and how the newly settled lands were subsequently exploited.

4.8.1 **Palaeogeography**

A recent attempt to reconstruct the landscape of Fenland suggested that the modern fen-edge was the Romano-British coastline, beyond which there were a series of low-lying offshore islands (Simmons 1993*a*; *b*: 21). In fact the landscape was far more complex with six broad topographically and ecologically defined regions, each of which was exploited in a different fashion:

- the fen-edge
- a freshwater peatland in the lowest-lying backfen
- an archipelago of dryland islands within the southern peatlands
- the seaward margins of the peatland where it was crossed by a series of tidal creeks
- the high coastal marsh traversed by more substantial tidal creeks with intervening areas of saltmarsh
- areas of lower saltmarsh and mudflats along the coast

The position of the Roman coastline is not clear, though most scholars have assumed that it was approximately along the line of the earliest medieval sea wall (e.g. Salway 1970: 3). It is unlikely that the shoreline remained static between the second and eleventh centuries AD, though it is equally not known whether erosion or deposition would have been the dominant process during the intervening period. In Figures 23, 24, and 58 the position of the medieval sea wall has, therefore, once again been taken as the approximate edge of the Roman high saltmarsh, though only through the lack of any alternative.

The character of the natural drainage system in the Roman period is also a matter of some conjecture. The Cambridgeshire, Suffolk, and Norfolk fen-edge is heavily indented with the flooded valleys of rivers flowing into Fenland. The exact line taken by these major freshwater rivers (the Ouse, Nene, and Welland) as they crossed the Fens in Roman times is not known, though the patterns of palaeochannels suggest they flowed into three major tidal inlets at King's Lynn, Wisbech, and Spalding, respectively. The Romano-British landscape between these inlets was dominated by dendritic networks of tidal saltmarsh creeks that had their origins during a period of marine transgression in

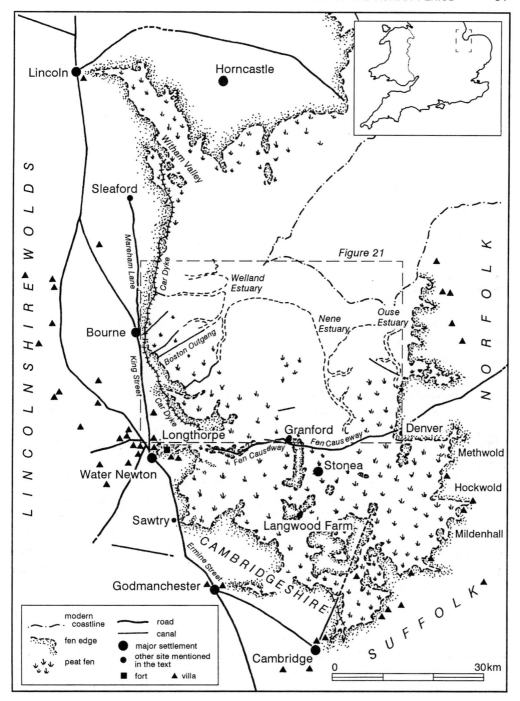

23. The Fenland and its hinterland during the Roman period (after Hallam 1970: map K; Ordnance Survey 1978; Waller 1994*a*: fig. 5.22). (Drawn by Sue Rouillard.)

the first millennium. By the Roman period the naturally-raised levee banks of these creeks provided the highest and driest land in the peat and silt-fens, though many of the creeks themselves were still active, being linked with canals, crossed by bridges, and the focus of salt production: in essence this was still an intertidal landscape.

4.8.2 **Fen-edge settlement**

Though the fen-edge was a favoured location for settlement, this was not consistently so all around Fenland. There were a number of probable small towns or other substantial nucleated settlements with Horncastle to the north, Bourne and Water Newton to the west, Godmanchester and Cambridge to the south, and Denver to the east (Figure 23). Bourne can be singled out as having particularly strong Fenland links, lying at the landward end of the Bourne to Morton canal, on the line of the Car Dyke (see below), and close to the junction of two Roman roads which ran from Water Newton to Sleaford and Ancaster (Hayes and Lane 1992: 135–6).

There were also a number of probable/certain villas around Fenland, though these were not evenly distributed along the wetland margin (Figure 23). Along the Lincolnshire and North West Norfolk fen-edge there were relatively few and it seems that the adjacent chalk and limestone Wolds were a much more favoured location for villa building (Gregory 1982; D. Hall and J. Coles 1994: 109–10; Hayes and Lane 1992: 20, 80; Lane 1993a: 83–4). In contrast, the Cambridgeshire/Suffolk fen-edge shows a marked concentration of villas between Cambridge and Mildenhall, while there was also a large number of substantial buildings along the southern part of the Norfolk fen-edge between Methwold and Hockwold (Gregory 1982; D. Hall and J. Coles 1994: 109–10; Reynolds 1994; Salway 1967). This area has a hinterland of poor Breckland soils.

Though much of the fen-edge does not appear to have been a focus for high status settlement, there was a greater frequency of lower-status agricultural farmsteads in certain areas (*Lincolnshire*: Hayes and Lane 1992; *Cambridgeshire*: Hall 1987; 1992; 1996; *Norfolk* Silvester 1988). In places the number of sites was quite remarkable: along the southern part of the Norfolk fen-edge, Late Roman settlements have been recorded at intervals of *c.* 400–800 m, comparable with the settlement densities found around the North Somerset Levels (Rippon 1997a: 87–90). However, elsewhere the fen-edge does not appear to have been a focus for even lower-status settlement. Hallam (1970: 41) noted that the northern fen-edge was strangely devoid of settlement, and a more recent survey has shown that not only was there relatively little settlement, but that even these never attained a high status (Lane 1993a). Another area of the fen-edge that appears to have lacked extensive settlement is between Water Newton and Godmanchester, in Cambridgeshire (*the Welland and Ouse Valleys*: D. Hall 1992). This lay next to the lowest-lying part of the southern peat fens, which would have provided a range of natural resources, such as fish, wildfowl, and reeds, but may have been too waterlogged to have been used for grazing.

4.8.3 **Transport and communications** (Figure 23)

Fenland was largely avoided by the Roman road network, with Ermine Street to the south-west, Kings Street (and its continuation at Mareham Lane) to the west, and the Icknield Way to the south-east. There were, however, a number of important roads and canals that crossed or skirted Fenland in what appears to have been part of a co-ordinated attempt to improve communications.

The Fen Causeway

The most important transport corridor across Fenland, the Fen Causeway, ran from Ermine Street and the first century AD legionary base at Longthorpe in the west, across several islands in the southern fen to Denver in the east. The Fen Causeway is in fact three separate features: two roads and a canal (Crowson 1994; D. Hall 1987: 41–4; Kenny 1933; Leah 1992: 53–4; P. Murphy 1992: 37; 1994: 28). The earliest road was laid across an active saltmarsh during the later first century AD, and may have been associated with attempts to subdue East Anglia after the Boudican revolt (Potter 1989: 158–9). To the south of the first road ran a canal, *c.* 10 m wide and 1.7 m deep, constructed during the second century and used until at least the mid-third century (Crowson 1994: 25). A series of salterns lay on the banks of the canal and beside the roadside ditches, indicating that this remained a tidal landscape (Gurney 1986: 93; Hall 1987: 42; Silvester 1991: 109–10). Following a period of marine flooding during the third century, which buried the earlier road under a layer of silt, a second road was constructed to the south of the first, on the southern bank of the earlier canal. Palaeoenvironmental evidence from the roadside ditches of the second highway, and layers of metalling intercalated with flood silts, show that it too crossed an active saltmarsh (Leah 1992: 53–4).

The only other major gravelled road in Fenland, the Baston Outgang, ran between Kings Street on the fen-edge and the putative estuary of the Welland (Hallam 1970: 30; Hayes and Lane 1992: 171–2). The rest of Fenland was served by a complex pattern of trackways that mostly appear to follow the raised ground afforded by naturally meandering creek-banks (e.g. Figure 25A). Other droveways were laid out in straighter lines across the intervening lower-lying areas, and these appear to have been primary landscape features around which field systems were subsequently arranged. However, there is no evidence for planning or regular land allotments defined by the droveways or the field systems. Just one block of fields, at Christchurch, may have been laid out using the Roman *actus*, though even this complex cannot be classed as *centuriation*. D. Hall (1996: 177) suggests that it may represent a less regular system of land division known as *limitatio*.

The Car Dykes

Two major earthworks survive along much of the western Fenland edge, both known as the 'Car Dyke' (Figure 23). The Lincolnshire Car Dyke ran north from the River Nene near Water Newton, past Bourne, to the Witham Valley near Lincoln, a distance of some 65 km. It comprises a low central channel *c*. 2 m deep and *c*. 12 m wide, with banks on either side *c*. 13 m wide and which survive to *c*. 1 m above ground level (D. Hall 1987: 28; D. Hall and J. Coles 1994: 105). The function of the Car Dyke is unclear though favoured interpretations are that it was either a canal, or a catchwater drain designed to prevent freshwater flowing off the uplands from flooding the Fens. The latter interpretation has been favoured since Pryor's (1978) survey which established that the channel is not completely horizontal, and Simmons's (1979) observation that longitudinal sections have revealed several causeways of un-dug bedrock (and see Salway 1980). However, the occurrence of banks on both sides of the central channel suggest that the Car Dyke could not have functioned as a catchwater drain, and the causeways may in fact have served the same function as locks in a canal, maintaining the water levels in individual stretches of the channel, so overcoming Pryor's objections with regards to slight variations in its altitude (D. Hall and J. Coles 1994: 109). Clearly, more work needs to be carried out on this important feature.

The Car Dyke in Cambridgeshire appears to link the River Cam with the Ouse and Old West River (D. Hall 1996: 123). It comprises an earthwork *c*. 20 m wide and *c*. 2 m deep, with banks on either side (Clark 1949; Macaulay and Reynolds 1993: 63–69; Thorpe and Zeffertt 1988–9). The Cambridgeshire Car Dyke appears to have been constructed in the second century (possibly during the Hadrianic period) and seems to have gone out of use by the mid- to late fourth century (Hartley 1970; Macaulay and Reynolds 1993; Thorpe and Zeffertt 1988–9: 14). Once again, functions as a catchwater drain and canal are possible, though the latter is more likely given the evidence for banks on either side and the absence of settlements in the southern Fens for it to protect from flooding. As a canal it would have considerably reduced the distance by river between Cambridge and Godmanchester. However, there is a third possibility for the nature of both Car Dykes: Mackreth's (1996: 234) suggestion that the Car Dykes represent boundary-features comparable to the *vallum* south of Hadrian's Wall, marking the edge of an imperial estate (see Chapter 6).

Other canals

In addition to the Fen Causeway, and possibly the Car Dykes, there are a number of other silted-up Roman canals in Fenland, several of which ran eastwards from the Lincolnshire fen-edge into the extensively-settled silt fen. One of the longest canals runs for 6 km from the Car Dyke at Bourne through the peat fen and into a natural creek at Morton (Hallam 1970: 255–6; Hayes and Lane 1992, figs. 74 and 82, plates IV–V). The canal was 13 m wide and 3 m deep, and contained high energy tidal waters (Lane 1993*b*: 42; P. Murphy 1993*a*: 38; 1994: 28). Canals in Rippingale and Deeping both run for *c*. 2 km from the fen-edge and across the peat to the siltland where they join the tidal creek system that enters the Welland Estuary (Hayes and Lane 1992: 84, 190). Various stretches of the modern drainage system have also been suggested as having a Roman origin, though such claims generally have little in their favour (D. Hall and J. Coles 1994: 107). The one exception may be the River Glen whose integration with other features in the Romano-British landscape 'leads to the tentative suggestion that [it] could have been re-routed along its present course during the Roman period' (Hayes and Lane 1992: 159; also S. Hallam 1970: 35). The Glen also runs from the fen-edge into a creek system that flows to Bicker Haven.

The Aylmer Hall canal in Norfolk was at least 5.6 km long, 12 m wide, and *c.* 1.7 m deep and contained tidal waters (Leah and Crowson 1993: 44–5; P. Murphy 1993*a*: 38; Silvester 1988: 54). It ran westwards from the Great Ouse river into an area that had a high density of settlement, where it was joined from the south by the shorter Spice Hills canal (Silvester 1988: fig. 122). Several other short lengths of canal are known in the southern Fens that appear to have either canalized stretches of natural watercourse (e.g. Figure 25B), or cut through large meanders in tidal rivers (e.g. Figure 25A).

The function of all these canals is not altogether clear, though similar structures for both drainage and navigation are found elsewhere in the Roman Empire (K. White 1984: table 6). The Fen Causeway canal runs across the southern fen from bedrock to bedrock and so cannot have aided the drainage of this area: it must have been primarily for transportation. The canals that flow east from the Lincolnshire fen-edge all link with tidal creeks, suggesting they could have served both a drainage and communications function, but without a sea wall to protect these areas from tidal inundation it hardly seems likely that freshwater run-off was really a major issue. It seems, therefore, that communication may have been the primary function of the canals suggesting a fairly concerted attempt at improving access to the Fenland, linking communities and transport networks along the fen-edge with settlements in the siltlands and on the coast.

4.8.3 The southern islands

The northernmost islands of the southern Fenland (notably March, Stonea, and Whittlesey) occupied a nodal location in that landscape, lying close to the major communication routes across the southern Fens (the Fen Causeway), and at the interface of the unoccupied peatland to the south and extensively settled siltlands to the north. Not surprisingly, there are several substantial settlements on these southern islands which may have played an important role in the exploitation of Fenland.

The island at Stonea appears to have fulfilled a 'central place' function from at least the eve of the Roman Conquest, for although there is little evidence for permanent occupation within Stonea Camp, a range of native British coins indicate that it was a place for meeting and exchange (Jackson and Potter 1996: 42–3; Malim 1992). Around *c.* AD 130–50 a substantial and carefully laid out Roman settlement was constructed *c.* 500 m to the north-east which included a substantial stone building of monumental proportions (discussed in Chapter 6). A second unusual stone building has been discovered in the settlement at Langwood Farm West, on Chatteris Island, which may also fall into the 'estate centre' category (Crowson *et al.* 2000: 25–36).

Another important settlement lay at the point where the Fen Causeway reached the western side of March Island at Grandford. The site covers some 30 acres adjacent to a possible fort next to the Fen Causeway, and originated *c.* AD 65–75 (Potter 1981). The subsequent settlement appears to have had a rudimentary street system, and shows an unusual level of wealth for the Fenland with ceramic roof tiles used during the late first and second centuries, and stone buildings constructed during the fourth century with window glass and plastered walls. The wealth displayed by these buildings may simply reflect the relatively security from flooding afforded by the islands compared with the adjacent marshes and fens, and such material elsewhere in Roman Britain might not warrant much comment. However, in the context of Fenland the site is certainly unusual, and may suggest that Grandford, like Stonea and Langwood Farm, functioned as an estate centre.

4.8.4 **Salt production**

There is evidence for salt production in Fenland from the later Bronze Age, and by the Middle Iron Age the industry was extensive, particularly in Lincolnshire (Lane 1993c). The late first and second centuries AD saw a significant increase in the number of sites throughout Fenland, though, in common with most of southern and eastern Britain, salt production appears to have declined by the mid- to late second century (Hallam 1970: 70). There is evidence for continued salt working on just a small handful of sites during the third and fourth centuries.[12] Sherds of Late Roman pottery have also been found on a number of earlier salterns, though it is not clear if this pottery is domestic refuse from Late Roman salt production, or whether it is derived from the re-use of earlier sites for some other purpose, perhaps because they offered small islands of raised ground in an increasingly wet landscape (Hayes and Lane 1992: 227; Nenquin 1961: 66). During the Roman period salt production mainly occurred close to 'quiet waters at the inland margins of the saltmarsh' (Figure 24; Lane 1993c: 26) though over time there was a slight shift in the location of production eastwards as the freshwater peat fen expanded (e.g. Hayes and Lane 1992: figs. 133–4; Simmons 1975: fig. 18).

4.8.5 **Settlement in the siltlands** (Figures 24–5, and 58B)

In the coastal marshlands and marsh/peat margins of the Cambridgeshire and Lincolnshire Fens, the plotting of earthworks, many of which now only visible on air photographs (S. Hallam 1970; D. Hall 1996; Palmer 1994; 1996a; b), and two major campaigns of fieldwalking (S. Hallam 1970; D. Hall 1988; 1992; 1996; Hayes and Lane 1992; Lane 1993a; Silvester 1988; 1991) have produced what probably amounts to the most detailed plan of a Romano-British landscape that we are likely to recover. As Palmer (1994: 34) has observed, 'But for a few gaps, [the mapped area] shows a pattern of past landuse that is more dense and continuous than any other . . . in Britain. This is part of the problem—there is almost too much to begin to understand'. Another major problem in understanding this landscape is that these major surveys have unfortunately not been matched by large-scale excavation and palaeoenvironmental analysis, though

---

[12] *Blackborough End, in the Nar Valley, Norfolk*: Crowson *et al.* 2000; *Denver, on the Norfolk fen-edge*: Gurney 1986: 93–148; *Norwood, north of March Island, Cambridgeshire*: Potter 1981: 104–16; *Old Croft in Littleport, north of Ely, Cambridgeshire*: Hall 1996: 27.

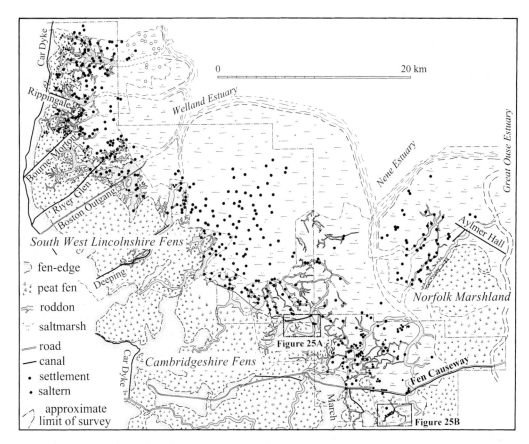

24. Central Fenland during the Roman period (after Hall 1996; Hallam 1970; Hayes and Lane 1992; Silvester 1988). (For location see Figures 23 and 53.)

work on the Fen Causeway and a number of other canals has at least confirmed that the marshes were an intertidal environment throughout the Roman period.

Settlement in the marshland concentrated on the slightly higher ground along the relict and still-active tidal channels. The Wash is a relatively sandy estuary, and over-bank flooding adjacent to the active tidal creek systems in Fenland would have led to the formation of naturally raised levees. These would have afforded better-drained ground compared with the lower-lying areas of marsh between the creek systems where finer-grained and more organic sediments accumulated. As these creek systems silted-up they would also have been filled with relatively sandy sediment leading to the formation of slightly raised creek ridges known as roddons.

During the Romano-British occupation of Fenland, many of these creek banks and roddons were flanked by ditches which presumably acted as catchwater drains during times of flood (Figure 25A), whilst also taking freshwater run-off from the adjacent, lower-lying, fields; an additional role managing livestock is also possible (Palmer 1996b: 12). The settlements comprised clusters of platforms, paddocks, and small enclosures, associated with surface scatters of domestic and building debris, sometimes

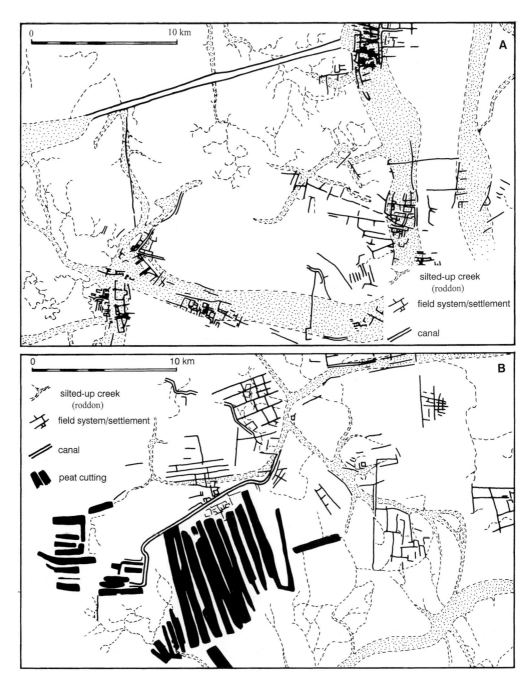

25. Romano-British landscapes in the Cambridgeshire Fens. (For locations see Figure 24.) A, settlements and field systems strung out along the raised ground afforded by relict creeks in Parsons Drove and Wisbech St Mary, Cambridgeshire (from Hall 1996: fig. 95); B, peat cuttings and associated canal in Elm and Upwell, Cambridgeshire (from Hall 1996: fig. 96). (See Figure 39.)

around what appears have been an area of open ground (e.g. Deeping St Nicholas in the south-west of the Lincolnshire Fens: Palmer 1994: fig. 3a). These settlements were linked by a network of ditched trackways, which also often took advantage of this higher ground. The trackways would have allowed the driving of livestock through the enclosed fields and paddocks that surrounded the settlement foci on the higher ground to the low-lying pastures between the roddons. The field systems were often laid out at right angles to the roddons and their flanking ditches, and many of the individual blocks of rectilinear fields were laid out within a broad coaxial framework. However, there is no evidence for any overall co-ordination: there are no extensive planned field systems (i.e. Figure 19C, not D) as can be found on the nearby uplands of East Anglia (Rippon 1991; Williamson 1987), or in a wetland context on the Wentlooge Level in Gwent (Fulford et al. 1994).

Most of the boundary systems peter out on the lower-lying areas between the creeks and roddons. The remaining open areas were presumably used for grazing, and since there is no sign of field boundaries, and as the wet conditions would make hedgerows unlikely, these areas may have been common land.

In a number of places attempts may have been made to prevent fresh water in the backfen from flooding the enclosed and settled marshes to the east. Hallam (1970: 30–1) identified several double-ditched linear features which ran roughly parallel to the fen-edge and close to the peat-marsh margins. She interpreted these features as droveways, though Hayes and Lane (1992: 210) observe that they make no sense as communication routes. The parallel ditches may represent quarries for a bank between them, which would have served the same function as medieval fen-banks (see Figure 51). However, in contrast to the medieval fen-banks that crossed many miles of fen in a single straight alignment, the Roman structures were on a much smaller scale. Along with the lack of overall planning in the road and field systems, colonization of the silt fen appears to have been a small-scale, un-coordinated, and piecemeal affair.

A characteristic of some siltland settlements is that although the pottery assemblages display a fair level of affluence—perhaps indicative of permanent as opposed to seasonal settlement—there is little evidence for substantial structures. Coldham, in Cambridgeshire, provides an extreme example with a remarkable collection of pewter and bronze vessels and other metal objects from a site which, upon (admittedly small-scale) excavation, revealed evidence for just wattle and daub buildings (Potter 1981: 93–8). There are few examples of possible stone buildings in the marshlands, though in Donington, Dunsby, Gosberton, and Quadring (Lincolnshire) several sites have produced scatters of ceramic and stone roof tiles (Hayes and Lane 1992: 54, 90; Hallam 1970: site 1,626). However, these sites are very much in the minority and contrast sharply with the relatively abundant evidence for buildings with stone walls and ceramic-tiled roofs along parts of the Lincolnshire fen-edge. What is odd is that, compared with these fen-edge sites, the pottery assemblages on Fenland settlements tend to be richer both in terms of the absolute amount of pottery and the proportion of fine wares (e.g. Hayes and Lane 1992: 74, 80, 90). It may be that these fen-edge settlements in Lincolnshire do have a relatively poor pottery assemblage: perhaps they were subsidiary elements of a larger estate based on the villas located on the limestone Wolds to the west. Alternatively, the Fenland sites may have unusually rich pottery assemblages: perhaps the constant threat of flooding meant that surplus wealth was invested in material culture rather than in masonry buildings.

4.8.6 Farming in the siltlands

There is a wide range of evidence that Fenland was not reclaimed during the Roman period. The distribution of salterns shows that the creek system carried sea water throughout the coastal marshes, while palaeoenvironmental analysis, their association with salterns, and the creation of substantial levee banks, shows that the major canals also contained tidal waters. As Fenland remained a tidal landscape during the Roman period, this raises important questions regarding the use to which these extensively settled marshes were put.

Ever since Stukeley's suggestion that the Car Dyke was built to facilitate the transportation of grain to the northern frontier, the traditional view of Fenland was that it represented a vast granary (e.g. Richmond 1963). This idea was gradually replaced by one that saw Fenland landuse as dominated by pastoralism (e.g. D. Hall 1982: 34; Phillips 1970: vii; Salway 1970: 14), though this too has been questioned in recent years (e.g. Silvester 1988: 156). It is always difficult to assess the relative contribution of arable cultivation and livestock husbandry in any rural economy, and in Fenland this is made even more difficult by the lack of excavations on the marshland settlements. However, a few threads of evidence do point to a mixed economy with a predominance of stock raising.

Very little is known about arable cultivation, though at Morton, for example, charred remains for barley, the most salt-tolerant cereal, has been found in association with saltmarsh weeds (Crowson *et al.* 2000: 138). More is known about the animal husbandry. The morphology of the Fenland field systems is suggestive of a strong pastoral element, with long droveways associated with open pastures and complexes of small paddocks and fields. Indeed, the lack of light pottery scatters associated with these Fenland field systems suggests infrequent manuring, which may also indicate a mainly pastoral use (D. Hall and J. Coles 1994: 119; Palmer 1996b: 8).

A series of excavations on settlements around the fen-edge and southern islands found roughly equal numbers of cattle and sheep bones (*c.* 40 per cent each).[13] This proportion of sheep is higher than average for rural sites in Roman Britain (e.g. Potter 1981: 130; and see Grant 1989). As sheep are vulnerable to foot rot and liver fluke in freshwater environments (French 1996: 653), it seems unlikely that they would have been grazed in the peat fen close to these settlements. It may have been that these fen-edge communities grazed their sheep on upland parts of their estate during the winter, but moved them down onto the coastal marshes during the summer, where saltmarsh conditions helped prevent foot rot and liver fluke (French 1996: 653; Stallibrass 1996; 591).

Both sheep and cattle appear to have been kept primarily for their secondary

[13] *Earith, Cambridgeshire*: White 1967; *Hockwold, Norfolk*: Salway 1967; *Golden Lion Inn, Stonea, Cambridgeshire*: Potter 1976.

products (milk, cheese, hide, and wool) rather than for their meat, though the predominance of sheep metapodials at the Golden Lion Inn site (Stonea Island) suggests the butchery of animals for consumption elsewhere (Potter 1981: 130). The main settlement at Stonea also appears to have been exporting butchered joints of meat, notably lamb (Stallibrass 1996: 604). Salt would have been an essential part of all these activities, used to preserve cheese and meat, and in the preparation of hides. Hartley (1970: 168) has noted that subjectively there appears to be 'far more examples of the vessel usually thought to be a cheese press for hard cheeses from the fens than from any other area of Britain'.

4.8.7 Third century floods

It has been known for many years that parts of Fenland suffered from a brief period of flooding during the third century AD (Bromwich 1970). This has been illustrated by a number of sites along the south western fen-edge and southern islands which had phases of abandonment marked by sterile layers of alluvium sealing a sequence of occupation deposits.[14] There was also a tendency for settlements to migrate up the fen-edge slope: second century occupation typically lay at *c.* 2.4–3.1 m OD, compared to *c.* 3.4 m OD during the third century, and *c.* 3.1 m in the fourth century (Bromwich 1970). Recent work at Throckenholt Farm in Parsons Drove (Cambridgeshire), out on the coastal marshes themselves, has shown that the site was also abandoned during the early third century when the field ditches were filled with silt (Bray 1994).

   The dating of the flooding was given by Bromwich (1970: 120) as early to mid-third century, while Churchill (1970: 140) suggests a slightly broader date range of *c.* AD 225–75: evidence from Earith, Grandford, Hockwold, and the Golden Lion Inn at Stonea would support the latter (Potter 1976: 46; 1981; 89; Salway 1967: 56–7; White 1967: 11).

   Palaeoenvironmental data from the flooded sites indicates a freshwater environment of deposition. The extensive third century abandonment might, therefore, have been caused by an acceleration in the expansion of the peat fen which is evident in Lincolnshire from the first millennium BC (Hayes and Lane 1992: 172, 208–10; Salway 1970: 14). Recent work has shown, however, that there also appears to have been an episode of marine flooding at this time closer to the coast. In Norfolk, a layer of marine sediment buries parts of the Fen Causeway and much of the Roman landscape either side, and the distribution of these silts suggests a source of flooding in the Wisbech tidal inlet (G. Fowler 1949; Leah 1992: 53–4; P. Murphy 1994: 28; Potter 1981: 118; Silvester 1991: 115). While the immediate cause of flooding in the southwestern Fens appears to have been an expansion of the freshwater bogs, this may ultimately have been due to an increase in marine flooding in coastal areas that caused freshwater discharges to become pounded-up. An episode of late second to early third century flooding has also been recognized in the lower Trent Valley, and may be due to the same factors (Van de Noort and Ellis 1998: 181; D. Riley *et al.* 1995: 263).

---

[14] *Earith, Cambridgeshire*: White 1967; *Hockwold, Norfolk*: Salway 1967; *Grandford and Flagrass on March Island, Cambridgeshire*: Potter 1981: 88; *Stonea*: Potter 1976.

4.8.8 Fourth century recovery

Settlement only appears to have recovered in Fenland during the late third century. Salway (1970: 15) suggests there was a *delay* in the recovery of settlement due to the political and economic problems facing the empire between the murder of Commodus in AD 193 and the accession of Diocletian in AD 284. Though this hypothesis cannot be dismissed, it would appear unlikely. First, it assumes that the whole of Fenland was a *directly managed* imperial estate during the third century, the evidence for which needs very careful examination (see Chapter 6). Second, there is no evidence for a *time lapse* between the flood waters subsiding and the recolonization of those areas affected: both could have occurred during the mid- to late third century. Third, the impact of widespread flooding on a landscape dominated by private estates, based around villas on the surrounding Wolds, may have been very similar to the impact on an imperial estate. In a free market individual owners could have taken the initiative to recolonize flooded lands at any time, but if the economic situation was poor there may not have been the resources available. If Fenland was not divided between villa estates, but was farmed by independent small-holders with even more limited resources, then this problem would have been accentuated. A parallel with Fenland might be found in Gaul, where peasants in the civitas of *Aeduorum* had become so burdened with debt, that they could not afford to maintain the drains and cut back the encroaching scrub, so that once fertile land reverted to marsh (A. H. M. Jones 1964: 817).

The recolonization of Fenland may have been related to a general package of measures that were taken in the Late Roman period to bring abandoned lands back into cultivation, rather than policies specific to an imperial estate. During the third and fourth centuries there was a growing problem within the Empire of deserted agricultural land (*agri deserti*), which resulted in a stream of legislation and imperial initiatives (A. H. M. Jones 1964: 812–3). Deserted lands were granted, sold, or leased on favourable terms, or compulsorily allocated, with their tax burdens, to individual landowners or the governing bodies of local communities: 'one thing which the government was reluctant to do, though occasionally it was forced to make this concession, was to write off deserted lands permanently.' (A. H. M. Jones 1964: 813).

The fourth century landscape in Fenland appears to have had a somewhat different appearance to that of the second century. The population may have fallen from *c.* 28.5 persons per square mile in the late second century, to 19.5 in the late third, 14.5 in the early fourth, and just 6.25 by the late fourth century (S. Hallam 1970: 72). Only certain areas of Fenland appear to have been reoccupied, notably the higher marshlands of Lincolnshire. The overall number of farm units fell by nearly a half between the late second and early fourth centuries and overall there was a decline in the size of settlements, though the number and proportion of large nucleations actually increased (S. Hallam 1970: 56; Potter 1981: 129). Though the settlement densities never returned to those of the second century, the Fenland communities were not too impoverished, as illustrated by the eleven fourth century coin hoards which have been discovered from both the southern islands and the silt fen (dating as late as the 390s: Potter 1981: tables 1–2, 120–7).

4.8.9 **Summary: the Fenland landscape**

Fenland comprised a number of distinctive environments including the fen-edge, freshwater peatlands within which lay a complex of islands, and an extensive coastal saltmarsh. Though there were a number of major engineering works concerned with water management, these appear to have been concerned primarily with transport rather than drainage. Indeed, the extent of salt production in Fenland, and palaeoenvironmental evidence from a range of sites, shows that the coastal marshes were still a tidal landscape during the Roman period. Though there was extensive local enclosure and drainage, Fenland was not reclaimed and there were no sea walls.

A key issue is the pattern of estate management which accounted for the colonization of Fenland. The fen-edge was extensively settled in many areas though there were few villas: if parts of Fenland lay within private estates then these were presumably based around the series of villas that lay on the Wolds of Lincolnshire and Norfolk. The traditional view is, however, that Fenland was an Imperial Estate and, though this interpretation has fallen out of favour in recent years, it still has much to commend it. This will be discussed in Chapter 6.

4.9 **The Lincolnshire coast**

The coastal plain between Skegness and Cleethorpes is distinct from Fenland in that during the Roman period it represented a long, narrow, strip of saltmarsh, possibly protected at least in part by a natural coastal barrier (Van de Noort and Davies 1993: 23). The marshes are currently up to 8 km wide, though erosion means that the position of the Roman coastline is unknown. The width of this coastal plain is such that it could not have been wholly exploited from the fen-edge: the distance to the coast would have been too great. A scatter of sites has been recorded across the marshes and as unstratified scatters of material in the intertidal zone (Eagles 1979), though had a string of settlements been located on the higher coastal land, they will have been lost to erosion. A number of Iron Age and Romano-British salterns are known in the Ingoldmells and Skegness area (Baker 1960: 27; 1975: 31–2; Lane 1993c; May 1976: 153; Swinnerton 1932; Warren 1932; Whitwell 1982: 28), though it is curious that the distribution of these early salterns is, at present, far more limited than in the medieval period (Healey 1993; Kirkham 1975, fig. 24).

4.10 **The Humber Estuary**

Though there are extensive areas of former tidal marshland around the Humber Estuary, which have yielded a number of important prehistoric boat finds (McGrail 1981; E. Wright 1990), very little is known about them in the Roman period. There are a large number of findspots of Romano-British material on the coastal marshes of North East

Lincolnshire, between Barton-on-Humber and Cleethorpes, though the character of these sites is ill-understood (Whitwell 1982: 125; 1988: 63). Several lay at the mouths of tidal creeks, such as Barrow Haven, Goxhill Haven, East Halton Skitter, and Killingholme Haven; a further site may lie next to Freshney Haven in Grimsby (Wise 1990).

In the coastal marshes of the Ancholme Valley, a settlement has been recorded in the South Ferriby brickyards. The main focus of occupation dated from the late first to second century, possibly associated with pottery production, and only a small amount of material dated to the late second to fourth century. The Roman occupation is associated with a dark brown, clayey peat, perhaps indicative of a brief period of drying of the marsh surface (Van de Noort and Ellis 1998: 232–6, 289–90).

In the Humberhead Levels, between the Trent and Ouse Estuaries, an expansion of settlement occurred during the later Roman period, as in Adlingfleet and Flixborough, where several scatters of second to early fourth century Romano-British pottery have been recorded on the banks of the Lower Trent (Van de Noort and Ellis 1998: 158–9, 166–83). At Adlingfleet-2 pottery and salt production may have supplemented the agrarian economy of a small Romano-British farmstead associated with a ditched drainage system (Van de Noort and Ellis 1998: 168–82). Further west, a series of ditched enclosures, occupied during the fourth century, was excavated at Sandtoft in Belton beside the old course of the River Don (Buckland and Sadler 1985; Samuels and Buckland 1978). A number of major artificial watercourses in the Humberhead Levels have been claimed as Roman in origin (e.g. Bikers and Turnbridge Dykes), though this is very doubtful (Van de Noort and Ellis 1997: 57, 66, 77, 460).

Several sites are known from the coastal marshes in the Vale of York, notably in Faxfleet and Melton on the higher coastal marshes adjacent to the Humber Estuary (Van de Noort and Ellis 1999: 209–12, 220). Two sites have been excavated. Faxfleet A was occupied from the Late Iron Age through to the Early Roman period, when it may have been abandoned in favour of the nearby Faxfleet B, which lay on slightly higher ground (Whitwell 1988: 65). Faxfleet B was occupied from the late first century AD, though the main phase of activity dates from the late second to third century and was associated with a series of drainage ditches (Sitch 1989; 1990: 162). Briquetage-type ceramics, probably associated with salt production were only found at Faxfleet A (Sitch 1989: 14). There is possible evidence for pottery production at Faxfleet, though a more extensive industrial area lay upstream at Holme-on-Spalding Moor, adjacent to the River Foulness. Here, a series of settlements were spread across a complex of small sandy islands surrounded by tidal creeks and estuarine marshes (Halkon 1989; 1990; Millett and Halkon 1988). Pottery, iron, and glass production were undertaken, although these were not purely specialized industrial settlements, as palaeoenvironmental evidence suggests that crops were processed on site (Millett and Halkon 1988: 43).

Numerous finds of coins and pottery in the lower Hull Valley suggest extensive activity, though until very recently few sites have been excavated (Dent 1990; Didsbury 1988; 1989). At Saltshouse Lane two first century AD enclosures and part of a ditched field system lay on a small island of glacial till (Challis and Harding 1975: 141, fig. 68), and traces of Late Iron Age occupation have also been recovered nearby (Evans and Steedman 1997: 120). At Greylees Avenue part of a ditched field system was used from the late second to fourth centuries, and the large animal bone assemblage suggests a primary butchery site (Didsbury 1988: 32; 1990; Eagles 1979). The Hull Valley marshes may have been tidal during the Roman period, as a late fourth century jar found in the alluvium at Thoresby Street has surface marks of ragworm, suggesting it was deposited in the intertidal zone (Didsbury 1988: 162). Possible evidence for Late Iron Age/(?)Early Romano-British salt production has also been recovered from Hull Cemetery (Ken Steedman pers. comm., 1999). Recent work just to the north of modern Hull has also revealed extensive evidence for occupation, with the focus of activity once again falling between the second and fourth centuries (Evans and Steedman 1997: 124; 2000: 197–9).

Overall, there is no evidence for more than localized drainage and enclosure on any of the Humber Estuary marshes during the Roman period. Most sites appear to have been ditched enclosures on areas of slightly raised ground, such as the banks of major tidal rivers, occasionally associated with other drainage ditches, though there is no evidence for enclosure on the scale of Fenland. Apart from 'dumped building materials' at Greylees Avenue (Didsbury 1990: 206) there is no evidence for any substantial buildings, or settlements of great wealth on the Humber marshlands. Salt production at a number of sites also suggests that these remained intertidal marshes.

4.11 Mainland North West European wetlands during the Roman period

The coastal wetlands of mainland North West Europe represented a diverse range of environments during the Roman period. In Belgium, an area of tidal flats, lagoons, and freshwater peatland formed behind a belt of sand dunes (Thoen 1975: 56; 1978; 1981: 245–6). In the western Netherlands, the near-continuous natural coastal barrier (the 'Older Dunes') was broken by four major estuaries: the Scheldt, Maas, Oude Rijn, and Oer IJ (Zagwijn 1986). Each estuary was fringed by saltmarshes and mudflats, with extensive creek systems extending into the freshwater peat bogs which developed in the sheltered conditions behind the sand dune barriers. Along the northern coast of The Netherlands and Germany there was a more open coastal plain with a zone of intertidal mudflats, saltmarshes, and extensive freshwater backfen swamps partly protected by an intermittent series of off-shore islands (Roeleveld 1974).

4.11.1 The Belgian coast

The coastal wetlands of Flanders saw little occupation during the Iron Age, though a number of settlements on the coastal dunes and along the fen-edge were associated with salt production and probably seasonal grazing of cattle on the tidal marshes e.g. De Panne (Ceunynck and Thoen 1981; Thoen 1978; 233). The area may have been abandoned at the end of the Iron Age but was reoccupied in the first century AD (Thoen

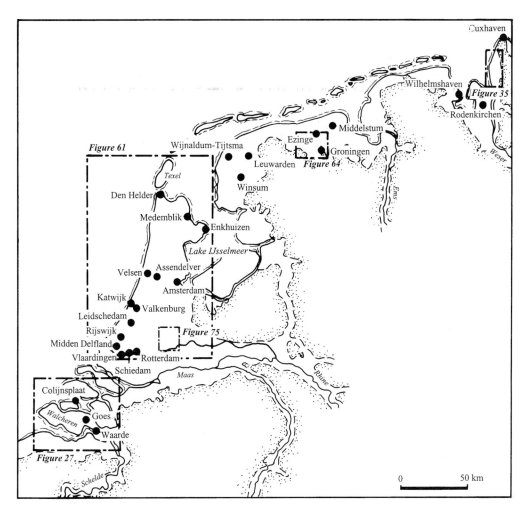

26. Location of continental case-study areas, and other key sites described in the text.

1978: 233). A similar pattern of landuse prevailed, along with a limited expansion of settlement along raised creeks banks into the better drained marshes towards the Scheldt Estuary. Though the extent of most ditched enclosure systems appears to have been relatively localized, a number of larger-scale drainage schemes were attempted in certain areas (Borger 1992: 134). During the late second/early third century there was also a marked increase in settlement, with occupation spreading into the peatlands (Thoen 1978: 237; 1981: 248–50). There appears to have been limited cultivation on both the marsh and peat areas, while pastoralism must also have been important. While cattle were most significant on the dunes, sheep predominated on the marshes, and documentary sources show that the coastal tribes, the Menapii and Morini, were important salt and wool producers (Thoen 1978: 234; 1981: 252). Peat was also cut in a systematic fashion during the Roman period (Borger 1992: 135).

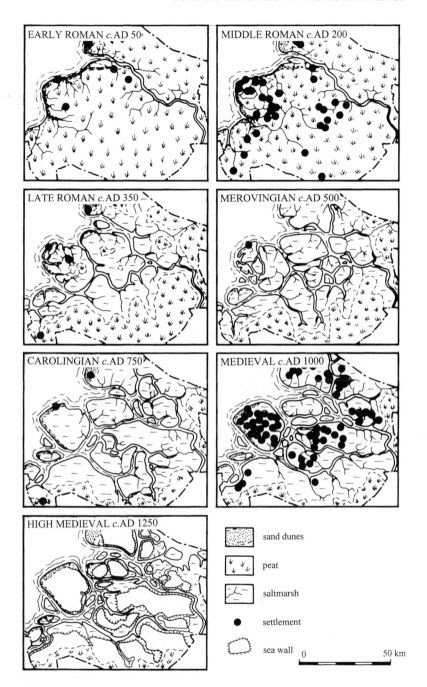

27. The expansion, contraction, and subsequent expansion of settlement into the coastal wetlands of Zeeland, South West Netherlands (after Vos and Van Heeringen 1997). For location see Figure 26.

4.11.2 **The western Netherlands: Zeeland and the Maas Estuary** (Figure 27)

In the western Netherlands, the coast was largely protected by sand dunes, broken only by major estuaries such as the Maas (the Roman *Helinium*). Behind the coastal barrier, the landscape was dominated by a vast peat bog dissected by a creek system created during the late first millennium BC 'Dunkirk I' transgression. A series of large-scale surveys and excavations have been carried out in both Zeeland to the south of the Maas,[15] and South Holland to the north, notably in Midden Delfland and Vlaardingen (between Rotterdam and Den Haag: Figure 28).[16] Together, these surveys have provided some of the most detailed information with regards to wetland exploitation in the western Netherlands.

Until the 1940s it was assumed that these coastal wetlands were not settled until the Roman period, though Iron Age occupation is now known to have been widespread (Abbink 1993; Van den Broeke 1993; Van Heeringen 1987; 1988; 1989*a-c*; Vos and Van Heeringen 1997). It was during the Roman period, however, that the greatest density of settlement was seen, with farmsteads and associated ditched drainage systems up to every 300 m strung out along the creek ridges in a very similar fashion to Belgium and the English Fenland (Figure 28). The majority of these farms lay directly upon the marsh surface, though a first to second century farmstead at Oostuurtse weg in Schipluiden near Delft, and a second to third century settlement at Rockanje, on Voorne-Putten, were on artificially raised mounds (Brinkkemper *et al.* 1995; Van Londen and Van Rijn 1999: 136).

The economy of these marshland settlements appears to have been mixed. Both cattle and sheep were kept, though the former were most important generally being killed in maturity (Prummel 1989). The presence of granaries suggests a significant level of arable production e.g. Rockanje (Brinkkemper *et al.* 1995), while palaeoenvironmental evidence indicate spring-sown barley and millet were cultivated both on the creeks banks and adjacent peat moors, along with fodder crops such as linseed (Brinkkemper 1962: 208; Brinkkemper *et al.* 1995: 146–55; Van den Broeke and Van Londen 1995: 26–40). Several sites have produced fragments of briquetage, though no salt production sites have been discovered from the Roman period (see Chapter 5). Evidence for pottery, iron, and textile production suggests these were largely self-sufficient communities.

During the later first to early second century, many of the settlements in Midden-Delfland were linked by curvilinear ditches running along the raised creek ridges, and during the second to third centuries rectilinear ditched field systems were laid out from these axial boundaries, creating field systems similar to those of Fenland (Figure 24). These ditches were largely restricted to the marshes, petering out as they reach the peat, though as in the Iron Age, there were some settlements in the peatlands between the creek systems. On Walcheren, Zuid-Beveland, and Stalhille (in Zeeland), rectilinear

---

[15] Brinkkemper 1962; Brinkkemper *et al.* 1995; Prummel 1989; Trimpe Burger 1973; Vos and Van Heeringen 1997.
[16] Abbink 1993; Van den Broeke 1993; Van den Broeke and Van Londen 1995; Bult 1983; Henderikx 1986; Van Heeringen 1987; 1988; 1989*a*; *b*; *c*; Van Heeringen and Van Trierum 1981; Van Londen and Van Rijn 1999; Modderman 1973.

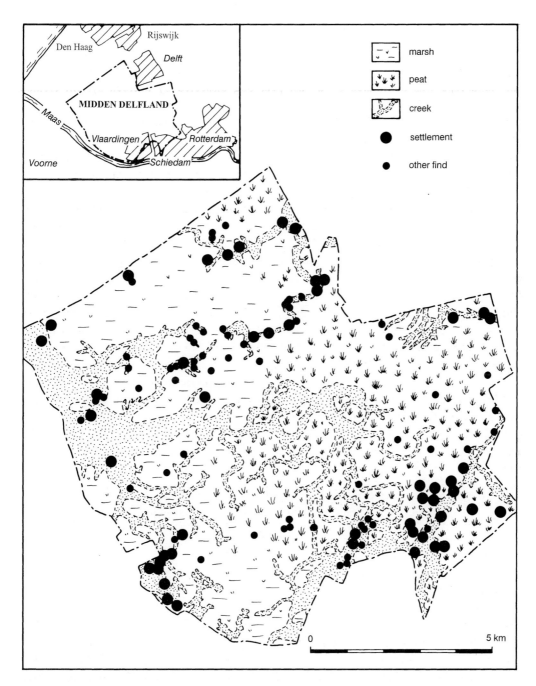

28. The distribution of Roman period settlement on raised creek banks in Midden Delfland, western Netherlands (after Bult 1983: fig. 6). For location see Figure 26.

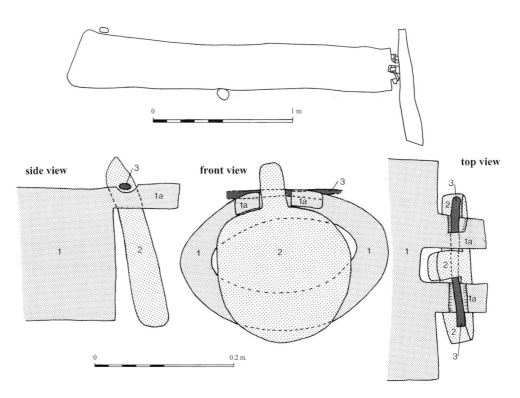

side view   front view   top view

29. Sluice structure, or 'duiker' from Valkenburg-Marktveld, western Netherlands: view from above (top), with detail of hinged flap-valve (below) (from Van Rijn 1993: fig. 13).

systems of ditches suggest a more systematic attempt to drain areas up to 25 km^2 of the peatland with long narrow field very similar to those on the Wentlooge Level in South East Wales (Thoen 1978; fig. 9; Vos and Van Heeringen 1997; 65, fig. 32). However, most of the Roman-period ditched field systems in Zeeland and South Holland would only have improved the drainage locally, and environmental evidence suggests that the drainage systems were subject to tidal influence e.g. Rijswijk (Jansma 1981).

While, however, there were no sea walls (i.e. full reclamation) attempts were made to control flooding through the construction of dams and sluices. At Vlaardingen-Hoogstad, a landscape very similar to that at Midden-Delfland has been uncovered, with Late Iron Age/Roman period settlements and their associated ditched paddock systems strung out along creeks which experienced tidal influence. In several places, dams were constructed either across ditches, where they discharged into the creeks, or across the creeks themselves (Figures 30–3; Brugge 1995; de Ridder 1997; 1998). The dams, up to 7 m long and 9 m wide, were constructed of clay sods with alternating layers of cut reeds and sedges, and revetted with sharpened timber stakes. Hollowed tree trunks allowed the flow of fresh water under the dam, though, to prevent flooding at times of high tide, hinged flap-valves were placed at the end of the timber pipe/culvert. Eight dams and four culverts (*duikers*) have been recorded at Vlaardingen, most of which date to the first century AD, though the earliest dam has been radiocarbon dated to *c*. 175 BC.

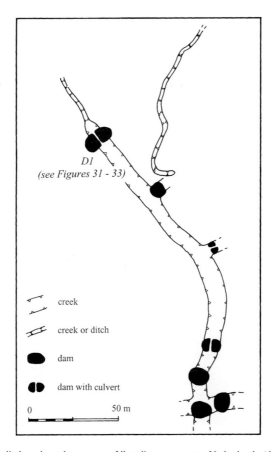

D1
(see Figures 31 - 33)

⌐⌐ creek

⊏⊐ creek or ditch

⬤ dam

◖◗ dam with culvert

0   50 m

30. Roman period ditch and creek system at Vlaardingen, western Netherlands (de Ridder 1997: 31).

Dendrochronology has produced a felling date of 17 BC for the oldest culvert, while another sluice at Rotterdam-Hartelkanaal has been radiocarbon dated to the late first century BC/early first century AD [17] and so could be pre-Roman (de Ridder 1997: 39).

There are now a total of twelve *duikers* recorded in The Netherlands, three with hinged flap-valves: Vlaardingen (Figures 30–3), Schiedam-Westabtjspolder, and Valkenburg (Figure 29); a fourth possible example has recently been found at Schiedam-Polderweg in Midden-Delfland (see below). All but two of the sluices have been found around the Maas Estuary, the exceptions being near the Roman fort at Valkenburg and under a Roman road at Vechten (Van Rijn 1993: 159). Indeed, the Vlaardingen example also appears to have been associated with a settlement of some status since it was associated with a dump of material including a lance point, enamel brooch, and wagon fittings (Brugge 1995: 386); the sluice at Schiedam may also have military associations (see below). It would appear, therefore, that this system of dams and sluices was a

[17] 2055±20 BP, GRn-13229, 100 cal BC-cal AD 75.

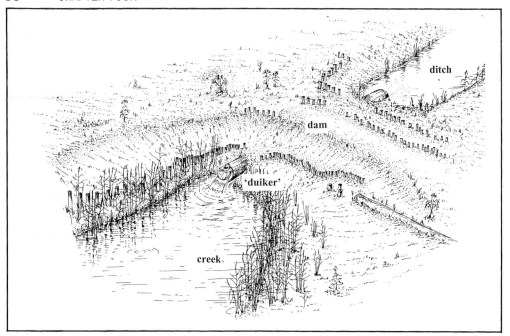

31. Reconstruction of Roman period dam (D1, *c.* 75–125 AD) across a tidal creek at Vlaardingen, western Netherlands (from Ridder 1997: fig. 9). The exterior end, with its hinged flap-value is to the left (see Figure 32). Total length of 'duiker', which comprises two hollowed tree trunks, one inserted into the end of the other, is *c.* 6.5 m (see Figure 33) (drawn by B. Koster, Vlaardingen Archeologisch Kantoor).

native tradition of water management which may then have been adopted by the Roman military authorities.[18]

The army may also have been engaged in larger-scale water engineering in the Central Rivers region of The Netherlands. Near contemporary writers Suetonius (see Motterhead 1986) and Tacitus (see Willems 1981: 52–62; 1984: 48–50) describe the construction of a canal (the *fossa Drusiana*) along with a dam (*agger* or *moles*) to control the flow of the Rhine during the Roman military campaigns of Drusus in 12 BC. There are a number of other possible canalizations including the *fossa Corbulonis* linking the Oude Rijn at Roomburg (near Leiden) to the *Helinium* (Maas) Estuary, part of which has recently been recorded near Leidschendam (Lambert 1971: 35; Willems 1984: 245; M. Dijkstra, pers. comm. 1998). Timber revetments recorded at Oostdijk Polder, on Goeree in Zeeland, may also represent an attempt to improve a natural river (Trimpe Burger 1973: 141). However, like the Fenland canals, these various works were concerned with communication rather than flood defence or land reclamation.

[18] The author has not yet found any parallels for these dams in Britain, though without waterlogged conditions, leading to the preservation of the timber *duikers* etc., the dams could appear simply as causeways across ditches/creeks. The Lincolnshire Car Dyke has a number of such causeways which, in section, appeared to be of un-exacavated natural gravel (Simmons 1979: 189). However, if the Car Dyke functioned as either a catchwater drain or a canal, some sort of sluice structure would have been required in order to maintain water levels in the various sections defined by these causeways. Perhaps further investigated is warranted in order to see whether there are any faint traces of timber structures within these features.

32. Exterior end of Vlaardingen 'duiker' (D1, *c.* 75–125 AD), showing fitting for hinged flap valve (photo: Tim de Ridder, Vlaardingen Archeologisch Kantoor).

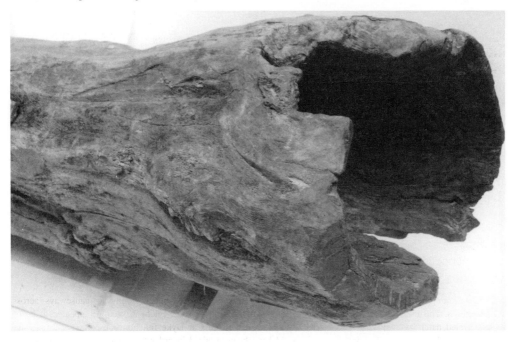

33. Interior end of Vlaardingen 'duiker' (D1, *c.* 75–125 AD), into which another hollowed tree-trunk was inserted (photo: Tim de Ridder, Vlaardingen Archeologisch Kantoor).

34. Roman period building, uniquely constructed of ash, at Schiedam-Polderweg, Midden Delfland (photo: copyright Heleen Van Londen).

Returning to Midden-Delfland, most of the settlements and their associated material culture appear to be wholly native in character, though one site at Schiedam-Polderweg may be different (Van Londen and Van Rijn 1999: 137–8). A series of farmsteads and associated ditched paddocks were strung out along the creeks system, part of which appears to have been dammed: several fragments of wooden piping tied together with rope were recovered, along with what may be the flap-valve from a sluice similar to those from Vlaardingen. One settlement complex, however, contained an unusually substantial building and the range of artefacts suggests a military connection (Figures 34 and 46; see Chapter 6).

4.11.3 The western Netherlands: Assendelver Polder

A second area of the western Netherlands that has seen intensive survey and excavation in recent years is the Assendelver Polder, north-west of Amsterdam (Brandt *et al.* 1987; Van Heeringen 1989*b*; T. Bloemers and L. Therkorn, pers. comm. 1998). This area of raised bog lay to the north-east of the Oer IJ, one of the few estuaries to breach the coastal barrier in the western Netherlands during the Iron Age and Roman periods. Marine flooding during the first millennium BC led to the creation of mudflats and creek systems around the Estuary, and as water levels fell the better drained fringes of the peat bogs and the raised creek-levees became available for settlement (Hakbijl 1989: 77; Hallewas 1987).

Brandt and Van der Leeuw (1987: 349) have modelled the way that this landscape appears to have been colonized. As the waters receded, communities living on the nearby coastal barrier made exploratory visits to the wetlands to exploit wild plants, waterfowl, and fish. Over time these visits were extended to become seasonal, and temporary encampments were established. Eventually, when the fringes of the peat bog and adjacent marshes had dried out sufficiently, settlements became permanent. Cattle raising appears to have been the most important activity (Brandt 1983; Van Gijn 1987; Seeman 1987), with some cultivation on the peat and creek-levees, notably of gold-of-pleasure (*Camelina sativa*); though other cereals were consumed, they appear to have been imported from elsewhere. This is also suggested by the absence of extensive field systems; settlement enclosures on the creek-levees were associated with small paddocks and potential garden plots, and recently similar features have been recorded on the peat (Therkorn and Abbink 1987; L. Therkorn, *et al.* 1998: 15–20). Cattle predominated).

4.11.4 **The northern Netherlands and Germany** (Figures 35 and 64)

Geomorphologically, the northern Netherlands/German coastal zone is very different to that of the western Netherlands. Although there was an intermittent off-shore barrier, the entire coastal frontage was exposed to tidal flooding leading to the now familiar pattern of elevated marshes along the coast and extensive freshwater peat bogs in the lower-lying backfen. Within the coastal marsh natural shore-parallel ridges, up to 0.5–1.5 m high, provided areas of elevated ground that were used by the earliest settlements, while a series of major rivers also crossed the marshes, whose raised levees were settled relatively early (e.g. Behre 1990*c*).

It was not just the physical landscape in these northern coastal marshes that was so different from the western Netherlands and Belgium, but also the way that human communities chose to exploit them. As the drainage improved, these coastal marshes were extensively settled, a process that started in The Netherlands during the Middle Iron Age (*c.* sixth century BC), and reaching the coast of North West Germany by the first century BC (Behre 1990*b*, 34; Behre *et al.* 1979, 103–4; Ey 1990; Krog 1979: 81; Schmid 1990*a*; *b*; Zimmermann 1995: 339–40; 1996: 18–19). Initially, farmsteads were built on the surface of the higher coastal marshes, the so-called *Flachsiedlugen* settlements (Waterbolk 1965–6), just as they were in the western Netherlands. As water levels rose some of these settlements were abandoned e.g. Middelstum, north of Groningen (Van Gelder-Ottway 1988) but most were not and, in order to counter the rising water levels, artificial mounds were constructed, known as *terpen* in Friesland, *wierde* in Groningen, *wurten* in Germany, and *vaerfter* in Denmark (Behre 1990*b*: 35; Larsen 1997: 1; Waterbolk 1965–6); for convenience, the generic term *terpen* is used hereafter. Conditions improved between the first centuries BC and the second century AD leading to another expansion of settlement, though rising water levels during the third century led to a further period of abandonment and *terp* raising. By the fourth century AD only the highest coastal marshes were still occupied (e.g. Figure 64; Streurman and Taayke 1989: 353–4).

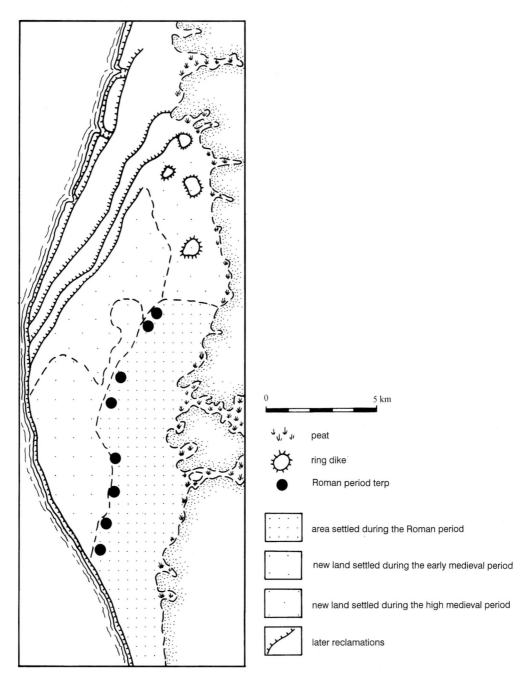

35. Development of the marshland landscape north of Bremerhaven, northern Germany, including line of Roman-period *terpen* on the edge of the contemporary higher coastal saltmarsh, and subsequent medieval reclamations. (For location see Figure 26.)

The *terpen* were located towards the seaward edge of the contemporary saltmarshes, often on slightly raised, shore-parallel ridges (e.g. Figure 35; Besteman *et al.*, 1999; Körber-Grohne 1981: 292; Vos, 1999). As the mid-first century AD writer Pliny observed, these were very much tidal landscapes:

> I myself have personally witnessed the condition of the ... regions of the far North. In those climates a vast tract of land, invaded twice each day and night by the overflowing waves of the ocean, opens a question that is eternally proposed to us by Nature, whether these regions are to be looked upon as belonging to the land, or whether as forming a portion of the sea?
>
> Here a wretched race is found, inhabiting either the more elevated spots of land, or else eminences artificially constructed and of a height to which they know by experience that the highest tides will never reach. Here they pitch their cabins; and when the waves cover the surrounding country far and wide, like so many mariners on board ship they are: when again the tides recede, their condition is that of so many shipwrecked men, and around their cottages they persue the fishes as they make their escape with the receding tide. It is not their lot, like the adjoining nations, to keep any flocks for sustenance by their milk ... With the sedge and the rushes of the marsh they make cord, and with these they weave nets employed in the capture of the fish. (Pliny's *Natural History* Book XVI, chapter 1).

Palaeobotanical and diatom evidence confirms that these settlements lay in the higher parts of the coastal saltmarshes, maybe 0.1–0.2 m below mean spring tide level, but as such they would not have been regularly flooded (Van Es 1968: 282–3, 286; Jansma 1981; Knol 1983: 146; Körber-Grohne 1981: 293; Streurman and Taayke 1989; Van Zeist 1974: 333). Even so it was only through skilful adaptation to these particular environmental conditions that the settlement and exploitation of the coastal marshes continued despite the deteriorating conditions.

A considerable amount of work has been carried out on the *terp* settlements themselves, and the botanical material found there, allowing detailed environmental reconstructions of the surrounding landscapes (Behre and Jacomet 1991; Körber-Grohne 1981; Van Zeist 1974). Less work, however, has been carried out on the physical characteristics of the countryside as a whole, notably any field systems or attempts at improving the drainage around the *terpen*. One exception is Heveskesklooster (beside the Dollart Estuary), which, during the Roman period, was associated with a rectilinear ditched field system on a raised creek-levee in what was still a tidal environment (Cappers 1993–4). Important work has also been carried out recently at Wijnaldum, located on the edge of a brackish saltmarsh beside what was then the Boorne Estuary (east of Leuwarden), and which would have been flooded a few times each year during the winter (Besteman *et al.*, 1999; Gerrets 1999). Traces of a sod-built embankment, *c.* 0.75 m high and 10 m wide, have been uncovered beneath a second century AD *terp*, which would have protected agricultural fields from summer flooding, but not from winter storms. Barley was the dominant crop grown. At Dongjum-Heringa nearby, another sea wall, initially just 2 m wide, has been recorded beneath a later *terp* (D. Gerrets, pers. comm. 1999).

Van Gijn and Waterbolk (1984) have suggested that the earlier settlement expansion into the coastal marshlands of the northern Netherlands may initially have been in the context of seasonal transhumance, though this is difficult to prove archaeologically. They cite Middelstum-Boerdamsterweg (north of Groningen) as an example of one such seasonal pastoral settlement, though Van Gelder-Ottway (1988) argues that even in the earliest phase of this site, the animal bone assemblage indicates that it was permanently occupied. In fact, Pliny was quite wrong to suggest that these communities were largely fisher-folk as most *terpen* communities appear to have practised mixed agriculture. The most common crops were hulled-barley for food, flax for textiles, and gold-of-pleasure for its oil bearing seeds, all of which can tolerate slightly brackish soils, while oats and horse beans are also encountered (Behre 1985: 91–2; Cappers 1993–4: 147; Van Es 1968: 282–3; Körber-Grohne 1981: 294–8; Schmid 1990*b*; Van Zeist 1974: 362). The presence of weeds indicative of brackish conditions, and absence of species typical of the sandy dryland soils of the nearby Drenthe/Geest, suggests that these cereals were cultivated on the marshes adjacent to the *terpen*. The exception is emmer wheat, present at a few sites including Middelstum and Paddepoel (in Groningen) in The Netherlands and Feddersen Wierde (near Bremerhaven) in Germany, which was probably imported from dryland areas since it is very intolerant of even slightly brackish soils (Van Zeist 1974: 113–14).

Animal husbandry on all *terpen* appears to have been dominated by cattle, with sheep, and to a much lesser extent, pig supplementing the diet (Van Gelder-Ottway 1988; Knol 1983; Milojkovic and Brinkhuizen 1984). Sheep were most important in the more brackish marshes typified by plant species such as *Limonium vulgare*, *Puccinellia maritima*, and *Salicornia europaea* (e.g. Elisenhof and Trisum), compared with the higher, less frequently flooded areas where these species are absent e.g. Feddersen Wierde and Paddepoel (Knol 1983: 171). Perhaps surprisingly, it appears that hunting, fishing, or fowling played relatively little part in the subsistence regime of these *terp* communities (Knol 1983: 168–9).

The evidence for Roman period salt production in the northern Netherlands and Germany is relatively slim (especially compared with Britain). Fragments of briquetage vessels have been reported from Paddepoel (Van Es 1968: 255–8), and several sites around the Jadebusen and Weser Estuaries (Först 1988; Zimmermann 1996: 23–4), though it is absent from most *terpen*, including Feddersen Wierde. At nearby Northum, however, several shallow pans associated with fire reddened floors may relate to salt production (H. Zimmermann, pers. comm.)

4.12 Discussion: strategies towards the exploitation of coastal wetlands during the Roman period

The evidence summarized above suggests that there were four clearly distinct strategies towards the exploitation of coastal wetlands in North West Europe during the Roman period (Figure 19). The first strategy was a major landscape *transformation*, including the construction of a sea wall, which appears to have been restricted to the Severn Estuary in South West Britain. At least two variants can be observed: first, the systematic drainage of the whole, or at least a large part, of the area protected by a sea wall (as was the case on Wentlooge) and, second, the piecemeal drainage of land associated with individual settlements (as occurred for example on the North Somerset Levels). A mixed economy was practised in these fully reclaimed landscapes.

A second strategy towards the exploitation of coastal wetlands was for a *modification* of the natural environment with partial settlement of the higher, usually coastal, marshes and levee-banks associated with localized drainage systems, but without the construction of a sea wall. This was far more widespread than reclamation, certainly being found in Fenland, around the Humber Estuary, and in the western Netherlands, while the presence of a number of substantial settlements on some of the Thames-side marshes may indicate a similar landscape there. As in North Somerset, areas were drained in a piecemeal fashion, though in these cases tidal waters were free to flow through the canals, creeks, and ditches. Cultivation would have been possible on the highest ground, though pastoralism was probably the main activity.

The third strategy towards the exploitation of coastal marshes during the Roman period was the establishment of *raised settlement* platforms. This tradition of *terpen* is mainly restricted to the northern Netherlands and Germany and, though two possible examples are known in the western Netherlands, there are none from Britain. In at least a few cases, limited attempts were made to improve the drainage of the surrounding marshes, some of which were cultivated, though the economy was largely pastoral.

A final strategy towards the exploitation of coastal marshland in North West Europe during the Roman period involved simply *exploiting* the resources offered by natural landscape, with the main activities being salt production and seasonal grazing. Two variants can be suggested: on the more substantial areas of coastal wetland (such as in the Brue Valley in Central Somerset, Romney Marsh, around the Thames Estuary, and along the Lincolnshire coast) communities probably lived on the marshes at least for the summer (hence the presence of burials), while the smaller tracts of marshes, such as those around Poole Harbour, Langstone/Chichester Harbours, and the Essex estuaries were probably exploited from fen-edge settlements.

In the following two chapters two key issues concerning the exploitation, modification, and transformation of coastal marshland will be explored. Firstly, Chapter 5 will consider the exploitation of natural resources, and in particular the reasons why salt production appears to have occurred so unevenly around the coast of Roman Britain. Then Chapter 6 will examine the reasons why certain marshes appear to have been modified through the localized drainage while others were transformed through reclamation.

Nature's rich harvest:

the exploitation of natural resources during the
Roman period

5.1 Introduction

Wetlands are physically inhospitable places, which raises the issue of why so many
ancient peoples were attracted to them. John Coles (1998: 7) argues that it was 'not
because people wanted to live in the wet, but because of the wealth in plants and
animals (wildfowl, fish, eels, mammals, reeds, withes, and plant foods), the ease of
travel and transport (in the absence of roads) and in some cases because of the isolation
and defense offered by certain wetlands'. On a global scale, human communities have
certainly been attracted to coastal wetlands because of their rich seasonal resources (e.g.
Bernick 1998), and this chapter will consider whether the same was true of North West
Europe in the Early first millennium AD.

This chapter examines one of the three strategies towards wetland utilization adopted
during the Roman period, that of natural resource exploitation. The extent of salt
production is summarized, and its location in the landscape is then examined. As an
inherently seasonal activity it is likely that salt was produced either by full-time crafts-
people or part-time farmers, and evidence for the exploitation of other coastal resources
including fish, shellfish, and peat is discussed. The occurrence of briquetage on inland
sites may also shed some light on the estate structure within which coastal marshes
were exploited. Attention then turns to the rise and fall of the Romano-British salt
industry, and what this tells us about the wider economy.

5.2 Natural resource exploitation during the Roman period

5.2.1 Salt production (Figure 36)

During the first and second centuries AD there is evidence for salt production around
most of the estuaries in southern and eastern Britain (Figure 36; see Chapter 4). The
extent of this industry may in fact have been even greater than is apparent today

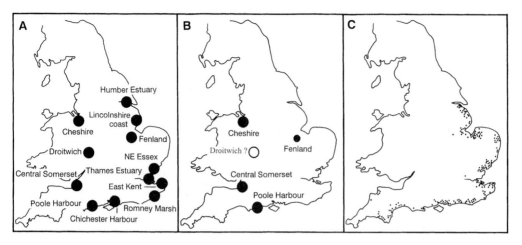

36. Salt production in Britain during: A, the Early Romano-British period; B, the Late Romano-British period; C, the 11th century AD.

because in some areas large tracts of coastal marshland appear to have eroded away since the Roman period, particularly off Lincolnshire and East Anglia. In contrast, by the Late Roman period coastal salt production appears to have been largely restricted to Poole Harbour and the Brue Valley in Central Somerset, though the inland brine springs in Cheshire and possibly Droitwich were also still exploited (see below). On the continent the situation is less clear as, despite epigraphic testimony for a salt industry during the first and second centuries AD, archaeological evidence is very scarce (see below).

A small number of coastal wetlands have not produced evidence for Romano-British salt production, though it is difficult to determine whether this reflects the contemporary situation or results from the limited opportunities for archaeological observation. The latter is the case for most of the Pevensey Levels, though it is strange that the urban expansion of Eastbourne onto the Willingdon Marshes has not revealed any saltern debris. The absence of salt production in the Severn Estuary upstream of Central Somerset may be due to low water salinity levels and high sediment loads (Pethick 1990: 56), though in the later Roman period extensive Romano-British reclamation would also have been a factor (with only the Brue Valley in Central Somerset left as a tidally inundated marsh: see Chapter 4).

5.2.2 The wider marshland economy

Salt production would have been a very seasonal activity (Bradley 1975), and this makes it unlikely that there were full-time professional salt-makers. There are three possibilities regarding who worked the salterns: full-time crafts specialists, part-time farmers, or communities which specialized in exploiting the whole range of rich natural resources in coastal marshlands.

In certain parts of Roman Britain it is possible that salt was produced as part of a wider crafts-based economy. For example, around Poole Harbour and Purbeck there were a wide range of industrial activities related to the area's rich natural resources, including chalk, iron, limestone, marble, mudstone, shale, pottery, and salt production (P. Cox and Hearne 1991; Farrar 1962*b*; 1977; Sunter and P. Woodward 1987). In North Kent there was an extensive pottery industry on the marshes (Monaghan 1982; 1987; Pollard 1988), though the evidence for pottery production from just across the Thames Estuary in Essex is very slim. W. Rodwell (1982) has suggested that several flues cut into the top of a saltern in Goldhanger (beside the Blackwater Estuary) may represent a Late Iron Age/Early Roman pottery kiln, while wasters of shell-tempered ware have been found on Canvey Island (Fawn *et al.* 1990: 7; W. Rodwell 1979: 165). Pottery production may also have been carried out in the Brue Valley of Central Somerset, though the evidence is very slim (Rippon 1997*a*, 71–2).

Other coastal wetlands have produced evidence for pottery production, though in most cases kilns were located along the fen-edge, for example at Caldicot by the Gwent Levels (Barnett *et al.* 1990), Congresbury by the North Somerset Levels (Lilly 1966), various locations around Fenland (D. Hall 1996: 114; D. Hall and J. Coles 1994:112–13; S. Hallam 1970: sheet K). However, of these only Fenland has also produced evidence for contemporary salt production, while there is little indication of pottery kilns associated with the salterns around Chichester Harbour and on Romney Marsh. Indeed, in Roman Britain as a whole the pottery industry shows no great bias towards the coastal zone (B. Jones and Mattingly 1990: maps 6.24–6), suggesting that its production was simply an option chosen by some fen-edge and marshland communities to supplement their seasonal incomes, but was not an essential pre-requisite of a successful salt industry.

Since the majority of salterns do not appear to be associated with other industrial activity or domestic debris, it is likely that these areas of marshland were exploited by fen-edge farming communities, with salt production carried out as part of an agricultural cycle that included seasonal grazing. Paul Sealey (1995) has recently shown that a number of Essex salterns where production ceased during the second century have yielded small amounts of third to fourth century pottery, though how this material came to be there is unclear. It is possible that these slightly raised areas were used as dairies, shepherds huts, and refuges for sheep at times of flood as was the case during the medieval period (see Figure 52 and Chapter 9).

Most Romano-British salterns have produced limited numbers of cattle and sheep bones, though these could simply represent meat taken to the sites for consumption by salt workers. However, evidence from several sites in Essex suggests that at least some were involved with animal husbandry. These assemblages are dominated by inedible parts of the carcass, such as skull and foot bones (N. Faulkner 1993*a*: 20; G. Lewin 1993; Reader 1908: 171, 187; W. Rodwell 1979: 165), and it possible that animals were being butchered on the marshes, with the meat preserved by salting before being transported elsewhere. There is often also a very high proportion of young individuals, particularly sheep. For example, excavations at Leigh Beck, on Canvey Island, have yielded a large animal bone assemblage from an Early Roman saltern and an overlying late third to mid fourth century occupation deposit. Both animal bone assemblages were dominated by sheep, with 35 per cent of the bones from lambs too young to have been butchered for meat (G. Lewin 1993). Faulkner (1993a: 20) suggests that this may indicate the culling of new-born lambs to ensure an adequate supply of ewe's milk for cheese production. Indeed, fragments of cheese-presses have been found at a number of Romano-British marshland sites e.g. Croft near Skegness in Lincolnshire (Eagles 1979: 363); Kenn Moor on the North Somerset Levels (Timby in Rippon, forthcoming a), while they are noted as being particularly common on Fenland settlements (K. Hartley and B. Hartley 1970: 168). Finds of Late Iron Age loom weights from individual salt production sites and coastal areas generally in Essex and Kent might also suggest the use of coastal marshes as sheep pasture (Hutchings 1988: 288; Sealey 1995: 69–71).

The extent to which natural food resources were exploited is, however, unclear. On marshland settlements in The Netherlands and northern Germany there is surprisingly little evidence for extensive wildfowling during the Iron Age or Roman period, which is in sharp contrast to earlier and later periods (Brinkhuizen 1979; Brinkkemper 1962; Clason 1967; Van Gelder-Ottway 1988: 125; Groenman-van Waateringe 1989: 99; Knol 1983: 168; Prummel 1989: 261: Seeman 1987: 96). The same is true in Roman Britain, and Luff (1993: 97), writing of the large faunal assemblage from Colchester, close to the Colne and Blackwater estuaries in Essex, comments that it 'has not yielded large numbers of wild birds, which is surprising considering its proximity to an estuarine environment'.

Marine fish were exploited in North West Europe during the Iron Age, and there appears to have been a greater interest during the Roman period, though not as great as in the medieval period (Chapter 10). This is reflected in the increased occurrence of fish bones and shellfish on Roman period settlements (see below), though recent stable isotope analysis of Iron Age and Roman human bones from Poundbury near Dorchester, Dorset (Richards et al., forthcoming) suggests that the consumption of protein from marine sources may have been largely restricted to the higher echelons of society.

Most Romano-British fish bone assemblages are dominated by freshwater species (particularly when compared with the medieval period), though very small numbers of estuarine and inshore marine fish have been recorded on some urban, temple, and villa sites particularly during the Late Roman period.[19] These inland examples of marine and estuarine species are likely to have arrived at those sites preserved through smoking, salting, or pickling, and a first century fish processing centre has been excavated at Pudding Lane in London that appears to have been producing garum (fish sauce) (Milne 1985: 87–91); several Late Roman deposits in Lincoln may be the product of making garum from eels (Dobney et al. 1995: 54).

The range of fish that have been recovered from Roman period sites could have

[19] Colchester: Crummy 1992: 278–80; Dorchester, Dorset: Woodward et al. 1993; Exeter: Maltby 1979; Gloucester: Heighway 1983; Gorhambury: Neal et al. 1990; Lincoln: Dobney et al. 1995: 53; London: Hill et al. 1980; A. K. Jones 1978; D. Jones 1980; Silchester: Fulford et al. 1997: 133; Uley: Woodward and Leach 1993; York: A. R. Hall and Kenward 1990: 409.

been caught with surface nets and hook-and-line from intertidal and inshore waters (Maltby 1979) though, in contrast to the medieval period, physical evidence for Roman fishing is extremely limited. A very small number of possible fishing weights have been recovered, including sheets of rolled lead from Heybridge, and Thorney Bay on Canvey Island (both Essex) (W. Rodwell 1966; Wickenden 1986: 26), and a small number of pyramidal weights from Kenn Moor on the North Somerset Levels (Rippon, forthcoming *a*). However, despite increasing evidence for early medieval fish weirs in both the Severn and Thames Estuaries there is almost no evidence for investment in fixed fishing structures during the Roman period or earlier in Britain: a wooden structure at Westward Ho! in Devon (Balaam *et al.* 1988: 174, 186), a fence-like structure in a palaeochannel at Coldharbour Pill on the Gwent Levels (Neumann and Bell 1996: 14–15), and a fragment of wattle hurdle from another palaeochannel across the Severn Estuary at Oldbury (Allen and Fulford 1992) could all be from fish weirs, though they could equally relate to trackways. On the continent, a number of Roman period fish baskets have been discovered from rivers within the wetlands, including three eel traps from a creek at Valkenburg-Marktveld (e.g. Figure 37), and other examples from Utrecht, Velsen, and Zwammerdam (Van Rijn 1993). However, as in Britain, there is no evidence for a specialist fishing industry on the scale of that seen in the medieval period.

Shellfish were certainly exploited during the Late Iron Age, though from the start of the Roman period there is a marked increase in consumption, notably of oysters. Their importance to the diet, however, should not be exaggerated: 52,267 oysters (22 bushels) have the same calorific value as one red deer carcass (Medlycott 1996: 168–9; Smoothy 1989: 25). It is not clear whether natural oyster populations were simply harvested, or whether they were cultivated at this time, though substantial dumps of oysters from London dated *c.* AD 100 certainly suggests that they were being collected and sold on a commercial scale (Brigham and Watson 1998: 46). At Pudding Lane a late first century assemblage showed considerable variation of size and shape, suggestive of a natural population being harvested, whereas the second century oysters were dominated by larger, more uniformly round shells that may suggest some sort of cultivation (Milne 1985: 91–2). However, Winder (1993) argues that this might simply reflect a different oyster bed being exploited or the long-term effect of fishing on a natural population, and she rejects evidence for oyster cultivation in Britain before the medieval period (and see Somerville 1997). Not surprisingly, a wide range of shellfish was eaten at coastal settlements e.g. Canvey Island in Essex (C. Faulkner and N. Faulkner 1993; W. Rodwell 1966) and Ower by Poole Harbour (P. Woodward 1987*a*: 68), and though a wide range of other shellfish were transported inland, including cockles, mussels, whelks, winkles, and even crab (Crummy 1992: 276–8; Drury 1978: 118; 1988: 123; A. Hall and Kenward 1990: 407; Lavender 1993: 18), it is only oysters that appear to have been traded inland over long distances in large numbers (Drury 1976: 62).

Taken with the evidence for limited fishing in tidal waters, the frequency with which oysters are found on inland sites suggests that coastal resources were exploited as part of a market-based economic system though, like salt production and grazing, these

37. Roman-period eel trap, constructed from one-year old unsplit and unpeeled willow, with a rope fastened to the handle fixed to the casing. From Valkenburg-Markveld, The Netherlands (from Van Rijn 1993: fig. 4; photo: copyright ROB).

activities would have been seasonal. This, along with the scale of coastal resource exploitation compared with the medieval period (see Chapter 10), does not really support the hypothesis that this was the sole means of subsistence for these coastal communities. Overall, there appears to have been *relatively* little use made of natural food resources at this time, and 'for the Roman period the scarcity of wild animal remains may be testament to the efficiency of the agricultural system, which was adequately feeding the population, and producing a surplus with which to pay the taxes demanded by the Roman administration and participate in local and international trade' (Grant 1989: 144).

5.2.3 **Inland finds of briquetage**

The economic links between coastal areas and their hinterlands are also demonstrated by the inland distribution of briquetage. There are a variety of contexts in which briquetage could have found its way inland depending on its character. Vessel fragments could be derived from the containers used to transport salt during both the Iron Age (e.g. Cunliffe 1984; Cunliffe and Poole 1991: 404–7; E. Morris 1985; 1994; Poole 1987; 1991; H. Rees 1986) and Roman periods (e.g. Buckley *et al.* 1987: 30; Havis 1993; Sealey 1995: 66; Wilkinson 1988: 97). It has also been suggested that certain shell-tempered, bucket-like vessels produced in northern Kent and southern Essex may have been used to transport salt from the Thames Estuary to London (Tyers 1984: 373), though this does not appear to have been confirmed by scientific analysis.

However, during the Early Roman period, inland finds of briquetage also include fragments of pedestals, pans, and other oven furniture (Barford 1990*a*; D. Bond 1988; P. Clarke 1998: 115; Drury 1988: 117; Eddy 1982; K. Rodwell 1983: 33–4; 1988: 81; W. Rodwell 1979; Sealey 1995: 68–9; Wickenden 1986: 52; 1992: 88–9; Wymer and N. Brown 1995: 96). Such fragments may have been used as salt licks for livestock (e.g. Barford 1990*a*), or could relate to the final stages of salt production such as refining and drying (Sealey 1995; Wallis and Waughman 1998: 164–6). As such, the inland finds of briquetage may be telling us about either the movements of saltworkers or the people who owned the rights to salt production (K. Rodwell 1988: 82; W. Rodwell 1979). If this is the case, salt certainly appears to have been distributed through the small town network,[20] and, though the number of villa excavations in Essex is limited, there may be a link with salt production as briquetage has been recovered from Chignall, Little Oakley, Rivenhall, St Osyth, and Wickford (Barford 1990*a*; P. Clarke 1998: 115).

5.2.4 **Roman period peat cutting**

The production of salt through boiling sea water requires a large amount of fuel and in Russia, for example, (where, as around the North Sea basin, solar evaporation played only a minor part in the process) it is recorded that one salt pan could consume a stack of logs '*c.* 7 foot long and *c.* 7 foot high' per year (R. E. F. Smith and Christian 1984: 32). In Roman Britain fuel was derived from a variety of sources. Oil-rich shales appear to have been used at Kimmeridge in southern Dorset (Farrar 1962*b*: 140), while at Denver in Norfolk it is possible that coal from County Durham was burnt (Gurney 1986: 133–4). It has often been assumed that peat was the main source of fuel in the prehistoric and Romano-British coastal salt industry (e.g. D. Hall and J. 1994: 115; S. Hallam 1970: 68–9), and it does appear to have been used at Banwell in North Somerset (Rippon, forthcoming *a*), Huntspill in Central Somerset (Leech *et al.* 1983), Nordelph in Norfolk (P. Murphy 1994: 27), and Norwood in Cambridgeshire (Potter 1981: 106).

---

[20] *Billericay*: Rudling 1990: 42; *Chelmsford*: Drury 1988:117; Wickenden 1992: 88–9; *Colchester*: Barford 1990: 79; Reader 1908: 201; *Heybridge*: Wickenden 1986; *Kelvedon*: Clarke 1988*a*: 36; Eddy 1982: 26; K. Rodwell 1988: 81–2.

38. Roman-period peat cuttings near Goes, Zuid-Beveland, Zeeland, The Netherlands. Two unexcavated balks of peat were left upstanding, and the site was subsequently flooded sealing the turbary with later alluvium (from Vos and Van Heeringen 1997: fig. 33; photo: copyright: ROB).

Small-scale peat cutting may have occurred throughout Fenland, and is also recorded in Flanders and The Netherlands, including Goes in Zuid-Beveland (Figure 38), Assendelves in North Holland (Therkorn *et al.* 2000:13), and Hemens-Teerns and near Leuwarden (D. Gerrets, pers. comm. 1999). In several parts of Fenland there is also evidence of peat extraction on a far larger scale, in the form of cuttings up to 600 m long (Figures 25B and 39). These major turbaries are largely found within the southern peat fens, with the largest examples in March, Stonea, and Upwell (D. Hall 1987: 43; 1996: figs 9, 96, 102; Silvester 1991: 107–8). There is some evidence that blocks of turbaries may have been carefully laid out using units corresponding to one, two, and four *actus* (35.5 m) (D. Hall 1996: 174), and their limited distribution also suggests that peat cutting was in some way regulated. It may be that the larger turbaries were located so that they could supply the substantial settlements at Bourne, Stonea, and Grandford, and take advantage of the major communication routes (e.g. the Fen Causeway and canal, Bourne-Morton canal, and Upwell canal: Figure 25B). However, if the distribution of peat cutting was simply determined by supply and demand, then further examples would be expected in the fens close to the extensive settlement and pottery industry at Water Newton. The apparent absence of turbaries in these areas suggests that

39. Romano-British turbary at Christchurch, Upwell, in the Cambridgeshire Fenland (TL 477 952). The dark lines represent uncut bulks of peat, *c.* 40 m apart and up to 600 m long. The cuttings themselves were flooded and filled with (lighter coloured) silt. The site is showing up as a soil mark in a ploughed field (photo: copyright: Rog Palmer). (See Figure 25B)

people were not free to cut peat on a large scale wherever they liked: perhaps the right to work turbaries, like many other mineral resources, was regarded as a state or private monopoly (see discussion on salt below).

Despite the abundance of peat in Romano-British coastal wetlands, timber and brushwood appear to have been the preferred fuel for salt production on many sites, perhaps because it was more suited to producing the heat required to boil brine. For example, at Cowbit in Lincolnshire wood and wood charcoal, along with some saltmarsh plants, appear to have been burnt rather than peat (P. Murphy 1993a: 38; 1994: 27–8; Potter 1981: 106), while at Morton Fen and Cross Drove Morton, the waste from local arable farming was used (Crowson *et al.* 2000: 134, 138). Recent work at Blackborough End in Norfolk suggests that young-grown stems, possibly from coppiced woodland, were burnt (Crowson, forthcoming), and this is supported by evidence from Essex where a number of sites have produced a range of wood charcoal dominated by oak, with lesser amounts of a wide range of other trees and scrubby species such as broom (de Brisay 1979: 35; Linder 1939: 150; Reader 1908: 187–8; 1910: 84–5). The relatively uniform diameter of much of the wood suggests that it may have come from coppiced woodland, while the list of species clearly points to a dryland source.

It would seem, therefore, that while the rich natural resources that coastal marshes had on offer were exploited to a certain extent, this does not appear to have been a landscape under enormous strain: although wetland resources appear to have been used more extensively than in the preceding Iron Age, their importance was limited when compared with the medieval period (see Chapter 10). Peat was used as fuel in the salt production process, but other sources were often preferred. Fish were caught, but there is little evidence for a large-scale, well-organized fishing industry inclined to invest in fish traps and move off-shore. Shellfish were collected on a commercial scale, but there is little firm evidence for their cultivation. Very little wildfowling appears to have been carried out. Only salt was exploited on a large scale, though by the Late Roman period even this industry was not evenly distributed around the coast. In fact, the history of salt production in Roman Britain illustrates some curious trends, and it is to the rise and fall of this industry that we must now turn.

5.3 **The growth and decline of salt production**

As described above, evidence for salt production is found on most of the coastal marshes of southern and eastern Britain. However, the industry only appears to have flourished during the Early Roman period, and around Chichester Harbour and the Blackwater/Colne Estuaries in Essex salt production ceased by the end of the first century AD. In Romney Marsh, South East Essex, most of Fenland, and along the Lincolnshire coast, the industry had largely ceased by the mid-second century, while in North Kent and a handful of sites in Fenland production appears to have continued on a reduced scale into the third century (Figure 36). Only in the Brue Valley (Central Somerset), and Poole Harbour did coastal salt production continue to flourish into the fourth century (though it also continued at the inland brine springs in Cheshire and possibly Droitwich). This diachronic cessation of the salt industry around much of the coast represents a dramatic change in the way that the landscape was exploited, yet it remains ill-understood. As there is no reason why demand for salt should have declined, a number of possible explanations can be suggested:

- environmental changes (increased freshwater flooding, or marine inundation);
- the development of a villa-owning rural class which found activities such as salt production distasteful
- the technology of production changed, and methods using briquetage were replaced by techniques which left less visible archaeological traces
- the marshes were reclaimed because agricultural land became more highly valued than the natural resources on offer
- there was increased competition from the inland springs in the West Midlands or the Continent
- salt production was a state monopoly, and so shifts in production may have reflected changes in procurement strategies or attempts to control the industry

5.3.1 **Environmental decline?**

A potential reason why the salt industry of southern and eastern Britain disappeared is that for some reason coastal salt became increasingly expensive or impractical to produce. It is possible, for example, that environmental change, such as falling relative sea level or increased storminess and flooding, led to the abandonment of coastal marshes.

Falling sea level cannot explain the end of salt production, as the solution to such a problem would simply have been to move the salterns closer to the coast. An episode of marine transgression would have been more of a problem, though the answer would once again have simply been to move the salterns, in this case to the fen-edge. Flooding can also not explain why salt production declined in North East Essex during the late first century, South East Essex in the second century, and North Kent in the third, or why pottery production on the North Kent marshes continued after the decline of the salt industry. Overall, environmental change cannot explain the decline of the Romano-British salt industry.

5.3.2 **A disapproving villa-owning class?**

W. Rodwell (1979: 159) notes that the North East Essex salt industry lay at the core of the pre-Roman Trinovantian territory and close to its oppida at Colchester, and that salt, a valuable commodity, may have been one of the goods that was traded with the Roman world in exchange for wine and manufactured goods. However, soon after the Conquest salt production showed a marked shift in location away from this region and towards the Thames Estuary. W. Rodwell (1979: 161) has suggested that this change resulted from the foundation of a Roman colony at Colchester, and that the 'owners of sea side villas would not want to be surrounded by salterns.' There was certainly a marked concentration of early villas in North East Essex (Going 1996: fig. 1; W. Rodwell 1978*a*), as in West Sussex that also saw the demise of its salt industry at this time.

However, very few of the North East Essex villas are actually very close to the coast. Several villas in this region are in fact associated with briquetage finds (see above), and in a number of other areas the growth of early villas is also matched by the appearance of the salt industry e.g. North Kent (E. Black 1987; Detsicas 1983). Throughout Roman Britain there are also examples of a direct link between villas and industries, such as iron and pottery production, both of which must have given off just as much unpleasant smoke as salt making (E. Black 1987: 63–4; Branigan 1989: 47–9; Fulford and Allen 1992; B. Jones and Mattingly 1990: 209). Overall, the emergence of a rural villa-owning class cannot explain the demise of the salt industry.

5.3.3 **The adoption of a less archaeologically visible technology**

Another possible explanation for the apparent cessation of salt making is that the technology of production changed, with methods using briquetage replaced by techniques that leave less visible archaeological traces (Barford 1988: 3–6; Brongers and

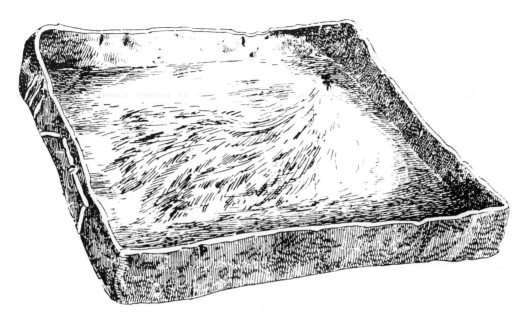

40. Romano-British lead saltpan found in Northwich, Cheshire, in 1864, and measuring approximately 1.11 m × 0.84 m × 0.12 m (from Kendrick 1865: 9; reproduced by permission of Stephen Penney, Cheshire Museum Service).

Woltering 1973: 34–5). Bradley (1992: 43–4; Bradley *et al.* 1997: 119) has noted that the use of briquetage first disappears close to the towns of Chichester and Colchester, arguing that innovation and investment in new technology (in the use of lead pans, for example) will have been greatest close to these early urban centres.

On several sites in Essex it has indeed been claimed that there is evidence of a change in the technology of production. At Goldhanger a series of flues was uncovered that had been cut into a levelled section of an earlier red hill (Reader 1908: 176; 1910: 69–77; and see Barford 1988: 3; Fawn *et al.* 1990: 24–5; W. Rodwell 1979: 153–4, 165). Though W. Rodwell (1979: 165) suggests these could relate to pottery production, their design can also be paralleled in early medieval salterns where similar structures are thought to have supported lead pans e.g. Droitwich (J. D. Hurst 1992). The early excavators at Goldhanger noted that these flues were only associated with very small amounts of abraded (?residual) briquetage, though Sealey (1995: 76) has questioned this. No pottery was directly associated with the flues, and nothing from the site is dated after the late second century (Fawn *et al.* 1990: 75); no lead waste was recovered either. Other examples of possible non-briquetage using oven-like structures in Essex may exist at Southminster near Burnham-on-Crouch (Crouchman 1977: 84), and Canvey Point (Eddy 1980: 61), though there is once again no dating evidence.

There are two arguments against the hypothesis that salt production continued on these coastal sites using a new technology. First, it is not just the use of briquetage that disappears, but ceramics as a whole: if these sites represent the missing third and fourth century salt industry, then we would expect them to be associated with at least a little domestic debris as was the case in the Early Roman period. Second, the only real alternative to using ceramic vessels is metal, particularly lead. Unlike ceramics, metal vessels could be repaired and recycled and so are likely to have left *fewer* archaeological traces, but traces there are. Lead pans are known to have been used during the Late Roman period in the West Midlands, with eight certain and two possible examples from Cheshire (e.g. Figure 40; Kendrick 1865; Penney and Shotter 1996; F. Thompson 1965): none, however, have been recorded from coastal areas. It is also known from medieval salterns in Kent, Lincolnshire, and Droitwich that the repair of vessels leaves droplets and scraps of lead (Healey 1975: 36; J. D. Hurst 1997: 17; M. Thompson 1956: 50), yet the evidence for lead waste from Romano-British coastal sites is meagre. In Essex, one site on Canvey Island has produced two small pieces of sheet lead (W. Rodwell 1966: 19), though the fact that one was rolled-up suggests it was used as a loom or fishing weight, rather than in repairing a lead pan. In North Kent, two second century Romano-British salterns at Funton Creek (Lower Halstow near the Upchurch Marshes) did produce drops of lead (A. Miles 1965: 261–3), though far less than on medieval salterns. Overall, therefore, the evidence for a change of technology on these coastal sites is very slim indeed.

5.3.4 **Late Roman reclamation?**

It is plausible that salt production ceased because the tidal marshes that once supported the industry were reclaimed for agricultural use, though there is almost no evidence that this was the case. Around Chichester Harbour, Romney Marsh, and most of the Thames Estuary it is not just salt production that disappears around the second century but almost all evidence for occupation. If the marshes had been reclaimed we would expect to see far more evidence for settlements, most obviously on the abandoned salt working sites that would have provided raised areas ideal for permanent occupation.

There are, however, a few notable exceptions. On Canvey Island in Essex and the Upchurch Marshes in North Kent there is some evidence for occupation of uncertain character into the third and fourth centuries, along with a number of sites that have yielded evidence for substantial buildings (see Chapter 4). Such material does suggest fairly permanent settlements, though similar sites in the coastal siltlands of Lincolnshire are known to have lain in a very high saltmarsh environment without the protection of a sea wall. Overall then, there is no evidence that the salt industry declined because of reclamation, though excavation and palaeoenvironmental analysis on some of the possible substantial buildings on the Essex/North Kent marshes is required to confirm or refute this hypothesis in those areas.

5.3.6 **Competition from alternative sources**

Another possible explanation for the decline of coastal salt production in South East Britain is competition from other areas, notably Poole Harbour, the Brue Valley in Somerset, and the inland brine springs. There is certainly evidence of trading contacts between Poole Harbour and South East England, reflected, for example, in the distribution of BB1 pottery that has even been found on Essex salterns e.g. Langenhoe near Colcester (Sealey 1995: 74). Further inland at Chelmsford (Essex) there were 86 sherds of South East Dorset BB1 which far outstrips closer mass-produced industries such as Alice Holt (North East Hampshire: 32 sherds), Oxfordshire (29 sherds), and New Forest ware (1 sherd) (Going 1987). It is not known whether these BB1 vessels were necessarily used to transport salt from Dorset to Essex, but they at least show that commercial links existed between the two regions.

Inland salt production in the West Midlands is another potential source of competition. Inland brine springs have a number of advantages over coastal waters (Bridbury 1955; Multhauf 1978: 7). First, the salt is far more concentrated: 25.3 per cent in inland springs compared with just 2.6 per cent in coastal waters. Second, the inland brine is far purer than sea water, with far fewer other chlorides and sulphates that give a bitter taste to the salt. Third, away from the dangers of winter storms, the inland springs could be exploited all year round.

The salt industry at Droitwich expanded during the first and second centuries AD though the evidence for later Roman production is slight (Anon. 1988; Burnham and Wacher 1990: 211–17; J. D. Hurst 1991; 1992: 8–13; E. Morris 1985; H. Rees 1986; Woodwiss 1992). A series of wooden barrels found at the Old Bowling Green Site may have been used for settling and storing brine, while settlements at both Droitwich and the adjacent villa at Bays Meadow certainly continued to be occupied into the fourth century. It may be that either the later Roman industry ceased to use briquetage, that the focus of activity shifted to an area not yet subjected to excavation, or that subsequent occupation has removed the Late Roman deposits. Roman salt production in Cheshire certainly continued into the late fourth century (Bestwick 1975; Burnham and Wacher 1990: 225–8; Petch 1987: 222–3; F. Thompson 1965: 97; and see B. Jones and Mattingly 1990: 224–5; Penney and Shotter 1996).

The possibility can also not be ruled out that salt was imported from the continent, as occurred during the late medieval period (Bridbury 1955; Pelham 1930). The importance of the salt industry south of the *Limes* during the Early Roman period is reflected in two inscriptions from Rimini, in Italy. They are dedications by the *salinatores civitatis Menapiorum* and the *salinatores civitatis Morinorum* (the two tribes occupying the coastal area of North West France and Belgium) to L. Lepidius Proculus, a centurion of the Legio VI Victrix in *Novaesium* (Neuss) during the reign of Vespasian (AD 69–79), for services to the trade in salt (Bloemers 1983: 168; Thoen 1975: 56). A number of late second/early third century altars have also been dredged up from the East Scheldt Estuary, off Colijnsplaat in Zeeland, including four dedicated by *negotiatores salarii* (salt merchants) and three by *negotiatores allecari* (traders in fish sauce, which used salt as a preservative) (Thoen 1981: 250–2). It is not clear in which direction this trade was going, though another altar mentions a *negotiator cretarius Britannicianus*, who was exporting pottery to Britain.

Unfortunately, there is relatively little archaeological evidence for Roman-period salt production on the Belgian and Dutch coast to support this documentary material (Van den Broeke 1995; 1996: 193). For example, in Midden-Delfland, briquetage was recovered from a series of Iron Age settlements, though just a handful of fragments has been found on Roman-period sites. What was thought to be briquetage of this date from De Panne in Belgium (Nenquin 1961: 93–5; Riehm 1961: 189) may in fact be residual material from an Iron Age salt production site below (Ceunynck and Thoen 1981). However, a second/third century saltern complex at Leffinge, on the Flanders fen-edge south-west of Oostende, appears to perpetuate the late prehistoric briquetage-using technology (Thoen 1978: 234–5; 1981). There are also a number of enigmatic second to third century AD rectangular wooden structures that may point towards a more industrialized salt production process at the coastal sites of Zeebrugge and Raversijde (near Oostende) in Belgium (Thoen 1975; 58–9). A number of Roman period ovens have also been recorded at 'S-Heer Abtskerke on Zuid-Beveland (South West Netherlands), associated with large amounts of ash (Vos and Van Heeringen 1997: 65–6). None of these sites were associated with briquetage although several have produced moulds of the type used during the Iron Age to produce salt cakes. Van den Broeke (1996) has also recently postulated that a particular form of thin-walled native pottery found on a number of Roman period settlements may in fact have replaced briquetage-fabrics as salt containers.

Though it remains possible that salt was imported into South East Britain from the continent during the Early Roman period, there is so little evidence for occupation in the coastal region of North West Europe during the late third and fourth centuries that it seems implausible that any salt trade would have continued. If competition, therefore, caused the decline of South East Britain's coastal salt industry, then it is probably to the west of the province that we must look. It is simpler to produce salt from the inland springs, but it was a long way from Dorset or Droitwich to London or Colchester, so if western sources did take over the markets in South East Britain that were formerly met by local production, western British salt must have been a lot cheaper to produce in order to make up for the transport costs. The introduction of a new technology, including the use of lead pans, may have played an important part, though this does not explain why similar technology was not introduced on the coastal sites in South East Britain. However, it is also possible that changing patterns in the production of salt reflect wider trends in Roman Britain, and to understand these we must look at the hinterlands of these coastal wetlands.

5.3.7 Political and economic geography

Even in the pre-Roman period certain areas of salt production appear to have been located close to particularly important political and economic centres. In Dorset, Hengistbury Head and Maiden Castle, both of which have yielded briquetage, lay within the broad hinterland of Poole Harbour, while the potential 'port of trade' at Ower lay beside the Harbour itself (P. Cox and Hearne 1991; Cunliffe 1984; 1987; 1995; Cunliffe and Poole 1991; P. Woodward 1987a). In Hampshire and Sussex the pre-Roman oppida at Selsey lay next to Chichester Harbour, while the most important centre of all,

Colchester, was close to the salterns in North East Essex. In Lincolnshire a number of high status settlements are known, though it may not be a coincidence that Old Sleaford, the closest of these sites to Fenland, is the only one of the Corieltauvian centres to have produced coin moulds (some 3,000 of them) (J. May 1984: 21; Whitwell 1982: 43). A few sherds of briquetage have also been recovered at Dragonby on the southern banks of the Humber Estuary (J. May 1996: 337). In Norfolk there is a marked bias in the distribution of high status sites away from the Fens, though the deposition of prestige metalwork close to the fen-edge does indicate a relationship between wetlands and power (J. Davies 1996: 71–3; Stead 1991).

Following the Roman Conquest the political and economic map of Britain changed, with new centres emerging, most notably London. The sudden growth of London is at first difficult to explain: there is no evidence for a Late Iron Age settlement, nor a Conquest-period fort, and it was not initially the provincial centre, nor a *colonia* or a *civatas* capital (Wacher 1995: 88). It had, however, a number of locational advantages for a major port of trade, notably its situation on a sheltered estuary which lay directly opposite the continent. Thus, while salt production may have flourished in North East Essex as the Trinovantes forged links with the Roman world, production may have become more concentrated around the Thames once London was established as the province's main port. The economic power of London did not last long as its commercial vibrancy may have declined as early as the second century (Millett 1990: 163), and the subsequent disappearance of the salt industry in South East Britain during the second and third centuries may also reflect a wider change in the region's economy. Monaghan (1987: 227) has discussed this in the context of the North Kent pottery industry. Flooding cannot have been a cause of the industry's decline since the kilns could simply have been rebuilt in a drier location on the fen-edge, and competition from other pottery industries may have been a factor: in London, for example, South East Dorset BB1, absent until the mid-second century, forms *c.* 6–12 per cent of third century assemblages (Allen and Fulford 1996: 24).

The decline of the North Kent pottery industry may also reflect a general economic decline in South East Britain. During the third century much of the province was affected by a recession (Fulford 1989: 191–5), and the South East in particular never appears to have fully recovered. For example, on Thanet in North East Kent, settlement continues until the end of the Roman period, but the island appears to have been far less populated after the mid-second century (P. Bennett and J. Williams 1997: 259; Hearne *et al.* 1995: 337; Monaghan 1987: 228). Across the Thames in Essex there also appears to have been a general decline in prosperity during the third and fourth centuries reflected in patterns of coin loss, a lack of investment in villas, the economic decline of towns such as Heybridge, and their lack of stone defences (Going 1996: 103–4; Wickenden 1996: 93). There are also signs of agricultural land going out of use during the fourth century at Mucking (Going 1996), Orsett (Carter 1998), Chigborough (Wallis and Waughman 1998: 106), and possibly North Shoebury (Wymer and N. Brown 1995: 42).

The signs of economic decline in South East Britain contrast sharply with parts of central southern and western Britain, including the area east of the Severn Estuary.

Here, considerable sums were invested in villas (Figure 42), mosaic schools flourished, urban life continued behind impressive defences, and the evidence from coin loss and hoards suggests there was no decline in the circulation of money during the late third and fourth centuries (B. Jones and Mattingly 1990; 222–4, map 6.41; Millett 1990; 195). The continuation of salt production in the west of Britain may, in part, be related to this period of prosperity. It may be significant that iron production in the Weald of Kent/Sussex also ceased during the third century, while it continued to flourish in the Forest of Dean until the end of the Roman period (B. Jones and Mattingly 1990: 192–3).

Overall, there does not appear to be a simple explanation for the changing geography of salt production in Roman Britain. The introduction of new technology on the inland springs, whose waters were more concentrated and contained fewer impurities, may well have been a factor, while the distribution of Late Roman saltworking also appears to correspond with the greater agricultural and urban wealth within western parts of the province. However, there must still have been demand for salt in South East Britain, and transport costs from, say, Cheshire to Essex cannot have been cheap. There seems to be no reason why coastal communities in the South East did not simply start using lead pans as seems to have occurred in Cheshire. Making salt by boiling sea water is not a complex process, and it is almost as if local populations were either unwilling or unable to use simple technology to produce salt locally. So are there non-economic factors at work?

5.3.8 The role of the state

As was discussed above, it is possible that during the Late Iron Age the coastal salt industry was somehow stimulated by the emergence of powerful political elites and increasing trade, including contact with the Roman world. Indeed, this may go some way towards explaining the lack of a substantial pre-Roman salt industry around the Thames Estuary, which as the distribution of pre-Conquest imported pottery and metalwork shows, was remote from the major political centres of that time (B. Jones and Mattingly 1990: map 3.16–17; Millet 1990: fig. 9).

Bradley (1975: 25; 1992: 43–4) has stressed the potential importance of salt as a tradeable commodity, and a number of Late Iron Age coins discovered on coastal salterns raises the question of whether they were exchanged for salt.[21] It may even have been that salt production during the Late Iron Age was at least partly controlled by the native political elite, in which case following the Conquest the right to these salterns may have become an imperial one. On the continent a similar phenomenon may be observed where the 'concentration of prestige objects found near the salt mines of Hallstatt and Hallein in Austria show to what great wealth control of the salt trade could lead.' (Van den Broeke 1995: 151). Salt was even worth going to war over as, for

---

[21] *Langenhoe, North East Essex*: Sealey 1995: 75; *Little Wakering, South East Essex*: Haselgrove 1987: 355, cf. Sealey 1995: 75; *Helpringham, Lincolnshire*: Whitwell 1982: 16.

example, in AD 58 when two tribes in Germany, the Chatti and Hermunduri, fought a battle over 'a river rich in salt' (Tacitus *Annals*, book XIII, chapter 57). The inhabitants of Ostia (in Italy) also went to war over salt (Meiggs 1973: 17), while the importance of its control was also reflected in the Roman state monopoly of its production which continued into the Byzantine and Ottoman periods (Grozdanova 1995: 195–9).

In the decades immediately after the Roman Conquest of Britain the coastal salt industry appears to have expanded rapidly, both in the earlier core areas (South East Dorset, Chichester Harbour, North East Essex, and Lincolnshire) and at new locations such as the Central Somerset Levels, Romney Marsh, and the Thames Estuary. In part, this expansion of production may have been related to the imposition of a large military force which would have required salt as a food preservative. The size of this military demand should not be exaggerated: the initial invasion force of *c*. 40,000 men was reduced to *c*. 10,000–20,000 by the Late Roman period and, along with their *c*. 50,000–200,000 dependents, they amounted to just 3.4 per cent of the population in Roman Britain (Frere 1987: 48; Millett 1990: 57, table 8.5). However, even this number would have consumed large amounts of preserved meat and other commodities that used salt in their preparation (see Chapter 3), and its procurement via regular orders from the Procurator would have been a stable source of income for salt producers.

During the initial decades of the Conquest, military dispositions had a distinctly coastal bias in southern and eastern Britain, stressing the importance of water transport (B. Jones and Mattingly 1990: fig. 4.23–4; Millett 1990: fig. 12). Important naval bases at Hamworthy by Poole Harbour, Fishbourne by Chichester Harbour, and Fingringhoe by the Colne Estuary in Essex, were no doubt primarily positioned to take advantage of the sheltered waters, though they also lay close to major salt production centres. By the late first century most troops were located in Wales and the North, where they remained for the rest of the Roman period, and this in turn may go some way in explaining the survival and even expansion of salt production in western Britain. Indeed, it may not be a coincidence that the only part of the Somerset Levels that appears to have been left unreclaimed and used for salt production lay next to the probably Roman supply route for BB1 from South East Dorset to the military establishment in South East Wales via Dorchester, Ilchester, and Crandon Bridge (Figure 41; Allen and Fulford 1996; Rippon 1997*a*: 54, 98, 121–2).

This raises the issue of just who was producing the salt: was it local communities simply responding to increased demand from the army, or was there more direct state involvement? The dedications by the *Salinatores* to L. Lepidius Proculus for services to the trade in salt might suggest the former (Thoen 1975: 56), though there is also a strong body of evidence to support the latter hypothesis: though the military establishment would have consumed a certain amount of salt, it may have been the control of that prized resource that was more important to the Roman authorities. During the Roman period the right to exploit mineral resources was regarded as an imperial one, just as areas which were brought under cultivation for the first time became *ager publicus* (state owned land) (Todd 1989: 14). The Roman State was the biggest owner of mineral resources within the Empire, and the salt industry was

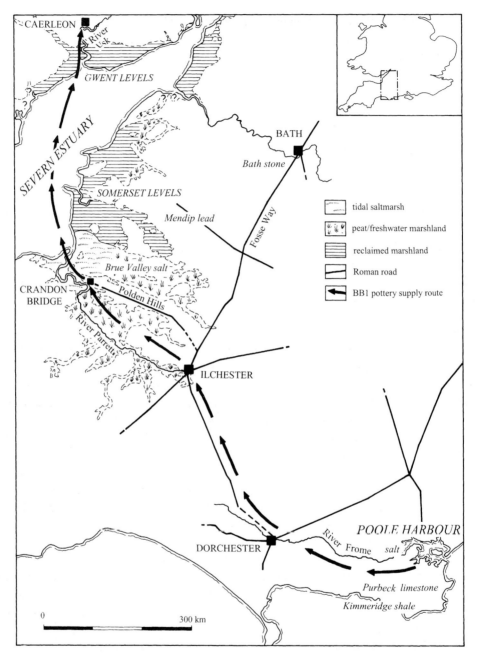

41. The potential economic links between South East Dorset and the Severn Estuary during the Roman period (after Allen and Fulford 1996 and Rippon 1997*a*). BB1 pottery from Poole Harbour appears to have been transported to the military establishment in South East Wales, possibly via a transshipment port at Crandon Bridge by the Parrett Estuary. The Brue Valley, to the north, was the only area of Romano-British salt production around the whole Severn Estuary.

carefully controlled through a monopoly (Broughton 1938: 566, 799; Frank 1927: 191; Petch 1987: 222; Multhauf 1978: 12; Rostovtzeff 1957: 340–2).

The way in which the authorities controlled mineral rights varied throughout the empire. In Gaul, for example,

> Rome did not concentrate all mines in her own hands, nor did she object to the discovery and exploitation of new ones on the estates of the Gallic nobility. When large mining districts in the new provinces passed into the possession of the state and emperors, the system of exploitation became more diversified through adaptation of the special conditions of each district. (Rostovtzeff 1957: 340–1).

A number of mechanisms were possible, ranging from renting whole areas to large capitalists, leasing individual mines to smaller entrepreneurs whose rent was collected by state officials or rent farmers, or direct exploitation by the state through contractors (e.g. E. Birley 1953: 95–6). However, over time, the trend was to increase state control through eliminating the larger capitalists and private entrepreneurs.

The State was certainly involved in the exploitation of mineral resources within Roman Britain. The discovery of tiles stamped with the monogram of the *Classis Britannica* at several iron working centres in the Kent/Sussex Weald suggests a long term military involvement with that industry (B. Jones and Mattingly 1990: 192), and it is plausible that they were also associated with the salt industry in Romney Marsh. Fulford (1996) has shown how the Second Legion, based at Caerleon, may have been involved in the exploitation of mineral resources throughout South West Britain, including lead (at Draethen, Machen, Risca, and Mendip), stone (Bath), and possibly gold (Dolaucothi), tin (Cornwall), iron (Forest of Dean), and the varied resources of South East Dorset (Figure 41; and see Elkington 1976; B. Jones and Mattingly 1990). The Mendip lead mines certainly appear to have come under military supervision within a few years of the Conquest via the fort at Charterhouse, though production appears to have been leased to private concerns by the mid-second century (Burnham and Wacher 1990: 208–11). The lead mines at Linley in Shropshire also appear to have been under military supervision via the fort at Brompton, though production in Derbyshire, Yorkshire, and North Wales may have been leased to civilian concerns within a few years of the Conquest (Manning 1979: 114; B. Jones and Mattingly 1990: 184–90). In the West Midlands there is also possible evidence for official involvement in salt production, in the form of forts at Droitwich, Middlewich, and Northwich (J. D. Hurst 1992: 8; Petch 1987: 222). In addition, South East Dorset produced not just salt, but shale, marble, and BB1 pottery which was used to supply the military establishment in western and northern Britain (P. Cox and Hearne 1991; Allen and Fulford 1996; Sunter and P. Woodward 1987). The hinterland of the legionary base at Chester not only produced salt, but pottery, glass, and bronze (B. Jones and Mattingly 1990: map 6.42).

It would appear, therefore, that the military establishment in Roman Britain was closely associated with the exploitation of mineral resources and, in the case of the legionary fortresses of Chester and Caerleon, this may have included salt. The decline of coastal salt production in the east of Britain is difficult to explain purely in economic terms, and it is tempting to see some official involvement in the gradual extinction of sprawling coastal industries in the east, and their replacement by smaller, more concentrated centres of production in the west which would have facilitated greater control.

5.4 Discussion: the exploitation of natural coastal resources during the Roman period

This chapter has examined one of the three ways in which coastal wetlands were utilized during the Roman period: the exploitation of natural resources without significantly modifying the environment. Throughout the prehistoric period, the rich natural resources that these landscapes had to offer attracted human communities to them, and the same was certainly true in the Roman period. It has been shown that there is surprisingly little evidence of wildfowling and, though the collection of both fish and shellfish was clearly an important activity in coastal areas, there is no evidence for a specialized fishing industry. In comparison with the prehistoric period there does appear to have been an intensification of natural resource exploitation, although, compared with the medieval period, the use of coastal landscapes as a source of natural food was fairly limited.

During the Early Roman period most coastal marshes were, however, used intensively for producing salt through boiling sea water, and the exploitation of other natural resources may have taken place alongside this seasonal activity. Only in a limited number of areas in western Britain did salt production continue into the Late Roman period, though the reasons for this are far from clear. Environmental deterioration can be ruled out: what happened to the coastal salt industry was a cultural phenomena related to human decision making. Three arguments—a disapproving villa-owing class, reclamation, and the adoption of new technology in coastal areas—can all be dismissed. More efficient methods of production at the inland springs, along with their naturally more concentrated brine, may have favoured the salt industry of the West Midlands, which was also ideally located to supply the army at Chester. So why was this technology simply not adopted elsewhere? Part of the explanation may lie in the changing regional economics of Roman Britain, which saw the South East eclipsed during the third and fourth centuries by the Wessex/Severn region. However, a substantial demand for salt would have remained in the South and East, and it would seem that non-economic factors were at work. Following the Roman Conquest the imperial authorities clearly took a close interest in certain mineral resources and the history of salt elsewhere in the Roman world would suggest that it too was regarded an imperial monopoly. Controlling an industry scattered around remote coastal areas would have been difficult, yet for some reason most of the British marshes ceased to produce salt. It may not be a coincidence that those areas which saw continued salt production also had a range of other resources that were supplied to the Procurator and his military establishment.

CHAPTER 6

Initiative and change:

marshland drainage during the Roman period

6.1 Introduction

Chapter 5 considered the varying intensity of natural resource exploitation on the coastal wetlands of North West Europe during the Roman period and, in particular, how changes in the distribution of salt production cannot simply reflect local supply and demand. Salt production was just one strategy towards the utilization of this particular type of environment, however, and this chapter examines another: the agricultural use of coastal marshlands, and especially the decision to modify such environments through drainage and reclamation. It begins with a summary of the various agricultural uses to which coastal marshlands were put. Spatial and chronological variations in these landscape utilization strategies are then examined and explanations sought in term of several possible factors: regional variation in estate structure and the changing patterns of agricultural wealth and innovation, the possibility of certain coastal marshes being imperial estates and, finally, the impact of military establishments. A key underlying theme that emerges is the need to understand who was taking the initiative in the process of settlement expansion and reclamation, a topic considered for the medieval period in Chapter 11.

6.2 The expansion of settlement into coastal marshes during the Roman period

Coastal marshes are clearly a physically marginal landscape in terms of permanent settlement and arable-based agriculture. So why did human communities leave the relative comfort and safety of dryland areas in order to occupy such harsh environments and increase the intensity with which their resources were used? Table 2 summarizes the different ways in which the coastal marshes of North West Europe were used during the Roman period.

An attempt will now be made to explore these marked spatial and chronological differences in marshland utilization strategies in terms of several possible factors:

Table 2a. The nature of marshland utilization during the Roman period

Area	Use	Mode of landscape utilization
Wentlooge (South East Wales)	Systematic reclamation	Transformation
Caldicot (South East Wales)	Unreclaimed	Modification
Inner and middle Severn Estuary	Reclamation (type unknown)	Transformation
Avonmouth Level	Reclamation (type unknown)	Transformation
North Somerset Levels	Unsystematic reclamation	Transformation
Central Somerset (Brentmarsh)	Reclamation (type unknown)	Transformation
Central Somerset (Brue Valley)	Unreclaimed: salt production	Exploitation
Pevensey Levels	Unknown	Unknown
Romney Marsh	Unreclaimed: salterns	Exploitation
North Kent	Unreclaimed: salterns and settlements	Exploitation and (?)modification
Essex Thames-side	Unreclaimed: salterns and settlements	Exploitation and (?)modification
Essex (eastern)	Unreclaimed: salterns	Exploitation
Norfolk Broadland	Unreclaimed (open water)	Unknown
Fenland	Unreclaimed: salterns and settlements	Exploitation and modification
Lincolnshire coastal marshes	Unreclaimed: salterns?	Exploitation
Humber Estuary	Unreclaimed: salterns and settlements	Exploitation and modification
Belgium	Unreclaimed: salterns and settlements	Exploitation and modification
Western Netherlands	Unreclaimed: salterns and settlements	Exploitation and modification
Northern Netherlands/Germany	Unreclaimed: settlements (raised)	Exploitation and (?)modification

Table 2b. The chronology of marshland utilization during the Roman period

Area	Use	Main period of activity
Wentlooge (South East Wales)	Systematic reclamation	2nd to 4th century
Caldicot (South East Wales)	Unreclaimed	1st/2nd to 4th century
Inner and middle Severn Estuary	Reclamation (type unknown)	3rd to 4th century
Avonmouth Level	Reclamation (type unknown)	1st/2nd to 4th century
North Somerset Levels	Unsystematic reclamation	3rd to 4th century
Central Somerset (Brentmarsh)	Reclamation (type unknown)	1st/2nd to 4th century
Central Somerset (Brue Valley)	Unreclaimed: salt production	1st to 4th century
Pevensey Levels	Unknown	Unknown
Romney Marsh	Unreclaimed: salterns	1st to 2nd century
North Kent	Unreclaimed: salterns and settlements	1st to 2nd/3rd century
Essex Thames-side	Unreclaimed: salterns and settlements	1st to 2nd century
Essex (eastern)	Unreclaimed: salterns	1st to 2nd century
Norfolk Broadland	Unreclaimed (open water)	Unknown
Fenland	Unreclaimed: salterns and settlements	1st/2nd to 4th century
Lincolnshire coastal marshes	Unreclaimed: salterns?	Unknown
Humber Estuary	Unreclaimed: salterns and settlements	1st/2nd to 4th century
Belgium	Unreclaimed: salterns and settlements	1st to 3rd century Western
Netherlands	Unreclaimed: salterns and settlements	1st to 3rd century
Northern Netherlands/Germany	Unreclaimed: settlements (raised)	1st to 4th century

regional variation in estate structure and patterns of agricultural wealth and innovation, the possibility of extensive coastal marshes being seized as imperial estates and, finally, the impact of a military frontier in The Netherlands.

6.3 **Coastal marshes and estate structure** (Figure 18)

In Chapter 3 the various territorial structures within which coastal marshes may have been exploited were outlined (Figure 18). However, as Todd (1989: 14) has observed: 'When we consider how important was the ownership of land in the Roman Empire, it is remarkable how ill-informed we are on the whole about the units in which land was owned and farmed' (and see Crawford 1976; Millet 1990).

For the medieval period, documentary evidence allows the pattern of estates within which coastal wetlands were exploited to be reconstructed (Chapter 11). For the Roman period we lack such sources, though analogy with the medieval period suggests four possibilities as to how coastal marshland may have fitted into different estate structures:

- if the distance was not too great, both the marshland and the sea shore could be exploited by communities living on the fen-edge (Figure 18A)
- if this distance was too great, then a settlement might be established on the marshes (usually on the higher ground towards the coast and tidal creeks) which was *subsidiary* to an estate centre on the fen-edge or further inland (Figure 18B). Such sites may initially have been used seasonally, for example by fishermen, shepherds, and salt makers, though later they may have become permanent agricultural communities but still attached to the fen-edge 'mother' settlement (being part of a 'multiple' or 'federative' estate: see below);
- extensive areas of coastal marsh could also be exploited by communities living in *independent* settlements on marshes which had previously been regarded as waste ground (Figure 18C). Such settlements may have emerged from formerly seasonal and subsidiary settlements that gained social and economic independence, or they may have been established on previously unoccupied land
- marshland may have been exploited as a *detached* holding of a settlement some distance away (Figure 18D). Certain coastal marshes were 'enclaved' in this way during the medieval period (e.g. Figures 57 and 69) and there is very limited evidence for a similar structure of landholding in at least the dryland areas of Roman Britain (Tomlin 1996)

Another potentially important factor was whether land was in private or public ownership. Three categories of public land can be distinguished in the northwestern provinces: military *prata* attached to legionary fortresses, estates of the emperor, and land which belonged to the state itself (D. Mason 1988; Todd 1989). Distinguishing between private and public land is not easy: if land was leased to tenants it may have been exploited in a similar way irrespective of whether the landlord was an emperor or a private villa owner. There have been several attempts at identifying imperial estates in Roman Britain on the

Table 3. The relationship between villas and the use of coastal wetlands during the Roman period

Area	Villa location			
	Marshland	Fen-edge	Distant	Absent
Wentlooge (South East Wales)	No	No	No	Yes
Caldicot (South East Wales)	No	No	Yes	No
Inner and middle Severn Estuary	No	No	Yes	No
Avonmouth Level	No	Yes	Yes	No
North Somerset Level	Yes	Yes	Yes	No
Central Somerset Level (Brentmarsh)	Yes	No	Yes	No
Central Somerset Level (Brue Valley)	No	No	Yes	No
Pevensey Levels	No	Yes	No	No
Romney Marsh		No	No	Yes
North Kent	No	Yes	Yes	No
Essex Thames-side	No	No	No	Yes
Essex (eastern)	No	No	Yes	No
Broadland	No	No	No	Yes
Fenland: NW Norfolk	No	No	Yes	No
Fenland: SW Norfolk to Cambridge	No	Yes	Yes	No
Fenland: SW Cambridgeshire	No	No	No	Yes
Fenland: SW Lincolnshire	No	No	Yes	No
Fenland: N Lincolnshire	No	No	No	Yes
Lincolnshire coastal marshes	No	No	No	Yes
Humber Estuary	No	No	Yes	No
Belgium	No	No	No	Yes
Western Netherlands	No	No	No	Yes
Northern Netherlands/Germany	No	No	No	Yes

basis of an absence of villas,[22] though such arguments have increasingly fallen out of favour because of the uncritical assumption that a lack of villas equates with a lack of private wealth, which in turn implies public rather than private property (Millett 1990: 120; Todd 1989: 14–15). Indeed, just as the absence of villas should not necessarily be taken as representing the presence of an imperial estate, so some villa-like buildings could simply have been bailiffs' residences on private or public estates.

Clearly, it is difficult to reconstruct an estate structure simply based on the upper part of the settlement hierarchy (villas), but this is at least a starting point which may lead to further research. The distribution of villas in the northwestern provinces was in fact very uneven, with extensive areas having a very high density, and equally large areas where they are absent. Table 3 describes the relationship between coastal wetlands and villas (Ordnance Survey 1978; Roymans 1996, fig. 18). Four types of settlement patterns are identified: villas on the marshes themselves, fen-edge villas, villas on adjacent uplands (within 10 km) whose estates may have extended onto the marshes, and a complete absence of villas from the region (within 10 km). It must be remembered that this relates to our present understanding of settlement types in each region, and although some villas undoubtedly lie undiscovered, these are unlikely to change the broad regional pattern in settlement types.

[22] *Southern Essex*: Rodwell 1978*b*; 1979: 164; *Salisbury Plain*: Collingwood and Myres 1937: 224; *Southern Somerset/northern Dorset*: Branigan 1976: 45–7.

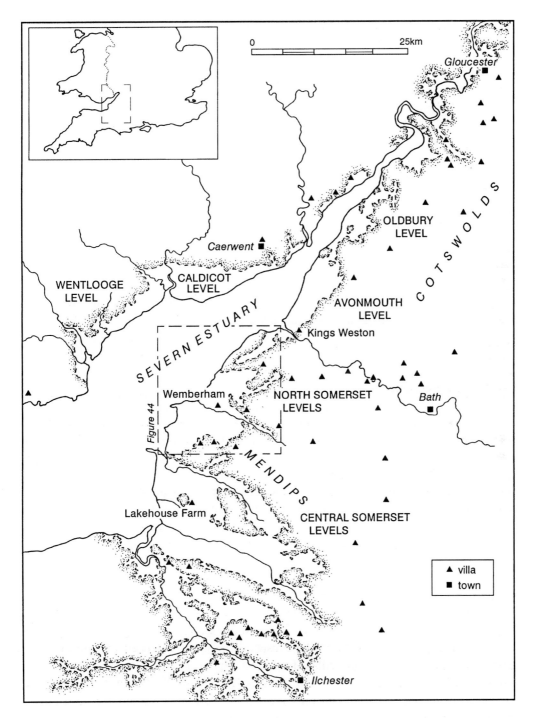

42. Distribution of Romano-British villas around the Severn Estuary (based on Ordnance Survey 1978). For a more detailed examination of North West Somerset see Figure 44. (Drawn by Sue Rouillard.)

Only two coastal marshes appear to have had villas constructed on them: Lakehouse Farm on the Brentmarsh area of the Central Somerset Levels, and Wemberham on the North Somerset Levels. It is surely no coincidence that both these areas were reclaimed (Figures 20 and 42).

Five areas are associated with fen-edge villas: the Avonmouth and North Somerset Levels on the English side of the Severn Estuary (Figure 42), the North Kent marshes, and South East Fenland; a single villa at Eastbourne lies close to the Pevensey Levels. Interestingly, each of these sets of villas looked out over a very different marshland landscape. The North Somerset and Avonmouth Levels appear to have been reclaimed. The North Kent villas were adjacent to extensive tracts of open marshland that appear to have been used primarily for salt and pottery production (and presumably seasonal grazing), while the villas by the South East Fenland lay beside a vast peat bog. The condition of the Pevensey Levels near the villa at Eastbourne is ill-understood.

Some of these and other marshland areas may have fallen within the estates of villas located on the adjacent uplands, of which the Inner and Middle Severn Estuary (Figure 42), Poole Harbour, and parts of Fenland (Figure 23) are the clearest examples. Finally, there are a number of wetlands that are in regions largely devoid of villas: Wentlooge, Romney Marsh, southern Essex, Norfolk Broadland, parts of Fenland, and the coastal wetlands of mainland North West Europe. Apart from Wentlooge, which was systematically drained (probably by the army) none of these other coastal wetlands, whose hinterlands were devoid of villas, appear to have seen any attempt at large scale landscape modification or transformation.

Clearly, the development of villa-based estates did not always lead to the reclamation of coastal wetlands though, apart from the military drainage of Wentlooge, all known reclamations either have villas on the marshes, on the fen-edge, or in the immediate hinterland. This may be accounted for by one of two explanations. First, there may have been a direct link: reclamation was, after all, a costly undertaking both in the initial act of embankment and drainage, and then the maintenance of that flood defence system. Second, it is possible that villas, reclamation, and the intensive settlement of coastal marshland are separate reflections of the general economic prosperity of a particular region during the later Roman period. In order to explore the latter possibility, the economic geography of Roman Britain must be explored.

6.3.1 **Regional economies** (Figure 43)

Roman Britain certainly displayed considerable regional variations in wealth and acculturation, but simple core–periphery models of economic development are no longer sustainable since they perpetuate a very static, usually London or South East England-centric view. A good example is given by B. Jones and Mattingly (1990: map 5.9) in their attempt to plot 'boundaries of acculturation as shown by the distribution of towns, villas and findspots of Roman material' (Figure 43). This map shows the highest levels of acculturation in an area from The Wash, through the East Midlands, to West Sussex (curiously avoiding Chichester and the early villas of the Sussex coastal plain), with a

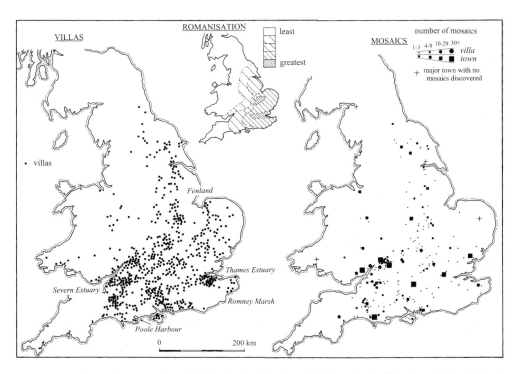

43. Measures of Romanization and wealth in Roman Britain: the distribution of all villas (from Millett 1990: fig. 48); a traditional model of acculturation (from Jones and Mattingly 1990: fig. 5.9); and distribution of later Roman mosaics (Millett 1990: fig. 76). The overall distribution of villas (from all periods) masks a marked shift away from the South East as seen in the wealth displayed in later Roman villas.

zone of lesser acculturation through middle England from the Humber through to the Severn Estuary. This may be a fair, if very generalized, reflection of the situation *c.* AD 100 (e.g. Dark and Day 1996: 66), but can the same be said of *c.* AD 300? The answer is clearly 'No', as the distribution of agricultural innovation, mosaics, villas, and urban prosperity show that South East Britain was eclipsed during the later Roman period by central southern England and the Cotswolds (Figure 43; B. Jones and Mattingly 1990: maps 6.39–41; M. Jones 1981; 1989; Millett 1990: figs 61, 68, 72, 76; J. Morris 1979; S. Rees 1979).

Reclamation represents a major agricultural innovation, and a considerable investment of resources, and, along with the associated expansion of settlement into coastal marshland, it may have been part of the more general phenomena of later Roman prosperity in the west of Britain. There are two possible scenarios for how this colonization may have been undertaken. Firstly, these marshland settlements may have had a mixed economy much like their dryland components of the estate: the reclaimed marshland was merely an extension of the dryland estate. Secondly, the marshland settlements may have originally been part of a seasonal pattern of transhumant grazing, and then become permanently occupied but specialized in their agricultural production, so forming part of a 'federative' estate.

6.3.2 **Unreclaimed marshes and seasonal settlements?**

The most obvious way in which coastal marshlands could be exploited as part of a seasonal agricultural regime is through transhumance, defined by H. Fox (1996*b*: 2–6) as 'the seasonal transfer of grazing animals to different pastures'. 'Lesser transhumance' involves the movement of stock and herdsmen over a relatively short distance in order to exploit local pastures that are only available for part of the year, in contrast to 'greater transhumance' which involves movement over longer distances, such as the several hundred miles that were covered in seasonal cycles around the Mediterranean (ibid.). There is plenty of evidence that during the medieval period upland areas of Britain and Europe were used as part of 'lesser transhumance' (e.g. Dyer 1996; H. Fox 1996*b*; Herring 1996), and place-name evidence such as 'Summerway' and 'Summerlease' indicate the seasonal movement of stock onto areas of coastal marshland such as the Gwent Levels (Rippon 1996*a*: 56).

However, during the Roman period we are not blessed with this documentary evidence, and must rely upon the archaeological record instead. One potential avenue is to look at the buildings, because in the medieval period there are a number of distinctive structures associated with seasonal use of landscapes such as shepherds' huts from upland areas (e.g. Dyer 1996; Herring 1996; Hooke 1997; A. Ward 1997) and fishing settlements in coastal locations (H. Fox 1996*b*; M. Gardiner 1998). Unfortunately, the scale of excavation on Romano-British marshland settlements is insufficient to say whether any distinctive building-types existed. On the continent, Waterbolk (1965–6) has suggested that the earliest marshland settlements may have been seasonal, though Van Gelder-Ottway (1988) rejects this in the specific case of Middelstum (north of Gröningen) on the basis of the animal bone assemblage. The extent of seasonal settlement on coastal marshes will probably remain one issue about which very little can be said.

6.3.3 **Marshland settlements as components of a multiple estate?**

Whether or not they were permanently occupied, marshland settlements may have been economically specialized, forming part of a larger estate which straddled several different ecological zones (Figure 18B). The concept of 'multiple estates' has received much attention from medieval landscape historians and archaeologists following the work of G. Jones (1979) on early medieval Wales. Jones observed the similarity between the formalized multi-tier estate structure described in thirteenth century Welsh law codes and certain territorial arrangements that survived well into the medieval period in various parts of Britain. He then argued that the Welsh estate structure reflected a pattern seen throughout southern Britain before the Anglo-Saxon Conquests, and by implication may well have roots in the Roman period or earlier. A key element of the Welsh estate structure was the seasonal use of pastures, which in an upland region was essential in order to conserve lowland grazing.

Jones's 'multiple estate' model has received some criticism (e.g. Gregson 1985; cf.

G. Jones 1985), and Bassett (1989: 20) dismisses it as 'unhistorical'. Blair (1991, 24) accepts that while 'it has long been recognized that "multiple" or 'federative' manors were a major element in the estate structure of pre-Conquest England ... we should not too readily adopt the multiple estate as a comprehensive model for British and early English land organization'. The phrase 'multiple estate' is certainly heavily laden with strict legal terminology, and the tiered hierarchy of territories need not interest us here. What is of interest is the simpler concept of an estate containing specialized settlements.

The phrase 'federative' (e.g. Blair 1991: 24; Lewis *et al.* 1997: 23; cf. G. Jones 1985: 354), is perhaps a better term to describe the idea that one estate could straddle a range of ecological zones offering a number of natural resources, with each environment being exploited by specialized settlements some of whose products were then redistributed within the estate. Indeed, 'one common response to the exploitation of environmental resources resulted in the type of "linked" territory which emerged in regions as far distant from each other as western Britain, the West Midlands and Kent' (Hooke 1989: 10). A. Ward (1997: 97) uses the phrase 'outstations' for the satellite settlements located to the seasonally exploited areas, suggesting that 'the use of outstations assists in managing the extra risk inherent in living in more marginal landscapes by diversifying the extra resources across contrasting environmental zones'.

These 'federative' estates certainly existed in the early medieval period (e.g. Everitt 1986: 65; Hooke 1988; 1989; 1994; 1997) and it has been argued that they had their origins in the Roman period or earlier. The continuity of estate structure from the Roman through to the medieval period has seen considerable discussion since Finberg (1955) postulated that the medieval parish of Withington, Gloucestershire may correlate with the territory of a Roman villa in that same parish. Other similar studies followed as continuity seemed to appear throughout the British landscape (e.g. Bonney 1979, cf. Goodier 1984; W. Davies 1979*a*, *b*; P. Fowler 1975; Leech 1982). In practice, it is likely that the survival of actual Romano-British estates into the medieval period will have shown much regional variation, depending upon the level of disruption that the Anglo-Saxon migrations brought (e.g. Williamson 1988). Whether or not the actual boundaries of Romano-British estates survived into the medieval period, however, the idea of a 'federative' estate with specialized settlements exploiting different ecological niches, well-attested in the medieval period, remains a logical model for marshland exploitation during *any* period.

One area for which this can be considered is the North Somerset Levels (Figure 44). Two marshland settlements, Banwell Moor and Kenn Moor, have seen excavations and both appear to have been cultivating wheat and barley, and keeping (or at least consuming) cattle and sheep. The lower-lying Banwell Moor, however, appears to have a more pastoral landscape with less evidence for intensive manuring of the fields (Rippon, forthcoming *a*). The lack of regional imports amongst the pottery assemblages at both sites, along with the scarcity of coins and items of personal adornment (despite an extensive wet sieving of midden material), indicate that both communities were of a very low status. The lack of fish bones, bird bones and marine shellfish, may also suggests that these communities did not have access to natural food resources. It is,

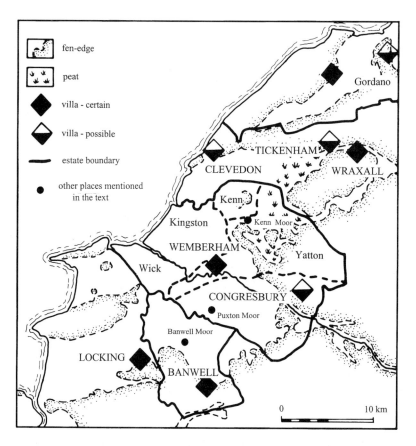

44. Possible villa-based federative estates around the North Somerset Level. (For location see Figure 42.)

therefore, tempting to postulate that these two communities were tenant farms of an estate based elsewhere, such as the villas at Wemberham (at the centre of the Levels), and along the fen-edge villas (including Banwell itself) (Rippon 1997a: 87–8). A range of evidence, including Saxon charters, allows the early medieval estates at Banwell and Congresbury to be reconstructed, both of which straddled dryland and wetland (Figure 44). Both have substantial Roman settlements adjacent to early medieval royal estate centres that were granted to the church, and the hillfort at Cadbury Congresbury was a high status centre during the intervening fifth and sixth centuries. This area must be a very strong contender for the continuity of estates and, even if the actual boundaries did not survive, the location of the fen-edge villas suggests that a 'federative' estate structure existed.

But how does Wemberham fit in, lying at the very centre of the Levels (as with Lakehouse Farm in Brentmarsh)? Like the settlements at Banwell Moor and Kenn Moor, it was established in the mid-third century, and the apparent lack of pre-villa occupation suggests that this was not one of several colonizing settlements, whose owner did particularly well and was able to invest in an impressive new home. The villa may simply represent the residence of an estate owner who used to live on the fen-edge, but after reclamation, possibly a collaborative venture by several villa-estate owners, relocated onto the marsh. Alternatively, reclamation may have been unrelated to the fen-edge settlements: it is possible that the open marshes were regarded as waste land, and that an entrepreneurial individual decided to embank and reclaim them, building a villa at the centre of their domain. We may never be able to distinguish between these models, though it is difficult to see how the reclamation could not have been in the context of some sort of villa estate.

6.4 The English Fenland: marshland colonization within an imperial estate?

A different type of land-holding may have existed in Fenland. The traditional view was that this area was an imperial estate: an area of unsettled land that was seized by the state, reclaimed for agriculture, and used to supply garrisons on the northern frontier with grain (Phillips 1970: vii; Richmond 1963: 128–30; Salway 1970: 9–19). The question of whether Fenland was an imperial estate is critical to our understanding of who was responsible for the marked intensification in how that landscape was used during the Roman period. The major arguments that have been put forward for Fenland being an imperial estate can be summarized as follows:

- as virgin land, Fenland would automatically be regarded as imperial property
- an inscription from Sawtry (close to the Cambridgeshire fen-edge) refers to 'public property', and along with the Car Dykes may represent the boundary of an estate
- large-scale land reclamation with drainage, artificial waterways, and roads are indicative of state involvement
- the main settlement expansion appears to have occurred during the Hadrianic period, and so may relate to that particular emperor's interest in land reclamation generally
- the character of the settlement pattern, comprising farmsteads as opposed to villas, suggests this was state owned land leased to tenants
- that salt production is likely to have been a state monopoly (see Chapter 5)

6.4.1 The right to new land

The principle that new land and the resources of wilderness areas belong to the state certainly existed in the Classical period (Purcell 1995: 185). Todd (1989: 14) suggests that any areas being brought under cultivation for the first time became *ager publicus* (land owned by the Roman state) though Salway (1970: 10) claims that virgin territory would have become the personal property of the emperor (*res privata*).

The Roman authorities certainly had a long history of reclamation in wilderness areas, reflected in the development of Rome itself and later large-scale drainage projects elsewhere in central Italy (Attema *et al.*, forthcoming; Purcell 1995: 184, 195). The state also actively encouraged the settlement of new lands, a policy pursued by Hadrian amongst others. He visited Britain in AD 122, and in addition to re-organizing the province's northern frontier, has been credited with a new wave of public building and the foundation of several new *civitates* (Salway 1981: 185–7; Wacher 1995: 378–407). Inscriptions show that in some parts of the Empire, such as Africa, Hadrian was also responsible for settling wastelands and extending cultivation into marginal lands (A. Birley 1997: 138; Frere 1987: 276), and it has been claimed that he may have done the same in Fenland (e.g. Salway 1981: 185–9).

6.4.2 **Car Dyke and the Sawtry inscription** (Figure 23)

Two strands of evidence may relate to the boundaries of an imperial estate. First, Mackreth (1996: 233–4) has argued that the enigmatic Car Dykes may be comparable to the *vallum* south of Hadrian's Wall, in acting as a boundary. Second, an inscription from Sawtry, Cambridgeshire, at the point where Ermine Street came closest to the fen-edge, reads *publicum* ('public property'). Inscriptions of this type usually represent the demarcation between areas of public and private land (Collingwood and Wright 1965: no. 230; Garrod 1940).

6.4.3 **Major works of engineering**

Ever since the hypothesis that Fenland was a vast imperial estate used to supply grain to the northern garrisons it has also been assumed that the Roman state must have undertaken 'extensive and systematic drainage' (Richmond 1963: 128). Hadrian certainly had an interest in water management, for example granting the city of Boeotia (in modern Greece) 65,000 *denarii* for a new drainage scheme on the town's surrounding floodplain (Reynolds *et al.* 1986: 140). However, the suggestion that large-scale land reclamation implies state involvement can be dismissed in the case of the English Fenland: there simply was no large-scale land reclamation since Fenland remained an intertidal marsh. Even the field systems and trackways appear to have grown organically and show no sign of any overall planning. Had this area been drained as part of a co-ordinated programme of work to improve the productivity of an imperial estate, we would expect evidence for regularity in land allotment and even centuriation (Millett 1990: 120–1; Salway 1970: 9–10).

There is just one major road that crosses Fenland (the Fen Causeway) but this need not indicate that the area was an imperial estate: there were roads all over Roman Britain built for the process of military conquest, subjugation, economic development, and the efficient conduct of administration and tax collection. In fact, the construction of the Fen Causeway may have had more to do with linking East Anglia with the rest of Roman Britain, rather than what was going on in Fenland itself.

The construction of the Fenland canals would have been a major undertaking, and if their function was indeed more to do with communication than drainage (as was also the case in The Netherlands and elsewhere within the Roman Empire: White 1984:

110–11, table 6), it is unlikely that an individual private landowner would have been responsible since a canal would do little to improve the productivity of their land. Elsewhere in the Empire, such major waterworks were the concern of both local communities and the imperial government. For example, Claudius invested the efforts of 30,000 men over some 11 years to bring 20,000 ha of wetland around Lake Fucine (east of Rome) into cultivation (Potter 1981: 12), while canals at Antioch (in Syria) were built during the reign of Vespasian with the encouragement of the governor (Reynolds *et al.* 1986: 140). A similar situation may have prevailed in Fenland. Though parts of the siltlands were extensively settled by the second century, the peatlands in particular must have been virtually impassable: Fenland represented a major barrier around which the road network of Roman Britain was forced to run. It would be expected that communities around Fenland would have wanted to make use of the river system for trade, and it is in this context that the canals may be seen. However, there is nothing inherently imperial in improving communications.

6.4.4 **The chronology of settlement**

The traditional view has been that while there was some Iron Age occupation on the southern islands (e.g. Potter 1981: 81), the major period of settlement expansion in Fenland was during the Hadrianic period (e.g. Potter 1981: 128; Salway 1981: 189). This model needs very careful examination. The Fenland Survey has confirmed that the southern islands were extensively settled during the Iron Age, and that there is no pre-Roman occupation in the Norfolk Marshland. However, it has also been established that there was some Iron Age activity in the South West Lincolnshire siltlands (Figure 58A; Hayes and Lane 1992: fig. 125). Many of these sites, which concentrated along the peat-silt interface, were associated with salt production and, for those which were not, 'It is tempting to think of the sparse scatters of Middle Iron Age pottery ... found on the levees of the creeks in the marsh as the isolated domestic debris of the herdsmen and shepherds who tended their stock on the grassy marshes during the summer' (Hayes and Lane 1992: 209). There is then a marked hiatus in the ceramic sequence recorded on the Lincolnshire Fens, until the appearance of Roman pottery during the late first century AD, despite there being a well-recognized range of Late Iron Age ceramics that survives in ploughsoil in the regions surrounding Fenland. It may be that Middle Iron Age styles simply continued in use as settlements on the silt fens were cut-off from the 'mainland' by encroaching freshwater peat fen (Hayes and Lane 1992; 233).

Another possible explanation for the apparent absence of latest Iron Age pottery in the South West Lincolnshire Fens, however, is that there was a genuine hiatus in occupation, perhaps equating with a brief marine transgression known to have affected coastal areas, depositing a layer of sediment known in Cambridgeshire as the Terrington Beds (D. Hall 1987: 8; Shennan 1986*b*: Wash VI deposits; Waller 1994*a*: 13–15, 75–9). Radiocarbon dates suggest a very late first millennium BC date for this flooding (Potter 1989: 153; Silvester 1988: 7; Waller 1994*a*: 78). Either way, the Iron Age activity is more suggestive of the seasonal exploitation of natural resources and is quite unlike the heavily modified landscape of the Roman period.

There is some evidence for late first century AD occupation on the southern islands, most notably at the major sites associated with the Fen Causeway, while certain locations in the South West Lincolnshire Fens may also contain some late first century material (Hayes and Lane 1992: 234–48). However, it does appear that the main colonization of the coastal marshes in Cambridgeshire, Lincolnshire, and Norfolk was indeed in the early second century (D. Hall 1996: 169; D. Hall and J. Coles 1994: 115; Hayes and Lane 1992; Potter 1989: 158; Silvester 1988; 1991: 109–10). For example, in the Norfolk siltlands, out of the sixty-eight dated Roman-British settlements just one may include first century material (Silvester 1988: 90).

6.4.5 **Stonea and possible Fenland estate centres** (Figure 45)

It was during the later Hadrianic period that the remarkable settlement on Stonea was laid out on a small bedrock island protruding through the Cambridgeshire peat fens (Jackson and Potter 1996: 678). The principal building was of unusual elegance with mosaics, painted wall-plaster, glazed windows, marble veneers and under floor heating: a building very much in the classical style (Figure 45). Its substantial foundations

45. Reconstruction of the possible imperial estate centre at Stonea in the Fenland. (Drawing by Stephen Crummy; reproduced from Jackson and Potter 1997; copyright: British Museum.)

suggest that it included a tower which, in the flat Fenland landscape, must have been visible for a considerable distance. The relatively affluent associated settlement, comprising thirty to forty buildings and a temple complex, was carefully laid out with plots alongside gravelled streets. The crop remains and animal bones suggest that the community living there was a consumer, not a producer, of food. The abundance of coins is in sharp contrast to the few other excavated Fenland settlements, and several pieces of military metalwork were recovered, which taken with all the other indications makes it difficult to conclude that Stonea was anything other than some form of estate centre. A second unusual stone building, which may have included a tower, has been discovered in the settlement at Langwood Farm West, on Chatteris Island, and could also fall into the 'estate centre' category (Crowson *et al.* 2000: 25–36).

Stonea was abandoned during the early third century, when the tower was demolished. At Langwood Farm there is a sharp decline after the mid-third century, while the other substantial Fenland settlement at Grandford was abandoned (D. Hall 1987: 43). It is possible that the functions of these possible estate centres may have been switched to one of the defended small towns that surrounded Fenland: Cambridge, Water Newton, Godmanchester, and Horncastle (Figure 23). The size of Water Newton, along with its very impressive public buildings and epigraphic evidence for some degree of self governance, sets it apart from the other small towns of Roman Britain. In particular, a large courtyard building has the appearance of either a mansio, proto-forum, or some sort of estate centre (Burnham and Wacher 1990: 81–91). Godmanchester was an extensive small town endowed with a range of public buildings including a bath house, mansio, temple, and a 'basilica-like building of official appearance' (Potter 1989: 172; Burnham and Wacher 1990: 125–7). The late third century walled area measured *c.* 350 m by *c.* 250 m, though in the early fourth century a smaller area *c.* 250 m by *c.* 150 m was defended, which included the public buildings. Unfortunately, little is known about Horncastle, though a small trapezoidal walled enclosure (*c.* 100 m by *c.* 180 m) appears to date to the late third or fourth century (Burnham and Wacher 1990: 245). There is a marked absence of material from within the defended area despite an extensive settlement lying to the south. A function concerned with the collection of taxation might account for the construction of this stronghold.

6.4.6 The character of the settlement pattern

It is not just the sudden expansion of settlement into Fenland during the early second century that is unusual, but the character of the resulting settlement pattern, as Romano-British Fenland was noticeably lacking in villas or other substantial buildings.

There are a small handful of fairly substantial buildings on the Fenland marshes, though they are few and far between. Near Whaplode Drove church, in the southern Lincolnshire siltlands, a substantial settlement has come to light through chance finds, including an altar, and a 'fair proportion' of brick and tile suggesting 'a building of some pretensions for the Fens' (Phillips 1970: 302). Another unusually substantial settlement lies nearby at Gedney Hill (Phillips 1970: 302–3). In the central Lincolnshire siltlands, around Gosberton, Quadring, and Dunsby, a number of surface scatters have yielded some building stone and ceramic roof tile, along with relatively high status pottery assemblages, though there is little to suggest anything other than a slightly above-average status rural settlement (Hayes and Lane 1992: 54, 90). However, it remains true that there are no known villas, and considering the long history of interest shown in the area by professional and amateur archaeologists, especially the amount of air photography and fieldwalking in an area of intensive arable farming, it seems clear that Fenland never supported villas. But need this suggest that Fenland was an imperial estate? Not necessarily. There is another explanation for the absence of villas from Fenland. It is clear that there were no sea walls and that tidal waters flowed in the creeks and canals. The higher roddons must have been sufficiently flood-free to make permanent settlement, and even agriculture, possible but the absence of proper flood defences must have made all areas vulnerable to occasional marine inundation. It may have been this physical insecurity that discouraged the construction of villas.

6.4.7 Discussion: an imperial estate in Fenland?

Fenland is certainly not alone in seeing a significant alteration in the way that the landscape was exploited soon after Roman conquest. In the Libyan Valleys of northern Africa there was a major change in the nature and scale of the area's exploitation, involving increased sedentism and a massive rise in population. However, there is no evidence to suggest that this was the result of Roman colonists being brought in from outside the area (G. Barker 1996: 319–21). Rather, Barker argues that there was enthusiastic support for participation in the Roman system of government on the part of the native population: 'Roman intervention in the structures of everyday life is nowhere more evident than in the resurveying and reallocation of the lands of submitted and conquered people. There is no doubting the extraordinary power that this aspect of conquest gave to Rome, nor should we underestimate the subtlety with which it could be exercised' (G. Barker 1996: 312). Examples of such intervention could include the promotion of private landholding as opposed to communal exploitation of the landscape, while the introduction of new social economic structures, notably a market economy, could encourage increased production.

Two broad interpretations of the Fenland landscape can, therefore, be proposed. The first is that the colonization of Fenland was simply the response of native communities to the changing social and economic circumstances brought about through Britain's assimilation into the Roman world, notably increased market exchange. Environmental factors could explain the lack of villas, or it may have been that Fenland fell within a series of private estates based on the surrounding dryland areas.

However, the more traditional model is that this region was imperial land leased out to tenants, and this still has much to commend it. The fact that in terms of agricultural production Fenland was the largest area of 'new land' in Britain, and that the expansion of settlement does broadly correspond to the construction of the Stonea complex during the Hadrianic period, might lend some support to the idea that the imperial authorities actively encouraged the area's colonization. But, the total lack of evidence for planning in the landscape, such as regular land allotment, suggests that at ground level, the settlement of the Fenland landscape was a piecemeal undertaking by native communities: unsystematic modification of the landscape, as opposed to systematic transformation. It appears more likely that farmers were attracted to the area by low rents or other incentives, rather than through a systematic policy of planned colonization, but either way, the view put forward by Richmond (1963: 130) that native peasant farmers were 'left to work the land in their ancestral fashion' appears as good an explanation as any.

6.5 Impact of the Roman army on coastal wetlands

6.5.1 Coastal wetlands and the military establishment in Roman Britain

So far, explanations for spatial and chronological variations in the use of coastal marshland have been sought in terms of two possible factors: regional differences in the patterns of agricultural wealth/innovation, and the possibility of coastal marshes in Fenland being developed in the context of an imperial estate. There is another potential factor that may have applied to certain regions: the impact of the military garrisons.

It has been shown how, in Britain, the presence of a substantial military establishment in and around South East Wales probably led to the intensive use of the Gwent Levels, including the embankment and systematic drainage of Wentlooge. This may have fallen within the military *prata* of the nearby fortress at Caerleon (D. Mason 1988), though the Second Legion may have had a significant role in the exploitation of mineral resources throughout South West Britain in general (see Chapter 5). Demand from the procurator's office also appears to have significantly affected the distribution of BB1 pottery, and potentially salt, from Poole Harbour in southern Dorset.

A contrast here can be drawn between the Severn Estuary and Romney Marsh in South West Kent. Despite lying adjacent to the iron works in the Weald and one of the Late Roman forts of the 'Saxon Shore' (Stutfall Castle: Cunliffe 1980), Romney Marsh does not appear to have been reclaimed in the Roman period, and indeed, salt production appears to have disappeared by the end of the second century. The implication is that the military community in South West Kent was supplied from outside the region, and that little interest was taken in improving the agricultural productivity of its immediate hinterland. Indeed, other Late Roman coastal fortresses in southern and eastern Britain lay in areas whose salt industry had disappeared by the time they were constructed, including Porchester by Chichester Harbour, Bradwell in Essex, and Burgh in Norfolk. It would appear that the authorities based in the late Roman 'Shore Forts' were not as interested in exploiting and improving the immediate hinterland of their bases as appears to have been the case earlier in the Roman occupation of Britain.

6.5.2 **The Roman *Limes* in North West Europe**

The impact of military garrisons can also be examined in The Netherlands. The coastal marshlands of mainland North West Europe straddle the Roman frontier and so it is inherently likely that demand for agricultural produce on the part of the army may have affected how that region was exploited. For example, during the first century AD four or more legions and auxiliary troops, some 30,000–40,000 men, were stationed in *Germania Inferior* (Bloemers 1988; 1989: 183), which may have impacted upon native communities in a number of ways (Kooistra 1996: 56–7).

First, native communities may have been relatively unaffected, as local production was not suited to the army's needs and so food was brought in from outside the immediate hinterland of the frontier. Certainly, native ideology amongst communities in the southern Netherlands was never transformed to the same degree as in northern Gaul, with comparatively little stratification evident in the settlement hierarchy and a strong emphasis remaining on cattle raising. Pastoralism was certainly 'an excellent strategy for making extensive parts of the landscape productive which were unsuitable for arable land' (Roymans 1996: 51, 79), and not only was the area unable to supply sufficient grain to meet the needs of the military and urban centres, but environmental conditions meant that it could not provide enough of the desired type of cereal—wheat—either.

The second way that the *Limes* may have impacted upon native communities was for the local agrarian system to have adapted itself in order to produce a small surplus with which to supply the new markets, whilst retaining their essential self-sufficiency. However, this could eventually have led to communities specializing in production for the market, making them no longer self sufficient. Groenman-van Waateringe (1983) supports the latter, arguing that the Roman occupation may have disrupted native economies by causing a move from small-scale mixed economies to large-scale specialized monocultures, and trading systems transformed into taxation networks.

There are signs of an intensification of arable farming in certain parts of the coastal marshes, such as the appearance of new crop species (e.g. rye and oats), substantial granaries, and large-scale field systems (Kooistra 1996, 64, 125; Roymans 1996: 76). For example, at Rijswijk, the number of farmsteads did not increase during second and third century, but the replacement of small four-post storage structures with granaries over 20 m long may reflect surplus production to supply the army, as the granary capacity suggests three to five times more could have been produced than was needed for subsistence (Bloemers 1979; 1989: 188–9). At the same time the area around the settlement was systematically divided into fields.

In the coastal wetlands of the western Netherlands there are also suggestions of direct military involvement. The correlation between 'duikers', with hinged flap-valves, and military establishments (Vlaardingen, Schiedam, and Valkenburg, with a fourth possible example from Midden-Delfland) has been discussed in Chapter 4 where it was suggested that this system of water management was a native tradition which may then have been adopted by the Roman military authorities, perhaps to increase agricultural productivity. An unusually substantial building at Midden-Delfland may also have

46. Roman military metalwork from Schiedam-Polderweg, Midden Delfland, western Netherlands (photos: copyright Heleen van Londen). Top: shield boss; bottom: spearhead; right: ballista bolt.

military associations. It was constructed of large timbers of uniform width, suggesting access to mature woodland—a rare commodity in the coastal zone (Figure 34). The timber was ash, not alder, making it even more unusual (Van Londen and Van Rijn 1999: 137). Nearby, a dump of refuse in a creek contained a large amount of military material including a distinctively military brooch, the metal butt from a dagger handle, a shield boss, balista bolt, and compass (Figure 46). A bone metapodial was sharpened to form a stylus and inscribed with *militis*: 'belonging to a soldier'. It is tempting, therefore, to see this as a military site associated with the exploitation of marshes in the hinterland of the Roman frontier.

It can be argued, therefore, that the military and urban populations that emerged during the Roman occupation of the southern Netherlands may have been partly supplied with food through an intensification of agriculture within that region. However, to a considerable extent this local production was supplemented with supplies from outside, notably the fertile loess regions to the south where a villa-estate system of agriculture had emerged and, to a lesser extent, the central rivers region that also saw the emergence of some villas and Roman-style farms (Groenman-van Waateringe 1989: 99–100; Kooistra 1996; Roymans 1996). Overall, the economic impact of the *Limes* and other centres of consumption in the central Netherlands appears to have been muted and this, in part, may explain the lack of reclamation on the coastal wetlands in this region.

6.6 Discussion: the intensification of marshland exploitation during the Roman period

Coastal marshlands are physically disadvantaged when it comes to settled agriculture due to their salty soils and regular flooding: they can be regarded as physically marginal. However, they are also rich in natural resources, such as the opportunity for salt production and seasonal grazing and, once drained, provided fertile and highly productive soils. The result is that coastal wetlands are attractive to human communities in a number of ways which, in the past, led to several different utilization strategies: exploitation, modification, and transformation.

This chapter considered marked regional variations evident in the extent of modification and transformation, and the resulting agricultural uses to which coastal wetlands were put. Saltmarshes represent a relatively uniform type of environment yet in certain areas they were embanked and systematically drained, whereas elsewhere they were left as tidal marshes and used for salt production and grazing. Spatial variations in the way that this one type of environment was exploited were not determined solely by nature, but were the result of human decision-making processes dependent upon that community's perception of the relative value of different resource utilization strategies. It is argued that spatial and chronological differences in the agricultural use of coastal marshland can be explained in terms of several possible factors: estate structure, the possibility of extensive coastal marshes being seized as imperial land and, finally, the impact of centres of consumption, notably military establishments.

The probable involvement of the state and military authorities in the physical transformation of certain coastal wetlands is not unexpected since reclamation represents a major investment of resources, both in terms of initial capital costs and the subsequent maintenance of flood defences. The Wentlooge Level in South East Wales appears to have been embanked by the military authorities based at Caerleon in the second century, and a distinctively planned system of drains was created. There are hints that the military authorities may also have been closely involved in procuring resources from other areas, such as Midden-Delfland in the western Netherlands, though Wentlooge appears to be unique in North West Europe in the extent to which the natural marshland landscape was systematically transformed.

By contrast, there is no evidence for military involvement in the reclamation which occurred during the third century on the English side of the Severn probably in the context of villa-based estates. Even around the Severn Estuary not all the coastal marshes were reclaimed, however, as the Central Somerset Levels were a divided landscape, reclaimed in the north and left as a tidal saltmarsh in the south. As has been shown elsewhere (Rippon 1997a: 65–77, 117–10) it would not have been a major feat of engineering to embank the latter (especially compared with areas such as the Gwent Levels) and so it seems that a conscious decision was taken to reserve this area for salt production. It may not be a coincidence that the Brue Valley lay next to the port of Crandon Bridge which appears to have been involved with supplying the military establishment in South East Wales (Figure 41; Allen and Fulford 1996).

The question remains of why no other coastal wetland was fully reclaimed. Romney Marsh may have been left as a saltmarsh because it was so remote: its immediate hinterland, the Weald of Kent and Sussex, appears to have been one of the most sparsely populated parts of South East Britain. However, the opposite applied to Essex, Kent, and the Fenland all of which had hinterlands with a relatively high settlement density, and a number of towns which would have consumed surplus agricultural produce. The obvious conclusion is that during the Early Roman period, there was not sufficient pressure on land to justify wetland reclamation in all areas. It was only in the south-west of Britain that conditions justified the investment of resources in reclamation, and this economic vibrancy is also reflected in the level of investment in villa building. In essence, for the Roman period, each individual area of coastal marshland needs to be understood primarily in its local context: at a time of stable or even falling relative sea level and a favourable climate, it was the differential impact of socio-economic changes brought about by the integration of North West Europe into the Roman world that may have been most critical in determining how these landscapes were utilized.

CHAPTER 7

Inundation and migration:

the late to post-Roman desertion of coastal wetlands

7.1 Introduction

During the Late to post-Roman period two major events affected the coastal wetlands of North West Europe. First, most if not all marshland settlements were deserted, and second, large areas of formerly settled land were flooded, resulting in their burial under a layer of sterile alluvium. This chapter summarizes the evidence for this marine transgression and the date when settlements were abandoned, and then explores the relationship between those two events.

7.2 Britain

There are hints that marshland settlements around the Severn Estuary may have been abandoned before the end of Roman rule as pottery and coin assemblages at certain sites lack distinctively late fourth century types (Locock 1997a; Rippon, forthcoming a). The evidence for a widespread marine transgression around the Severn Estuary during the Late to Post-Roman period is now considerable (summarized in Rippon 1997a; and see C. Hollinrake and N. Hollinrake 1997; Locock 1997a; Locock and Walker 1998; Rippon, forthcoming a; A. Young 1998). In both the Central and North Somerset Levels, flood waters appear to have extended up to 10 km inland, burying both the reclaimed and unreclaimed Roman landscapes under up to c. 0.7 m of alluvium. Recent palaeoenvironmental work has established that this marine transgression resulted in the establishment of brackish conditions over what had been a freshwater landscape (Figures 47 and 48). Further up the Severn Estuary, the Avonmouth and Caldicot Levels were also affected by flooding, though the extent of inundation on Wentlooge is less clear (Allen 1996b; cf. Rippon 1996a: 35; 1999: 109).

In Romney Marsh several Romano-British horizons have been observed stratified beneath c. 0.7 m of later alluvium (Bradshaw 1970: 169; R. Green 1968: 18; Woodcock 1988: 184). All known sites date to the first and second centuries with almost no evidence for third or fourth century activity. Recent palaeoenvironmental work has

47. Sequence of buried landsurfaces on Banwell Moor, North Somerset (NGR: ST 389 616). The lower buried ground surface (at a depth of *c*.1 m) dates to the Late Iron Age (early first century AD), while the clearer, upper, buried soil (at a depth of *c*.0.5 m) dates to the third century AD. The latter was associated with a ditched enclosure system that was blanketed by sterile alluvium deposited during the Late/post-Roman period. (See Figure 48.)

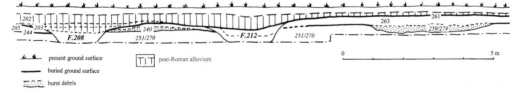

48. The 1st millennium AD sequence at Banwell, North Somerset Levels. The lower buried ground surface was associated with a Late Iron Age saltern (stippled Layers 240, 259/279), which was sealed beneath estuarine alluvium (Layer 263). Reclamation led to the formation of a soil during the later 3rd century ad (Layer 261), which was associated with two drainage ditches (F.208 and F.212). This landscape was in turn sealed beneath *c*.0.5 m of later estuarine alluvium (hatched). (See S. Rippon, forthcoming *a*.)

confirmed that around *c*. AD 300 there was a widespread episode of marine flooding (Long *et al*. 1998).

On the North Kent Marshes the Roman ground surface lies under 0.9–1.2 m of later alluvium and, although both settlement and salt production appear to have declined towards the end of the second century, the pottery industry continued into the third (J. H. Evans 1951*a*: 1953, 120–3; Haverfield *et al*. 1932: 132; I. Hume 1954; I. Hume and A. Hume 1951; A. Miles 1975).

In Essex most salt production sites were abandoned by the end of the second century, although a number of substantial settlements on the Thameside marshes appear to have been occupied into the fourth century. There was subsequently a period of flooding, such as at Tilbury where the Romano-British horizon lies *c.* 2 m below the present ground surface (Spurrell 1885; 1889–90: 216). On Canvey Island there is 1.2–1.5 m of post-Roman alluvium (Linder 1939: figs 1 and 6; Reader 1908: 165; W. Rodwell 1966) and elsewhere around the Essex coast red hills are similarly buried by up to 1.5 m of later sediment certainly deposited under saltmarsh/mudflat conditions (de Brisay 1979; Wilkinson and Murphy 1995: fig. 114). In some of the Essex estuaries, however, this marine transgression appears to have resulted in freshwater flooding as riverine discharges were disrupted. For example, around the inner Crouch Estuary a series of red hills may be associated with an oxidized, 'blocky', ripening horizon within the alluvial sequence. This land surface is succeeded by *c.* 0.25 m of freshwater clay sealed by a peat dated to between the fifth and seventh centuries AD[23] which, in turn, is buried by estuarine or marine clay (Wilkinson and P. Murphy 1995: 40, 181–3, 198, 201, fig. 38). This gives a *terminus ante quem* of sometime before the fifth century for the flooding that affected that Roman landscape.

Fenland saw an initial period of settlement contraction in the third century due to flooding, followed by a partial recovery (see Chapter 4). The occupation of most areas appears to have continued well into the fourth century, though the Romano-British landscape in coastal areas was subsequently buried by estuarine alluvium (Hayes and Lane 1992: 29, 54, 113–4: 237; Lane 1993a: 5; Leah 1992: 53; Silvester 1988: 154, fig. 110). The position of the Roman coastline is not known, though if it was similar to that in the tenth century (when the medieval sea wall was built: see Chapter 8) then the Late to post-Roman flooding reached 5–6 km inland (Silvester 1988: fig. 110). In the Lincolnshire Fens, two radiocarbon dates from the top of a thin peat at Swineshead, near Boston in Lincolnshire, suggest that marine conditions returned by the late fourth or fifth century AD[24] in an area where the ceramic evidence suggests occupation ceased at precisely the same time (Lane 1993a: 88; Lane and Hayes 1993, Silvester 1988; Waller 1994a: 79, 288–95).

Though no proper stratigraphical recording has been carried out on Romano-British horizons in the Lincolnshire coastal marshes, pottery has been recovered from buried land surfaces up to 1.8–2.4 m deep (Eagles 1979: 363; Owen 1984: 46). Elsewhere the depth is so great that the material may have fallen into palaeochannels.[25] In places occupation of the marshes appears to have ceased in the third century (Swinnerton 1932: 252), though elsewhere it continued until at least the mid-fourth century (Eagles 1979: 363, 364, 373, 379, 381, 388, 395, 396).

Late to post-Roman marine transgressions also appear to have affected a number of coastal locations around the Humber, such as South Ferriby in the Ancholme Valley,

---

[23] Bottom: 1610±70 BP (HAR-5225, 380–540 cal AD); top: 1380±80 BP (HAR 6589, 604–681 cal AD).

[24] 1660±60 BP (Q-2556; 315–425 cal AD) and 1590±60 BP (Q-2558; 395–535 cal AD).

[25] Chapel St Leonards, east of Louth, 3.1 m; and Saltfleetby St. Peter, north of Skegness, 3.6 m deep (Eagles 1979: 362, 388). For analogous arguments relating to deeply buried material from the Somerset Levels see Hawkins (1973); Nash (1972/3); Rippon (1995c).

where a Romano-British settlement was occupied until the fourth century and then sealed by over 1 m of later estuarine alluvium (Eagles 1979: 149; Van de Noort and Ellis 1998: 97, 233; Whitwell 1988: 57). The Roman landscape at Faxfleet, abandoned *c.* AD 370, and various sites in the Hull Valley occupied into the late fourth century, are similarly overlain by *c.* 1 m of alluvium (Didsbury 1988; 1990; Eagles 1979: 437, 444; Sitch 1990; Evans and Steedman 2000: 197).

7.3 The Netherlands and northern Germany

During the early third century there was an expansion of settlement into the Belgian marshes, though this was abruptly reversed around AD 260 when the entire area was deserted (Thoen 1978: 235; 1981: 250). Settlements on the Assendelver Polder (North Holland) were abandoned by the later second century, possibly due to a deterioration of the drainage caused by peat shrinkage (Hallewas 1987: 35–6), though elsewhere in the western Netherlands settlement continued into the third century. However, water levels appear to have been rising from *c.* AD 200, evidenced at Katwijk (near Leiden) and Rijswijk (near Den Haag) by the raising of hearths in buildings, thin layers of clay washed into nearby ditches, and renewed peat growth in the surrounding landscape (Bloemers 1989: 192). Throughout the western Netherlands there are signs of a decline in settlement from *c.* AD 240, and most sites appear to have been abandoned by *c.* AD 260/270 (Figure 27; Henderikx 1986: 478; Vos and Van Heeringen 1997).

Palaeoenvironmental work in a number of areas has established a marine source for the flooding that subsequently affected this region, particularly the peat areas which had subsided during the Roman occupation (Vos and Van Heeringen 1997: 67–8). On Voorne and Putten (in Zeeland), a series of sites where the latest material culture dates to *c.* AD 260 were buried by flood silts which were, in turn, sealed by a peat yielding radiocarbon dates in the mid- to late third century AD[26] suggesting that there cannot have been a significant time lapse between settlement desertion and the onset of flooding (Brinkkemper 1962; Brinkkemper *et al.* 1995: 125; Bult and Hallewas 1990: 73; Henderikx 1986: 451). At Goes, on Zuid-Beveland, peat cuttings were inundated at around the late third and early fourth century[27] (Vos and Van Heeringen 1997: 67).

In the northern Netherlands many settlements were abandoned during the third century[28] though occupation on other, mostly coastal, sites continued into the fourth century.[29] Though a synchronous Late Roman marine transgression ('Dunkirk II') can now be dismissed, there certainly was flooding in certain areas, most notably the lower-lying backfens (Van Es 1965-66: 39; Roeleveld 1974: 112; cf. Streurman and Taayke 1989). At Paddepoel the settlements were sealed beneath *c.* 0.2 m of sterile clay which, in turn, was sealed by an organic rich horizon that has produced radiocarbon

---

[26] *Nieuwenhoorn IV*: 1695±30 BP, GrN-15227; *Simonshaven*: 1720±25 BP, GrN-12215; *Lodderland*: 1725±65 BP, GrN-1093; *Rockanje*: 1790±65 BP, GrN-14594.

[27] 1680±30 BP, GrN-20007, 262–429 cal AD.

[28] e.g. Leuwarden-Oldehove (Van Es and Miedema 1970/1: 117), Paddepoel, near Groningen (Van Es 1968).

[29] e.g. Driesumerterp, Hatsum, Hoogebeintum, and Wijnaldum-Tjitsma (Cappers 1993/4; Gerrets 1996: 42; 1999: 121).

49. Sequence of buried landsurfaces, at Rodenkirchen, on the banks of the Weser between Brake and Nordenham, northern Germany. The thick dark horizon half way down the section dates to the Roman Iron Age; the excavation is of a Late Bronze Age house.

dates in the third or fourth century AD.[30] Once again, there cannot have been a significant time lapse between the archaeologically attested abandonment of the settlements and their subsequent flooding (Streurman and Taayke 1989). Only on the higher coastal marshes was continued settlement possible until the early fourth century, and even here it was restricted to heightened *terp* mounds in an environment that was regularly flooded (Figure 64). For example, at Wijnaldum-Tjitsma (east of Leuwarden), lenses of sandy clay intercalated with the lateral sides of the *terp* and associated ditches indicate continued occasional flooding, though there is no lithostratigraphic evidence that its abandonment was due to a particular increase in inundation (Vos, 1999).

In North West Germany a similar pattern is seen with settlements on the coastal marshes being built on raised mounds from as early as the first century AD, though here they were occupied into the mid-fifth century before being abandoned (Behre 1990*c*; Ey 1990; Schmid 1990*a*; *b*). The Roman-period landscape was once again sealed by estuarine alluvium (Figure 49).

7.4 Discussion: the causes of landscape desertion

From the evidence described above it appears that, firstly, most settlements on the coastal wetlands of North West Europe appear to have been abandoned at some stage

[30] 1790±60 BP, GrN-15464; 1665±55 BP, GrN-6030; 1580±40 BP, GrN-15468.

between the third and fifth centuries AD and, secondly, that most of these areas were subsequently affected by marine transgressions which buried the Roman-period landscapes under sterile layers of alluvium. This was also a time of great socio-political instability—the onset of the migration period—and traditionally the desertion of coastal wetlands has been attributed to these two phenomena: barbarian raids and marine flooding (Bloemers 1988: 22; Van Es 1965–66; A. Lambert 1971: 47; Roeleveld 1974: 112; Schoute 1984: 169–70; Thoen 1981: 248). There are, however, a number of possible explanations including:

- the disappearance of archaeologically datable material culture rather than the actual desertion of settlements
- environmental deterioration, including marine transgression, due to rising relative sea level and/or breaches in natural and man-made barriers
- insecurity caused by barbarian raids
- epidemic disease
- economic decline linked with the collapse of the Roman frontier and the market-based economy
- Anglo-Saxon migrations from the Continent to Britain

7.4.1 Datable material culture and the desertion of coastal wetlands

One plausible explanation for the *apparent* abandonment of settlements in any region is that communities living there simply no longer used easily datable material culture. When coastal marshlands in Britain were abandoned before the end of the fourth century this explanation can be dismissed for there is a well-dated and continuous ceramic sequence up until this time. In these areas settlement desertion was a genuine phenomena.

On the continent the situation is less clear, as some coarse wares of the late third and fourth centuries are difficult to distinguish from earlier fabrics (Willems 1984: 143). However, distinctively Late Roman pottery and coins were still circulating during the fourth century yet they are absent in the coastal zone of Belgium and exceedingly rare in the western Netherlands; only a very light scatter of fourth and fifth century artefacts have been recovered from the coastal barrier (Figures 27 and 61; Besteman 1990: 98; Brinkkemper *et al.* 1995: 125; Bult and Hallewas 1990: 73; Vos and Van Heeringen 1997: 67–8; Woltering 1975: 28; 1979: fig. 23). The survival of a few archaic Roman place- and river-names also hints at some continued exploitation of this landscape, but while the area may not have been completely deserted, it was clearly used far less intensely than in the preceding centuries (Besteman 1990: fig. 4; Bult and Hallewas 1990: fig. 4; Henderikx 1986: 479; Vos and Van Heeringen 1997: 68).

On the *terpen* of the northern Netherlands and Germany datable material culture disappears during the fourth and fifth centuries respectively, though many sites were subsequently reoccupied. This is a period when datable material culture was still in use in those wider regions, and very occasionally material found its way onto the *terpen*, though in insufficient quantities to indicate significant activity. For example, at

Leuwarden-Oldehove Van Es and Miedema (1970–71: 117) claim that the site was abandoned during the third century and reoccupied from the eighth century, though a few sherds of fourth to seventh century pottery are dismissed as indicative of occupation 'from time to time but never continuous'.

Overall, therefore, the disappearance of datable material culture cannot explain the abandonment of coastal marshlands in North West Europe, starting at varying dates between the third and fifth centuries. We must now turn, therefore, to the possible causes of these episodes of landscape desertion: environmental deterioration, economic collapse, and folk migrations.

7.4.2 **Environmental deterioration: marine transgression and the desertion of coastal wetlands**

In recent years the simplistic concept of a synchronous 'Dunkirk II' transgression, which explains the desertion of coastal landscapes during the Late to Post-Roman period, has been rejected. For example, in Zeeland, Henderikx (1986: 479) argues that:

> The depopulation in the lower-delta region and elsewhere along the coast was further aggravated by severe flooding at the beginning of the Dunkirk-II transgression period, as has been assumed by many, does not appear very probable . . . in Zeeland and the coastal plain of Flanders severe flooding did cause profound changes in the landscape, but it remains uncertain whether this flooding already occurred in the middle of the third century, or at a later date; in any event, the flooding itself cannot be considered as having been a major cause of the depopulation of that region, although it may have contributed to the area remaining uninhabited for a long period of time.

Vos and Van Heeringen (1997: 34–6) also dismiss the Dunkirk II transgression in Zeeland, while for North Holland and the northern Netherlands Heidinga (1997: 16) states perceptively that 'The increasing wetness of the coastal area at this time is generally seen as the most important factor [in the area's desertion], but this explanation which assumes that people are a plaything of their circumstances, is no longer satisfactory. We will have to look at the socio-political developments within the society itself.'

However, this reaction against a Late to Post-Roman marine transgression may have gone rather too far. There were important environmental changes during this period which may have had a detrimental impact upon the capacity of coastal landscapes to support human communities. The problem with the traditional 'Dunkirk' transgression is that in the search for synchroneity, local variablity has been lost. As described in Chapter 2, marine transgression simply represents a period of increased marine influence and should be considered simply as a landscape event—an environmental change—which might be brought about by a wide variety of factors, only one of which is rising sea level. Three key issues need to be resolved:

- Was there a widespread episode of marine transgression (of whatever cause)?
- Was this a synchronous event?

- If so, what was its cause? (Only at this point should relative sea level be considered.)

In answer to the first of these questions, the evidence described above clearly shows that the vast majority of Roman period coastal landscapes around Britain, and some parts of the western Netherlands, do show stratigraphic and palaeoenvironmental evidence for marine flooding after a phase of occupation in the Roman period: these areas were subjected to transgression (for whatever reason). In a number of cases radiocarbon dates from deposits overlying these settlements suggest that the time lapse between *settlement abandonment* and the *onset of flooding* was so brief that there must also have been a causal link between the two events (e.g. Swineshead in Fenland, Paddelpoel, and on Voorne and Putten: see above).

The available dating evidence suggests that these transgressions occurred during the Late Roman/Early Post-Roman period, though in most cases the latest datable material culture from deserted landscapes can only give a *terminus post quem* for the flooding. In eastern Britain, the western Netherlands, and the backfens of the northern Netherlands, evidence points to an increase in flooding from the third century; coastal areas of the northern Netherlands were abandoned around the early fourth century, and in the Severn Estuary the transgression appears to have begun after the mid-fourth century. In Germany the coastal marshes remained occupied until the mid-fifth century. This was not, therefore, a synchronous event over the whole of North West Europe.

This leads to the third question of why there was increased tidal influence in these areas at slightly different times: was there an actual rise in sea level, or were there other, local, factors at work such as the breaching of coastal barriers? The Holocene movement in sea level appears to have included a series of short-term minor fluctuations set against a long term upward trend. The fluctuations appear to have been most marked during the early and mid-Holocene (Figure 12) and a series of broadly correlative peats, but with diachronous lower and upper surfaces, were created during periods of sea level stability and fall. In contrast, during the post-Roman period, the thick layers of alluvium suggest that the trend in relative sea level has been continuously upwards, and in Chapter 2, a wide range of evidence was brought together to show that around Britain and the North Sea during the past 2,000 years it appears to have risen *c.* 2 m. However, this rise need not have been at a uniform rate, and there may well have been fluctuations about this upward trend, but which were weaker than before and were not sufficient to allow peat to form.

So, was the abandonment of coastal landscapes in North West Europe due to an acceleration of sea level rise? Around the Severn Estuary the extent of reclamation means that it is potentially possible that cultural factors led to the flooding, most notably a failure to maintain sea defences. However, this, nor a sudden increase in storminess causing barriers to be breached, cannot wholly explain the Late or Post-Roman transgression seen all around the Estuary as the flooding also affected areas that were not embanked and did not have natural coastal barriers. For example, in the Central Somerset Levels Romano-British landscapes both to the north of the River *Siger*, protected by a natural barrier of sand dunes and artificial embankments, and to the south, where there were extensive intertidal saltmarshes and no barriers, were inundated and buried under later alluvium. Other British coastal wetlands such as Fenland and the Thames Estuary marshes show no evidence of ever having been protected by natural or man-made barriers, yet are also buried under later alluvium clearly dated to the few centuries immediately after the Roman period. There must have been an actual rise in relative sea level during the Late to post-Roman period and this was a major contributor to the widespread flooding seen in coastal areas.

What this does not explain, however, is why human communities decided to abandon these areas. During the Roman period a variety of measures were taken in coastal areas to adapt to the high water levels including the construction of embankments, digging of drainage ditches, and building settlements on raised mounds. In the Late to post-Roman period the decision was clearly taken that it was no longer worth investing resources in this way. Quite simply, marine transgression is not the whole story.

7.4.3 Epidemic disease

Coastal wetlands were unhealthy areas to live, and during the post-medieval period, when we have accurate records of death rates, mortality in marshland districts could be up to two or three times higher than on dryland areas (Dobson 1998a; b). This was notably due to the risk of malaria, though there was also a higher incidence of bubonic plague and smallpox. Climatic fluctuations may have made conditions worse, but although epidemic disease is known to have occurred in North West Europe during the Late to post-Roman period, there is no real evidence that the later third to fourth centuries were particularly severe (Todd 1977).

7.4.4 Socio-economic factors and the desertion of coastal wetlands: insecurity and barbarian raids

It is always important to see any particular landscape in its regional context, and in the case of the desertion of coastal wetlands during the Late to post Roman period this is particularly informative. For example, the alluvial sequence on the North Somerset Levels indicates that at the same time as the formerly reclaimed coastal marshes were abandoned and flooded, there was an increase in dryland tree pollen (Rippon, forthcoming a). In The Netherlands it was similarly not just the coastal marshes of Zeeland and Holland that saw a pronounced decline in occupation at this time. Pollen, dendrochronological, and place-name evidence all suggest that there was woodland regeneration on the coastal barrier of the western Netherlands in the third century just as marshland settlements were being abandoned (Bult and Hallewas 1990: 75; Jelgersma et al. 1970: 130–2). The Central Rivers area similarly saw a contraction of settlement around the mid-third century, with around 70 per cent of sites abandoned (Willems 1981: 76, fig. 23), while pollen evidence suggests a decrease in arable cultivation and an increase in woodland cover (Figure 50: Bloemers 1983: 185; de Jong 1970–71; Smit and Janssen 1983; Törnqvist 1990; Willems 1984: 143).

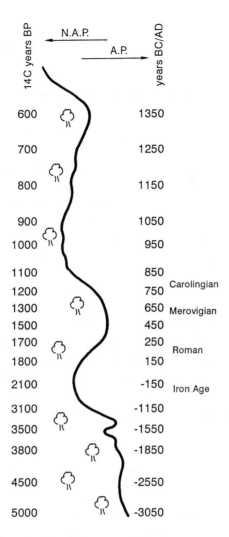

50. Simplified pollen diagram from the Central Rivers area of The Netherlands, showing forest clearance from the mid-2nd millennium BC into the Roman period, but then a marked regeneration. AP, arboreal (tree) pollen; NAP, non arboreal pollen (after Willems 1984: fig. 137). (Drawn by Sue Rouillard.)

In North West Germany, dryland areas were also abandoned during the fifth century at the same time as the adjacent coastal marshes were deserted. Pollen diagrams suggest that the intensity of landscape exploitation started to decline in the fourth century and woodland subsequently regenerated between the late fifth and seventh centuries (Behre 1990*b*: 22–3, fig. 5; Behre and Kucan 1990; O'Connell 1990; Zimmermann 1990). A marine transgression cannot account for this: there must be a cultural explanation.

In explaining this widespread hiatus in the occupation of several landscape zones there is a danger of replacing one simplistic monocausal explanation—marine transgression—with another—barbarian raids and migrations. For example, Henderikx (1986: 478) states simply that 'repeated raids by Germanic tribes in the area south of the

Rhine border, and the Roman abandonment of the *Limes* along the Neder [lower] Rhine . . . [caused a] large proportion of the provincial-Roman population to seek refuge in the south.' Barbarian raids are certainly well documented during the first millennium AD, and the mid-third century does appear to have been the start of a period of particular unrest. However, what effect would this have had on rural populations in the coastal zone? A number of settlements do appear to have been destroyed at this time, such as Aardenburg and Ouddorp in Zeeland, though there is no such evidence on the majority of abandoned settlements (Trimpe Burger 1973: 138). There are three possible explanations for the desertion of this majority of sites: first, that they were destroyed during raiding but that this has not left any archaeological traces; second, that they were not destroyed but that almost the entire population of this extensive region simultaneously decided to migrate south because of a general sense of insecurity; or third, that it was not the raids themselves that were the problem. The latter is the most plausible, suggesting that we must look elsewhere for an explanation of why these areas were abandoned.

7.4.5 Economic decline and the collapse of the Roman frontier

The desertion of coastal marshes may also have resulted from disruption to regional socio-economic systems caused, for example, by the collapse of the Roman frontier. The southern Netherlands lay on the edge of the Romanized world: this was a 'transitional zone', on the 'fringes of the Roman Empire, outside the urbanized core, but within the frontiers of the Imperium' (Groenman-van Waateringe 1983: 147). The stable Roman frontier in North West Europe, known as the *Limes*, was established in AD 47 after the campaigns in Germany were halted (Willems 1981: 25). A heavily garrisoned frontier was maintained up until AD 268 when the emperor Postumus died, after which a static 'frontier of exclusion' was replaced by a system which relied on 'defence in depth' (Willems 1981: 26–7). The abandonment of the frontier garrisons could have had a profound impact upon the region, if that area had become economically integrated with the Roman system.

Kooistra (1996) has examined the effect that alternating centralization and decentralization of power had on food production, of which the advent and collapse of the Roman frontier in The Netherlands provides a good example. It appears that during the Roman occupation, although there was some increased agricultural production, including surplus grain with which to supply the army and urban populations, the native communities did not specialize to the extent that they lost their self-sufficiency. As such, it is unlikely that the collapse of the Roman economic system would have caused so much disruption to these communities that they deserted their fields and settlements: they would simply have reverted to more subsistence-based forms of agriculture. What is more probable is that in *combination* with other factors, such as insecurity in the face of barbarian raids and the increased frequency of flooding, the economic changes brought about by the ending of the *Limes* made the coastal areas an increasingly unattractive area in which to live.

In Britain, the occurrence of pottery imported from outside the immediate hinterland of areas such as the Fenland and Somerset Levels, suggests that these areas were economically well-integrated with the rest of the province. The relationship between the exploitation of coastal marshlands and villa-based estates was considered in Chapter 6 and, although a clear link could not be established in all areas, the occurrence of villas at the centre of reclaimed wetlands in both the Central and North Somerset Levels suggests that reclamation may have occurred in order to produce surplus agricultural goods for sale at market. As a result, the decline and eventual collapse of that market system must have had an effect on how the utilization of coastal marshes was perceived by the communities living there. The returns would have diminished due to the disappearance of profits from market exchange, while if flooding was an increasing problem, productivity would also have been in decline. This decreasing return from wetland utilization must also be seen in the light of the relatively high cost, in terms of maintaining the drainage system, and high risk, in terms of flooding. As the Late to Post-Roman period appears to have been one of rising sea levels leading to transgressive events (see above), then these costs and risks would have been increasing just as the returns from agriculture were decreasing. The abandonment of coastal marshes was, therefore, not necessarily due to any one of these factors in isolation, but to the way in which a number of environmental, political, social, and economic factors interacted to change communities' perception of the cost, risk, and return equation.

7.4.6 Migrations and the desertion of the German coastal marshes

The coastal marshes of North West Germany were not finally abandoned until the late fifth century, around 100 years after the English Fenland and two centuries after the western Netherlands. The predominant explanation in Germany for this final act of desertion is migration, as is described so succinctly by Behre (1990*b*: 21): 'In the coastal region the occupation phase of the Roman and Migration period came to an end around AD 500, probably because the people left the area for England.' This is, in fact, not an explanation: it may (or may not) describe what happened, but certainly does not account for *why* it happened. For a settled community to uproot themselves and travel to a relatively unknown island a considerable distance away implies that there were either very strong reasons to leave their homeland ('push' factors), or very strong attractions that they were aware of in their destination ('pull' factors).

The traditional view is that the marsh-dwellers were encouraged to leave by the rising water levels (e.g. Van Es 1965–66: 58–66), yet, as described above, the evidence for this is disputed and cannot explain why the adjacent dryland areas were also abandoned. Indeed, if flooding was becoming more of a problem, colonization of the adjacent dryland areas would have been a far simpler solution than sailing all the way to Britain. Instead, it is likely that developments in both wetland and dryland areas were related and cannot be divorced from the wider social upheavals of the early medieval (or 'migration') period. Rather than a simple translocation of population from northern Germany to eastern Britain, the later fifth century appears to have seen a more complex reshuffling of the peoples in North West Europe, which also resulted in the recolonization of coastal marshes in the northern Netherlands. Though Boeles suggested as long ago as 1906 that there was Anglo-Saxon immigration into the northern Netherlands, this view was dismissed by later scholars. However, recent excavations have shown that, in keeping with many other settlements in the region, the *terp* of Wijnaldum-Tjitsum, west of Leuwarden, was deserted during the fourth century only to be reoccupied during the fifth century. The excavators argue that the distinctive material culture relating to this second phase of occupation suggests an origin for these peoples in the Schleswig-Holstein/Elbe-Wesser regions (North West Germany), and that changes in settlement layout seen here and on *terpen* such as Ezinge and Tritsum, also indicates a phase of Anglo-Saxon colonization (Gerrets 1996; 1999; Knol 1993: 244; Knol *et al.* 1995-96). Thus, it is argued, that the 'Frisians' whom Roman writers described as occupying this coastal region during the first and second centuries AD were not the same 'Frisians' documented during the sixth to eighth centuries. Overall, this complex pattern of abandonment, migration, and colonization should be seen as part of the complex socio-political milieu of fifth century northern Europe.

7.5 Conclusions

This chapter has examined a critical period in the history of the coastal wetlands in North West Europe: the near complete desertion of these once populous landscapes during the third to fifth centuries AD. The most widespread assumption is that abandonment of marshland settlements was the human response to a rise in relative sea level and the resulting marine transgression. Any such monocausal, geographically-deterministic, explanation needs to be treated with great care, though in many areas there does indeed appear to have been increased flooding which blanketed Roman period landscapes under sterile alluvium. Where good dating evidence exists there was very little time between the abandonment of settlements and the onset of sedimentation, suggesting that there was a causal link. While breaches in natural coastal barriers and man-made sea walls are possibly factors in certain areas (e.g. the North Somerset Levels), the fact that this flooding is also seen in areas that lacked such barriers (e.g. Fenland) indicates that the most likely cause of this flooding was an increase in the rate of relative sea level rise.

This raises the issue of why rising water levels were not countered through improvement to the flood defence systems such as the construction of embankments (as appears to have been the case around the Severn Estuary). It may have been that communities in certain areas were unaware of this technology, though it is more likely that other factors were at work making the occupation of these physically marginal environments increasingly unattractive.

The desertion of coastal wetlands must be seen in the context of the major socio-economic upheavals that North West Europe experienced at this time. During the later third century the western Netherlands saw barbarian raids and the collapse of the Roman *Limes*, though evidence for the physical destruction of settlements is extremely limited and the extent to which the coastal region had become economically dependent on the Roman frontier is questionable. However, if flooding was becoming an increasing problem, then the political insecurity and disruption to markets caused by these events could have made the continued occupation of environments that, although highly productive, were liable to flooding, an increasingly unappealing prospect. The same may well have been the case in Roman Britain, where the exploitation of coastal marshland was more closely tied in with the production of surplus agricultural goods for the market, particularly on villa-based estates. The economic decline seen in Britain from the later fourth century may well have made the exploitation of environments such as coastal wetlands, with their high costs and high risks, progressively unattractive.

The fifth century desertion of the North West German marshlands appears to have been due neither to increased flooding nor to the collapse of the Roman economic system. It must be seen in the context of the more widespread abandonment of the adjacent dryland areas, for which the most plausible context is the general migration of the Anglo-Saxon peoples westwards, into Frisia and eventually Britain. The causes of these major demographic upheavals are beyond the scope of this study, though suffice to say that as both wetland and dryland areas were abandoned at this time, factors specific to the coastal marshes are likely to have played only a small part. Overall, there are no simple monocausal explanations for the apparently straight-forward desertion of coastal marshland in the mid-first millennium AD: instead, these landscapes must be seen in their context during what was a dynamic and troubled period for the people of North West Europe (see Table 4).

Table 4. Summary of the major factors leading to the abandonment of coastal marshes during the Late to post-Roman period

Coastal marshes	Period	Factors leading to abandonment
Chichester Harbour, Romney Marsh, Thames Estuary	2nd/3rd century: cessation of salt production	Competition from alternative sources in western Britain? Effect of procuratorial/military patronage? Changes in the regional economies of Roman Britain as a whole?
Flanders and the Western Netherlands	Later 3rd century: sudden and pronounced desertion of coastal marshes	Marine transgression, insecurity caused by barbarian raids, and changing socio-economic circumstances caused by the collapse of the Roman frontier make settlement of this physically marginal environment no longer sustainable
Poole Harbour and the Brue Valley (Central Somerset)	Late 4th/early 5th century: decline of salt production	Collapse of Roman market economy
Severn Estuary, parts of the Thames-side Marshes, Fenland, the Lincolnshire coast, and around the Humber Estuary	Later 4th century: abandonment of marshland settlements and salt production	Marine transgression and economic decline at the end of the Roman period make settlement of this physically marginal environment no longer sustainable
Northern Netherlands/ Northern Germany	Later 5th century: abandonment of *terpen* settlements	Abandonment of marshes part of wider period of population migrations

CHAPTER 8

Pushing back the frontiers:

early medieval recolonization of coastal wetlands

8.1 Introduction

Following the tidal inundations that affected most coastal marshes around North West Europe starting in the third century AD, the early medieval period saw a gradual process of recolonization, representing a second occasion when human communities substantially modified and transformed these physically marginal environments. In Chapters 4 to 6 it was shown that during the Roman period these coastal marshes had been extensively settled, with modification and exploitation being the main approaches towards wetland utilization, and reclamation being restricted to the Severn Estuary. During the early medieval period, all three strategies towards the exploitation of these marshland landscapes—exploitation, modification, and transformation—were once again adopted, though now reclamation appears to have been the usual strategy. This chapter focuses on the early stages of this process—the initial recolonization of coastal wetlands in the last few centuries of the first millennium AD. The continued expansion, particularly into the low-lying backfens, is considered in Chapter 9.

Note on nomenclature: the term early medieval is used here for the period between the fifth and eleventh centuries, though the older British terms 'Early Saxon'(*c.* AD 400–650),

51. (*Opposite*) Models for the reclamation of coastal marshes: A–G from Rippon 1997*a*: fig. 4; and an alternative scenario for the earliest stages of saltmarsh colonisation (1–4): A, tidal saltmarsh, partly protected by a belt of sand dunes, with a freshwater reed swamp in the lowest-lying part of the backfen; B, construction of a continuous sea wall along the coast and the major tidal rivers, protecting most of the saltmarsh from tidal inundation. (See Figure 51: 1–4 for an alternative scenario); C, initial settlement of the newly reclaimed areas, based on small 'infield' enclosures and subsequent 'lobe-shaped' intakes from the relatively open landscape. Both open and enclosed fields. Settlements linked by tracks and droveways; D, further enclosure and drainage, leaving just the lowest-lying backfen as common pasture. The enclosed lands are protected from freshwater run-off by a fen-bank. Settlement expansion down the droveways. Enclosure of riverside marshes; E, further rudimentary enclosure in the backfen and recently formed saltmarshes seaward of the earliest embankments; F, drainage of the newly enclosed areas of backfen and saltmarsh. Piecemeal enclosure of some open fields. Coastal erosion forces the managed retreat of certain sea walls; G, systematic enclosure of the surviving backfen commons, roadside waste along the droveways, and the remaining open fields. Imposition of a railway on the landscape. 1, tidal saltmarsh, partly protected by a belt of sand dunes, with a freshwater reed swamp in the lowest-lying part of the backfen; 2, small areas of marsh enclosed and protected from summer floods by ring dikes; 3, further areas of marsh seasonally drained through extension of ditched enclosure system; 4, protection of entire marsh from tidal flooding through the construction of a continuous sea wall.

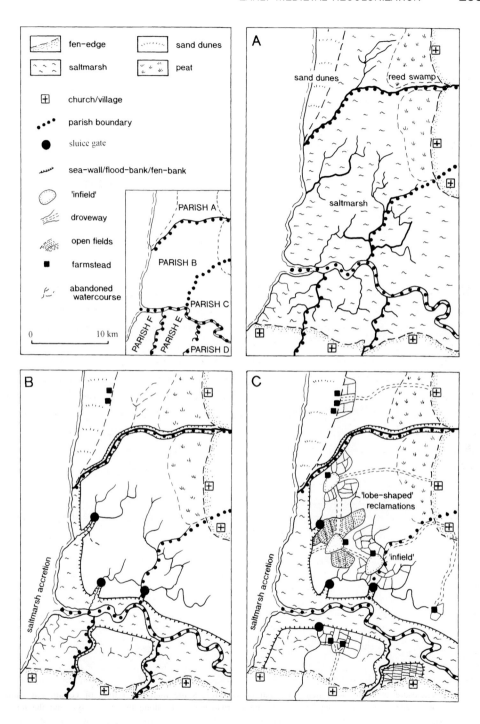

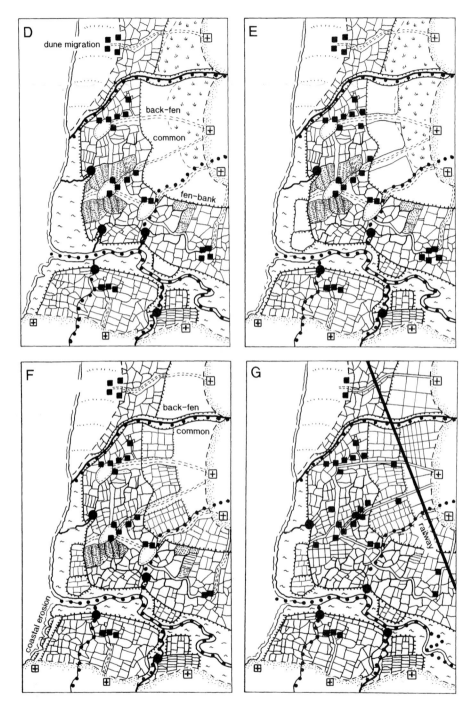

51. (*Continued*)

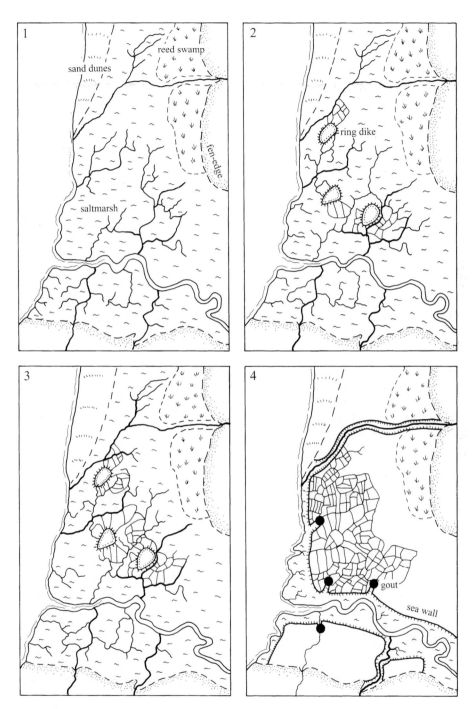

51. (*Continued*)

'Middle Saxon' (*c.* 650–850), and 'Late Saxon' (*c.* AD 850–1100) is retained in places where the dating of sites relies upon pottery classified using this system. Similarly, the terms 'Merovingian' (*c.* AD 525–725) and 'Carolingian' (*c.* AD 725–900) are used in reference to mainland Europe as appropriate.

8.2 The Severn Estuary

The early medieval recolonization of the Severn Estuary Levels has recently been reviewed elsewhere (Rippon 1994*a*; 1996*a*; 1997*a*) and what follows is simply a brief summary of that work, up-dated where appropriate. Domesday shows that the higher coastal marshes in Somerset were extensively settled by the late eleventh century, while the extent of cultivation suggests that reclamation had occurred. That a number of independent manors existed on the higher coastal ground implies that there were permanent, as opposed to seasonal, settlements by that time. When this landscape came into being is unclear. The description of estate boundaries in a number of tenth century charters suggest that reclamation was already underway, while a large number of settlement-indicative field- and place-names potentially of the same date suggest a dispersed settlement pattern, parts of which were later abandoned. Just one settlement has been excavated—Puxton—which was certainly occupied from at least the tenth century (Rippon 1997*c*: 1998).

On the Avonmouth Level, features described in the boundary clauses of several charters indicate that the northern area was embanked and possibly settled, though no settlements are recorded in Domesday as they were subsumed within the entry for the inland manor of Henbury which held most of the area (Rippon 1997*a*: 175). In contrast, recent excavations at Seabank Industrial Site (further south) indicate a landscape that had simply been modified through the digging of a ditched drainage system on a high saltmarsh (Insole 1996). Further up the Estuary, a scatter of tenth century or earlier pottery from Elmore in Gloucestershire suggests that at least some of the smaller areas of alluvium further up the Estuary were also settled (Allen 1997*b*: 72).

A detailed dissection of the historic landscape (the present pattern of fields, roads, settlements, and flood defences) has led to a hypothetical model for the process of medieval reclamation around the Severn Estuary (Figure 51). It was originally argued that the initial act would have been to build a sea wall along the coast and embank the major rivers (Figure 51B; Rippon 1997*a*: fig. 7). Settlements, perhaps initially seasonal but presumably very soon permanent, would subsequently have been established and, in a flat landscape with few other features, early intakes from the marsh would probably have assumed an oval shape (as is the case with pioneering assarts in woodland and moorland areas; Figure 51C). There is, however, another explanation for these oval-shaped 'infield' enclosures: they may represent 'summer dikes' on what was a high tidal marsh, but which were subsequently incorporated into the post-reclamation landscape (Figure 51: 1–4). This is currently under investigation on one such site, at Puxton, near Weston-super-Mare on the North Somerset Levels (Rippon 1996*c*; 1997*c*; 1998).

8.3 **Landscape exploitation: the Pevensey Levels**

In the Pevensey Levels it appears that neither landscape modification nor transformation had taken place prior to the twelfth century. In AD 772, Offa, King of Mercia, granted certain lands at Bexhill (including Barnhorne on the south-east margins of the Levels) to Bishop Oswald, and the bounds make reference to a saltmarsh extending as far into the Levels as Hooe Stream (Figure 65; S.108; F. Barker 1947: 92–3; Dulley 1966: 26). The second charter, dated AD 947, is more informative, and relates to a grant by King Eadred to one Edmund, of lands at Hankham on the northern side of the Pevensey peninsula. The bounds run through the northern part of the Willingdon Level which is described simply as 'marsh', before turning north across the peninsula and down into the marshes between Ersham and Horse Eye, where they joined a river called the 'Landfleot' (later re-named Pevensey Haven), by which there was a saltworks (Figure 65; S.527; F. Barker 1949; Dulley 1966: 26–8).

Further evidence for the unreclaimed state of the Pevensey Levels comes from Domesday, in which the presence of over a hundred saltworks, and the scarcity of meadow compared with areas such as the Ouse Valley to the west of Eastbourne, suggests that there had been little reclamation. The earthworks of medieval salterns, still survive in a number of places (e.g. Figure 52).

8.4 **Romney Marsh: a divided landscape**

Romney Marsh is fortunate in having a wide range of evidence relating to the early medieval period including a large collection of charters with boundary descriptions (Figure 54; G. Ward 1931; 1933a; c; d; 1940), and a series of late eleventh century surveys related to Domesday (the Exchequer version itself (Morgan 1983; J. Morris 1976), the *Excerpta* describing the lands of St Augustine's Abbey (E. Campbell 1962), and the Domesday *Monachorum* which lists estates of Christ Church Canterbury (Neilson 1932: and see Ballard 1920; Douglas 1944; J. Morgan 1983)). There have also been several fieldwalking surveys (M. Gardiner 1994; Reeves 1995a; b) and an extensive programme of palaeoenvironmental work (e.g. Long *et al.* 1998).

The historic landscape also contains a range of physical evidence into which the documentary detail can be fitted. A critical, yet poorly understood feature is an undocumented sea wall that ran from the fen-edge at Appledore to the shingle barrier at Romney, along what is now called Yoke Sewer (Figures 53, 56, 57, and 67C–D). This was first recognized by Green (1968) and was given further consideration by the author following a field visit with John Allen and other members of the Romney Marsh Research Trust. Allen (1996a) followed N. Brooks (1988) in subsequently, and possibly erroneously, naming the feature after the *Rumenesea*, a river mentioned in a charter of AD 920 (S.1288). This important landscape feature was in fact the original boundary between Romney Marsh proper and Walland Marsh, though since at least AD 1309 a second major artificial watercourse, the Rhee Wall, was taken as the boundary (see Chapter 9; Teichman Derville 1936: 7).

52. Medieval saltern mound north of Horse Eye on the Pevensey Levels (NGR: TQ 628 086). Early topographical writers describe how such mounds were used by sheep as refuges at times of flooding, and this is still the case.

53. Yoke Sewer, the boundary between Romney Marsh proper (left) and Walland Marsh (right). From south of Snargate church (NGR: TQ 992 287).

8.4.1 **The shingle barrier** (Figure 54)

Romney Marsh formed in the sheltered conditions behind a natural shingle barrier which is documented in the bounds of three Saxon charters as 'a wood called *ripp*' in mid-eighth century Lydd (S.24), *Ad Hlidum* in late eighth century Lydd (S.111), and *fealcing rip* near *Gamelanwyrthe* in mid-ninth century Burmarsh (S.510). *Hlidum* is derived from *hlid*, or hillside, while the term *Ripp* refers to the shingle beaches (Wallenberg 1931: 55–6; G. Ward 1931).

The shingle ridges south-west of Lydd are still called the Ripes, and have an extensive covering of holly trees. The Lydd charter of AD 774, which may have been doctored in the tenth century (N. Brooks 1988: 99) refers to three plough lands 'lying in the west part of the region which is called the Marsh, where it is named *Ad Hlidum* (S.111; Wallenberg 1931: 55–6; G. Ward 1931). The charter bounds state that to the east lay the sea, while to the south land called Denge Marsh extended as far as the 'stone at the end of that land'. The latter may be another reference to the shingle ridges as is the case with the current terms Littlestone, Great Stone, and Holmstone in the same area (N. Brooks 1988: 100).

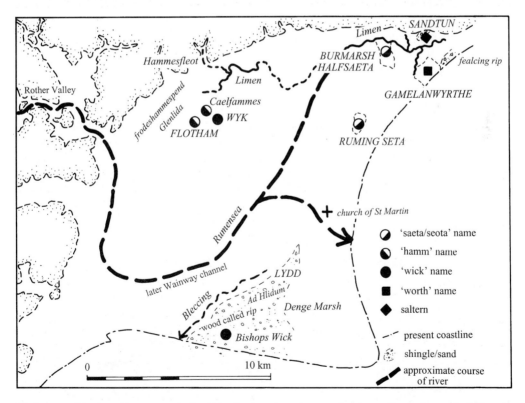

54. Romney Marsh: evidence contained within the boundary clauses of early medieval charters including the original line of the River *Limen* (the 'proto-Rother') via an estuary by 'Sandtun' (near Hythe), and its later diversion to a new estuary by the church of St Martin at Romney.

8.4.2 **The changing river system** (Figures 54 and 67)

The changing pattern of natural drainage on Romney Marsh was critical to the history of reclamation, yet there has been little agreement on how the major rivers that crossed the Marsh changed their courses (cf. Allen 1996a; Brooks 1988; C. Green 1988; Rendell 1962; C. Spencer 1996; Tatton-Brown 1988). A series of rivers enter the Marsh from the west which appear to have flowed into a major watercourse termed here the 'proto-Rother' (in order to avoid confusion with the bewildering number of names attributed to the same watercourse during the medieval period, including the *Limen*).

Several pre-Conquest charters refer to a River *Limen* , though they appear to relate to at least two watercourses, with estuaries at Hythe and Romney (Brooks 1988; R. Green 1968; C. Green 1988; C. Spencer 1996; C. Spencer *et al.* 1998a; b; Tatton-Brown 1988; Wass 1995). One of the rivers called *Limen* appears to have been a tidal creek that ran east to west across the northern part of Romney Marsh proper (S.21; S.23; S.39; S.270; S.1180; S.1193; S.1414), and can be identified on R. Green's (1968) soil map as a palaeochannel which discharged its water through a breach in the shingle barrier at 'Sandtun' near Hythe (Figure 54). This channel has been subject to palaeoenvironmental analysis indicating a 'sheltered arm of a tidal inlet which opened eastwards' (Wass 1995: 76), and does not appear to have taken the freshwater discharge from the Rother Valley. The existence of continuous peat in the northwestern part of Romney Marsh also discounts any major palaeochannel extending directly east from the Rother Valley (Green 1968: fig. 6; Long *et al.* 1998; C. Spencer *et al.* 1998).

The second river called *Limen* (termed here the 'proto-Rother') appears to have turned southwards as it flowed out of what is now known as the Rother Valley, crossing Walland Marsh, and then turning north-east up a substantial palaeochannel later known as the Wainway (Figures 54, 56, and 67). The Wainway in its present form is late medieval, though a recent programme of palaeoenvironmental work has confirmed the existence of a substantial predecessor, presumably the palaeochannel of the *Limen* (C. Spencer 1996; C. Spencer *et al.* 1998). In AD 741 (S.24) there is reference to fishermens' houses and the church of St Martin at the mouth of the *Limen* (in New Romney), though originally it appears to have discharged its water via the estuary south of 'Sandtun', near Hythe. This earliest line of the *Limen*/'proto-Rother' is reflected in an arm of relatively recent calcified alluvium which stretches through Newchurch towards Old Romney (Figure 55), and a number of abandoned embankments in the Newchurch area (Figure 56). The pattern of parish boundaries south of Newchurch also contains a large number of detached parochial parcels indicative of relatively late enclosure of formerly common land, which may also have occupied the line of the former river course (see below; Figure 57). As Newchurch, which lies on the line of this palaeochannel, was established as a hundredal centre around the tenth century, the old course of the 'proto-Rother' must have entirely silted up by that time.

Another river-name, the *Rumenesea*, is recorded in AD 920 (S.1288). N. Brooks (1988: 98) argues that the name was derived from Romanus, a priest known to have owned land south-west of Lydd sometime before AD 741, and possibly the same cleric recorded in

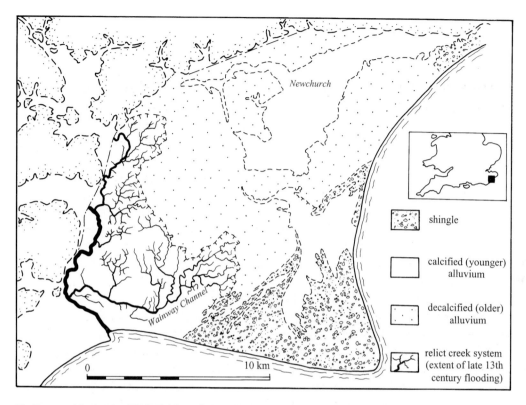

55. Romney Marsh: simplified division of the soils into older/decalcified and younger/calcified, along with the surviving shingle ridges and extent of late 13th century flooding (after Green 1968).

Kent by Bede in *c.* AD 660 (*Bede*: III.25). The route taken by the *Rumenesea* between the Rother Valley and the coast has been much debated. N. Brooks (1988: fig. 8.7) and Allen (1996*a*) favour a direct line along what is termed here the Yoke Sewer palaeochannel, but this is clearly not sufficient to have taken the discharge from the Rother Valley and the existence of continuous peat in the northwestern part of Romney Marsh precludes this direct line (Green 1968: fig. 6; C. Spencer *et al.* 1998). Thus, C. Green (1988), Tatton-Brown (1988), and G. Ward (1953) would appear to have been correct in arguing that the *Rumenesea* was simply another name for the river *Limen* (i.e. the 'proto-Rother' and its course via the Wainway). In the Rother Valley, what is now known as the Rother was called the *Limen* as late as the fourteenth century (AD 1317: *CPR* 1313–17: 695; AD 1321: *CPR* 1317–21: 609), and during the thirteenth and fourteenth centuries this same river appears to have had a third name, the 'river of Newenden' (*CPR* 1247–58: 635–6, 662; *CPR* 1313–17: 134; and see Eddison 1983*a*; 1985; 1995*b*; 1998).

8.4.3 Romney Marsh proper: a reclaimed landscape

Since the Roman landscape on Romney Marsh appears to have been abandoned by the third century and subsequently flooded, we must assume that in the Late Roman/early

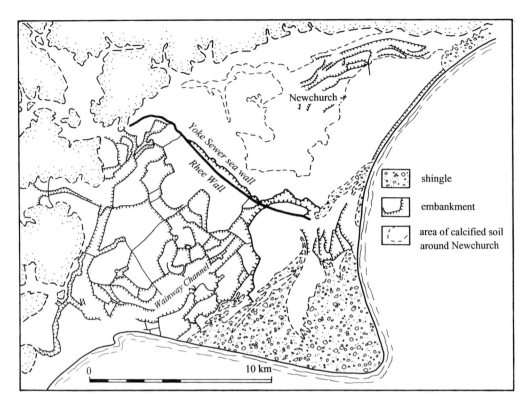

56. Romney Marsh: extant and relict sea walls and flood banks, including old course of the 'proto-Rother' via the Wainway channel and Newchurch (after Green 1968; Reeves 1995*b*; and air photographs in the National Monuments Record).

medieval period much, if not all, of **Romney Marsh** was a tidally inundated saltmarsh crossed by a series of creeks, rivers, and streams. The date when reclamation occurred is unclear. By the tenth century, Romney Marsh proper was divided into a large number of estates with well-established boundaries; the charter for *Rumening seta* even states that 'we do not set down the boundaries because they are well known to the country folk all around' (Jenkins 1859: 20; G. Ward 1936: 11). However, this well-parcelled landscape does not exclude the possibility that it was still a regularly inundated saltmarsh, since the tidal marshes along the Essex coast were divided into numerous well-defined blocks throughout the medieval period (Figure 69). There was also extensive arable farming, with references in charter bounds to ten corn fields in *Gamelanwyrthe* (AD 946: S.510), two ploughlands in Ruckinge either side of the *Limen* (805: S.39), and three ploughlands in Lydd 'on the marsh' (AD 774: S.111). In Domesday, an un-named parcel of land on the Marsh in Newchurch Hundred was 'assessed in Tinton [on the uplands to the north of Romney Marsh], because it is ploughed with the lordship ploughs from there' (Morgan 1983: 9.8). Although these areas of arable could also plausibly have lain on a very high tidal marsh, a landscape divided into small, well-defined estates, with cultivation extending to the very edges of those estates, points to reclamation having already been undertaken.

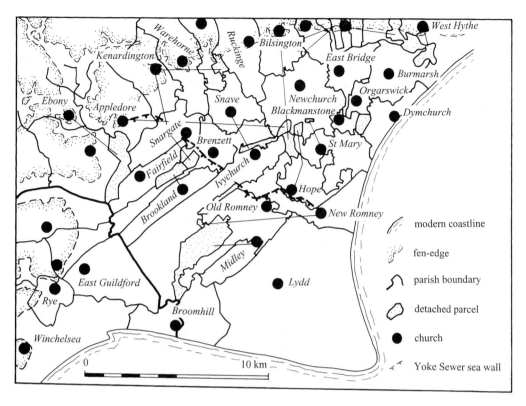

57. Romney Marsh: parish boundaries, including detached parcels (after Brooks 1988: fig. 8.2).

Domesday, the *Excerpta*, and the Domesday *Monachorum*, along with the fieldwalking that has been carried out around Newchurch and Old Romney (M. Gardiner 1994; Reeves 1995) show that by the eleventh century Romney Marsh proper was well populated, with a highly dispersed settlement pattern (Figure 67B). These pottery scatters indicate that these settlements conform to the pattern of existing roads, implying that the framework of the present landscape already existed by the tenth century.

The creation of an administrative system in Kent based on 'hundreds' also probably dates to the mid-tenth century (Jolliffe 1933). Three hundreds lay wholly on Romney Marsh (Aloesbridge, Langport, and Worth: Brooks 1988; 94), which itself suggests a substantial area of permanently-settled and flood free land with a large population. A fourth hundred, Newchurch, straddled both the Marsh and the adjacent dryland, though the choice of Newchurch itself as the hundredal centre is significant since it shows that the marshland was free from flooding and sufficiently populated to warrant the construction of a church. That it was called *New*church when the hundred was created in the mid-tenth century implies either an older church on the same site, or other churches in the area. By the eleventh century Romney Marsh proper was certainly well-endowed with churches, and of the medieval parish churches on Romney Marsh proper (north-east of the Yoke Sewer sea wall), only Burmarsh, Snargate, and Snave are not recorded.

There are two possible references to artificial watercourses in the northwestern part of Romney Marsh, though neither can be located with any certainty (Figure 54). A charter of AD 811 (S.168) refers to *Frodeshammespend*, possibly meaning an embanked river channel (Brooks 1988: 102). The name element 'pend' is found is later sources, such as the embanked River Chene north of Broomhill, which is referred to as *Chenespend* in the fifteenth century (Neilson 1928: 201–5). A charter of AD 845 (surviving in an eleventh century form) refers to land at Warehorne and *Flotham* (between Warehorne and Snargate: S.282). The western boundary of this estate was *Genlida*, which literally means a 'counter-channel' (N. Brooks 1988; 102) and implies some form of water management. The location of *Genlida* is unknown, though it must have lain very close to the line of the putative Yoke Sewer sea wall.

8.4.4 **Landuse and economy in Romney Marsh proper**

The references to arable cultivation have been mentioned above, and a number of charters also reflect the importance of pastoralism. Around AD 669/700, pasture for 300 sheep is recorded at *Rumening seta* (S.21), and there was pasture for 150 cattle near Bishops Wick on the marsh in Lydd in AD 741 (S.24). The Burmarsh charter of AD 1016/20 refers to 150 acres of land along with 30 oxen, 20 cows, and 10 horses (S.146).

Just one early medieval settlement on Romney Marsh has been excavated, located on a sand dune at *Sandtun* just north of the *Limen* Estuary near Hythe, and dating to the eighth and ninth centuries (Figure 54) (Clutton-Brock 1976: 376; G. Dunning *et al.* 1959: 21; Macpherson-Grant and Gardiner 1998). Pottery included imported wares from the continent, and the impression of a trading settlement is confirmed by recent finds of eighth and ninth century coins minted in England and Frankia (Cross 1997: 6).

The former estuary of the *Limen*, represented by the area of calcified soil to the south of Newchurch (Figures 54–5), may have been one of the last parts of Romney Marsh proper to be enclosed and drained. As Reeves (1995a: 88–9) has noted, this area falls at the junction of many parishes, while large areas were detached portions of other marshland and fen-edge parishes (Appledore, Bilsington, Brookland, Hope, St. Mary; Figure 57). This complex parochial organization may reflect the parcelling-up of an area of former common land, as seen in other former intercommoned pastures such as Canvey and Foulness Islands in Essex (Chapter 9, Figure 69), parts of the Somerset Levels (Rippon 1997a: 207–9), and the Norfolk Fens (Silvester 1988: figs 115 and 119).

Kent had a well-established tradition of detached territories providing specialist resources for distant estate centres, of which the Wealden swine pastures are the best known example (Campbell 1962: 527–32; Everitt 1986; 32–9). Coastal resources appear to have been treated in the same way. From at least the eighth century, parts of Romney Marsh were held as detached parts of distant estates, providing them with valuable summer pasture. St. Mary's monastery at Lyminge (absorbed into Christ Church Priory at Canterbury in AD 965: Jenkins 1859) held a series of marshland estates in Dymchurch, Lydd, Lympne, Orlestone (Ham), Romney, and Ruckinge (S.21; S.23; S.24; S.39; S.153; S.1180; S.1203). Another early monastery, St. Eanswith's in Folkestone, also held a number of estates near Burmarsh which are referred to in the bounds of *Burmarsh halfsaeta* (S.1193) and *Gamelanwyrthe* (S.510), while Brenzett Church is dedicated to St. Eanswith. St. Augustine's Abbey in Canterbury was another significant landowner on Romney Marsh with estates in Burmarsh, Snave, and *Sturton* (S.1651; S.1650; S.1656; Ballard 1920; S. Kelly 1995: 92–5; Morgan 1983: 7.29; Tatton-Brown 1989: 260). Canterbury Cathedral's eighth/ninth century acquisitions on the Marsh included Lydd (S.111), land near Snargate (S.168), *Lambahamm* south of the *Limen* (S.1414), and an estate adjacent to *Gamelanwyrthe* (S.510). From the eighth century, Ruckinge on the fen-edge belonged to Ickham near Canterbury (S.1180) and Denge Marsh was attached to Wye near Ashford (S.111: G. Ward 1931; cf. Everitt 1986: 58).

This pattern of detached landholdings was partly fossilized in the nineteenth century by the large numbers of distant parishes which had detached parts on the Marsh (Figure 57; N. Brooks 1988; fig. 8.2; Reeves 1995*a*: fig. 5.2). For example, in the nineteenth century, Sellindge parish (which lies to the north of Aldington and Lympne) held a detached portion west of Dymchurch, which has been identified as the pasture for 300 sheep called *Rumening seta* granted to the church at Lyminge in AD 697/700 (Figures 54 and 57; S.21; N. Brooks 1988: 93, 98; G. Ward 1936). *Seata* or *seota* is a common place-name in the pre-Conquest charters of Romney Marsh, and probably refers to lowland pasture equivalent of the Wealden 'dens' (Wallenberg 1931: 80–1; G. Ward 1936: 22).[31]

There area also a number of 'wicks' mentioned in the early charters, probably representing dairies. A charter of AD 858 refers two *Wiwarawics* on Romney Marsh: 'dairy farms of the men of Wye' (S.328; G. Ward 1940: 24). They produced 40 *statera* of cheese, 20 lambs, and 10 fat sheep each year. These wicks came to be part of the manor of Westwell (near Ashford in central Kent) which in the post-Conquest period still owned a number of detached holdings on Romney Marsh which can be identified near Hope All Saints and St. Mary's in the Marsh (G. Ward 1940: 26; 1953: 16). Other 'wicks' include 'Bishops Wick' in Lydd (S.24), *Wyk* (Snavewick?: S.1651), and *Hremping wiic* (unlocated: S153). Orgarswick is first recorded in *c.* AD 1100 (Wallenberg 1934: 463).

Romney Marsh proper, therefore, appears to have been reclaimed, extensively settled, and used for both arable cultivation and pasture by the tenth century. Many areas appear to have been held by distant manors, notably those belonging to the numerous Kentish monasteries. However, to the south-west of the Yoke Sewer sea wall lay Walland Marsh, which had a very different landscape.

8.4.5 Walland Marsh: a tidal saltmarsh

The south-east corner of Walland Marsh (south of the 'proto-Rother') appears to have been reclaimed by the eleventh century, as Domesday records three places there: Lydd,

[31] Other examples include *Hafingseota* (alias *Hremping wiic*) and *Bobingseata* south of the *Limen* (S.153), *Halfsaeta* in Burmarsh (S.1193), *Hiredes seota* (possibly Hamme in Orlestone; S.1203), and *Caping saeta* in Romney (S.1286). Brenzett (*Brenseta* in Domesday) has the same origin (Wallenberg 1931: 224), and the common local field-name 'seed' could be a modern derivation (Ward 1936: 22).

Midley, and Old Romney (Figure 67B). There may also have been some inning on Denge Marsh since there are two entries for it in Domesday, and it was included in the original foundation grant of Battle Abbey (N. Brooks 1988: 100; Vollans 1995: 122–3). However, the main body of Walland Marsh, to the north of the 'proto-Rother', does not appear to have been reclaimed until after the Norman Conquest: there are no Domesday entries, no churches referred to in the Domesday *Monachorum*, and no unequivocal references in charters. It has been suggested that an unidentified property *inter torrentem heorat burnan et haganan treae* ('between the stream Hartbourne and Hagana's tree') in a charter of AD 785 may refer to Agney, south-west of Old Romney (S.123: possibly an early ninth century copy; N. Brooks 1988: 100; Wallenberg 1931, 64–5), but names suffixed '-bourne' are otherwise absent on Romney Marsh, being typical of the chalk uplands of Kent and Sussex (N. Brooks 1988: 100). Agney also occupies the line taken by the 'proto-Rother' which was still flowing past Romney in the eighth century (Figure 67C, D).

Another place that it has been claimed may have lain in Walland Marsh is an un-named estate possibly to the west of Snargate (AD 811; S.168). The bounds included *Frodeshammespend* and *byttlinc hopa*. The latter's name is now preserved in Bedlinghope Sewer to the south-west of Yoke Sewer, though the Bedlinghope after which this long watercourse is named could have lain elsewhere.

The only other possible indication of reclamation in Walland Marsh is a charter of AD 833–58 which refers to various lands including Ebony on the Isle of Oxney and *Mistanham* (S.1623). N. Brooks (1988: 100) and Wallenberg (1931; 171–2) agree that *Mistanham* was Misleham in Brookland parish even though other evidence clearly points to that area having been reclaimed in the twelfth century (see Chapter 9). The place-name is simply derived from two very common features in a wetland area, 'mistel' (mistletoe) and 'hamm' (meadow), and which could have lain almost anywhere on the Marsh (Wallenberg 1934: 477). Overall, there is little indication of reclamation on Walland Marsh, north of the 'proto-Rother', until the twelfth century.

8.4.6 **Discussion: a divided landscape?** (Figure 67B)

By the eleventh century a range of archaeological and documentary evidence, linked with physical evidence still preserved within the landscape, shows that Romney Marsh proper was divided into a complex series of well-defined estates that were extensively settled and cultivated, or were held as areas of detached pasture by inland manors. The initial recolonization appears to have begun by the eighth century or earlier, and was confined to the area north-east of the Yoke Sewer sea wall. The date when Romney marsh proper was transformed from a tidal marsh into a freshwater landscape is unfortunately unclear, though the presence of several churches and four hundredal centres by the tenth century suggests a substantial population living in a flood-free environment. Two possible artificial watercourses are referred to in the ninth century which might indicate that reclamation was underway by that time.

The construction of the Yoke Sewer sea wall led to Romney Marsh becoming a divided landscape: reclaimed to the north and open saltmarsh to the south. The conscious decision to reclaim only part of a wetland was also seen in the Roman period, when half the Central Somerset Levels were protected by sea walls and reclaimed, while the other half was left as a tidal saltmarsh and intensively exploited for salt (Rippon 1997a: 65–77). Not surprisingly, considering it was reclaimed, Domesday records relatively few salt pans under manors on or adjacent to Romney Marsh proper (Bilsington had 10, Eastbridge 8⅓, and Langport in Old Romney had 7) in contrast to Rye, adjacent to Walland Marsh, which held 100 salt houses; a similar number are recorded on the unreclaimed Pevensey Levels (E. Campbell 1962: 540; H. S. King 1962: 455; J. Morris 1976: 5.1).

So, was Walland Marsh deliberately left unreclaimed because of its value for salt production? In the case of early medieval Romney Marsh a more plausible explanation is the natural pattern of drainage. There were two main sources of flooding: firstly, a series of major rivers that enter the Marsh from the west and; secondly, tidal flooding via the estuary of the 'proto-Rother'. Once the latter's tidal inlet had shifted to Romney from Hythe, Romney Marsh proper was largely flood free, whereas Walland Marsh remained open to tidal influence. Put simply, Romney Marsh proper was relatively easy to reclaim, whereas Walland Marsh would have been more difficult.

8.5 The North Kent marshes

The various coastal marshes in North Kent, though collectively extensive, were individually of relatively limited extent. This meant that in the medieval period they differed significantly in how they were exploited compared with both Fenland and Romney Marsh, in that very few settlements were actually located on the marshes themselves, and there were no wholly marshland communities.

Though relatively little has been written about reclamation in North Kent, a general consensus has been reached that it was a largely twelfth and thirteenth century affair (Bowler 1968; Evans 1953; Hasted 1797–1801: vol. II, 217; R. A. L. Smith 1943). J. H. Evans (1953: 116) clearly saw little likelihood of there having been any pre-Conquest drainage: 'It is difficult to imagine that the Saxons of this age [seventh to tenth centuries] had the resources to build river embankments (supposing that it was necessary to do so) around the great areas described in the Charters, and since works of this kind are never mentioned as convenient land boundaries we may assume that they did not exist' (J. H. Evans 1953: 116). Bowler (1968: 127) was even more emphatic in her denial of pre-Norman reclamation: 'There is no direct evidence that any of the marshland was protected along the Thames before 1200 in North West Kent [from Woolwich to the Medway].'

This traditional view is not altogether correct. The history of reclamation in Fenland, Romney Marsh, and on the Somerset Levels shows that Evans's first assumption is wrong: the technology to reclaim coastal wetlands did exist. Evans is also wrong in his second statement: there is evidence in the charters for drainage having taken place as early as the eighth century (see below). Finally, and in answer to Bowler, it must always be remembered that a lack of references to reclamation in a certain period need not imply a lack of reclamation: the documentary record is far from complete.

The best evidence for at least limited drainage on these marshes comes from the Cliffe Marshes, with a series of charters recording the gradual accumulation of lands by the Bishop of Rochester (Bowler 1968: 106–15; J. H. Evans 1953: 133; Jessup 1942). Two charters of AD 778 and AD 779 relate to land at *Bromgehege*, probably Bromhey in Frindsbury, beside the Medway north of Rochester (A. Campbell 1973; Sawyer 1968: 80; cf. Wallenberg 1931: 56–9 suggests Broomey in Cooling). The grant included arable fields near a meadow called *Hreodham*, and a marsh called *Scaga* lying 'between dryland and the banks of the *Iaenlade*' (S.35–6; Bowler 1968: 109–10; A. Campbell 1973: 11–13; J. H. Evans 1953: 134). *Hredham* (reed-ham) suggests a freshwater landscape as opposed to a tidal saltmarsh, while the adjacent arable fields are also most likely to have occurred in a landscape free from tidal inundation. In AD 789 another charter extended the previous grants at *Bromgehege*, and the bounds also refer to the marsh called *Scaga* along with a number of ditches (S.130; Bowler 1968: 112; A. Campbell 1973: 16–17). A charter of AD 801, also relating to lands in *Bromgehege*, describes arable cultivation on the marshes (S.157; A. Campbell 1973: 19–20; J. H. Evans 1953: 134).

Elsewhere on the North Kent Marshes, a number of other eighth and ninth century charters also refer to meadows including *Meadham* and *Bulenham* in Higham (S.110; J. H. Evans 1953, 133–4; Jessup 1942) and at *Strood* and *Bioccanlea*, presumably Bickley near Lower Higham (S.1276; Bowler 1968: 114; J. H. Evans 1953). Further east along the North Kent coast embankments are referred to a charter of AD 811 relating to Graveney near Whitstable (S.168; Witney 1989: 29). The place-name may mean 'a stream that feeds a canal' or 'dug river' (Fenwick 1978: 179): either way an artificial watercourse is implied. Overall, the impression is that many of the North Kent marshes had some arable cultivation and extensive freshwater meadow by the eighth and ninth centuries, implying that some improvements had been made to the drainage and flood defence. However, unlike in the Roman period, there is no evidence for settlement.

8.6 The Essex marshes

On the opposite side of the Thames Estuary, the coastal marshes of Essex are very similar to those in Kent in that while they are collectively extensive, few are individually of any great extent: there was just one wholly marshland community, on Foulness Island, which emerged during the thirteenth century (Chapter 9). Unfortunately, a scarcity of pre-Conquest documentary sources means that we know relatively little about the Essex Marshes during the early medieval period. In AD 958 King Edgar granted five *mansiunculae* to Aethelstan at *Hamme* (later East and West Ham, beside the Thames east of London) (Hart 1957a: 12). The place-name means 'land in a river-bend promontory, dry ground in a marsh, river-meadow, cultivated plot in marginal land, perhaps also a piece of valley bottom land hemmed in by higher ground' (Gelling 1988:

112; Reaney 1935: 94)). Though the place-name is not unequivocal in implying embankment of the coastal marshes, the estate bounds do refer to an *eadelmes dic*.

8.7 Fenland

Through the historical research of Darby (1940*a*; *b*; 1983) and Hallam (1954; 1965), Fenland has become one of the best documented examples of medieval reclamation in Britain, yet the early stages of this process remained obscure. Though Domesday shows that the coastal zone was well-populated by the eleventh century, the traditional view was that during the early medieval period Fenland was 'an overgrown and waterlogged landscape of choked drains and desolate crumbling settlements' (Salway 1970: 18). This impression must have been influenced by contemporary writers, such as Bede, who described how 'since the district of Ely was surrounded on all sides by sea and fens ... it resembles an island surrounded by water and marshes, and it derives its name from the vast quantities of eels that are caught in the marshes' (*Bede:* IV.20). St Guthlac described the landscape around Crowland Island during the early eighth century as 'a hideous fen of a huge bigness which, beginning at the banks of the river Gronte, extends itself south from the north even to the sea ... now consisting of marshes, now of bogs, sometimes of backwaters overhung by fog, sometimes studded with wooded islands, and traversed by the winding of tortuous streams' (Godwin 1978: 108; Hallam 1954: 5; Raban 1977: 47). However, these early writers were describing just one of the distinctive environments that made up Fenland: the small islands of bedrock that protruded through the freshwater peat bogs in the low-lying backfens. These writers said little about the higher coastal marshes, and it was only through a programme of archaeological survey and excavations, started in the late 1970s and completed in the mid-1990s, that the extent of early medieval settlement in Fenland became clear.

8.7.1 The evolution of the settlement pattern

During the early medieval period there were three areas of settlement in Fenland: the margins of the expanding freshwater peat bogs, the islands of bedrock that protruded through the freshwater backfens, and the coastal marshes adjacent to The Wash. Each of these settlement zones would appear to correlate with communities listed the Tribal Hidage of the later seventh century: respectively, the *Spaldas* in South West Lincolnshire, the *Sweordora* around Whittlesey and the southern islands, and the *Wixna/Wissa* around Wisbech and the coastal marshes (Courtney 1981; Darby 1983: 5).

Communities living in the first of these settlement zones continued the Iron Age and Romano-British tradition of exploiting both the freshwater backfen and intertidal marshes. In Norfolk, a single Early Saxon pottery scatter, in Tilney St Lawrence, has also been located on the margins of the backfen (Figure 59A; Silvester 1988, 60). Activity at the site was clearly short lived (Middle Saxon pottery was absent) and excavations failed to reveal any sub-surface features, suggesting very ephemeral

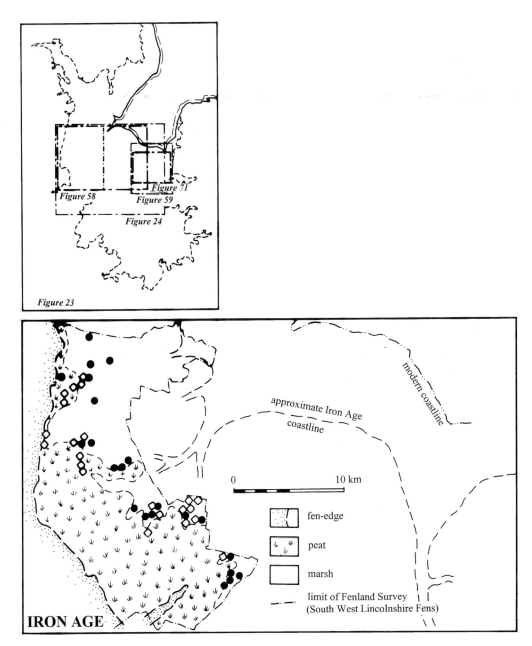

58. The South West Lincolnshire Fens. A, the Iron Age; B, Romano-British period; C, Early to Middle Saxon period; D, medieval period (after Hallam 1965; Hayes and Lane 1992: figs. 125–8).

occupation destroyed by later ploughing (Crowson *et al.* 2000: 211–13). There were no drainage ditches, and the community living there could only have exploited the natural fenland resources without attempting to modify their environment.

The evidence for fifth to ninth century occupation in the South West Lincolnshire

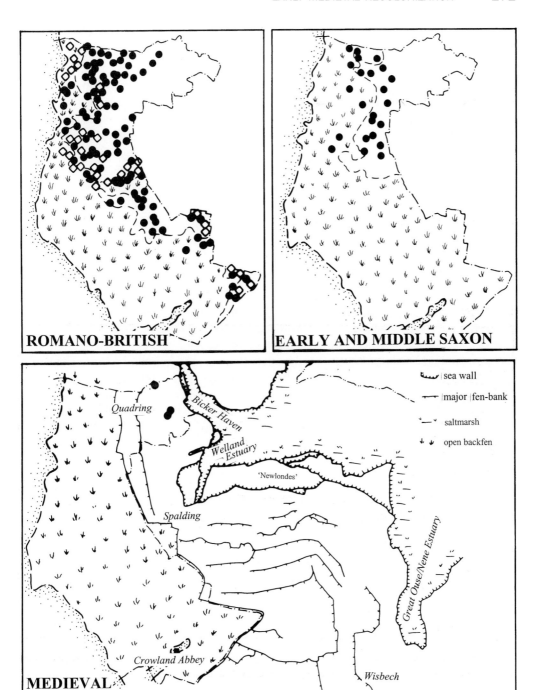

58. (Continued)

fens is far more abundant (Figure 58). Several locations have produced scatters of both Romano-British and Early Saxon pottery, though this is rare: Iron Age to Roman continuity was far more common than Roman to Saxon (Hayes 1988: 324; Hayes and Lane 1992). However, it is not clear whether there was a significant hiatus in occupation at the end of the Roman period, or simply that the main area of settlement had shifted eastwards, continuing the trend seen within the Roman period when the focus of occupation migrated some 2 km towards the coast (Hayes and Lane 1992: figs. 126–7; 1993: 65, figs. 5.4–5). This expansion of the freshwater backfen over former saltmarsh areas is reflected in the change of environment at Third Drove Gosberton, where the intertidal Romano-British landscape was replaced by freshwater conditions during the Early Saxon period (Crowson *et al.* 2000: 110–1). Pottery suggests a hiatus in occupation between the mid-fourth century and the Early Saxon period, and ditches of the two periods were on different orientations. In contrast to most other Early Saxon sites along the margins of the backfen, there was no Middle Saxon pottery, which suggests that this may have been an early victim of the eastwards expansion of the freshwater fen. Only a small part of the site was excavated which revealed two small isolated sub-rectangular enclosures defined by slight gullies and of unknown function: there was little domestic refuse and phosphate analysis showed little patterning indicative of stock pens. Nearby, at Leaves Lake Drove, Pinchbeck, a settlement associated with shallow ditches and gullies and also of Early Saxon date appears to have lain in an environment associated with alternating freshwater and intertidal conditions (Crowson *et al.*, 2000: 145; Lane 1994).

A number of other recently excavated sites have revealed a range of landscape exploitation and modification strategies during this period, including the extent of cultivation in this still intertidal environment (Crowson *et al.* 2000: 112–19). The Early to Middle Saxon site at Chopdike Drove, Gosberton, is one of a number that lay on slightly raised creek banks close to the landward edge of the marshland. In its earlier phase the site appears to have had an industrial function: a number of pits appear to have been used for hemp-retting, while three other features were associated with possible salt-working debris. Later, an agricultural settlement was established which, although lying in a saltmarsh environment, was associated with cereal cultivation dominated by the salt-tolerant barley, along with smaller amounts of wheat, rye, oats, horsebean, and flax/linseed. A number of substantial ditches in both phases may indicate attempts to improve the drainage of the site. At Mornington House, Gosberton, a somewhat indistinct phase of Early Saxon activity was followed by a Middle Saxon agricultural settlement, possibly associated with salt production, also lying on a slightly raised creek bank. A number of substantial ditches indicate attempts to improve the drainage of the site.

During the initial Fenland Survey, many of the sites associated with Middle Saxon pottery appeared to be on 'low mounds, which do not appear to have formed naturally and on which the surface soil was stained black' (Hayes and Lane 1992: 31). It was tempting to see these raised areas as a human response to increased flooding similar to the contemporary *terpen* of the northern Netherlands and Germany, and may have been created by immigrants from the continent. However, the excavations of one such site (Chopdike Drove in Gosberton) showed that mound to be a natural creek bank.

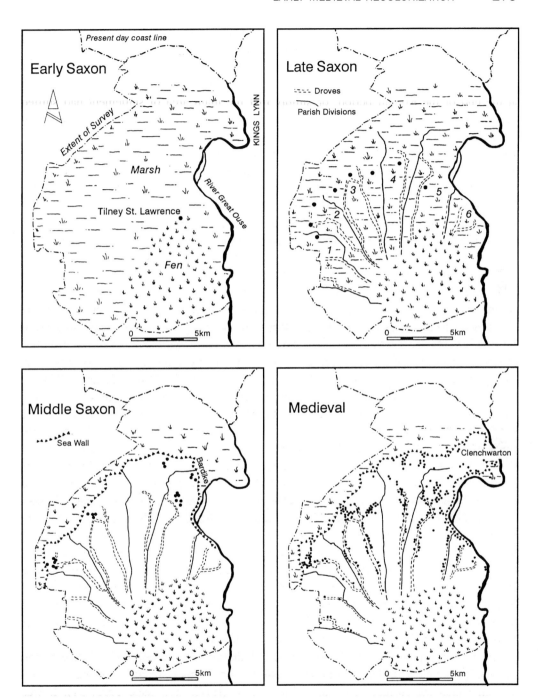

59. The Norfolk marshland. A, Early Saxon period; B, Middle Saxon period; C, Late Saxon period; and D, medieval period (and see Figure 60) (from Silvester 1988: figs 113–15). The early estates are: 1, Emneth; 2, Walsoken; 3, Walton; 4, Walpole; 5, Terrington; 6, Islington/Tilney. (For location see Figure 58; drawn by Sue Rouillard.)

The margins of the peat bogs in South West Lincolnshire were finally deserted between the seventh and the ninth centuries as the dispersed scatter of settlements was eclipsed by a far more regularly arranged series of more nucleated settlements which had already started to appear on the higher coastal marshes, and which were to become the major Fenland villages (Hayes and Lane 1992: 34, 215). Though the *Wixna/Wissa* recorded in the later seventh century Tribal Hidage may have occupied the area around Wisbech, there is very little evidence for settlement in these areas before that time: two Early Saxon brooches and some burial urns have been found in Wisbech, which presumably represent a cemetery (D. Hall 1996: 182), and two of the coastal Middle Saxon settlements in Norfolk have produced sherds of a pottery fabric that *may* be Early Saxon (Silvester 1988: 156). However, it was only during the period when Ipswich Ware was in use (in the seventh to ninth centuries) that the coastal marshes of Fenland were extensively colonized (D. Hall 1996: 182; Hayes and Lane 1992: 31; Healey 1979; Silvester 1993: 28).

The clearest evidence for the character of the Middle to Late Saxon settlement pattern in Fenland comes from the Norfolk Marshland, with a series of pottery scatters located on naturally raised creek banks, regularly spaced *c.* 1.5 km and 2 km apart in an arc parallel to the nearby contemporary coast (Figure 59; Silvester 1988: 156–60). The quantity of pottery and animal bone suggests that these were permanent settlements, though they may have originated as temporary accommodation for those over-seeing the summer pasturage of livestock (D. Hall and J. Coles 1994: 126; Silvester 1988: 158). The Norfolk Marshland appears to have been carved up into six long, narrow, estates—Emneth, Walsoken, Walton, Walpole, Terrington, and (?)Islington/Tilney—which extended from the higher marshes towards the lower-lying backfen (Clenchwarton and the Wiggenhall parishes were later creations). Certain elements of the regularly arranged series of Middle Saxon sites then faded away, as settlement appears to have become consolidated into fewer, larger settlements that went on to become the medieval villages.

Excavations at three settlements on the coastal marshes in Norfolk (Hay Green in Terrington St Clement, Rose Hall Farm in Walpole St Andrew, and Ingleborough in West Walton) show that the Middle Saxon phases of occupation lay on a tidal saltmarsh (Crowson *et al.*, 2000). Each settlement was located on naturally raised areas on the banks of former creeks, and attempts had been made at all three to improve the local drainage through digging substantial ditches. However, environmental evidence such as foraminifera indicates that these ditches were subject to regular tidal inundation: the landscape had been modified but was not yet transformed through reclamation. Large amounts of butchered animal bone suggests a role of stock raising, and there is circumstantial evidence for salt production in the form of ashy deposits at Ingleborough and a number of steep-sided pits at Rose Hall Farm which could have acted as settling tanks: the analysis of foraminifera suggests higher than normal levels of salinity. Fragments of poorly fired ceramic vessels may represent an early medieval form of briquetage. As in the South West Lincolnshire Fens (see above), there is also evidence for some cultivation, particularly of salt-tolerant barley. The amount of imported Ipswich Ware and range of other domestic debris suggests that these were not impoverished communities (Leah 1992: 55).

8.7.2 **The date of reclamation and construction of the sea wall**

There has been much speculation over the origins of the sea wall that protected medieval Fenland, though its construction need not have been a single event. The medieval coastline was heavily indented, with estuaries at King's Lynn, Wisbech, and Spalding, and each area of marshland between them had to be embanked quite separately: the transition from saltmarsh exploitation, through modification, to transformation could have happened at different times in different places.

The best dating evidence for the origins of the first sea wall comes from Norfolk. The place-name group Walpole, Walsoken, and Walton are first recorded in the tenth century, and it is possible that they incorporate the Old English place-name element *weall* or wall (though the names could also be derived from the Anglo-Saxon *w(e)alh* referring to the presence of a native British population: Silvester 1988: 160). In Tilney St. Lawrence and Walpole St. Peter the sea wall appears to overlie scatters of Middle Saxon pottery, giving a *terminus post quem* of the seventh century for its construction (D. Hall and J. Coles 1994: 127; Silvester 1988: 60, 67, 75).

The medieval sea wall itself has been excavated at Clenchwarton (Norfolk), and was found to contain eleventh century pottery (Crowson *et al.* 2000: 225–30). However, various strands of evidence suggest that this parish was a later intake of saltmarsh seaward of the earlier flood defences which may have run along the Bardike (which forms the western side of the parish: Figure 59C; Silvester 1988: fig. 10). Domesday recorded a single holding of no more than 40 acres, worth six shillings, at Clenchwarton and though it has been suggested other land in the parish was subsumed in entries for adjacent vills such as Islington (Silvester 1988: 17), it may be that this Domesday entry is a genuine reflection of the very early stages of reclamation. Fieldwalking revealed evidence for eight pottery scatters. Three were associated with mounds, yielding tenth to twelfth century pottery, and though their function is unclear, they are different in character to salterns (Silvester 1988: 118–19). They bear no relationship to the historic landscape, and it is tempting to see these as small raised platforms for settlements, perhaps seasonal and related to grazing, exploiting the marsh before its embankment. Five other pottery scatters were recorded in Clenchwarton, all of which lay beside roads that form part of the historic landscape and, as such, must relate to the post-reclamation landscape; none contained eleventh century material, just two yielded twelfth century material with the rest being thirteenth century in date. Taken altogether, this points to the reclamation of Clenchwarton as occurring around the eleventh century, giving a *terminus ante quem* of that date for the initial embankment of the Norfolk Marshland including the construction of Bardike. Excavations of Middle Saxon settlements at Terrington, Walpole St. Andrew, and West Walton show that they lay on a tidal saltmarsh (see above), whereas the Late Saxon settlements at Terrington and West Walton lay in a wholly freshwater landscape, giving a *terminus ante quem* for the construction of a sea wall of around the tenth century.

The line of this earliest sea wall is not known as the later medieval sea wall appears to have been superimposed upon the pattern of fields and roads, suggesting that it

60. The Norfolk marshland: the historic landscape (from Silvester 1988: fig. 124). (Drawn by Margaret Mathews and reproduced by permission of Bob Silvester.)

represents an early example of 'managed retreat' (for a similar phenomena around the Severn Estuary see Allen 1988; Allen and Rippon 1997a; Rippon 1996a: 97–9, fig. 4, plate 14).

8.7.3 Drainage and enclosure in early medieval Fenland

The Early and Middle Saxon settlements in Fenland do not appear to have been associated with systematic attempts to drain the surrounding land: the ditches that have been recorded in excavations would have improved the drainage locally, but had little impact upon the wider landscape. These sites are also unrelated to the present pattern of roads, suggesting that they pre-date the creation of the 'historic landscape' (the present pattern of fields, roads, and settlements).

In Cambridgeshire, Lincolnshire, and Norfolk (Figure 60; cf. Figure 51) broadly three types of historic landscape can be recognized. On the highest coastal areas there is an irregular pattern of fields, with narrow winding lanes and small irregular greens at their junctions. Further from the coast, towards the lower-lying backfens, there are more regular blocks of often long narrow fields, laid out between broad, linear droveways that linked the coastal settlements with the open pastures of the backfen. Finally, there are the highly rectilinear blocks of fields that resulted from the drainage and enclosure of the lowest-lying ground. Whilst there are differences in detail, these three zones are broadly comparable with the irregular, intermediate, and regular landscapes identified on the Gwent Levels and elsewhere around the Severn Estuary (Rippon 1996a: figs. 14–16; 1997a: fig. 39). The close spatial relationship in the higher coastal marshes of both Lincolnshire and Norfolk between Late Saxon settlement foci and roads in the historic landscape, suggests that the irregular landscapes that still characterize these areas started to form during the ninth and tenth centuries (Hayes and Lane 1992: 31–8; Silvester 1988: figs. 23, 56, 86, 69–70). The morphology of this landscape suggests a relatively piecemeal approach to reclamation, with small areas of land being enclosed and drained as required (e.g. Figures 13I and 19C).

8.7.4 Discussion

Three themes relating to Fenland during the early medieval period have been discussed: the evolution of the settlement pattern, landuse and environment, and the date at which the marshes were finally embanked and enclosed. The coastal parts of Fenland were certainly abandoned during the post-Roman period though in South West Lincolnshire this hiatus may have been brief, and settlements were re-established on the fringes of the freshwater backfen by the fifth/sixth centuries. During the seventh and eighth centuries, scatters of Middle Saxon pottery indicate that in addition to the margins of the peat bogs, a second area of the Fenland landscape was colonized: the higher, coastal, parts of the saltmarsh. This is evident in Lincolnshire and Cambridgeshire, but most clearly demonstrated in Norfolk where a series of regularly spaced settlements were laid out on the saltmarsh in a line close to what must have been the contemporary coast. These settlements appear to have been exploiting the rich natural resources of this landscape though there was limited arable cultivation, for which a number of substantial ditches would have improved the drainage. By the ninth century the marsh-backfen interface was finally abandoned as the settlement pattern appears to have condensed into fewer, nucleated villages restricted to the higher coastal siltlands. At about this time there was also a marked change in environment with saltmarshes replaced by freshwater conditions indicative of reclamation. Overall, a two stage process is evident: a phase of colonization of the coastal marshes during the seventh and eighth centuries, followed by a re-structuring of the landscape during the ninth and tenth centuries: a classic example of the transition from landscape exploitation, through modification, to transformation.

8.8 Belgium and the western Netherlands

8.8.1 Belgium

Following the Late to Post-Roman flooding of the coastal marshes in Belgium, a layer of clay was deposited over large parts of peat-filled backfen (Dewilde *et al*. 1995: 220; Tys 1997: 157). These marshes were subsequently exploited for seasonal grazing, particularly by sheep, illustrated for example the ninth century place-name Lampernisse near Veurne ('wet meadow suitable for sheep': Dewilde *et al*. 1995: 220), and reference in AD 992 and AD 995 to two *terrae ad oves* (sheepland) at Testerep near Oostende (Tys 1997: 157). The earliest settlements on the Belgian marshes, also dating from the ninth century, were located on the banks of still active or silted-up creeks. Localized embankment appears to have started around the eleventh century, though the area remained in use as extensive sheep pastures until at least the early twelfth century (Nicholas 1992: 98). One example of such an embankment is when Testerep was protected by the Kaaidijk, which is still preserved within the historic landscape dividing the early reclamation characterized by an irregular pattern of fields and roads (the 'Oudland'), and the more regularly laid out twelfth century reclamations in the 'Nieuwlands' (Tys 1997).

8.8.2 Zeeland (Figure 27)

Further north, in Zeeland, the marshes were largely deserted during the Late to Post-Roman period. Although there was subsequently some expansion of occupation on the coastal barrier (e.g. on Walcheren), the marshes and peat bogs remained deserted until the eighth century when the tidal marshes started to dry out and the creeks silted up, eventually allowing the area's reoccupation (Figure 27; Vos and Van Heeringen 1997: 67–8). Settlements tended to be located on raised mounds and documentary references imply that flooding was still common. Seasonal grazing of sheep was the main activity, while salt production was also important, reflected in the inclusion of salterns in several eighth and ninth century charters (Besteman 1974: 172). However, traces of plough furrows have been found beneath the ramparts of the late ninth or tenth century fortresses at Middelburg and Souburg (both on Walcheren) indicating that the raised creek ridges upon which they were built were already under cultivation (Vos and Van Heeringen 1997: 68). A similar relict soil associated with ninth and tenth century pottery has also been recorded at nearby Domburg on the coast (Trimpe Burger 1975: 215).

The main expansion of settlement came in the tenth century, with settlements associated with cereal cultivation located directly on the marsh surface (*Flachsiedlungen*), suggesting that flooding was no longer such a problem (Figure 27; Van den Broeke and Van Londen 1995: 41; A. Lambert 1971: 102; Vos and Van Heeringen 1997: 67–70). This may have been due to improvements in the natural environment or the construction of artificial embankments, though renewed flooding during the eleventh and twelfth centuries led once again to the raising of dwelling mounds. Place-names, such as *Tubindic* and *Isendycke* (on Zeeuws-Vlaanderen in Zeeland) suggest that embankments had been constructed locally by the eleventh century, though systematic reclamation did not begin before the twelfth century (Vos and Van Heeringen 1997: 69–70).

8.8.3 **South Holland** (Figure 61)

Further up the coast in South Holland, there was once again an almost complete settlement desertion between the late third and early sixth centuries, with just a light scatter of stray finds of this period on the coastal barrier and banks of the major tidal rivers such as the Maas and Oude Rijn (Figure 61; Bult and Hallewas 1990: 73, fig. 4). A number of distinctive place-names, and an increase in the number of archaeological finds, suggests an expansion of settlement in the later sixth century, though occupation was still largely restricted to the dunes and major river banks (Bult and Hallewas 1990: 75, figs 76–7; Henderikx 1986: 483; Van der Linden 1982). Flooding remained a problem with a series of storm surges, notably in the ninth century, though the traditional view of a distinct marine transgression in the ninth and tenth centuries can be dismissed (see Chapter 2).

As in Zeeland, the number of settlements on the sand dunes and higher estuarine marshes increased during the tenth century, when for the first time there was also some expansion into the peatlands, as a number of places there are recorded as having to make *botting* payments to the Count of Holland, an obligation that was abolished for reclamations after *c.* AD 1000 (Bos 1990: 121; Bult and Hallewas 1990: 79, fig. 2; TeBrake 1985: 194–200). These early medieval settlements were usually located on raised creeks ridges, and the presence of revetments along rivers and drainage ditches show that some attempt was made to modify what remained an essentially high intertidal environment. In the tenth century reclamation may have started beside the Maas, for example at Merwede (around Vlaardingen) and the royal estate of Maasland (around Schipluiden), though the main period of embanking followed the twelfth century floods (Bult 1986: 23; Henderikx 1986: 495; Van den Broeke and Van Londen 1995: 41). Work on reclaiming the peat backfens only started in the eleventh century and is described in Chapter 9.

8.8.4 **North Holland** (Figure 61)

In North Holland the coastal barrier was almost continuous, and the lack of tidal inlets led to a landscape dominated by freshwater peat (Figure 61). As with South Holland, the whole region appears to have been abandoned between the later third and sixth centuries, with just occasional settlement on the coastal barrier and Island of Texel (Besteman 1990: 96–9, fig. 4). Both archaeological and place-name evidence shows that during the seventh century there was an increase in settlement in the dune region, along with an expansion into the marshes adjacent to the Zuider Zee (Besteman 1990: 99–110, fig. 6). Animal bone assemblages from these settlements suggest that sheep grazing was particularly important, with the age at death indicative of dairy and wool, rather than meat, production (Besteman 1990: 103, 106; Besteman and Guiran 1987: 300–1). The

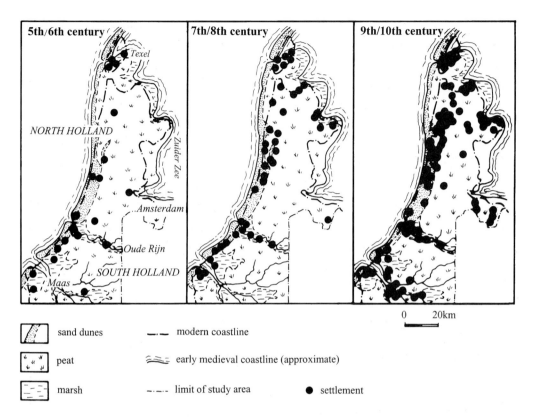

61. The expansion of settlement in early medieval Holland (after Bos 1990: figs. 4, 6–7 and Besteman 1990: figs. 4, 6–7). (For location see Figure 26.)

marshes remained intertidal, as at Het Torp, in Den Helder, which lay in a brackish environment with direct tidal influence at extremely high tides, though cultivation was possible with barley and vetch being the main crops (Van Es 1973a; b; TeBrake 1985: 150; Van Zeist 1973). In the eighth and early ninth centuries settlement expanded further and the peatlands were extensively settled for the first time, illustrated, for example, by the place-names -heem (equivalent to the Old English '-ham') and -more (OE 'moor': Besteman 1988: 338; 1990: 111; Besteman and Guiran 1987: 299–300; Hallewas 1984: 300; Van der Linden 1982: 42–3).

The agricultural productivity of these areas is also reflected in the growth of the trading station at Medemblik from the eighth century, where imported goods were exchanged for wool/cloth, hides/parchment, dairy produce, and fish (Besteman 1990: 197–110; Schoorl 1997). Whether salt was also traded is unclear as, although a number of peat cuttings are known in this area, they do not appear to have become saturated with salt and so were presumably worked simply as a source of fuel (Marschalleck 1973: 139–42; cf. Besteman 1974).

By the ninth century the earliest dikes were also constructed, notably enclosing small areas of marshland immediately behind the coastal dunes (A. Lambert 1971: 94).

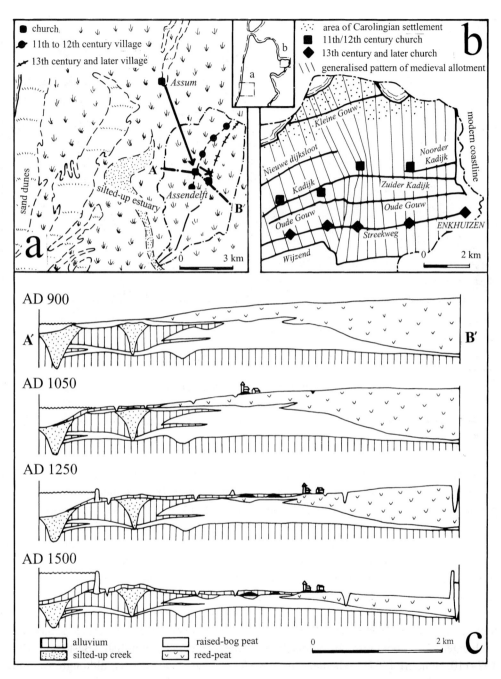

62. Early reclamation in North Holland. (For locations see Figure 26.) A, The 11th/12th and 13th century settlements of Assendelft, on the peat bogs east of the coastal sand dunes (after Besteman and Guiran 1987: figs. 14.3–4). The settlement shifted eastwards as drainage caused the peat to shrink. B, The sequence of 11th/12th and 13th century settlements west of Enkhuizen (after Besteman 1988: fig. 6). C, Cross-section through the Assendelver reclamation showing how the enclosed and settled areas shifted eastwards as drainage causes the peat to shrink (after Besteman 1988: fig. 20). (For location see Figure 62a above.)

This early phase of colonization was carried out in a fairly piecemeal fashion, and it was only from the tenth century that large-scale land reclamation of the peatlands occurred both eastwards, from the dunes, and south and westwards from the banks of the Zuider Zee (Besteman 1990: 110–17; Hallewas 1984: 300–1; Therkorn *et al.* 1998: 21; Van der Linden 1982: 43). Settlements, such as Assendelft (Figure 62) were initially founded on the banks of active or relict tidal creeks. A series of long parallel ditches were dug at right angles to the creek bank and extending into the peat fen, with each farmstead in the long linear settlement having its own plot of land. The natural vegetation was cleared, and low banks constructed around the perimeter of the ditched area (Besteman 1990: 111–17, fig. 15; Besteman and Guiran 1987). Place-names suggest that these peatland settlements may originally have sprung from 'mother' settlements back in the dune region (e.g. Assum–Assendelft: Figure 62a).

8.9 The *terp* landscapes: northern Netherlands and North West Germany

The coastal marshes of the northern Netherlands started to be reoccupied from the mid-fifth century, and during the sixth and seventh centuries the area became the focus for one of the great early medieval cultures: the kingdom of Frisia (Gerrets 1999: 120; Heidinga 1997; Knol 1993). The power of the Frisian kings extended from the Schelde in Zeeland to the Weser in Germany, perhaps even around into Jutland, though the focus for their power lay in the northern Netherlands (Heidinga 1997: 9–10). The political history of the Frisians is not of particular concern here, although it does have a landscape dimension: though their wealth was based on trade and their role as middle men in the early medieval prestige goods economy, this relied ultimately upon the exploitation of natural and agricultural resources. In the case of the Frisians these were, in particular, cloth and salt, two products for which the coastal marshes in their homeland were ideally suited to producing.

A major feature of these marshland landscapes during the early medieval period is the continuation of earlier settlement-building traditions using raised *terp* mounds (e.g. Figure 63). Though the basic concept of *terpen* as raised settlements is very similar throughout Frisia, there is marked regional variation in their development. For example, the coastal marshes of the northern Netherlands appear to have been abandoned in the fourth century, and remained largely deserted until the later fifth/sixth century when many of the old mounds were reoccupied. In contrast, the north German marshes were settled up to the fifth century before being abandoned until their seventh/eighth century reoccupation. There are also regional variations in the size and layout of raised settlements: for example, in the modern province of Friesland (around Leuwarden) *terpen* were generally small and supported individual farms and hamlets, whereas further east, in Groningen and Germany, they were larger, and supported radially planned villages (A. Lambert 1971: 79; Zimmermann 1995: 347). The eighth and ninth centuries saw an expansion of settlement, notably along the rivers that extended into the backfen peatbogs,

63. The *terp* and church at Ezinge (north of Groningen) looking west.

and these settlements were the starting point for the reclamation of the peatlands from the tenth century (Figure 64; Knol 1993: 244; Miedema 1983: figs 268–9).

Though the evolution of the *terpen* themselves is relatively well-understood, their wider landscape context has received less attention (but see Vos, 1999). The early coastal settlements were usually located on naturally raised areas close to the contemporary coast, such as the banks of tidal creeks and shore-parallel ridges, within a very high tidal saltmarsh environment (Behre 1985: 91; 1990*b*: 35–6; Behre and Jacomet 1991; Knol *et al.* 1995–96: 364; Van Zeist 1974). These raised areas, along with parts of the *terpen* themselves, were used for agriculture with the main crops being salt-tolerant barley, along with beans, oats, flax, turnip, and hemp (Behre 1985: 91; Besteman *et al.*, 1999; Cappers 1993–4: 147–9; Van Zeist 1974). However, this was largely a pastoral landscape, with sheep and wool production of particular importance, and late eighth and ninth century land charters granting various estates to monastic institutions make few references to ploughlands (A. Lambert 1971: 81; Zimmermann 1995; 1996: 25–30).

The *Egils saga*, a detailed account of a Viking raid into Frisia during the mid-tenth century, describes one area in considerable detail (A. Lambert 1971: 79; TeBrake 1985: 146–7). The landscape was very flat, but water-filled ditches, enclosing fields and meadows, had been dug over a large area. It would appear, therefore, that attempts to modify this landscape through locally controlling flooding may have begun as early as the tenth century, and other sources indicate that the earliest coastal embankments also date to this time (A. Lambert 1971: 81–6; Vos 1999). The earliest dikes may have originated simply as raised trackways (*dijkwegen*) running between *terpen*, though these were found to afford some protection from tidal flooding and so gradually extra banks

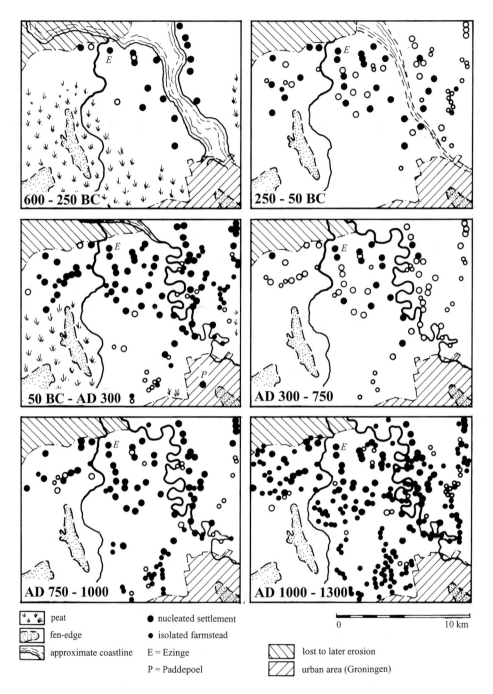

64. The expansion and contraction of settlement on the marshes of the northern Netherlands north of Groningen (after Miedema 1983: figs. 265–70; Roeleveld 1974: figs. 63–4). The earliest occupation lay on the banks of a major estuary, though over time settlements spread into the lower-lying areas inland, until increased flooding during the 3rd and 4th centuries forced a retreat. A second period of expansion started around the 6th/7th centuries, which eventually led to the colonization of all but the lowest-lying backfens. (For location see Figure 26.)

were constructed to enclose whole blocks of land. This was generally a piecemeal process with individual marshes enclosed separately, though by the eleventh century larger tracts of land were being protected by a single dike.

In Germany, another tradition of embanking has been identified from around the eleventh century, with low 'summer dikes' constructed in order to improve conditions for agriculture during the growing season, but allowing flooding during the winter months. These 'ring dikes' did not form a continuous line, but only protected the lands of individual *wurten* (Figures 13D and 35). Only around the twelfth or thirteenth century were higher 'winter' dikes constructed in an attempt to keep the tide at bay all year round (Behre 1990*b*: 38–9; Mayhew 1973: 48; Schmid 1990*a*: 96).

8.10 Discussion: the recolonization of coastal marshes during the early medieval period

As described in Chapter 7, the Late Roman/Early post-Roman period saw an extensive marine transgression throughout the coastal wetlands of North West Europe, re-creating extensive areas of saltmarsh. By the eighth and ninth centuries recolonization was well-underway in most areas, and it is notable that around the tenth century there was a further expansion of settlement and initial attempts at embankment throughout North West Europe (Table 5). It was during this period that in many areas of wetlands, notably the higher coastal marshes, that the foundations of the present, 'historic', landscape were laid. However, much remained to be done and, in the subsequent two centuries, attention shifted from the coast towards the unreclaimed backfens which forms the focus of Chapter 9.

Table 5. The date of early medieval recolonization and initial reclamation

Location	Date
Central Somerset Levels	Recolonization and embankment by the 11th century
North Somerset Levels	Recolonization and embankment by the 11th century
Gwent Levels	Recolonization and embankment starting in the 12th century
Pevensey Levels	Recolonization and embankment starting in the 12th century
Romney Marsh	Recolonization from the 8th century; embankment by 9th/10th century
North Kent	Embankment from the 8th century
Essex	Some embankment by 10th century?
Halvergate Marshes	Not recolonized or embanked
Fenland	Recolonization from the 7th/8th century; embankment in the 10th century
Belgium	Recolonization by 8th/9th centuries; embankment from 11th century
Zeeland/South Holland	Recolonization by 8th/9th centuries; embankment from 11th century
North Holland	Recolonization by 8th/9th centuries; embankment from 10th century
Northern Netherlands	Recolonization late 5th/6th century; embankment from 10th century
Germany	Recolonization 7th/8th century; embankment from 10th century

CHAPTER 9

Pressing on:

continued expansion during the high Middle Ages

9.1 Introduction

By the eleventh century the predominant strategy towards the utilization of coastal wetlands throughout much of North West Europe had become transformation, with most substantial areas of saltmarsh having been embanked, and the process of drainage and enclosure well underway. Despite these early achievements, much remained to be done and reclamation, notably in the freshwater backfens, continued well into the high medieval period. By the thirteenth century a 'high water mark' of expansion had been reached, with arable cultivation probably at its most extensive. However, this logical sequence—with the simple exploitation of natural resources being replaced by landscape modification, and finally transformation—was not always followed, and in certain areas reclamation proceeded at a much slower pace, suggesting that local factors must have affected the decision whether or not to transform those wetlands.

This chapter describes the major developments in each major coastal wetland of North West Europe during the twelfth to fourteenth centuries, with particular attention paid to areas with good primary evidence that has seen relatively little synthesis (e.g. the Pevensey Levels and Romney Marsh), and briefer summaries for those regions that have seen recent study (e.g. the Severn Estuary, Fenland, and The Netherlands). Chapters 10 and 11 then explore a number of themes related to landuse and the exploitation of natural resources, and why broadly similar types of environment in different areas were utilized in very different ways.

9.2 The Severn Estuary

The history of reclamation on the Severn Estuary wetlands has recently been considered elsewhere (Rippon 1994a; 1996a; 1997a) and a brief updated summary will suffice here. As described in Chapter 8, the early medieval sources are not good, and all that can be said with confidence is that reclamation was well underway in Somerset and Gloucestershire by the time of Domesday. The main coastal embankments were in place, though during the twelfth and thirteenth centuries there was an expansion of enclosure and drainage into the freshwater backfens. By the thirteenth century what had been meadow and pasture was even being put over to arable as the landscape was used ever more intensively (e.g. Musgrove 1997; Musgrove, forthcoming). There was also an expansion of settlement, both in terms of the growth of existing hamlets (e.g. Rippon 1994a; 1997a: table 7.3; 1997c; 1998), and the establishment of new settlements, usually in the form of scattered farmsteads (e.g. Allen 1997b; Locock 1997b). The extent to which new land was also won from saltmarshes in front of the original sea wall is less clear as this part of the landscape has been lost to later erosion which appears to have affected both sides of the Severn Estuary during the late medieval period (Allen 1988; Allen and Rippon 1997a).

On the Gwent Levels reclamation appears to have started during the late eleventh/early twelfth century, the most plausible context for which was as part of the new Anglo-Norman marcher lords' policies of estate improvement. This also saw the introduction of English colonists to the region, the foundation of boroughs, and the replanning of landscapes associated with the establishment of nucleated villages and open fields more typical of Midland England (Chapter 11; Rippon, forthcoming c; Sylvester 1969).

9.3 The Pevensey Levels: post-Conquest reclamation (Figure 65)

The scarcity of Domesday meadow compared with areas such as the Ouse Valley in Sussex, and abundance of salterns, suggests that there was little or no early medieval reclamation on the Pevensey Levels (Dulley 1966). Numerous salt works can be identified in the field as earthwork mounds, c. 1–1.5 m high, roughly oval in plan, and c. 50 m in diameter and, although none has been excavated, occasional cases of soil erosion show that they are made of the same clay as the rest of the marsh (Figures 52 and 65; Dulley 1966: 28). The mounds occur next to many of the naturally meandering rivers that cross the Levels, and they clearly pre-date earthen embankments that were constructed alongside these watercourses when the Pevensey Levels were reclaimed: sometimes the mounds were left inside the embankments, other times outside, and occasionally they were actually incorporated into the flood defence.

During the twelfth and thirteenth centuries extensive areas were embanked and drained and it is to this period that the basic framework of the present landscape belongs. The process of reclamation appears to have been as follows: each of the rivers that flow off the adjacent uplands became constrained by embankments which may have resulted from one of two processes. First, they may have been deliberately embanked all the way from the fen-edge to the coast (i.e. the rivers were the focus of attention) or, more probably, individual areas of marsh between them were enclosed in a piecemeal fashion which eventually had the cumulative result that each stream was confined to an embanked channel. These rivers were still tidal a considerable distance inland, illustrated by an early thirteenth century reference to the Waterlot Stream (*Fletum de Hooe*) in

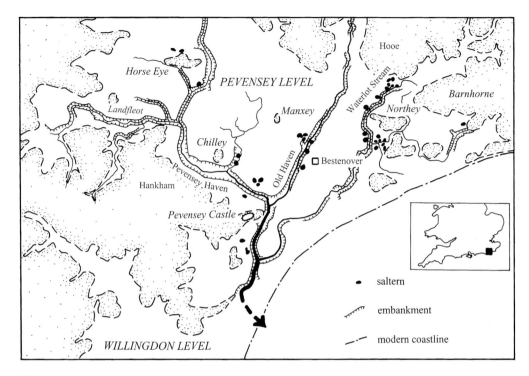

65. Pevensey Levels: the embanked tidal rivers, and mounds of saltern debris (after Dulley 1966, fig. 2; and air photographs in the National Monuments Record).

Hooe, upon the banks of which there were several saltworks (Figure 65; Brandon 1971*b*: 78–9; Dulley 1966: 28–9).

The rivers and streams that crossed the Pevensey Levels were relatively insubstantial and, on other coastal wetlands, such minor watercourses would simply have discharged their water via sluices under a substantial sea wall that ran all along the coast. The lack of such a continuous embankment until the late thirteenth century, when a sluice was constructed across Pevensey Haven (*CPR* 1281–92: 404), could not have been due to any technical difficulty: the coastal frontage, between the peninsula at Pevensey Castle and the cluster of bedrock islands south-west of Barnhorne, is very short relative to the area of marshland behind it. Rather, it appears to be yet another indication of the piecemeal approach to reclaiming the Pevensey Levels, with the various landowners unwilling or unable to co-operate in constructing a single flood defence along the coast. Thus, by the mid-thirteenth century, although the maintenance of flood defences was a communal responsibility, as laid down in the Pevensey Custumal (Larking 1851), much of the work was still carried out by private agreement. For example, in AD 1248 the Abbot of Battle granted part of his marshland at Barnhorne to his neighbour, William de Northeye, in return for the right to cut a drain through William's demesne, which lay between Barnhorne and the sea, in order to aid the drainage of the Abbot's land (Dulley 1966: 31).

One reason for this piecemeal approach towards reclamation may have been the highly fragmented nature of landholding on and around the Levels. Though a number of major ecclesiastical houses such as Battle, Lewes, and Michelham held extensive estates, so did many local families (Hudson 1892: 161). Due to a lack of documentation relatively little is known about these non-monastic estates, though by the thirteenth century holdings on the Levels were certainly much sought after and an active land market had developed (Searle 1974: 65–6, 130–1). Unlike the Welsh marcher lords who controlled much of the Gwent Levels, or Glastonbury Abbey which held large parts of the Somerset Levels, there was, therefore, no dominant landholder at Pevensey.

Following the reclamation of the Pevensey Levels, a number of settlements were established on the small islands of bedrock that protruded through the marshes such as Northey (Bloe *et al.* 1937: 119; Burleigh 1973: 72; Holden 1962*a*; 1965; E. Turner 1867), Manxey (Holden 1962*b*; Hudson 1892; Mawer and Stenton 1969: 444), and Hydneye (Turner 1867). In addition to these small island hamlets, there are a two moated enclosures at Bestenover (Figure 66; Dulley 1966: 31; Mawer and Stenton 1969: 444) and Kentland Fleet, though both are more likely to be stock enclosures as opposed to settlements. In AD 1471 Mankseye is described as a parish, and there was also a medieval chapel at Northeye, both of which have now disappeared along with their associated settlements (E. Turner 1867: 4). However, while this suggests that there has been a certain amount of late or post-medieval depopulation, overall, it is the relative absence of medieval settlement on what was a substantial area of embanked marshland that is striking. This probably reflects the fact that large areas of the Levels were used as summer grazing by estates based elsewhere.

The best documented estates are those of Battle Abbey, notably its manor of Barnhorne, whose abundant records have received considerable scholarly attention (Brandon 1971*a*; *b*; 1972; A. Evans 1941; 1942; Scargill-Bird 1887; Searle 1974; 1980; Searle and Ross 1967; Swift 1937). Barnhorne occupies a peninsula of dryland protruding into the eastern part of the Pevensey Levels in the parishes of Bexhill and Hooe (Figure 65). Land there was included in the Abbey's foundation grants (*DB Sussex* 8:12), and the estate was greatly extended during the early twelfth century when Abbot Ralph (AD 1107–24) purchased further land there (Brandon 1971*b*: 70; Searle 1980: 211). The Abbey was subsequently given part of 'St Martin's Marsh' adjoining Ralph's acquisitions, where much effort was expended on reclamation and buildings, including the construction of a mill (Searle 1980: 119, 211).

These acquisitions formed part of a coherent policy pursued by the early abbots to make good deficiencies in their original endowments (Searle 1974: 40–1, 144). In the early twelfth century the monks had very little good arable land close to the abbey, while the coastal location of Barnhorne was also ideal for the creation of meadow. Even into the thirteenth century, Battle was still acquiring and reclaiming land on the Levels, as in the mid-thirteenth century when the abbey was granted a wall and ditch 'together with whatever can be acquired from the sea adjacent' (Brandon 1971*b*: 78; Searle 1974: 161–2). Battle Abbey's investment in its marshland holdings may even have prompted the estate centre, or *curia*, to shift westwards from its earlier site at 'Oldeton' to its present location at Barnhorne Manor Farm (Brandon 1971*b*: 70). The uses to which these estates were put are discussed in Chapter 10.

66. Bestenover moated enclosure, possibly for livestock (marked out as a vegetation mark) on the Pevensey Levels (NGR: TQ 661 060, looking south-west).

There is little in the physical landscape to distinguish the reclamation undertaken by Battle Abbey, and the Pevensey Levels as a whole have a highly irregular landscape indicative of gradual and piecemeal reclamation. The one exception is around Bestenover which appears to have been inned during the thirteenth century, and has a more regular arrangement of ditches (Salzman 1910: 40–1).

9.4 **Romney Marsh**

As described in Chapter 8, Romney Marsh was a divided landscape by the eleventh century. To the north-east, Romney Marsh proper appears to have been protected from tidal flooding by a sea wall running along the line of the Yoke Sewer, while Walland Marsh to the south-west remained a tidally inundated saltmarsh (Figure 67B). A number of early medieval charters, along with Domesday and several other eleventh century surveys, show Romney Marsh proper to have been extensively settled and cultivated, with a number of religious houses in Canterbury being the major landowners.[32] By the twelfth century, these pre-Conquest ecclesiastical institutions were joined by several post-Conquest foundations which also acquired extensive estates on the Marsh.[33] The

[32] The three Canterbury houses were Christ Church Priory (which had also acquired the lands of St Mary's in Lyminge), St Augustine's Priory, and the Archbishop. A late 13th century survey records that in Romney Marsh proper, the Archbishop owned 5,450 acres and Christ Church Priory 1,690 acres, out of a total of 17,300 acres (Brooks 1988: 90; Smith 1943: 172),. (and see Adams 1993; Gross and Butcher 1995; Sheppard 1876; 1877; 1881; 1883; Smith 1940; 1943; Turner and Salter 1915; Ward 1933c; Woodruff 1917).
[33] Battle Abbey was endowed with the North Kent manor Wye which included Denge Marsh and, from c. AD 1100, it started to acquire land in Broomhill (Muhlfeld 1933; Searle 1974: 40). Robertsbridge Abbey also held extensive

excellent archival material relating to these estates, along with the archives of the Cinque ports of Hythe,[34] Lydd,[35] Romney,[36] Rye,[37] and Winchelsea,[38] make Romney Marsh one of the better documented areas of coastal marsh in Britain.

9.4.1 Diversion of the 'proto-Rother'

Just as it was probably the diversion of the 'proto-Rother' from its original outfall at Hythe to a newly-formed inlet at Romney that encouraged the colonization of Romney Marsh proper (see Chapter 8), it may have been the diversion of this river even further south, to a new tidal inlet at Winchelsea, which left Walland Marsh relatively flood-free and available for reclamation (Figure 67C, D). Traditionally the diversion of this river has been attributed to the storms of the mid-thirteenth century. For example, Camden states that:

> It [New Winchelsea] is seated on a high hill of gravel and sand, and on the west side has a pretty large haven, that was guarded against most winds before the sea withdrew itself. But in the reign of Edward I, AD 1287: when the sea, driven forward by the violence of the winds, overflowed this tract, and for a great way together destroyed men, cattle, and houses, threw down Promhill [Broomhill], a little populous village, and removed the Rother (which formerly emptied itself into the sea here) out of its channel, stopping up its mouth, and opening for it a nearer passage into the sea by Rhie [Rye]; then it began by little and little to forsake this town, which has decayed by degrees ever since, and has lost much of its populousness and dignity. (Camden 1637: 350–1)

Camden appears, however, to be incorrect in assuming that the Rother was diverted as late as the mid-thirteenth century. Geomorphological studies indicate that the shingle barrier was breached near Old Winchelsea c. 700–1,000 years ago (Long and Hughes 1995). In AD 1258 tidal waters are recorded as flowing from Winchelsea up to Appledore (W. Robertson 1880b: 264), while during the early thirteenth century there is reference to 'the great fleet which goes towards Rye' (M. Gardiner 1988: 112). The old course of the 'proto-Rother' past Old Romney was certainly abandoned before the thirteenth century because the estate of Agney, which occupies the line of the palaeochannel, was reclaimed by c. AD 1225 (Figure 67D; Tatton-Brown 1988: 105). Eddison (1998: fig. 5.10, 68) argues for a late twelfth or thirteenth century date for the creation of the Winchelsea inlet, based on documentary evidence for reclamation on Walland Marsh which, it is argued, cannot have taken place *without* the protection of a

lands in Broomhill, along with 'Woderove', west of Snargate (Gardiner 1988; Vollans 1988: table 11.2). Bilsington Priory held land in Brenzett, Brookland, Lydd, Newchurch, Snargate, and Snave (Neilson 1928: 56; Stringer 1880: 250), while Horton Priory held land in Eastbridge (Scott 1876).

[34] Riley 1874b.
[35] Riley 1876b.
[36] Riley 1874c; 1876c; Robertson 1880a; c; Tatton-Brown 1987; Walker 1880.
[37] Dell 1962; 1965/6; Page 1937a; Riley 1876a.
[38] Dell 1963; Gardiner 1995; Homan 1949; Lovegrove 1994; Page 1937b.

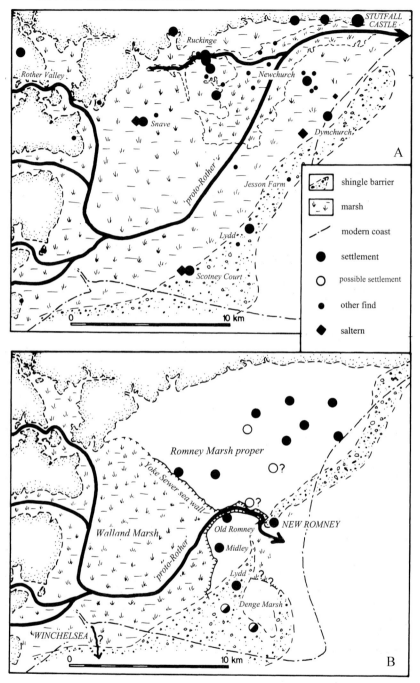

67. The evolution of Romney Marsh. A, Romano-British (1st to 2nd century AD), including original course of the 'proto-Rother' via an estuary south of Hythe; B, *c.* 11th century AD, following the diversion of the 'proto-Rother' to a new outfall at Romney, and the construction of the Yoke Sewer sea wall; C, 12th century innings, rooted on the Yoke Sewer sea wall, in Walland Marsh; D, The 13th century Rhee Wall, and further inning in vicinity of Agney and Old Cheyne Court on the line of the old course of the 'proto-Rother' (the Wainway Channel).

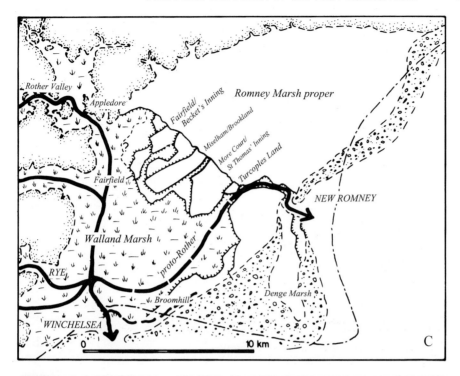

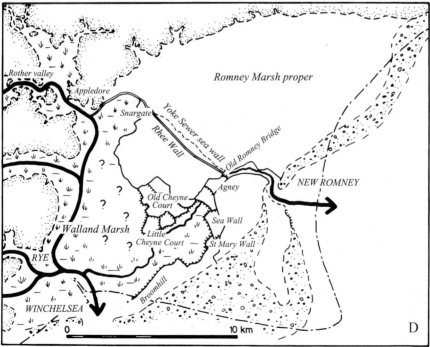

67. (*Continued*)

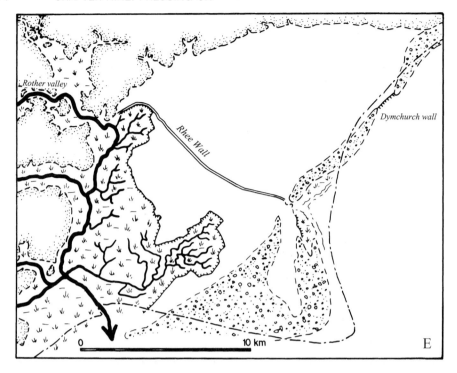

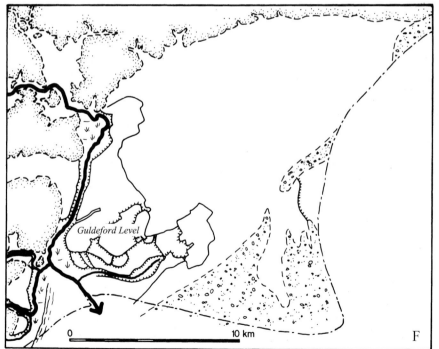

67. (*Continued*)

coastal barrier. However, it is argued here that it was in fact the *breaching* of this barrier, and the resulting diversion of the 'proto-Rother', that made reclamation possible. The history of the port towns of Rye and Winchelsea suggests this happened around the eleventh century. Though not among the original Cinque Ports, they were added to the federation by Henry II (AD 1154–89) (Tatton-Brown 1988: 106) and, to have functioned, there must already have been a tidal inlet/harbour. Despite its omission in Domesday, Winchelsea is first documented in AD 1040–2 when a charter of AD 1028–35 was confirmed, granting the Abbey of Fécamp 'two parts of the tolls of the port which is called Wincenesel'. Eddison (1998: 68) dismisses this as a forgery but, although the original charter is dubious, the confirmation of AD 1040–2 is regarded as authentic (Sawyer 1968: no. 982). It would appear, therefore, that a new breach had occurred in the shingle barrier by the mid-eleventh century, and that this eventually captured the 'proto-Rother', reducing the tidal flooding of Walland Marsh.

9.4.2 **The inning of Walland Marsh** (Figure 67)

Whereas the basic framework of Romney Marsh proper dates to the early medieval period, the landscape in the eastern part of Walland Marsh owes its origins to twelfth and thirteenth century reclamation, with a series of innings that are still enclosed by impressive embankments. Once the larger part of Walland Marsh had been deserted by the 'proto-Rother', reclamation proceeded at quite a pace, starting with a sequence of innings that, since the work of Elliott (in Lewin 1862), have been attributed to Archbishops Becket (AD 1162–70), Baldwin (AD 1184–90), Peckham (*c.* AD 1229), and Boniface (AD 1240–70). This traditional view has, however, been challenged on a number of grounds (Eddison 1983*a*; Tatton-Brown 1988) and the close integration of documentary evidence with the patterns of soils, field boundaries, and sea walls (Figures 55–7) is used here to suggest a new sequence for the reclamation of Walland Marsh. Up to three distinct stages can be identified (Figure 67C, D; cf. Allen 1996*a* and Eddison and Draper (1997) suggest slightly different sequences):

- first, a series of individual intakes of marshland each rooted in the Yoke Sewer sea wall (not the Rhee Wall as Edison and Draper (1997) and Tatton-Brown (1988) have claimed)
- second, the enclosure of these individual reclamations by a new sea wall
- and third, further innings seaward of this sea wall

One of the earliest reclamations rooted on the Yoke Sewer sea wall was an area just across the 'proto-Rother' from Old Romney called 'Turcolpule's Land' (Figure 67C). It was included in the original endowment of the Leper Hospital in New Romney, confirmed in *c.* AD 1186–90 and by Papal Bull in AD 1211 when it was described as '80 acres called *terra Turcopule*' (Tatton-Brown 1988: 106). In fact, this reclamation must have occurred before AD 1154–89 since it stratigraphically pre-dates St Thomas' Inning to the north-west, a large lobe-shaped reclamation also extending from Yoke Sewer within which lay More Court that existed by the time of Henry II (AD 1154–89) (Figure 67C; Tatton-Brown 1988: 106).

North-west of St Thomas' Inning, in Brookland parish, lies a large sub-rectangular reclamation once again rooted on Yoke Sewer, but which was created independently of St Thomas' Inning. This area was known as 'Baldwin's Inning' due to its association with a tenant, Baldwin Scadeway, not Archbishop Baldwin (Elliott in Lewin 1862: cxi). In AD 1155–67: Christ Church Canterbury granted Baldwin Scadeway and his heirs all their land of Misleham which lay in the marsh, in so far as Baldwin could enclose it against the sea at his own expense. Scadeway held the land free of service for two years, and thereafter paid 4 pence per acre. Subsequent grants and agreements by Christ Church were subject to their tenants agreeing to maintain the sea walls, and by *c*. AD 1200 'Baldwin's Inning' was divided into small parcels of *c*. 35 acres farmed by 'the men of Misleham' (Eddison and Draper 1997: 82–3; Neilson 1928: 45, 54; Tatton-Brown 1988: 106–7). Even though the area was originally called Misleham, and a farm of this name lies at the centre of the inning, most settlement became nucleated around the church some distance away which became known as 'Broke' [Brook] (Wallenberg 1934: 477), and later 'Brookland' (Eddison and Draper 1997: 84). Mills (1991: 55) suggests that the name means 'cultivated land by the Brook', though it is more likely to mean 'new land'.

North-west of Baldwin's Inning in Brookland lay the parish of Fairfield. 'New land' is recorded at Fairfield during the twelfth century (Eddison and Draper 1997: 85), and this lobe-shaped intake from Walland Marsh, once again rooted on the Yoke Sewer sea wall, became known as 'Becket's Inning', a name probably derived from church dedication to St Thomas Becket rather than this inning being the work of that Archbishop (cf. Furley 1874; 1880: 189). The area between Becket's Inning in Fairfield and Baldwin's Inning in Brookland was left open, being occupied by a creek (shown on Green's (1968) soil map).

All these early intakes rooted on the Yoke Sewer were completed independently of each other, though a subsequent sea wall was then constructed in order to enclose all the early reclamations and the channels between them (Figure 67C). There were subsequently further reclamations to the south and west of St. Thomas' Inning, including the old channel of the 'proto-Rother' which became a long narrow strip of Old Romney parish (splitting Midley in two) that eventually extended down the abandoned river channel for *c*. 4 km (Figures 57 and 67D). The earliest apart of the channel to be reclaimed, the estate of Agney, certainly existed by AD 1225 when livestock and a plough team is recorded as having been taken there (Tatton-Brown 1988: 105). On the basis of their decalcified or slightly decalcified soils, several other reclamations can be identified as pre-dating the great floods of the late thirteenth century. These included a second parcel of the old river channel to the south of Agney called 'Great Brack', but which was traditionally known as 'Archbishop Peckham's Inning' (Tatton-Brown 1988: 105). As Peckham held office between AD 1279 and 1292, he may have been responsible for the restoration of the sea wall following the flood of AD 1287 (hence the name 'Great Brack' = breach), rather than the area's initial embankment. Other possible reclamations pre-dating the floods include the areas enclosed by 'Sea Wall' and 'St Mary Wall' to the south of, and secondary to, 'Peckham's Inning' (M. Gardiner 1988: fig 10.2), and the area of Old and Little Cheyne Courts (cf. Tatton-Brown 1988: fig 9.1).

68. The Rhee Wall at Mock Mill, Walland Marsh (NGR TQ 981 294), looking east.

The line of sea walls that marked the edge of these innings represents the division between older decalcified soils to the east and younger calcified soils to the west, indicating that these embankments marked the limit of the extensive late thirteenth century floods described by Camden. It is not known if there were any further twelfth/thirteenth century reclamations that have been totally buried under the later alluvium, though one such area may lie to the north west of Fairfield in Snargate. When Robertsbridge Abbey was founded in AD 1176 they were given 700 acres of land in Snargate, which Christ Church later claimed was part of their manor at Appledore. The dispute was resolved by Robertsbridge getting 100 acres 'lying next to the bank of the Abbot and Convent [of Robertsbridge] near the land of Adam of Caring' (Tatton-Brown 1988: 106), and this area is now covered with calcified soils.

9.4.3 **The Rhee Wall** (Figures 67D, E and 68)

Walland Marsh supports a major feat of medieval water engineering—the Rhee Wall— which represents a classic example of human response to environmental change. The Rhee Wall comprises two earthen banks *c.* 50 m apart, either side of a watercourse some 6 miles long, running between Appledore and Romney. It was not a sea wall, but was designed to carry freshwater from the Rother Valley, across Walland Marsh, in order to flush out the ailing tidal inlet at Romney.

It is clearly not a simple single-phase structure. Based on its plan it can be divided into three sections (Vollans 1988: 128): the first between Appledore and Snargate; the second between Snargate and Old Romney Bridge, where it cuts through the 'Archbishop's Innings'; and the third from Old Romney Bridge to New Romney where it changes direction and cuts across the line of the old 'proto-Rother' from where it proceeds to the tidal inlet at New Romney. The earliest unequivocal reference to the Rhee Wall (though not named as such) is in AD 1258, when the king commanded Nicholas de Hadlo to 'bring the river [Newenden] back to the port [of New Romney]'; this important document is worth quoting in full:

> As the king has understood that the port of Romenal is perishing, to the detriment of the town of Romenal, unless the course of the river Newenden, upon which the said port was founded, and which has been diverted by an inundation of the sea, be brought back to the said port, and now hears by inquisition made by N. de Haudlo whom he sent to those parts to provide measures for bringing the river back to the port by the old course or by another, that the river cannot be brought back or the port saved unless the obstructions in the old course be removed, and a new course made through the lands of certain men of those parts, near the old course, to wit, from a cross of the hospital of infirm persons* of Romenal which stands near Aghenepend as far as Effeton, and from Effeton to the house of William le Wyll, and so to Melepend and from Melepend down to the said port; so that a sluice be made below Apeltre [Appledore] to receive the salt water entering by inundation of the sea from the parts of Winchelse, and retain it in the ebb of the sea, that such water with the water of the river may come together by the ancient course to the new course, and so by that course fall directly into the said port; and so that a second sluice be made at Sneregate [Snargate], and a third by the port where the said water can fall into the sea, to retain merely the water of the seas inundation on that side that it enter not the said course; reserving nevertheless the ancient and oblique course from the said cross to the port. (*CPR* 1247–58: 635–6)

The Rhee Wall appears to have developed as follows (Figure 67D, E). Upland waters from the Rother Valley originally flowed via the 'proto-Rother' along the Wainway channel, past Old Romney, to a tidal inlet at New Romney; this was the 'river of Newenden' of the AD 1258 account. This channel started to silt up (as, presumably, part of the discharge from the Rother Valley was now flowing through a new tidal outfall at Rye/Winchelsea), and so the first two stretches of the Rhee Wall were constructed in order to take some of the upland waters across the now partly reclaimed Walland Marsh in order to flush out the tidal inlet at Old Romney Bridge. This reclamation had begun by AD 1155–67: giving a *terminus post quem* of the mid-twelfth century for the Rhee Wall's construction. Subsequently, the channel between Old and New Romney also silted up, and in order to maintain the haven at New Romney, the Rhee Wall was extended eastwards in AD 1258. However, it was not a success and by AD 1337 the channel had silted up (Homan 1938: 204, 219).

* One of the lands through which the middle stretch of the Rhee Wall passed was *terra Turcopule* which was owned by the Hospital in New Romney, and so may have been the location of this cross (Tatton-Brown 1988: 106).

9.4.4 **Reclamations in the south of Walland Marsh**

In addition to the 'Archbishop's Innings', there was a second area of reclamation in Walland Marsh, at Broomhill (Figure 67C). The history of drainage in this area, to the south of the 'proto-Rother' and east of the tidal inlet at Old Winchelsea, has been reviewed by Gardiner (1988). Reclamation appears to have started in the twelfth century, and a church was established at Broomhill by AD 1200 (or possibly AD 1129–39: Gardiner 1988: 119; 1989; Salzman 1937: 150). The earliest phase of reclamation appears to have been undertaken by wealthy entrepreneurial landowners and tenants, followed by a period of considerable monastic involvement, notably Battle and Robertsbridge Abbeys. However, their grants and purchases soon led to disputes with the local 'men of Broomhill' such as in AD 1201–4 when the two abbots came to an agreement over 500 acres of disputed land only for the men of Broomhill to claim rights there (Salzman 1937: 148–9). The issue of who took responsibility for reclamation in Broomhill is discussed further in Chapter 11.

9.5 **The East Kent marshes**

The East Kent marshes appear to have seen a major period of embanking in the twelfth and thirteenth centuries following the expansion of sand and shingle coastal barriers and resulting silting of the Wantsum Channel (Hearne *et al.* 1995: 243, 268). St Augustine's Abbey had a major interest in the area, holding the manor of Northbourne near Deal and the marshes west of Thanet, which they were actively inning in the AD 1270s (Dowker 1990: 115; Neilson 1928: 51). Christ Church Priory, Canterbury, also owned 405 acres of embanked marshland, mostly retained as demesne and used for pastoralism. There was considerable expenditure during the late thirteenth/early fourteenth century on the construction and repair of embankments and drainage ditches, amounting to 13.9 per cent of annual manorial income (R.A.L. Smith 1940: 36; 1943: 184–5).

9.6 **North Kent: the southern Thames-side marshes**

Though the traditional view that most reclamation on the North Kent marshes started in the twelfth and thirteenth centuries can be questioned (see Chapter 8), there was certainly some activity during the high medieval period. The pre-Conquest ecclesiastical landlords continued to expand their estates through purchases, exchanges, and leases, and eventually Christ Church Priory came to dominate the Cliffe Marshes, St Augustine's the marshes at Plumstead, and St Andrews (Rochester) on the Isle of Grain. These were joined by a series of new foundations both in Kent[39] and further afield,[40] leading to the church dominating this landscape as it did in Romney Marsh.

[39] Boxley Abbey at Little Hoo, Allhallows, High Halstow, and Burntwick Island; Lesnes Abbey in Erith; Lillechurch Nunnery in Higham; and the College of All Saints Maidstone, which owned a house in their marsh at Hoo (Bowler 1968: 121; Evans 1953: 141).

[40] Holy Trinity (Norwich) at Chalk; Holy Trinity (Aldgate, London) at Erith; Bermondsey Abbey (London) at Chalk; Reading Abbey at St Marys; and the Bishop of Bath and Wells at Greenwich (Bowler 1968: 130, 140, 146; Evans 1953: 141).

However, although the documentary record is certainly biased in favour of these ecclesiastical landlords, it is evident that certain lay families also built up extensive marshland estates during the thirteenth century, such as the Cobham family around the southern shores of the Medway Estuary (J. H. Evans 1953: 141).

From the twelfth century there are numerous documentary references to 'embanking', though this could represent one of three processes: the initial inning of a saltmarsh, the extension of an earlier sea wall to enclose further areas of saltmarsh, or improvements to existing sea walls. In practice all three processes appear to have been going on. Work is particularly well documented for the estates of Canterbury Cathedral Priory at Barksore (near Lower Halstow), Cliffe (near Gravesend), Seasalter (near Whitstable), and Monkton (on Thanet) during the late thirteenth/early fourteenth century (J. H. Evans 1953: 140; R. A. L. Smith 1940; 1943: 185–8). The works described are usually the maintenance, repairs, and upgrading of existing embankments, though there does appear to have been some increase in the reclaimed area. There were marked differences in the degree to which the Priory directly managed its estates, and the use to which they were put. At Cliffe, a considerable effort in labour and resources was also expended by the Priory on embanking, but as soon as the land was reclaimed it was leased to tenants (R. A. L. Smith 1943: 117–8, 188). By contrast, at Monkton, most of the marshland remained as part of the demesne, and in AD 1302 just 53.5 out of 366 acres were leased to tenants (R. A. L. Smith 1943: 185). In the early fourteenth century the area of embanked marshland increased from 257.5 to 366 acres, and was used for cattle and sheep grazing. The amount of arable cultivation actually declined, as 'the rich grazing value of the Isle of Thanet and the high profits to be drawn from such a practice were fully realised' (R. A. L. Smith 1943: 187).

After the AD 1230s most references to work undertaken on the North Kent marshes are concerned with maintaining existing sea defences, though occasionally new areas were enclosed, such as in AD 1325 when some 700 acres of marshland in Boughton, Hernhill, Graveney, and Seasalter (between Faversham and Whitstable), previously used for salt production, were embanked for the first time (M. Thompson 1956: 47).

The relatively narrow strips of wetland that fringed the estuaries of North Kent could easily be exploited by fen-edge communities, which explains the almost total absence of medieval settlement on the North Kent marshes. However, a number of 'wick' place-names are recorded as early as AD 823 (J. H. Evans 1953: 145), and which presumably represent dairies and shepherds huts. Occasionally, the raised mounds of former Romano-British salt productions sites have yielded medieval material and may have been used for this purpose.[41] The local dialect for these raised mounds used as refuges for sheep at times of flooding was 'coterells' (M. Thompson 1956: 44), though the term 'sheep cote' was also used (Hasted 1797–1801: vol. IV, 256; vol. VI, 215).

---

[41] Burnt Wick, Milfordhope, and Slayhills on the Upchurch Marshes (Harrison 1949: xlv; Hume 1954: 78; Payne 1905); Black Shore near Cliffe (Anon 1966); and Wallend Farm on the Isle of Grain (Harrison 1949).

9.7 **The Essex marshes**

As in Kent, many of the Essex marshes were moderate in extent and were often utilized from fen-edge settlements. There were, however, a number of more extensive areas including Canvey and Foulness Islands, that could, based on their size, have supported wholly marshland communities. However, different communities in Essex made very different decisions with regard to how they utilized their coastal marshes, with certain areas being embanked and cultivated, other marshes being embanked but only used as pasture, and certain extensive tracts of marshland being left unreclaimed.

9.7.1 **Medieval reclamation around the Essex coast**

The Island of Foulness is the best documented of the major Essex marshes (Table 6). A large part of the island was certainly reclaimed by the early thirteenth century, since the manor of Foulness is recorded from AD 1235. Sea walls are mentioned in AD 1270–1 and references thereafter often distinguish 'carucates of land', presumably drained arable, and marsh. By AD 1385 a chapel had been established but it had 'little endowment, and the Chaplain made little or no residence there' (J. Smith 1970: 23; see Gramolt 1960 for the later period).

It is clear from Table 6 that the term 'marsh' on its own could refer to both saltmarshes and reclaimed land, which is rather unfortunate as so many references to coastal wetlands in Essex are simply to 'marsh', without specifying its condition (for example, '1 messuage, 1 garden, 60 acres of land, 6 acres of meadow, 100 acres of pasture, 20 acres of wood, and 300 acres of marsh' in Goldhanger: *FF Essex IV*, 272). Since the 'marsh' is distinguished from 'land', 'meadow', and 'pasture', it was clearly something different, but this could have been an open saltmarsh or a freshwater grazing in an area with rudimentary flood defence. The practice of distinguishing 'saltmarsh' and 'freshwater marsh' only appears to have become common practice during the sixteenth century.

However, if the cultivation of crops or the production of hay can be taken as an indication of at least rudimentary flood protection, then many Essex marshes had been embanked to a certain extent, particularly alongside the Thames. For example, in AD 1135 the foundation grant of Stratford Langthorne Abbey included 11 acres of meadow at West Ham (R. Fowler 1907: 129) and, in AD 1198–9, 82 acres of land in Hamme included 1 acre in 'Fardensmede', 6 acres in 'Wicmede', 5 acres in 'Riedmede', and 4 acres in 'Fardensmede' (*FF Essex I*, 16). In AD 1202–3 half a virgate in West Ham was described as lying in 'Brademade, Sagodesmade and Monemade to the north of la Wic' (*FF Essex I*, 27). By the early fourteenth century, large areas of former saltmarsh in East and West Ham appear to have been embanked, and certain areas at least were cultivated: for example, in AD 1421 reference is made to 101 acres of arable land, which was part of a 145 acre marsh (*CPR 1416–22*: 374). 'Wheatcroft' and 'Wheatfield' are recorded in Trinity Marsh (Powell 1973*b*: 75).

Attempts were also made to cultivate marshes in Aveley, Barking, Rainham, and

Table 6. The marshlands of Foulness Island, Essex

Date	Reference
c. AD 1190	Earliest reference to Foulness ['Fulenesse'] (Reaney 1935: 183)
AD 1198	Marsh of 'Borewerde' [Burmarsh] (Reaney 1935, 183)
AD 1218/19	'a marsh called Barnflete in the marsh called Fuelnesse' (*FF Essex* I: 51)
AD 1235	Reference to the manor of Foulness (*CPR* 1232-49: 101)
AD 1247	Marsh called 'Great Rugeward' in Foulness held by Thomas de Plumberrow as part of his manors of Plumberow and Sutton Hall [in Hawkwell] (Morant 1763/8: 288)
AD 1270/71	'two carucates of land . . . with appurts, sands, issues, marshes, as well within walls as without' (*FF Essex* I: 275)
AD 1274	168 acres of arable and 120 acres of marsh in Foulness (Morant 1763/8: 269)
AD 1279/80	60 acres of land and 90 acres of marsh in little Burgherthe [Little Burwood] (*FF Essex* II: 26)
AD 1304	The holdings of manor of Rochford in the 'marsh of Foulnesse' included 'Estwodewik' (*CIPM* V: 99)
AD 1309	The holdings of manor of Rochford in the 'marsh of Foulnesse' included 'Eastwood-wick' (Morant 1763/8: 269)
AD 1313/14	'a messuage and one carucate of land in Middelwyk in Fulnesse' (*FF Essex* II: 153)
AD 1324	a survey describes 'all the marshes in Fughelnes', which included 'Thurkellesmerse', 'Estwodemerse', 'Pertrichesmerse', 'Gorgotes', 'le Spert', and 'all other marshes within and without the walls' (*CChR* 1300-26: 461)
AD 1362	Manors of Rochford, Foulness, and Middlewyk, and 'marsh of Bernemerssh' (*CIPM* X: 526)
AD 1385	2 messuages, 2 carucates of land, 6 acres of meadow, 300 acres of pasture, 100 acres of marsh . . . in the island of Foulness . . . and the advowson of the . . . chapel of Foulness' (*FF Essex* III: 203)
AD 1407	A chantry was established in the chapel and endowed with 'a rood of land on which the chapel is situated, an acre of land for [the chaplain's] mansion . . . and a messuage and certain land called Litelbourewerde containing 80 acres of fresh land and 160 acres of saltmarsh' (*CPR* 1405-8: 386)
AD 1517	Lovetotes in Great Wakering held 600 acres of marsh called Small Gore and Temple-Gore in Foulness (Morant 1763/8: 306)
AD 1534	Reference to manor of Shelford (*FF Essex* IV: 194)
AD 1540	Reference to 'Southwyke, Estwyke, Ormondeswyke, Newyke, Ormondeswyke alias Ormonswyk, Arundelys Mershe alias Arundellys Mershe, Monkbarne alias Monkenbarne, Rugworthe, and Naswyke' on Foulness (*FF Essex* IV: 234)

Sutton (Grieve 1959: 10–11; Oxley 1966: 25; Powell and Knight 1983*a*: 10; Ransome 1978: 134; J. Ward 1987: 103). In AD 1321 the accounts for Dagenham and Westbury include 'For whetting the shares of 3 ploughs while they were ploughing in the marsh at the time of the sowing of corn, of beans, of winter barley, and of oats,' along with the general maintenance of the sea walls, the mending of a breach, and 40 perches of new wall (Grieve 1959: 11). Work on reclaiming the marshes in Wennington had begun by AD 1198–9 when there is reference to '1 carucate of land with appurts in the marsh of Weninton . . . to wit in Newland 19 acres, in Anns Feld 10 acres and in the two fields next to the house 18 acres' (*FF Essex I*, 16). In the same year, there is reference to 1½ acres of meadow bounded to the south by a wall (*FF Essex I*, 17) while, in AD 1201–2, 10 acres of land are described as lying in 'the fresh Marsh called "the Falge" next to the Wall' (*FF Essex I*, 24). In AD 1210–11 there was a dispute over reclamation in Rainham marshes mentioning 'walls, gutters and ditches' (*FF Essex I*, 45). In AD 1201 the Abbot of Stratford was in dispute over a dyke in Little Thurrock that had been damaged (Grieve 1959: 6) while in AD 1228–9 Simon de Fenbrugge held 40 acres of marsh in 'Fenbrugg' (Fambridge) including 'the mill in the same marsh, with the road, pond, walls and all easements' (*FF Essex I*, 84).

In AD 1280 the first Commission *de Wallis et Fossatis* was appointed to Essex with the job of ensuring that banks and ditches on the Abbey of Stratford's marshes at West Ham were maintained, after the Abbot complained that his lands were in danger of inundation as his neighbours had neglected to maintain their flood defences (*CPR 1272–81*: 380). By the early fourteenth century the Commissions had been extended to all the Thames-side and coastal marshes as far north as the Blackwater, implying the fairly widespread presence of flood defences (Grieve 1959: 10).

9.7.2 **The unreclaimed Essex marshes**

Though many of the Essex marshes appear to have been embanked, certain areas were not. For example, in AD 1473 the manor of Paglesham included 200 acres of arable land, 100 acres of pasture, and 100 acres of saltmarsh beside the Roach Estuary west of Foulness (Morant 1763–8: 311). In AD 1570 the manors of Great and Little Wakering included 1,000 acres of arable along with 100 acres of meadow, 1,000 acres of pasture, 3,000 acres of fresh marsh, and 2,000 acres of saltmarsh in the same area (Morant 1763–8: 307). The fourteenth century bailiffs accounts for Langenhoe, beside the Colne Estuary south of Colchester, record the expenditure on bridges, hurdles, and raised causeways that were constructed in the saltmarshes to allow sheep to escape at times of exceptionally high tide (Grieve 1959: 5–6; J. Smith 1970: 25). Possible examples of such trackways have been recorded at The Stumble in the Blackwater Estuary, and Alresford Creek (Wilkinson and Murphy 1995: 203–5).

One of the reasons why extensive tracts of saltmarsh were left unreclaimed is that they were so highly prized for their excellent sheep pasture which produced famous cheeses. For example, in the late sixteenth century Norden (1594) described how:

> The hundreds of Rocheforde [and] Denge (see Figure 70) ... which lie on the sowthe-easte parte of the shire, yelde milke, butter, and cheese in admirable abundance: and in those partes are the great and huge cheeses made, wondred at for their massiuenes and thicknes.

The most extensive area of unreclaimed saltmarsh, at least in the sixteenth century, was Canvey Island (Figure 69). Not recorded in Domesday, by the eleventh century it appears to have been divided between numerous adjacent dryland manors who held 'pasture for sheep' there (Round 1903: 368–73) and, by the post-medieval period many parishes, scattered throughout South East Essex, had detached portions on the Island (Figure 69). Extensive areas of marshland further east around Wallasea Island was similarly 'enclosed'. In AD 1594 Norden described how Canvey was then a series of islands and 'low merishe grounds; and for that the passage over the creeks is unfitt for cattle, it is onlie conuerted to the feeding of ewes, which men milke, and therof make cheese (suche as it is), and of the curdes of the whey they make butter' (Norden 1594: 10). In the seventeenth century, Camden described how:

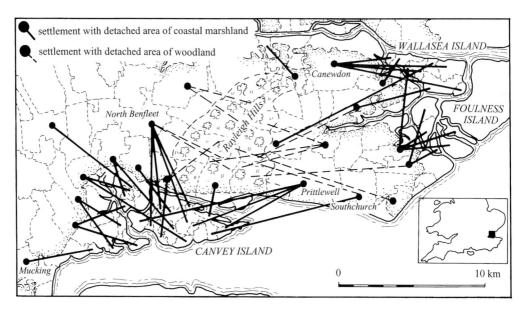

69. Detached parochial parcels and enclaved woodland in South East Essex (after Rackham 1986*b*: fig. 14; Round 1903; Jerram-Burrows 1980).

> [Canvey is] . . . so low lying that often-times it is quite overflowne, all save hillocks cast up, upon which the sheepe have a place of safe refuge. For it keepeth about foure thousand sheepe, whose flesh is most sweet and delicate taste, which I have seene young lads taking women's function, with stooles fastened to their buttockes to milke, yea and to make cheeses of ewe's milk in those dairy sheddes of theirs that they call there "wickes". (Camden 1637: 441).

Curiously, there is no evidence for medieval salt production on Canvey.

9.7.3 Settlement on the Essex marshes

The extent of medieval settlement on the Essex marshes is very difficult to establish, though not surprisingly much of it appears to relate to sheep farming. There are two potentially settlement-indicative place-name elements commonly associated with the Essex marshes: 'cote' and 'wick'. 'Wicks' appear to have been dairies, cheese making sheds, and shepherds huts, and occur in considerable numbers particularly in the south east of the county (e.g. Table 7; Figure 70; see Camden above; Cracknell 1959: 11–14). They often lay on slightly raised areas, including early Roman salt works, a number of which are surrounded by later ditches;[42] one such ditch at Langenhoe has produced medieval material (Reader 1908: 169–71; 1910: 76). Other red hills have produced

---

[42] For example, Goldhanger, Langenhoe, Saltcott and Tollesbury Creek (Fawn *et al.* 1990: 33; Reader 1908: 169–71, 180; Wilkinson and Murphy 1995: 167).

assemblages of medieval pottery,[43] while at Leigh Beck, on Canvey, a medieval occupation deposit overlying a Late Iron Age and Romano-British red hill yielded a large animal bone assemblage dominated by sheep, with almost 50 per cent of the bones derived from lambs too young to have been butchered for meat. Faulkner (1993*b*: 19) suggests this may indicate the culling of new-born lambs to ensure an adequate supply of ewe's milk for the cheese industry. The association of 'wicks' with sheep farming is also illustrated by names such as 'Wetherwick' in Tillingham, while a link between wicks and cotts is suggested by 'Kitcott marsh alias Southchurchwick' on Canvey Island (Reaney 1935: 150, 230). Rarer examples indicate an association with cattle farming, illustrated by a handful of 'Rether(e)wyk' names (Reaney 1935: 594).

Other 'wicks' are prefixed with place-names reflecting the common practice of inland manors holding grazing rights of the coastal marshes. For example, Rochford held marshes called 'Nassewyk', 'Partricheswyk', and 'Tokhalle' on Foulness (*CIPM* II, 46). The holdings of Eastwood on Foulness are reflected in the names 'Estwodewik' (*CIPM* V, 99) and 'Estwodemerse' (*CChR 1300–26:* 461), while the manor of Barrow Hall in Eastwood held 'Alford Nashe Marsh' in Wallasea Island (Morant 1763–8: 283). Ringworth and Sherworth Marshes in Wallasea were held by the manors of Scottys and Pudsey in Canewdon (Morant 1763–8: 315–6). The bailiff of Writtle manor (in the very centre of Essex) accounted for 110 year-old lambs and 8 'multoni' (male sheep kept for wool, meat, and skins) sent to Foulness Island (Smith 1970: 11). Stratford Abbey (in West Ham) held detached dairies in Corringham ('Warrewyke'), Little Thurrock ('Grangewyke'), and Hadleigh ('Clerkynwyke') (Morant 1763–8: 18). In certain cases, individual marshes, or sheepwalks, assumed the names of the 'wicks', illustrated in AD 1222 by St Paul's Cathedral's marshes at Tillingham: 'In the marsh are four sheepwalks, of which one is called Howich and can carry 180 head of sheep, another is called Middelwich and can carry 130 head, the third is called Doddeswich and can carry 132 head, and the fourth is called Pirimers and can carry 110 head.' (Grieve 1959: 5).

The distribution of wick names on the Essex marshes shows marked patterning, with very few examples west of Corringham (Figure 70). In this respect it is interesting to note that field-names indicative of meadow such as 'mead' and 'ham' are more common west of Corringham.

'Cote' appears to have had two meanings in the context of coastal marshes: as a dairy/raised refuge for sheep, and as salt producing sites, both of which relate to the seasonal use of these coastal marshes. For example, in AD 1547 a weller (saltmaker) from Hockley left his son a 'saltcote and four lead pans belonging to the said Salthouse' (Barford 1988: 7). 'Saltcote' place-names are recorded in Brightlingsea, Burnham, Saltcott, Tollesbury, Wigborough, and Woodham Ferrers (Christy 1906: 193, 198; Reaney 1935: 305, 322–3). 'Sheepcote' place-names are found in Cricksey (Morant 1763–8: 363), Hockley (Reaney 1935: 188), and Southminster (Reaney 1935: 226), while on the Isle of Grain (just across the Thames Estuary in Kent) there is a reference to a 'becary or sheep cote' in AD 1189 (Hasted 1797–1801: vol. IV, 256).

---

[43] For example, Goldhanger (Reader 1980: 176), Great Wakering (Helliwell 1971: 26), Benfleet Creek (Rodwell 1976*a*), and Canvey Island (Linder 1939: 149–50; Rodwell 1965*b*; 1966; Wymer and Brown 1995: 169).

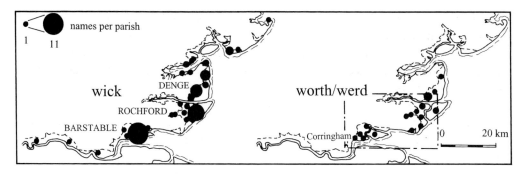

70. Distribution of 'wick' and 'worth'/'werd' place-names on coastal marshland in Essex. (Based on Tables 7–8.)

Table 7. Medieval '-wick' names on the Essex marshes

Modern place-name	Medieval '-wick' name
Bradwell-on-Sea	Misyke, Tomlyns Wike, West Wick (Morant 1763/8: 377; Reaney 1935: 211).
Burnham	Dammerwick, East Wick, Wesuuic [Westwick] (*DB Essex*, 30, 51; Morant 1763–8: 364; Reaney 1935: 212)
Canewdon	Gorewyk, Necollewyk (Reaney 1935: 180–1)
Canvey Island	Castlewick, Clerkingwick, Furtherwick, Knightswick, Munkeswyke [Monkswick], Northwick, Sharewyke, Southchurchwick, Southwick, Sunderwyke, Westwick (*WAM Lease Book* III, f.152; Cracknell 1959: 12; Reaney 1935: 149)
Corringham	Warrewyke (Morant 1763–8: 18)
Dengie	Bridgewick, Landwick (Reaney 1935: 214)
Foulness Island	Eastwoodwyke, Eastwyke, Middelwyk, Nassewyke, Newyke, Ormondeswyke, Partricheswyk, Southwyke: *CIPM II*: 46; *FF Essex* II: 153; Morant 1763/8: 269)
Great Clacton	Jay Wick (Reaney 1935: 335)
Great Wakering	Landwick (Reaney 1935: 204)
Hadleigh	Clerkynwyke (Morant 1763/8: 18)
Harwich	Herdwic (Reaney 1935: 339)
Little Thurrock	Grangewyke (Morant 1763/8: 18)
Little Wakering	Pottingwick [Potton Island] (Reaney 1935: 205)
Fobbing	Nasshewick, Nazewick (Reaney 1935: 156)
Rainham	Berwick (Reaney 1935: 128)
Rochford	Stadwkye (Reaney 1935: 197)
St Lawrence	Ramsey Wick (Reaney 1935: 224)
St Osyth	Cocket Wick, Holewyke, Jaywick, Lee Wick (Grieve 1959: 5)
Southminster	Bradwyerdewyk, Middlewick, Monnsalewyk, Mowick, Ray Wick, South Wick (Morant 1763/8: 371; Reaney 1935: 226)
Steeple	Stansgatewick (Reaney 1935: 228)
Tillingham	Doddeswich, Howich/Mowick, Middelwich, Muthwyke, Wetherwick (Grieve 1959: 5; (Reaney 1935: 230).
Tollesbury	Wick (Reaney 1935: 306)
Tolleshunt	Longwick, Skinner's Wick, Todwyk (Reaney 1935: 308–9)
Wallasea Island	Grapnellewyk (Reaney 1935: 206)
West Ham	Laywick, Wicmede (*FF Essex* I: 16; Powell 1973b: 94)

Another important place-name on the Essex marshes is 'worth', or variants thereof ('ward', 'werth' and 'wood'; Table 8; Figure 70). The earliest form is *werde* (documented from *c.* AD 1170), which remains the common form until the thirteenth century, after which it is gradually replaced by *warde* and *werth* (Reaney 1935: 149). Reaney (1935: 149) states *werde* is derived from Old High German *warid/werid*, meaning 'island in a river', and related to Old English *warod/werod*, meaning coast or bank. In The Netherlands this led to the terms *weerd* and *waard* being used for islands, peninsulas, and land which had been diked. The significance of these names is twofold. Firstly, they are mainly restricted to South East Essex, notably the hundreds of Barstable, Rochford, and Dengie, with very few examples west of Corringham (Figure 70; Reaney 1935: 148). As they are mainly thirteenth century and later in date, they might reflect that inning occurred rather later in South East Essex than on the Thames-side marshes.

Overall, a broad division can be drawn within the Essex Marshes, roughly at Corringham near Canvey Island. To the west, many of the marshes appear to have been embanked by the early fourteenth century and, while there was some cultivation, there was also an abundance of meadow (reflected in the abundance of 'mead' and 'ham' names. To the east, extensive tracts of marshland were left un-embanked, and the concentration of 'werde'/'werth'/'worth' names indicates that reclamation there occurred far later than along the inner and middle Thames Estuary. 'Wick' names also concentrate in this eastern region reflecting the use of these marshes for dairying. Indeed, even around AD 1300 when population pressure was at its greatest, the majority of Essex's coastal wetlands, even if embanked, were used as pasture, notably for sheep. The reason why this was the case is explored in Chapter 10.

Table 8. Medieval '-werde', '-werth', and '-worth' names on the Essex marshes

Modern name	Medieval '-werde', '-werth', and '-worth' names
Benfleet/Canvey	Humelesworth (*FF Essex* I: 30)
Bradwell	Grenewerde (Reaney 1935: 148)
Burnham	Colewerde, Labworth, Redward, Twyselworth (Morant 1763/8: 364, 377; Reaney 1935: 211–12).
Buttsbury	Sudhanewerde (*FF Essex* I: 42)
Canvey Island	Labwerde (Reaney 1935: 148)
Corringham	Horswerd, Radewrth (Reaney 1935; 151–2)
Fobbing	Estylward, Westelword (Reaney 1935: 156)
Foulness Island	see Table 6
Paglesham	Taward Marsh (Morant 1763/8: 311).
Shopland	Heghwerd Marsh (Morant 1763/8: 309)
Shoebury	Shelword Marsh (Morant 1763/8: 302),
Southchurch	Bradwyerde (Reaney 1935: 126)
Southminster	Loward Marsh (Reaney 1935: 148)
Stanford-le-Hope	Rogewerde (Reaney 1935: 171)
Sutton	Bradewerde Marsh (Morant 1763/8: 292)
Tillingham	Chyngilworth (Reaney 1935: 230)
Little Wakering	Littlebingworth Marsh (Morant 1763/8: 306)
Wallasea	Ringworth Marsh, Shernwards, Tilwerde (Morant 1763/8: 315–6)

9.8 **The Norfolk Broadland**

The most extensive tract of coastal marshland in Norfolk, the Halvergate Marshes, have recently been studied by Williamson (1997), and what follows is simply a brief summary of his conclusions. No settlements on the Marshes are mentioned in Domesday, though the large flocks of sheep recorded in nearby manors were probably grazed there. The presence of salterns, many of which were also held by distant manors, indicates that this remained an intertidal landscape. By the twelfth century, place-names indicate that the marshes were divided into a series of discrete parcels, many of which were held by distant communities: as with the Essex marshes, the rich wetland resources of Halvergate were a valued resource. A number of low mounds, often located on the banks of what were probably still tidal creeks, may have supported the cottages and dairies of shepherds and saltworkers. Several have yielded assemblages of building debris and medieval pottery which in certain cases dates back to the ninth/tenth centuries. There are also occasional references to sheep 'cotes'.

By the twelfth and thirteenth century large flocks of sheep were grazed on the marshland parcels of fen-edge or more distant manors into whose economies the wetland resources were carefully integrated. For example, the Norwich Cathedral Priory flock remained on the Marsh all year round apart from ten weeks after the harvest when it was fed on the stubble of dryland fields. The Earl of Norfolk's marshes supported 1,800 sheep that were penned up at night, after which the dung was collected up, taken to the upland part of his estate and spread over the arable fields to improve their fertility.

9.9 **The Fenland**

By the eleventh century, Fenland consisted of two very different landscapes: extensively reclaimed and settled marshes towards the coast, and vast open peat bogs in the backfen (the latter being exploited both from coastal and fen-edge villages). During the twelfth and thirteenth century demand for new land meant that further areas were reclaimed both from the rapidly-accreting saltmarshes in front of the original sea wall, and more particularly the freshwater backfen. This has been the subject of detailed research by H. Hallam (1954; 1965), and what follows is simply a brief summary of those points that are relevant to this study.

In Norfolk, Cambridgeshire, and Lincolnshire eleventh century settlement was focused in a series of loosely nucleated villages located on the slightly higher siltlands in a line roughly parallel to the coast (Figures 58, 59, and 71). Each village was at the head of a long narrow parish that extended from the coast into the lower-lying backfen, and as population increased and land became scarce, blocks of this backfen were also enclosed and drained. Farmsteads gradually expanded down a series of linear droveways that linked the coastal villages with the remaining areas of common pasture in the backfens, resulting in linear 'fen hamlets'. In Cambridgeshire and Lincolnshire the droveways appear to have been laid out as reclamation proceeded into the backfen, whereas in Norfolk some at least of the droveways are demonstrably later than the field systems through which they pass, notably Walpole East Drove and Tilney Drove (Silvester 1988: 80). The Norfolk droveways are also much wider (up to 300 m) than those in Cambridgeshire (*c.* 150 m) and Lincolnshire (*c.* 30 m) (Silvester 1993: 31, 33). In order to protect these newly occupied areas from freshwater flooding a series of fen banks were constructed that ran perpendicular to these droveways (and so parallel to the coast), the combined effect of which was to give a highly rectilinear feel to the landscape (Figures 51 and 60).

Though most effort was devoted to enclosing and draining the freshwater backfen, the eleventh to thirteenth centuries also saw limited reclamation of saltmarshes that lay outside the early medieval sea wall. In Norfolk, one example is the creation of the parish of Clenchwarton, described in Chapter 8 (Figure 59), while in Lincolnshire a series of smaller 'Newlondes' can be identified running along most of the coast (Figure 58D; Hallam 1965).

Medieval Fenland also saw water management on a grand scale. A number of rivers were canalized in order to improve drainage and navigation including the Witham, Glenn (the 'Baston Ea'), Welland, and Ouse (D. Hall and J. Coles 1994: 136). Some wholly artificial rivers were also dug, such as the 12 km canal dug through a narrow neck of land at Marsh in order to link the Nene and Old Croft rivers (D. Hall 1987: 46). Lesser artificial watercourses (often known as 'lodes') were also dug such as 'Monkslode', in Sawtry, that was designed 'to preserve the lands, meadows and pastures of the men of Walton, Sawtry, and Connington from the waters descending ... and for the navigation of corn, turves [peat] and other things' (D. Hall and J. Coles 1994: 137). The initial construction of these canals and lodes is rarely documented, though the earliest references to them are often early thirteenth century.

The development of the Norfolk marshland landscape provides an excellent case-study of how the Fenland landscape developed at this time (Figures 59, 71, and 72; Silvester 1988; 1993). A series of coastal villages had their origins in a number of settlements created during the seventh/eighth century, that were subject to some nucleation around the ninth/tenth century (see Chapter 8). These settlements were originally restricted to the raised banks of silted-up creeks (roddons), though by the eleventh century they started to expand along the trackways that linked the various villages. In the twelfth century settlement drifted towards small greens in the lower-lying ground between the roddons, which are likely to have been the last surviving areas of common pasture that were left over as the coastal marshes were enclosed. During the twelfth and thirteenth centuries, farmsteads also spread down the droveways towards the backfen, and these linear settlements eventually grew to the extent that new parishes were created (e.g. Terrington St John was carved out of Terrington, and Tilney St Lawrence out of Tilney).

This rapid phase of reclamation and settlement expansion into the backfens was probably completed in Norfolk by the early thirteenth century by which time Chancellor Dike and Smeeth Bank were constructed to mark the limit of 'West Fen', the remaining area of backfen which was an important source of summer pasture (Silvester 1988: 32, 160–9; 1993: 29). Such areas were usually common land, some of it the property of

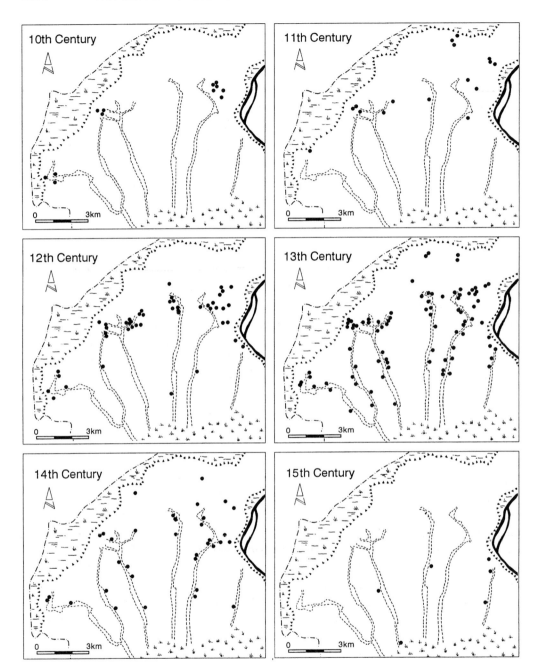

71. The expansion of medieval settlement in the Norfolk marshland, shown by date of settlement foundation (after Silvester 1993: fig. 3.3). (For location see Figure 52.) (Drawn by Sue Rouillard.)

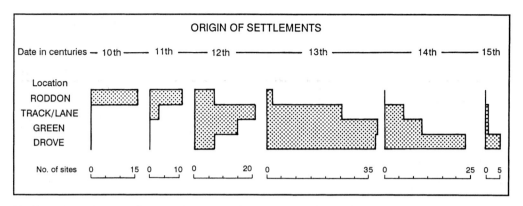

72. The date and location of new settlements founded in the Norfolk marshland (after Silvester 1988: fig. 117). (Drawn by Sue Rouillard.)

individual communities, such as Borough Little Fen that belonged to the inhabitants of Peterborough, while others were open to the wider community, such as Great Fen that could be used by all the inhabitants of Peterborough Hundred (D. Hall and J. Coles 1994: 138). In the West Fen of Norfolk marshland, however, earthworks suggest that there may have been a brief, and unsuccessful, attempt to enclose areas of the common by extending the droveways (Silvester 1988: fig. 20), marking a 'high water mark' of the high medieval 'expansion into the margins' (a similar phenomena may be evident in the Somerset Levels: Rippon 1997a: 210–12; 1997c: fig. 3).

9.10 **The Lincolnshire coast**

Whilst the reclamation of Fenland has seen considerable scholarly attention, the marshes that fringe the rest of the Lincolnshire coast have not. The coastal wetlands of this region form a narrow coastal plain partly fringed by an intermittent belt of sand dunes (e.g. Figure 73; Grady 1998; D. Robinson 1970: fig. 1). Middle Saxon pottery has been recovered from several villages e.g. Marsh Chapel and Trusthorpe (Vince 1993), and the area was certainly extensively settled by Domesday. Many of the villages lie on raised mounds that are probably the debris from salt production, and may have originated as the seasonal residences of saltworkers and shepherds. As the marshes continued to accrete the saltworks also migrated seaward, while abandoned mounds of debris were linked together by the first sea wall to be constructed. Its date is unclear, though sea banks are first documented in the later twelfth century (Figure 73; Grady 1998; Owen 1952; 1984: 46; 1986: 61), and the area protected from inundation appears to have been largely enclosed and drained by c. AD 1200 being used primarily for pasture and meadow (Owen 1996: xv, xvii).

Even after the construction of this sea wall, extensive areas of saltmarsh up to 5 km wide were left unreclaimed and used for grazing sheep and producing salt (Figures 73 and 79; Grady 1998; Healey 1993; Owen 1993; 1996). A series of monastic houses in

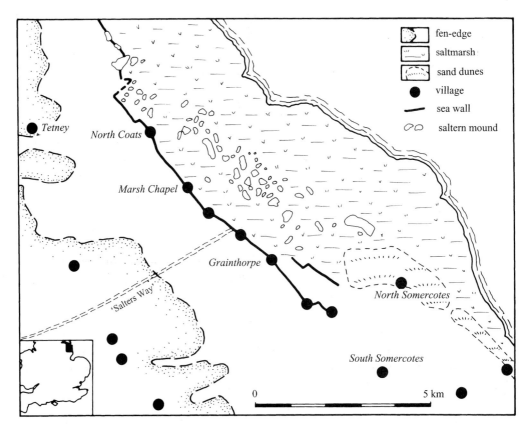

73. Settlement and salt production along the Lincolnshire coast (after Grady 1998; Robinson 1970: fig. 1).

eastern Lincolnshire held extensive tracts of this open marsh, such as Louth Park Abbey, Bullington Priory, and Markby Priory that in total held rights of pasture for 2,130 sheep in Huttoft alone: assuming a stocking level of 1.5 sheep per acre, this suggests 1,420 acres of saltmarsh which would have extended some 1.5 km beyond the sea wall. The formation of intermittent natural coastal barriers, possibly during the twelfth and thirteenth centuries (Grady 1998: 90) would have made embanking this marsh a relatively simple task, though a conscious decision had clearly been taken not to reclaim these areas as they were valued for their grazing.

9.11 **The Humber Estuary**

The history of embanking and drainage around the Humber Estuary has seen some documentary research (e.g. Lythe 1938; 1939; J. Sheppard 1957; 1958; 1966), though as most of the available material relates to the maintenance of flood defences that had already been created by the twelfth/thirteenth centuries, the initial phases of reclamation are poorly understood. The available documentary material is also very much biased towards monastic reclamation.

The earliest written reference to the condition of the Ancholme Valley is in AD 1288 when drainage work was undertaken (Straw 1955). In the Humberhead Levels, around the estuaries of the Rivers Aire, Don, Ouse, and Trent, there is little evidence for occupation before the twelfth century, though Domesday records one settlement with a church, fourteen tenants, and three ploughs, besides the Ouse at Adlingfleet (Van de Noort and Ellis 1997: 21). It is possible that other marshland settlements existed but were subsumed in the entry for another manor, Snaith, of which all the communities on the Humberhead marshes apart from Adlingfleet were later chapelries. Buckland *et al.* (1989: 28) also note the predominance of '-thorpe' names in this area, suggesting that they represent outlying farmsteads associated with settlements on the nearly dryland. Following the establishment of these other communities along the southern bank of the Ouse by the twelfth century, the reclaimed area expanded southwards into the lower-lying backfens where it was associated with the establishment of numerous moated sites (M. Beresford 1986: 152; Van de Noort and Ellis 1997: 21, 429–38). This reclamation appears to have been carried out by a number of monastic landlords, notably Selby Abbey, and their tenants (Van de Noort and Ellis 1997: 21, 429–38).

The estuary-side saltmarshes in the Vale of York, within the lordship of Howdenshire, were certainly settled by Domesday (Cotness and Yokefleet), but the major period of reclamation appears to have been during the early twelfth century, when Hugh de Pudsey who, as Bishop of Durham was Lord of Howdenshire, granted a series of manors to various individuals who proceeded to embank and drain the land (Figure 74; J. Sheppard 1966: 15). It is to this period that the present structure of the landscape owes its origins. A series of villages were established on the higher coastal areas, at the head of long narrow parishes that stretched into the lower-lying freshwater backfens (e.g. Blacktoft and Faxfleet). Each parish was divided by a major artificial watercourse (or 'dam') which stretched from the Humber Estuary as far inland as the Foulney River. Beyond Foulney, the backfen saw little improvement to its drainage and remained common land.

Many of the dams were named after the individual manorial lords who were presumably responsible for their construction: Hansardam after Gilbert Hansard owner of Blacktoft, Thornton Dam after the Canons of Thornton who owned Thornton Land, and Temple Dam after the Knights Templars who owned Faxfleet. Like Fenland, as enclosure and drainage proceeded, there was a need for fen-banks to be constructed and in the Vale of York these also appear to have been the result of collaboration between several communities e.g. the Scalby dike (J. Sheppard 1966: fig. 4). During the thirteenth century these dams, and the roads that ran along their banks, became the foci for a number of linear fen hamlets such as Gowthorpe, Clemthorpe, and Gilberdike.

Just one area of the coastal marsh—Wallingfen—was left as unreclaimed common land. Sheppard (1966: 16) assumes that this was because it was particularly ill-drained, though there is little in its physical character to suggest that this was the case. Rather, this may represent another example of a conscious decision by local communities not to

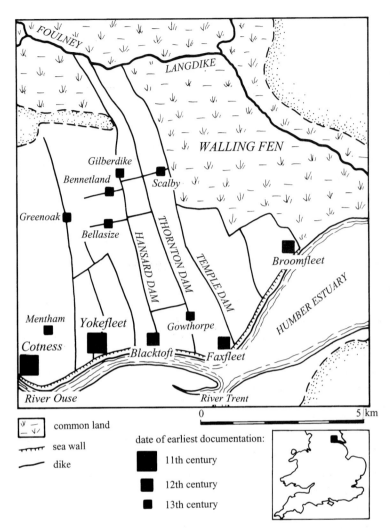

74. The reclamation of coastal marshes in Howdenshire, Vale of York (after Sheppard 1966: figs. 3–6).

reclaim an area of marsh because it was so highly valued as common land and/or because there were strong communal rights there (another example being Caldicot Moor on the Gwent Levels: Rippon 1996a: 77–8).

In the Hull Valley, Sheppard (1958: 1) argues that until the twelfth century the southern, coastal, end was covered by unreclaimed saltmarshes whereas to the north of the small bedrock islands of Sutton, Tickton, and Wawne there were extensive freshwater swamps and carr woodland. Communities living on the adjacent drylands subsequently embanked the marshes and, by the thirteenth century, a number of new hamlets had emerged including Wyk (re-named by Edward I as Kingston-upon-Hull). In AD 1150 the Abbey of Meaux was founded on one of the small bedrock islands and within a few years the monks had constructed a number of artificial watercourses to improve navigation, though their east–west orientation meant that they cannot have made a major contribution to improving the drainage (Van de Noort and Ellis 1993: fig. 3.15; J. Sheppard 1958: 3).

In southern Holderness, the area of marshland between the Hull Valley and Spurn Point was also partly settled by the eleventh century as Tharlesthorpe is mentioned in Domesday (*DB Yorks.* 2:1). Sheppard (1966: 5) claims Friskmersk, Penisthorpe, and Orwithfleet also came into being at that time. During the twelfth century the settlement pattern expanded with a scatter of farmsteads established such as Meaux Abbey's grange at Ottringham. Land was embanked and some of it cultivated, but little else can be said about this reclaimed landscape because it has been lost to later erosion; the present structure of the landscape relates to the subsequent accretion of new marshes and their reclamation in the post-medieval period (Berridge and Pattison 1994; J. Sheppard 1966).

9.12 The western Netherlands and Belgium

Though colonization of the marshes in Belgium began during the later ninth to tenth centuries, the earliest embanking appears to have been in the eleventh century. This was very localized in its extent, and it was only during the twelfth century that systematic attempts were made to protect areas at a regional scale. From the twelfth century extensive tracts of marsh were granted to various monastic houses and, although much of the drainage was undertaken in order to create good sheep pastures, there was also extensive arable cultivation notably of oats (Dewilde *et al.* 1995: 220; Nicholas 1992: 98–100; Tys 1997; Verhaeghe 1981: 98).

The first systematic attempts to embank the Zeeland marshes appears to have followed major flooding in AD 1134 and, by the end of the twelfth century, this task was largely complete with the major estuaries and islands within them having been protected (Figure 27; A. Lambert 1971: figs 36 and 41; Van den Broeke and Van Londen 1995: 41). Three conditions appear to have encouraged this rapid phase of reclamation: first, the marshes had naturally silted to a relatively high level and so were flooded fairly infrequently; second, a flourishing wool industry made sheep farming very profitable; and third, the growth of several major monastic houses, including the Cistercian Abbeys of Ten Duien and Ter Doest, and the abbey of St Peter's in Ghent, meant that there were institutions with the political influence, resources, and organization to invest in reclamation on a large scale (Tys 1997; Vos and Van Heeringen 1997: 71). From the thirteenth century the original sea walls were abandoned as 'newlands' were created through the reclamation of the remaining areas intertidal marsh (De Bakker and Kooistra 1982: 29; Vos and Van Heeringen 1997: 71).

9.12.1 Reclamation in the peatlands of North Holland

In North Holland, reclamation was well underway by the tenth century (Figure 62), and this was followed by further peatland reclamation during the eleventh and twelfth centuries. Once an area of peat was drained, subsidence meant that it became lower than the unreclaimed bog, and so a bank had to be constructed in order to prevent freshwater flooding from the unenclosed areas, and settlements were raised on artificial mounds. Eventually, the reclaimed land became so low-lying and waterlogged that it could no longer be cultivated, prompting further reclamation by simply extending each drainage ditch in the open peat bog a certain distance and then constructing a new fen-bank. Arable cultivation shifted onto the newly enclosed areas, while the earlier reclamation was given over to pasture. This led to the cultivated lands being further and further away from the original settlements and, in many cases the villages, along with their churches, would move onto the newly reclaimed peat (Figure 62; Besteman 1988; Besteman and Guiran 1987; De Bont 1994: 63–4; A. Lambert 1971: 97–100).

Documentary and palaeoenvironmental evidence, along with excavated examples of plough marks, confirm that the peat was indeed used for arable cultivation (Besteman 1988: 356–7; Besteman and Guiran 1987: 300; Van Geel *et al.* 1983). In certain cases communities appear to have had a relatively specialized economy, such as the twelfth century peatland settlement Midwoud which produced flax. As flax requires deep fertile soil rich in lime, clay was presumably dug from pits and spread over the peaty soils (Pals and Dierendonck 1988).

Whereas during the tenth and eleventh centuries the major flooding problem was freshwater run-off from the peatbogs, from around the twelfth century tidal flooding was increasingly becoming a problem. This led to the raising of settlements on artificial mounds and the construction of embankments alongside the tidal estuaries and Lake Almere (now the IJsselmeer). Though largely prompted by a deterioration in the natural environment, this was also a period when the Counts of Holland were re-asserting their authority over the region, and they appear to have encouraged dike building wherever possible (Besteman 1988: 360–1; A. Lambert 1971: 108–9).

9.12.2 The 'cope' reclamations in South Holland

The vast peat bogs of South Holland were amongst the last major wetlands in The Netherlands to be reclaimed (Figure 75). The Crown had given its 'regalian' right to exploit this wilderness area to the Bishops of Utrecht and Counts of Holland and, from the eleventh century, they began the task of drainage and enclosure. This was a carefully planned exercise with blocks of land granted to knights, groups of peasant reclaimers, or religious foundations in return for a very nominal rent or simply a formal acknowledgement of allegiance. Work started from the relatively well-drained ground afforded by creek ridges which were used as a base-line, from which were laid a series perpendicular drainage ditches. These divided the peat bogs into regularly-sized blocks often 30 *roeden* wide (*c.* 105 m) and 6 or 12 furlongs long (1,250 and 2,500 m) which were then settled by colonists whose farmsteads lay at the head of each strip on the higher ground. At the end of all the plots, a terminal dike was laid out parallel to the base-line and, when the next portion of bog came to be reclaimed, this terminal dike was used for the new settlement. This type of reclamation became known as the 'cope'

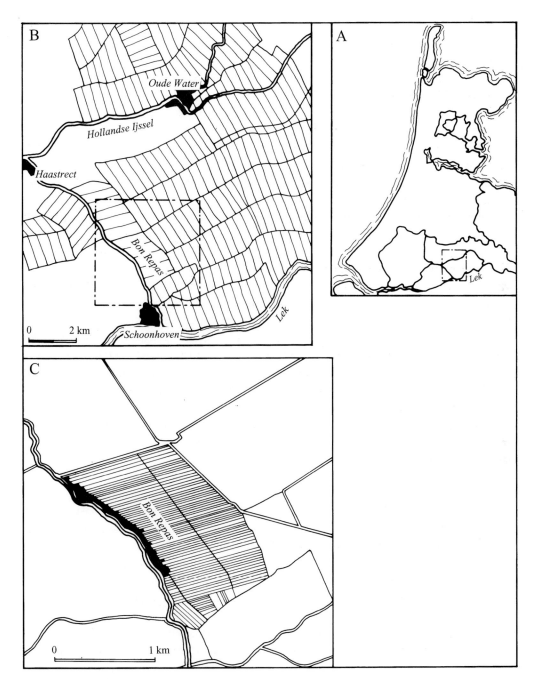

75. Example of 'cope' reclamation in South Holland (after Van der Linden 1982: figs. 1, 3–4). (For location see Figure 26.)

system, from the Dutch word *kopen* (to buy), and was characterized both by its physical layout (Figure 75) and the legal rules associated with it (De Bont 1994: 67; Bos 1990: 121; Besteman 1988: 338–9; 1990: 116–7; A. Lambert 1971: 104–6; Van der Linden 1982: 50–8; TeBrake 1985: 206–20). By the thirteenth century the reclamation of these peatbogs was virtually compete.

Initially, the natural system of rivers would have provided sufficient drainage for the reclaimed areas, but from the twelfth century additional measures were needed because of increased tidal flooding, the silting-up of one of the natural tidal inlets that had drained the area (the Oude Rijn), and greater freshwater flooding from the east as the increasingly well-drained peat bogs could no longer soak up freshwater run-off (TeBrake 1985: 213). The human response was to develop a complex system of dams, embankments, sluices, and canals. One of the earliest works to have more than simply local significance was the 'Zwammerdam', built across the Oude Rijn at the eastern edge of the Rijnland district (to the north of Gouda). However, this simply shifted the flooding problem eastwards to the lands of the Bishopric of Utrecht and, in AD 1165, the Emperor ordered that the dam be removed (A. Lambert 1971: 102; Van der Molen 1982: 108; TeBrake 1985: 214). To try and deal with the flooding problem, a number of substantial canals were constructed in order to improve the discharge of freshwater rivers, and eventually the Count of Holland and Bishop of Utrecht, along with the communities of both areas, co-operated in these major undertakings. A number of substantial embankments were also constructed, initially enclosing individual areas but culminating in *c.* AD 1220 with the *c.* 30 km long 'Zijdwinde' which divided Rijnland and Maasland (TeBrake 1985: 215–7).

9.12.3 **The northern Netherlands and Germany**

In Friesland and Groningen the construction of raised *terpen* settlements represented a fairly passive response to the problem of flooding, which was replaced from the tenth century by a more active policy of landscape modification through the construction of ring dikes, or raised trackways, leading from *terp* to *terp* which were gradually extended to form a closed system of sea defence. As a result, few new *terpen* were built after *c.* AD 1000 and in some areas farmsteads left their mounds and moved out into the newly reclaimed landscape. By the twelfth century the coastal marshes were wholly embanked and work had also started on enclosing, draining, and settling the peat backfens (Cappers 1993–4; A. Lambert 1971: 81; Roeleveld 1974: 113; Schoorl 1997: 26; Vos, 1999). Behind these protective embankments settlement expanded rapidly, and by the thirteenth century it had spread deep into the lower-lying backfens (e.g. Figure 52).

On the North German marshes dike building appears to have begun around the eleventh century in the form of ring dikes built around individual settlements and their fields (Figure 35). It was only during the thirteenth and fourteenth centuries that continuous sea walls were built along the coast, that were designed to keep the entire area flood-free even in winter, a process possibly related to the introduction of Dutch colonists (Figure 35; Behre 1985: 94; Behre *et al* 1979: 105; Ey 1997; Mayhew 1973: 48; Streif 1982). Once again, farmsteads tended to shift away from the *terpen* following reclamation, and many of the old village mounds were abandoned by the fourteenth century (Zimmermann 1995; 1996: 34).

9.13 **Discussion**

The recolonization of most coastal wetlands started during the early medieval period, when the foundations of the present landscape in these areas were laid. The twelfth and thirteenth centuries clearly saw a steady intensification of wetland utilization throughout North West Europe, notably through continued embankment of coastal marshes, and large-scale enclosure and drainage of the freshwater backfens. There appear to have been three strategies towards wetland utilization:

- Continued enclosure and drainage in the backfens of areas that had already been embanked by the tenth/eleventh centuries—the Somerset Levels, Romney Marsh, parts of the North Kent marshes, Fenland, the Humberhead Levels, North Holland, and the northern Netherlands
- Areas of coastal marsh embanked for the first time from the late eleventh century—the Gwent Levels, Pevensey Levels, Walland Marsh, the East Kent marshes, parts of the North Kent marshes, many of the Essex Thames-side marshes and some areas along the east coast including Foulness, certain marshes on the Lincolnshire coast, Howdenshire in the Vale of York, the Hull Valley, the Belgian marshes and Zeeland, the peat bogs of South Holland, and the German marshes
- Areas left as open saltmarsh—Caldicot Moor (in the Gwent Levels); some of the Essex coastal marshes (notably Canvey Island); the Halvergate Marshes (Norfolk); the outer marshes of the Lincolnshire coast; Walling Fen (Howdenshire in the Vale of York)

Clearly, the dominant policy was embankment and reclamation and, in most areas, coastal marshes were enclosed, drained, settled, and used for mixed agriculture. There were exceptions, however, with some embanked marshes being used relatively un-intensively, mainly as sheep pastures (e.g. East Kent and Essex), and a handful of marshes that were not embanked at all (see above): the reasons why apparently very similar areas of marshland were used in such different ways, and who was responsible for taking those decisions, is explored in Chapter 10.

CHAPTER 10

Under pressure:

the use of coastal resources during the medieval period

10.1 Introduction

Chapters 8 and 9 examined the recolonization of coastal wetlands in North West Europe during the medieval period, and the following two chapters examine certain general themes relating to this period. Chapter 11 considers why human communities decided to invest such considerable resources in transforming their landscape, but first this chapter explores the uses to which coastal resources were put during the medieval period, and in particular how patterns in wetland utilization suggest that the landscape of North West Europe was coming under increased strain. This was a period of rising population and rising prices. Throughout North West Europe the intensity with which the landscape was being exploited increased (Duby 1968; Postan 1972) and coastal areas were no exception.

Firstly, an examination of coastal fishing shows the extent to which a hungry population was increasingly driven towards the exploitation of off-shore species. The growth and decline of the salt industry is then considered, as another coastal resource that was widely exploited during the medieval period. A review of the uses to which embanked marshes were put reveals that arable cultivation was extensive in many areas, though this was only ever part of a mixed economy. In other areas, however, both embanked and unenclosed marshes were used largely for pasture, and a variety of explanations for this seemingly surprising phenomena are put forward.

10.2 Medieval fishing

The extent of fish consumption during the Roman period has been reviewed in Chapter 5 and, though it appears to have increased compared with the preceding Iron Age, it was still at a relatively low level. This appears to have changed during the medieval period, as the survival of substantial intertidal fish weirs and evidence of animal bone assemblages, particularly from towns, indicates a marked increase in fish consumption. For example, at Southwark (in London), 41 Roman samples were sieved yielding 89 identified fish bones, compared with 10 medieval samples which produced 475 fish bones (P. Hinton 1988: 431–33; and see A. G. Jones 1982).

The increase in fish consumption during the medieval period is partly explained by religious teachings. Even though the strict ordinances, which stated that members of monastic communities should abstain from the meat of four-footed animals, were gradually liberalized, the consumption of red meat was still controlled making fish a vital year-round source of protein (anon. 1997: 5; G. Black 1976: 135; J. Bond 1988; Dyer 1988: 28; Ervynck 1997: 73–5). While fish did form a more significant part of the diet of monastic communities compared with the rest of the population, there is also a marked increase in fish consumption on both urban and rural settlements. The sources of that fish changed with an increasing use of offshore as opposed to freshwater or inshore fish stocks. This is so pronounced that it might suggest a rising demand for food by communities living in an ever more crowded landscape, and as such forms part of the general shift towards the exploitation of what were previously regarded as 'marginal' resources.

One manifestation of the increased economic importance of fishing is the construction of fixed fish weirs which, as a costly undertaking, represents a conscious and long-term investment of time and resources. Unless the absence of pre-medieval fish weirs is due to later processes of erosion, then it suggests that before the medieval period demand for fish was not sufficiently substantial to warrant the construction of fixed fishing structures. In the Severn Estuary fisheries are documented from the late seventh century (Sawyer 1968: no. 77), though the most detailed early reference dates from *c*. AD 1060 when a charter of Bath Abbey describes 104 fish weirs at Tidenham in Gloucestershire, comprising 100 'cytweras' and 4 'haecweras' (Sawyer 1968: no. 1555). 'Haecweras' appear to be 'hedge weirs', later known as kiddles: large V-shaped structures, comprising wattle fences, or stone/boulder walls that funnelled fish towards a basket at the structure's apex. The remains of such kiddles still survive in the inner Bristol Channel off Minehead (Figure 76; J. Bond 1988: 78; McDonnell 1980). Large kiddle-like fish weirs dating from the early medieval period are also known off the Isle of Wight, at several locations in Essex (Figure 77) and the Deel Estuary, Fergus Estuary and in Strangford Lough in Ireland (C. Clarke 1993; B. Crump and Wallis 1992; O'Sullivan *et al.* 1997; O'Sullivan and Daly 1999: 181; Strachan 1996; 1998*a*; 1998*b*; Wallis 1993). At least in Essex, several of these early sites may be related to early monastic foundations (Rippon 1996*b*: 124; Strachan 1998*b*: 281). It is at about this time that archaeological evidence suggests an increased investment of resources into inland fishing, with the appearance of fish weirs in a number of major rivers, notably in the English Midlands (Salisbury 1991; 1992).

The Tidenham 'cytweras' probably equate with large baskets later known as 'putts', secured by small V-shaped arrangements of posts (Figure 78; J. Bond 1988: 78). Another late ninth century fishery is documented nearby, close to a royal *Llys* site at Portskewett (W. Davies 1979*a*: no. 235b; J. G. Evans 1893: 378; Rippon 1996*a*: 35–7), and several tenth to eleventh century examples of 'cytweras'-type fish traps have recently been excavated there (Godbold and Turner 1994; and see C. Green 1992; Nayling 1996).

While the medieval period certainly saw an intensification in the use of the intertidal zone for fishing, there was also a marked increase in the exploitation of off-shore

76. 'Kiddle'-like fish weir in the Bristol Channel off Minehead, West Somerset (NGR: SS 972 472), looking south.

77. Early medieval 'Kiddle'-like fish weir, in the Blackwater Estuary, off The Nass, in Tollesbury, Essex (NGR: TL 999 110) (see Strachan 1998*b*: 276). (Photo: David Strachan; copyright: Essex County Council.)

78. 'Putt'-type fish weir in the outer Severn Estuary off Kingston Seymour, North Somerset (NGR: ST 374 684), looking north.

species such as cod, haddock, and herring, which by the twelfth century are dominant on high status, urban, monastic, and rural settlements in both Britain[44] and on the continent.[45] The major period of expansion in off-shore fishing appears to date around the tenth to twelfth centuries. Hence, at West Stow in Suffolk, freshwater species predominated throughout the fifth to seventh centuries (Crabtree 1989: 27), and though herring have been recovered from a sixth century site at Thetford (P. Andrews 1995), freshwater fish were dominant once again. In towns such as Ipswich, Northampton, Norwich, Thetford, and Winchester halibut, herring, and ling appear around the tenth century (Andrews 1995; Fasham et al.1980: 128; Locker 1997: 3; J. Williams 1979: 335; J. Williams et al. 1985: 78–9).

York provides a further example of how off-shore fishing reached pre-eminence around the eleventh century (O'Connor 1994: 145). During the eighth to mid-tenth centuries, the fish bones are largely of eel, though with increasing numbers of carp, herring, salmon, and pike. In the mid- to late tenth century there are signs that the diet became more diverse with herring increasing in importance and cod making an appearance. This might suggest that pressure on inland resources was forcing communities to seek ever more distant food sources, though in this case there is an alternative interpretation: the eight to ninth century trading settlement at York may have been carefully regulated and the inhabitants could have been prevented from exploiting the full range of local resources (O'Connor 1994: 141).

[44] *High status settlements*: Albarella and Davis 1994a; Levitan 1984: 121. *Towns*: Atkins 1985: 223, Ayers 1987: 114–17; 1994: 42–4; Ayers and Murphy 1983: 32–3; Dobney *et al.* 1995; Hinton 1988: 431–3; Locker 1997; Maltby 1979: 74–80; O'Connor 1982: 44-6. *Monasteries*: Hare 1985: 185; Mellor and Pearce 1981: 173–5; S. Rahtz and Rowley 1984: 126. *Rural settlements*: Albarella and Davis 1994b.

[45] For example, Haithabu and its later medieval successor Schleswig in northern Germany (Heinrich 1983).

The access to rural resources of the potentially regulated trading settlement at York can be compared with the seventh to tenth century (probably royal) site at Flixborough, next to the Trent marshes in northern Lincolnshire (Loveluck 1997: 9). Numerous bones of freshwater fish, along with crane, duck, and various wading birds, suggest that the diet was supplemented through fishing and wildfowling, while oyster shells, marine fish, porpoise/dolphin, and whale bones indicate the exploitation of intertidal and marine resources. Whale bones are occasionally found on inland urban and high status sites during the medieval period, though it is unclear whether they were from joints of meat, or curiosities picked up on the beach and used in bone working or as chopping boards (Albarella and Davis 1994a: 24). Documentary references from c. AD 1000 suggest boats were used for whaling off Dorset, while there are possible butchery marks on a number of medieval whale bones from Romney Marsh (Gardiner et al. 1998).

During the medieval period sea fish were traded throughout inland England. For example, the accounts of Abingdon Abbey (Oxfordshire) include herring, mackerel, and oysters, while Pershore Abbey (Worcestershire) bought fish from as far afield as Bristol and Gloucester (S. Rahtz and Rowley 1984: 126). Excavations at Leicester Friary revealed cod, ling, haddock, and plaice/founder but no freshwater species (Mellor and Pearce 1981: 173–5), while in twelfth century and later Northampton a few eel and salmon were the only fish that may have been caught locally (J. Williams 1979: 335; J. Williams et al. 1985: 78–9). Imported fish must have been preserved, and documentary evidence suggests salting, smoking, and drying was used (Grant 1988: 172). The introduction of smoking during the thirteenth century would have meant that fish could be stored and transported much more easily than through salting (Ayers 1987: 116) while from the fourteenth century, fish were salted onboard ships allowing them to sail further from the coast and exploit ever more distant fisheries.

The growing importance of fishing is also reflected in the emergence of specialized fishing settlements from around the tenth century e.g. Great Yarmouth (Suffolk) (Rogerson 1976), and by the thirteenth/fourteenth century large numbers of ports, both large and small, were heavily involved in the exploitation of deep-sea fish stocks e.g. Hull (P. Spencer 1993), Kings Lynn (H. Clarke and Carter 1977), and London (Schofield 1981). These major ports were at the head of a settlement hierarchy which led down to numerous smaller local ports. This can be seen in Essex where, for example, Barking, Colchester, Harwich, Maldon, and Manningtree all had an interest in sea fishing (Britnell 1986: 15; Glenny 1907: 439–43; Petchey 1991: 134). By the fifteenth century professional fishermen in areas such as Essex appear to have been involved with fixed intertidal fishing weirs as well (B. Crump and Wallis 1992: 39).

Assuming that this increased evidence for off-shore fish on tenth to twelfth century settlements does not simply reflect patterns of refuse disposal, it may suggest improved technology (such as the introduction of drift nets), movements of fish stocks making them easier to catch, or increased economic pressure to produce more food (Andrews 1995). The latter has much to commend it for, by the twelfth and thirteenth centuries, the consumption of freshwater fish (apart from eels) was largely restricted to the aristocracy, and the high prices paid for freshwater fish suggest that supply simply could not keep pace with demand (C. Dyer 1988: 27–33; Moorhouse 1988: 479–80).

10.2.1 Shellfish

This increased pressure on resources is also reflected in the range and frequency of shellfish that was consumed, particularly from around the tenth and eleventh centuries (e.g. Norwich: Atkin 1985: 228; Ayers 1987: 118; Ayers 1994: 48–9; Ayers and Murphy 1983: 34; D. Evans and Carter 1985: 69). During the medieval period oysters were a relatively common food (Grant 1988: 173) and oyster fisheries are found around many parts of Britain, especially the Thames Estuary (Christy 1907a; Goodsall 1965). Documentary evidence suggests that the emergence of oyster cultivation dates to around the early twelfth century with the Colne Estuary, near Colchester, being the earliest recorded example (Benham 1993: 1). Archaeological evidence, such as a shellfish processing sites (e.g. Cox and Hearne 1991: 82; N. Faulkner 1993b: 16–18; Horsey and Winder 1991; P. Smith et al. 1983) and food debris assemblages (e.g. H. Brooks 1992: 48; C. Clarke 1988b, 80; Fenwick 1984; Medlycott 1996: 168–9; Wymer and Brown 1995: 144) also suggest an expansion of oyster cultivation and consumption at this time. Most commercial fisheries were dominated by oysters, though a wider variety of species were exploited in areas such as the Thames Estuary, notably mussels (Milton 1309: 15; Christy 1907a; Glenny 1907: 442; Nichols 1932). At Pevensey Castle, a large shellfish assemblage shows a marked diversification of species around the twelfth century (including whelks that must be caught in pots and so, require a greater effort and input of resources) (Sommerville, forthcoming).

10.2.2 Wildfowling

There also appears to have been a greater interest in wildfowling, when compared with the Roman period, though reclamation meant that it was increasingly restricted to river floodplains and areas of unenclosed backfen. The right to hunt wild birds was legally protected and it was only on common land that peasants were allowed to catch fowl. Wild birds were, indeed, relatively scarce on rural settlements (Coney 1992: 59; Davis 1992; Grant 1988: 168–9). This contrasts sharply with urban and high status sites, where a wide range of species are found, including wetland and coastal species such as gannets (Albarella and Davis 1994a: 23–31; Bramwell 1977; Bult and Hallewas 1990: 86–7; Grant 1988: 169).

10.3 Medieval salt production

Salt production during the medieval period has been rather neglected. This is reflected in its absence from two reviews of medieval industry (Blair and Ramsay 1991; Crossley 1981; but see Keen 1989) and, unfortunately, this is not the place to correct that deficiency. However, certain aspects of the growth of coastal salt production are important in the context of this study: firstly, the strong interest that monastic institutions had in this coastal resource and, secondly, its geographical extent.

From the eighth century onwards there are a series of charters in Britain and the Netherlands which record grants of land from the crown to the church and leading thanes for the purpose of saltmaking. For example, in Somerset a charter of *c*. AD 737 record a grant of land to the Bishop of Winchester for the purposes of constructing salt pans at 'Cearn' on the Parrett near Bridgwater (Dunning and Siraut 1992: 79–80; A. Turner 1953: 121). In Dorset the earliest documentary evidence for salt production is in AD 774, when King Cynewulf of Wessex granted a small piece of land on the west bank of the River Lym to the Bishop of Sherborne for saltworking (S.263; Keen 1987: 25). In Romney Marsh a charter of AD 732 records a grant by Aethelberht (King of Kent) to the church of St Mary in Lyminge of a saltern at 'Sandtun' (now Sampton) near West Hythe, beside the former tidal inlet of the *Limen* (Sawyer 1968: no. 23; Wallenberg 1931: 175; Ward 1931). In North Kent salt pans are recorded at Stoke (on the Medway estuary) in AD 738 (J. Evans 1953: 136; Fenwick 1972: 14), while two charters of AD 786 describe salt production at Seasalter (near Whitstable) and the woodland resources that were required for fuel (S.125; G. Ward 1944). The importance of these resources is shown by the way that manors many miles inland held coastal salterns e.g. Mersham and Great Chart in Kent (E. Campbell 1962: 539), Nether Wallop in Hampshire (Welldon Finn 1962: fig. 100), and Netherfield in Sussex (Darby and E. Campbell 1962: 457). In the same way, many distant places held salt pans in the inland brine springs at Droitwich e.g. Bampton and Great Rollright in Oxfordshire, and Risborough in Buckinghamshire (Darby 1962: 608; Darby 1977: 261).

On the continent, notably in the South West Netherlands, there are a similar range of eighth and ninth century charters, as in AD 776 when the abbey of Lorsch was granted seventeen salterns in Zeeland (Besteman 1974: 172; A. Lambert 1971: 131; Vos and Van Heeringen 1997: 73). An Old Saxon epic poem, the Heliandlund, testifies to the production of salt from peat along the North Sea coast of Frisia during the mid-ninth century (Marschalleck 1973: 127).

By the eleventh century, coastal salt production was extremely extensive, with most areas of intertidal marsh being used, either as a source of salt-impregnated intertidal muds and sands, in Britain (Figure 79) or salt-saturated peat, on the continent (Figure 80). Around 1,200 salterns are listed in Domesday around much of the British coast but notably on the Pevensey Levels, Romney Marsh, Fenland, and along the Lincolnshire coast (Bridbury 1955: 19; Keen 1989: 140).[46] In certain areas, however, the great survey appears to be defective, for example in Essex, where all the recorded salterns (bar one in the Lea Valley) are in the north-east of the county (Christy 1906: 196–7; 1907*b*; Darby 1977: 265). It is difficult to believe that there were no eleventh century salterns on the other marshes, where there was certainly a flourishing industry in the twelfth and thirteenth centuries (Barford 1988: 4; Christy 1906: 194; 1907*b*; Christy and Dalton 1925: 28: 30–40, 53–6;

---

[46] Most of the Domesday salterns were in Sussex (294, mostly on the Pevensey Levels and Romney Marsh), Norfolk (285; mostly west of King's Lynn), and Lincolnshire (260, mostly around Bicker Haven, and the Somercotes–Tetney part of the Lincolnshire coast), but also Kent (139), Devon (73), Essex (56, although this figure is probably incomplete), Dorset (32), Hampshire (26), Suffolk (18) and Cornwall (10).

79. Medieval saltern mounds in Marsh Chapel and Northcoates, on the Lincolnshire coast. (National Monuments Record RAF photograph CPE/UK/1746 frame 5013, copyright Ministry of Defence.)

Garwood 1995: 29; Pearson 1996; Wilkinson and Murphy 1995: 197). One suspects that we are simply witnessing one of the many inconsistencies of the Domesday survey and, if the density of salterns in North East Essex is repeated all around the coast, then a number approaching 100 can be supposed. Another area in which Domesday is deficient is Cambridgeshire where no salterns are mentioned despite there being 260 in Lincolnshire

80. Medieval peat extraction in order to produce peat using the *darinck delven* method, in the intertidal zone, near Waarde, Zeeland, The Netherlands (from Vos and Van Heeringen 1997: fig. 39; photo: copyright ROB).

and twenty-seven around King's Lynn in Norfolk. Saltern mounds have been identified between Tydd and Leverington, an area with documented salt production in the thirteenth and fourteenth centuries (D. Hall 1996: 183–5; Owen 1975: 43).

In most cases, the handful of salterns recorded for any one manor probably provided enough salt for the community's own consumption, with a little surplus for sale at the market. In other cases, however, there was clearly a more specialized industry, such as at Ower (Dorset) where, in Domesday, all the recorded population was engaged in salt production (Keen 1987: 26). The marked concentration of eleventh century salterns in certain locations, such as Walland Marsh (where there were over a hundred), around Bicker Haven in Lincolnshire (ninety-three), and West Walton in Norfolk (where there were thirty-seven salterns on just one manor) also suggest the emergence of specialized salt-making communities. In several parts of Lincolnshire such salt-making communities grew so large that they established permanent settlements with their own chapels e.g. Bank Village in North Somercotes, Marshchapel in Fulstow, and Northcotes in Thoresby and Autby (Figure 73; Rudkin 1975: 38). Salt was transported overland along roads that became known as saltways, which radiated from the production centres (Figure 73F. Gurney 1920: 169–70; Hewitt 1929: 113; Hooke 1981: fig. 8.5; Mawer and Stenton 1927: 6; E. Morris 1985: 345; D. Robinson 1970: fig. 1; A. H. Smith 1964: 19–20). As with the emergence of specialized fishing communities, the development of the salt industry is testament to the intensity with which coastal resources were now being exploited.

One major area of coastal wetland that saw very little medieval salt production is the Severn Estuary. No salterns are mentioned in Domesday, and the abundant records of Glastonbury also fail to mention any salt production in Somerset. One explanation might be the high sediment load and low salinity levels of the Severn (Bell 1990: 71) though this cannot have been a major factor since there was a flourishing salt industry in Somerset during the later prehistoric and Roman period, and the Bishop of Worcester is recorded as holding over 186 salt pans on his Henbury estate in AD 1165/6 (Hollings 1937: 411). The main reason why medieval salt production was so limited around the Severn is probably competition from Droitwich, where salt production was certainly flourishing as early as the seventh century (S.77; S.102; S.1822; Hooke 1981: 125; J. D. Hurst 1992; 1997; Woodwiss 1992: 187). Indeed, Domesday shows that by the eleventh century, much of central and western Britain obtained its salt from the inland springs at Droitwich, with manors as far away as Oxfordshire and Buckinghamshire having salt-pans there (Bateson 1913; Berry 1975; Darby 1977: 261; Mawer and Stenton 1927: 4).

10.4 **Landuse on reclaimed coastal wetlands**

Reclamation represents a major investment of resources both in terms of the initial capital outlay, in materials and particularly man-power, and in terms of the regular maintenance that the drainage and flood defence systems required. Reclamation can also be considered as a high cost strategy towards landscape utilization because it led to the loss of the natural resources that such environments had to offer, such as rich grazing and the opportunity for salt production.

Reclaimed coastal marshlands are sometimes regarded as having been primarily used for pasture. For example, in Everitt's (1986: 60–61) account of Romney Marsh he states, quite simply, that:

> The marsh has always been utilized chiefly as pastureland, and for the most part as sheep pasture. Even in the Napoleonic Wars, when the acreage under corn greatly expanded and probably reached its maximum extent, there seems to have been very little ploughland ... but whatever the explanation, there can be little doubt that there was no real parallel in Kent to the populous fenland villages of medieval Lincolnshire and Cambridgeshire, with their big arable fields and numerous substantial peasant families. The Kentish Levels belonged essentially to a different type of pays: their economy was based on sheep and their society was mainly composed of sheep-farmers fishermen, and lookers or shepherds: in other words they were marshlands pure and simple.

There is no question that, in the late medieval period, distinctive regional economies did emerge throughout Britain, and Romney Marsh certainly became one of the many distinctive *pays* that resulted. But the situation in, say, the sixteenth century, does not necessarily reflect that of the eleventh century: reclamation in most areas was not undertaken simply to improve the grazing, and this major investment of resources was more commonly associated with a mixed agricultural system which included a significant proportion of arable and meadow.

One major reason why reclamation was undertaken was that it increased the value of land enormously. In AD 1311, for example, the upland parts of Battle Abbey's Barnhorne estate were valued at between 3 pence and 6 pence per acre, whereas the reclaimed marshes on the Pevensey Levels were worth 12 pence; unreclaimed backfen was worth 4 pence if flooded, rising to 10 pence if properly drained (Dulley 1966: 37). Glastonbury Abbey owned a series of estates in and around the Somerset Levels and, once again, they show a marked differentiation between the value of dryland versus marshland (Table 9). On the marshland manors, all of which except Withy (east of Huntspill) lay on the higher coastal ground, arable formed a similar proportion of the demesne compared to the dryland/fen-edge estates, though it was much more highly valued (further examples can be found in Chapter 3). Brent was Glastonbury Abbey's most valuable manor in Domesday with 22 hides and 35 ploughlands valued at £56; nearby Shapwick had 30 hides and 60 ploughlands valued at £38 on the dry land of the Polden Hills.

Figures for crop yields also show how productive marshland could be if properly drained (Table 10). For example, the records of Canterbury Cathedral can be used to compare the productivity of estates on a variety of geologies throughout Kent and the Romney Marsh manors, particularly the better drained Agney, Fairfield, and Orgarswick, which had very high yields for barely and oats.

At a broader scale, the success of reclamation can be seen by comparing regional patterns of wealth. During the twelfth and thirteenth centuries, coastal wetlands such as the Somerset Levels, Romney Marsh, and the English Fenland showed some of the biggest increases in wealth in the country (Darby *et al.* 1979: 250). For example, in AD 1334 the Norfolk marshland was valued at around 30 shillings per square mile, in

Table 9. Land values on selected Somerset manors owned by Glastonbury Abbey in *c.* AD 1300

	Acres	%	Value per acre (shillings)
Dryland/fen-edge manors			
Ashcott	324	77	0.3
Greinton	36	80	0.4
Shapwick	502	76	2.2
Marshland manors			
South Brent	257	80	0.9
Berrow	282	92	0.9
Lympsham	287	84	0.9
East Brent	227	79	0.8
Withy	42	21	1.0

Source: Keil 1964: table A.

Table 10. Crop yields (in bushels) per bushel sown on Canterbury Cathedral's Kent estates in AD 1291

	Wheat	Spring barley	Oats
Chalklands	3.0	2.5	2.1
Thanet Beds/Brickearths	3.3	3.3	2.7
Claylands	3.5	2.6	2.9
Greensand	2.5	2.6	2.9
Romney Marsh:			
all manors	3.0	3.3	3.3
Romney Marsh:			
Agney, Fairfield, and			
Orgarswick	3.1	3.4	3.1
Lyden	2.7	2.4	2.0
Average	*3.0*	*2.7*	*2.5*

Source: Smith 1963.

contrast to the rest of Norfolk most of which ranged between 10 and 29 shillings (Glasscock 1973: fig. 35). Fenland, as a whole, had an extra-ordinarily high number of places with an assessed wealth of over £225 (Glasscock 1973: fig. 41). A similar situation is seen in the Central Somerset Levels which were one of few areas within that county valued at between 20 and 29 shillings per square mile; most of the county was valued at between 19 and 29 shillings (Glasscock 1973: fig. 35). Clearly, reclamation was worth the costs and risks.

10.4.1 Mixed economies

Relatively few reclaimed marshland were used primarily for arable cultivation. Glastonbury Abbey's Brent estate is one example, where 85 per cent of the demesne in *c.* AD 1300 was down to arable, with the remaining 15 per cent used for meadow (Keil 1964: table A).

Fenland is another example. H. Hallam (1965: 174–96) has collated the evidence for agricultural regimes in the Lincolnshire Fenland and adjacent fen-edge manors during the thirteenth century, though great care needs to be taken as some of the sources are clearly incomplete: for example, it is inconceivable that manors such as Tydd St Mary would have had no pasture in AD 1249. However, on average, arable accounted for 68.9 per cent on siltland manors, in contrast to 64.1 per cent on the fen-edge (Table 11). There were, however, significant variations between different areas. For example, in the Elloe region, arable was particularly important in Pinchbeck, Spalding, and Weston. In the pastoral sector, dairy production was most important in Spalding and Weston, whereas sheep dominated in Holbeach, Fleet, and Tydd St Mary. On the whole, the manors in Kirton and particularly Skirkbeck Wapentake appear to have seen even more arable cultivation that Elloe (Tables 11 and 12).

On many other reclaimed coastal wetlands, the system of agriculture appears to have

Table 11. Landuse on selected marshland manors in the Lincolnshire Fens

Manor	Date	Arable		Meadow		Pasture	
		Acreage	%	Acreage	%	Acreage	%
Wapentake of Elloe							
Pinchbeck	1291	84	100.00	–	–	–	–
Spalding and							
Weston	1330	1,651	89.4	195	10.6	–	–
Holbeach	1293	298	48.2	20	3.4	300.0	48.4
Fleet	1294	257	36.2	62	8.7	391.0	55.1
Gedney	1294	192	38.5	121	24.2	186.0	37.3
Tydd St Mary	1249	70	88.1	9.5	11.9	–	–
Tydd St Mary	1273	158	54.2	20	7.3	95.0	38.5
Tydd St Mary	1298	126	84.0	8	5.3	16.0	10.7
Tydd St Mary	1303	180	61.9	15	5.2	96.0	32.9
Wapentake of Kirton							
Gosberton	1265	120	80.0	30	20.0	–	–
Gosberton	1280	40	71.4	16	28.6	–	–
Wigtoft	1265	6	37.5	10	62.5	–	–
Wigtoft and							
Bicker	1265	47	85.5	8	14.5	–	–
Frampton	1257	190	70.9	72	27.0	6.0	2.1
Frampton	1280	161	62.3	39	15.1	58.5	22.6
Frampton	1303	130	54.6	80	33.2	28.0	12.2
Frampton and							
Wyberton	1265	60	87.0	9	13.0	–	–
Wykes (Donington)	1280	226	87.1	–	–	33.5	12.9
Wapentake of Skirbeck							
Boston	1249	24	92.3	2	7.7	–	–
Boston	1273	33	100.0	–	–	–	–
Boston	1298	40	100.0	–	–	–	–
Boston	1303	60	100.0	–	–	–	–
Fishtoft	1257	307	83.2	44	11.9	18.0	4.9
Fishtoft	1303	103	77.4	25	18.8	5.0	3.8
Fenne	1265	22	73.3	–	–	8.0	26.7
Fenne	1272	56	71.8	18	23.1	4.0	5.1
Freiston	1272	94	87.9	13	12.1	–	–
Freiston	1287	329	72.1	127	27.9	–	–

Source: Hallam 1965: tables 2–4

Table 12. Comparison of landuse on marshland and fen-edge manors in Lincolnshire

Region	Total acreage	Arable		Meadow		Pasture	
		Acreage	%	Acreage	%	Acreage	%
Elloe	3,941	2,615	66.4	311	7.9	1,015	25.7
Kirton	1,334	948	71.1	223	16.7	163	12.2
Skirbeck	931	710	76.3	188	20.2	33	3.5
Northern fen-edge	253	140	55.3	45	17.8	68	26.9
Western fen-edge	3,211	2,100	65.4	754	23.5	357	11.1
Siltland total	6,206	4,273	68.9	722	11.5	1,211	19.6
Fen-edge total	3,464	2,240	64.1	799	23.1	425	12.8

Source: Hallam 1965: 195

been mixed with, very approximately, 40 per cent of the land used for arable. On the Pevensey Levels, for example, the older marshes were put down to arable with the newly reclaimed areas used for grazing sheep. The earliest accounts are those for the Pevensey Castle demesne in AD 1283–94. Out of 277 acres, 177 were down to pasture, grazed by 25–30 cattle, and 400–600 sheep valued for their wool and cheese rather than their meat. The remaining 100 acres (36 per cent) was down to arable, with 34.5 per cent oats, 19.7 per cent wheat, 16.4 per cent beans, and 0.7 per cent barley, with 28.7 per cent left fallow (Dulley 1966: 36). A series of fourteenth century accounts illuminate the agricultural system at nearby Barnhorne (and see Moffat 1986). An infield/outfield system was practised, with fields close to the estate centre being heavily manured and ploughed most years; fields further from the centre, including those on the Levels, were cropped for three to five years and then left fallow for a similar length of time (Brandon 1971b: 75). The crops grown varied from year to year: in AD 1382 there were 59 acres of wheat and 5 acres of legumes, compared to AD 1384 when there were 90 acres of oats and 30 acres of wheat (Brandon 1971b: table 1).

There was a similar picture on Romney Marsh. At Orgarswick in AD 1292, 108 acres were under cultivation, rising to 163 acres by AD 1327 which amounted to 42 per cent of the parish (Reeves 1995a: 89; R. A. L. Smith 1943: 183). Oats were the main crop (34 per cent of the arable), with legumes as close second (31 per cent), and wheat third (26 per cent; R. A. L. Smith 1943: 183). Cultivated land was not only producing food for human consumption. During the later thirteenth century between 20 and 40 per cent of the demesne at Agney was sown with legumes, such as peas, beans and vetch, probably as a deliberate policy of increasing the fertility of the soil; in AD 1315/16 it is specifically mentioned that a newly reclaimed area of Agney was cultivated with oats and vetch (Gross and Butcher 1995: 109; R. A. L. Smith 1943: 183). A more detailed examination of the cultivation of beans on coastal wetlands is to be published elsewhere (Rippon, forthcoming d).

Legumes may also have been grown as fodder (Gross and Butcher 1995: 113; Percival 1902), which reflects the very mixed character of Romney Marsh farming. Both sheep fattening and dairy production were important, with the latter increasing throughout the thirteenth century. In AD 1285/6, for example, Agney and Orgarswick sent 7 cheeses to Canterbury, while in AD 1291/2 the number had risen to 10: reaching a peak of 33 in AD 1323/4 (R. A. L. Smith 1943: 157). A survey of AD 1257 records that, on Battle Abbey's manor at Denge Marsh, wheat, barley, and beans were cultivated, while there were 10 oxen, 12 cows, 9 two-year and 13 yearlings, 132 sheep, 15 lambs, 8 suckling pigs, and a flock of swans (Searle 1974: 253). The probate inventory of Robert de Pere of Romney, taken in AD 1278, shows a similarly mixed pattern of husbandry; 16 horses, 11 oxen, 20 cattle, 286 sheep, and 48 pigs. He left 80 seams of barley, 60 of oats, 60 of beans, 20 of peas, and 10 of tares, along with unspecified amounts of flax and hay (Woodruff 1934: 27–31).

Recent excavations on a rural settlement at Lydd Quarry suggest that the peasant economy was also based around mixed farming (L. Barber 1998). The assemblage of some 3,000 animal bones from several thirteenth/early fourteenth century settlements included 30.5 per cent cattle, 20.6 per cent sheep/goat, and 15.8 per cent pig. The animals were mainly killed in maturity suggesting that they had been kept for their secondary products such as dairy produce and wool. A wide range of cereals were recovered, dominated by hulled barley, with bread wheat next in importance, and lesser amounts of club wheat, rye, and oats, though it is unclear whether the latter were wild or cultivated.

A. Smith (1963) has used the account rolls of Canterbury Cathedral's estates throughout Kent to examine the patterns of landuse on different soil types: the chalk downlands, the Thanet Beds and brickearth terraces, the clay vales, Lower Greensand, and coastal marshes. Of the marshland manors, only Fairfield, Agney, and Orgarswick lay wholly on alluvium, with the other Romney Marsh manors (Appledore, Ebony, and Ruckinge), along with Lyden and Monkton (both in East Kent), and Cliffe (North Kent) straddling both dryland and marshland areas. A. Smith (1963) includes Cliffe and Monkton in her 'Chalkland' region since most, if not all, of the arable appears to have lain on the dryland part of each manor.

Table 13 shows the areas sown with wheat, barley, and oats. Fairly consistent proportions of wheat were grown in most regions. The overall figure for Romney Marsh is relatively low because it includes fen-edge manors such as Appledore and Ebony, whose areas of marsh were restricted to the lowest-lying backfens; this can be contrasted with Agney, Fairfield, and Orgarswick on the higher coastal ground which had, on average, the same proportion of wheat as dryland manors. All of the marshland areas had a very low proportion of barley (as was the case on the Pevensey Castle demesne). Romney Marsh had a relatively large area under oats (once again, as was the case on the Pevensey Levels) and the marshland manors also had a slightly higher than average occurrence of other crops such as rye and legumes. Clearly, careful judgements were made as to what were the most appropriate crops to be grown in each area.

10.4.2 Pastoral economies

Traditionally, the high medieval agricultural economy has been seen as dominated by arable (e.g. Postan 1972) but this was not always the case. Coastal wetlands are a case

Table 13. Crop acreages sown on Canterbury Cathedral's Kent estates in AD 1291

Region	Wheat		Barley		Oats		Total acreage
	Acreage	%	Acreage	%	Acreage	%	
Chalklands	1023.00	40	1016.0	40	526.00	20	2565.00
Thanet Beds/Brickearths	92.00	47	83.0	42	22.25	11	197.25
Claylands	73.50	46	20.0	13	65.00	14	158.50
Greensand	392.50	47	65.5	8	381.25	45	839.25
Romney Marsh	104.75	25	28.75	7	282.50	68	416.00
Lyden	98.00	79	10.0	8	16.00	13	124.00
Totals	1783.75	39	1223.25	29	1293.00	30	4300.00
Fairfield, Agney and Orgarswick	49.25	39	20.25	16	57.50	45	127.00

Source: Smith 1963.

in point. Certain areas of marshland, although embanked, appear to have been used primarily for pasture. For example, Christ Church Priory held extensive tracts of reclaimed marshland in East Kent, most of which was retained in the demesne. Little land was cultivated, and the bulk of the manorial income was derived from the sale of stock and dairy produce. During the late thirteenth/early fourteenth century there was considerable expenditure on the construction and repair of embankments and drainage ditches (13.9 per cent of annual manorial income), though, once again, this was largely for the benefit of pastoralism; the acreage under arable increased from 56 to 77 acres between AD 1305 and AD 1330 while the number of sheep increased from 214 to 490 (R. A. L. Smith 1943: 185).

Across the Thames Estuary in Essex, Christ Church Priory's manor at Milton Hall in Prittlewell included another coastal marsh that appears to have been embanked, but which was primarily used for pasture (Nichols 1925; 1926–8; 1930; 1932; and see Frances 1930; 1932). In Domesday it is recorded that there was pasture for 124 sheep, which is thought to imply coastal marshland (Darby 1977: 149–58). In AD 1327 there is reference to a breach in the sea wall (Nichols 1930: 28), indicating that an embankment had been constructed, though little else can have been carried out to improve the drainage since the detailed account roll of AD 1299 and extent of AD 1309 refer to just one hay meadow (5½ acres in 'Sutzmede': *Milton 1309*: 14; Nichols 1926–8: 14: 29–30), and no labour services or expenditure concerned with drainage or flood defence (in stark contrast to other marshland manors held by Christ Church: Smith 1943). There was, however, a 'sheep marsh' for 120 sheep and reference to a sheepcote (*Milton 1299*: 130–1; Nichols 1926–8: 26). In AD 1299, the income from this marshland was made up of £4 18s 1d from the sale of wool, £4 1s 6½d from the sale of wethers, ewes and lambs, and 30s from the sale of ewes milk.

Table 14 compares the acreages, values, and income of different landuses within Milton manor *c*. AD 1300. Clearly, the marshland was not highly valued. This is borne out in the valuations placed upon individual pieces of parcels of land within the manor, given in the extent of AD 1309 (Table 15; Nichols 1926–8). Clearly, the unimproved marshes were not valued in monetary terms as highly as the arable fields, but the Priory was quite happy with what they yielded in terms of balancing the manorial economy. It is critical to see these pastoral-based manors in the context of what was often a much larger agrarian/economic unit (i.e. a 'federative' estate).

10.4.3 Seasonal grazing

In Chapter 9 it was shown that while, in many regions, reclamation was the way that medieval communities decided to utilize their coastal wetlands, this was not always the case even at this time of high population and grain prices. In Essex, Norfolk, and along the Lincolnshire coast, large areas were left as intertidal saltmarsh, while smaller areas of unreclaimed marsh survived at Caldicot, on the Gwent Levels, and Wallingfen in the Vale of York. The technology to embank and drain these areas certainly existed and, in certain cases they were in the hands of the same monastic houses that elsewhere were

Table 14. Landuse on Canterbury Cathedral's estate of Milton, Essex, *c.* AD 1300

Landuse	Area (acres) (1309)**	Value (1309)*	Value per acre (1309)*	Income (1299)**	Income per acre (1299)**
Arable	380	£13 12s 0d	0.72s/acre	£23 0s 9¾d	2.2s/acre
Meadow	5	5s	1.0s/acre	-	-
Woodland	15	6s	0.40s/acre	-	-
Marsh	240***	10s	0.04s/acre	£10 9s 1½d	0.41s/acre _

*	Nichols 1926–8.
**	Nichols 1932.
***	pasture for 120 sheep: Nichols 1930, 28; Nichols 1932, 123.

Table 15. Land values on Canterbury Cathedral's estate of Milton, Essex, *c.* AD 1300

Landuse	Name	Acreage	Value	Value per acre
Arable	Pyrfeld	97 acres	48s 6d	6d
	Henedfeld	23 acres	23s 0d	12d
	Kyngestonesfeld	57½ acres	38s 4d	8d
	Halvehide	43 acres (+3 roods)	43s 9d	12d
	Abramsland	13 acres	6s 6d	6d
	Westwille	5 acres	2s 6d	6d
	Northfield	116 acres	£4 16s 8d	10d
	Goselond	20 acres	10s 0d	6d
	Sutzmede	½ acres	2s 9d	6d
	Total	380 acres (+3 roods)	£13 12s 0d	
Wood	Middelton Wood	15 acres	6s 0d	5d
Hay meadow		5 acres	5s 0d	12d
Several pasture	Bradefeld	11 acres	7s 4d	8d
	Sheep pasture	(120 sheep)	10s 0d	0.5d*

* The pasture for 120 sheep amounted to 240 acres (Nichols 1930, 28; Nichols 1932, 123).

actively involved with marshland drainage (e.g. Canterbury's holdings at Lyden and Milton). So, why should these coastal wetlands have been left in what would appear to have been such an under-developed state for so long?

The simple answer is that the owners and tenants were happy with the marshes as they were. For example, during the AD 1230s a large part of the marshland in Erith and Plumstead (North Kent) was flooded. The Abbot of Lesnes Priory, who held large parts of the marshes in Erith, undertook to re-embank his lands and, during the AD 1280s, was also commissioned by St Augustine's Abbey to re-defend their lands in Plumtree. Both these episodes led to disputes with the local community, since it was claimed that the Abbot enclosed other marshes without the owner's consent, and that the abbey retained those marshes until the owner had repaid the cost of inning. However, many owners of small parcels of marshland claimed that they were happy with the condition of the land as it was, though the Abbot claimed—and the jury accepted—that he had undertaken the work at the request of, and in the interests of, the whole community. The jury concluded that the Abbot of Lesnes had behaved quite properly, and that it was for the village elders to agree to actions such as these (the reclamation) and that they had done so (Bowler 1968: 61–2). In the early fourteenth century the Abbots of Lesnes and

St Augustine's were once again in trouble, after the local community complained that reclamation had led to the blocking of public rights of way, and that the Abbot of Lesnes had enclosed common land without permission. This time a jury found in favour of the community (Bowler 1968: 149–50).

There are a number of possible reasons why the smaller landowners were happy with the marshes the way they were, including avoiding the costs of maintaining flood defences. However, this is also telling us that coastal marshes were valued resources, providing a specialized environment which formed part of the complex agricultural economy. This is illustrated in Domesday, for example, by the numbers of inland manors that held coastal marshes described in terms of the number of sheep that they could support (seen most clearly in Essex, see Chapter 9; but also at Cooling and Higham in North Kent). This practice of inland manors holding detached parcels of coastal marsh continued well into the medieval period in both Romney Marsh and Essex, and this approach to exploiting the varied resources within a region is also reflected in the practice of manors holding detached woodland. In South East Essex, for example, some of the manors that held detached areas of coastal marshland also held woodland enclaves on the nearby Rayleigh Hills (Figure 69; Rackham 1986b: 103: 107; Rippon, forthcoming b).

One cause of a fragmented pattern of landholding such as this, was the tradition of intercommoning by which numerous local communities, many several miles inland, had rights of pasture on the Thames-side marshes. Once the marshes were enclosed, the various parishes whose occupants formerly had rights of common pasture each received a parcel of land. For example, the three islands of Canvey, Foulness, and Wallasea, in South East Essex, were divided between eighteen parishes (Figure 69; Cracknell 1959: 10–11; Round 1903: 369; J. Smith 1970: 9).

Another cause of the fragmented patterns of landholding seen on the Essex marshes was the process of land acquisition which, in itself, reflects how highly valued the marshes were. By the late twelfth century an active land market had developed in Essex, with lay and ecclesiastical landlords alike actively acquiring marshland (J. Ward 1987: 98). This was particularly the case near London; in Barking, for example, the 1,601 acres of marsh were divided into 182 parcels owned by 48 landowners (O'Leary 1966: 282; Oxley 1966: 215), and in Havering, c. 150 tenants, many of them commoners, held parcels of marshland (McIntosh 1986: 205; 1991: 124–5). A survey of the marshes in South West Essex, made around AD 1560, noted that 'those tenants of marsh holdings who actually lived in the Thames-side area were improperly obliged to assume full responsibility for the repair of the marsh walls, since so many of the marsh units belonged to outsiders—particularly butchers, innholders, and other citizens of London' (McIntosh 1991: 125).

The activities of Westminster Abbey on Canvey Island serve as an example. The coastal manor of South Benfleet, in South East Essex, was granted to Westminster by William I (B. Harvey 1977: 340), giving the Abbey extensive areas of marshland, but it later embarked upon a policy of active land acquisition on the adjacent Canvey Island.[47]

---

[47] The following section is based upon the unpublished research of Bob Delderfield.

In AD 1258/63 the Abbey was granted a marsh called 'Dybershope' (*WD*, f.605: 616) while, by AD 1315, they had acquired marshes called 'Monkswyk' and 'le Shore' (WD, f.609). In AD 1354 they received a further 100 acres of marsh in South Benfleet (*CPR 1354–8*: 5; *FF Essex III*, 102; *WAM* 5406), while in AD 1364/5 40 acres of marsh called 'Bartlescote', in 'Great Bemflete', was purchased (*WAM* 5703: 19,859); in AD 1392 this marsh was specified as being in Canvey Island (*CPR 1391–6*: 133). A marsh attached to the landlocked vill of Thundersley, given to the Abbey in AD 1258/83 also lay in Canvey (*WD*, f.605: f.616). In AD 1550 the Abbey's holdings on Canvey included 'Monkeswyke', 'Sharewyke', and 'Sunderwyke' (*WAM* Lease Book III, f.152).

These examples of gradual and piecemeal acquisition show that the marshland of Canvey was already divided into relatively small parcels, and that no one landowner would have been able to control, and so improve, large tracts of land. The construction of a sea wall, and its subsequent maintenance, would have been uneconomical for small parcels of marsh where the length of embankment per acre reclaimed was high.

Another factor that may have discouraged reclamation was the considerable profits that landlords could make simply from grazing sheep on a saltmarsh. This was particularly the case close to London (which provided a huge market for agricultural goods, especially fresh dairy produce: Thirsk 1967: 49). Landowners in Essex, in particular, appear to have exploited their geographical location, and a strong coastal economy developed in parts of the county. During the medieval period we have just fleeting glimpses of the developing network of small ports around the Thames, which appear to have been concerned mainly with fishing and local trade (Oppenheim 1907). The picture becomes clearer in the sixteenth century when, although larger vessels were restricted to a limited number of ports, notably Leigh and Harwich in Essex, and Rochester in Kent (Oppenheim 1907: 274), the coast was lined with numerous smaller landing places. In AD 1564/5 a survey revealed that Colchester had the most vessels (35), followed by Leigh (31), Barling (23), Burnham (21), Harwich (17), Maldon (16), Brightlingsea (12), Wivenhoe (12), Prittlewell (10), South Benfleet (5), Mersea (2), and Shoebury (1) (Oppenheim 1907: 276). Several years later vessels are also recorded at Canewdon, Hullbridge, Little Wakering, Paglesham, and Milton (Burrows 1909: 68), along with Swalecliffe and Herne, Whitstable, Queenborough, Milton, Upchurch, and Halstow in North Kent (Gibson 1993). In AD 1575 a survey was carried out of 'all the Ports, Creeks and Landing Places in England and Wales'. Essex was recorded as having 135 compared with 29 in Suffolk, 18 in Kent, 17 in Suffolk, and just 12 in Norfolk (Darby *et al.*1979: 257–8).

While the abundance of small ports partly reflects the heavily indented coastline of Essex, it must, to a great extent, reflect the emphasis that was placed upon maritime trade with London which is documented from at least the thirteenth century (J. Ward 1987: 105). All the Home Counties clearly supplied the large urban market in London, although coastal areas were at a particular advantage due to the ease of transportation. In Essex, the meat trade with London was established by the fourteenth century (e.g. West Ham: Powell 1973*b*), while cereals and hay were also shipped along the Thames (e.g. Barling, Milton, and Wakering: Burrows 1909: 25; H. Hallam 1981: 52; N. Moore

1918: 241; Wymer and Brown 1995: 169). For example, St Bartholomew's Hospital imported grain, beans, and hay from its Rainham estate as early as *c.* AD 1200 (Ransome 1978: 134). Agricultural goods (including dairy produce) were even shipped directly from Thames-side manors, such as Barking, Fobbing, and Rainham, to the continent, for examaple in AD 1367 when John Burgeys of Fobbing obtained a royal licence to ship 60 weys of cheese to Flanders (Ransome 1978: 136; J. Ward 1987: 104).

Another extensive area of marsh that was left unreclaimed during the medieval period was the Norfolk Broadland, for which a very similar range of explanations can be identified. Land ownership was highly fragmentary and large areas were common ground, neither of which is conducive to reclamation, and there were substantial markets for fresh dairy products in nearby Norwich and Yarmouth (Williamson 1997: 59–60). Above all, in a region dominated by arable farming, Broadland provided a valuable environment offering alternative resources.

Along the Lincolnshire coast north of Skegness there were also large areas of saltmarsh that were left unreclaimed. They were extensively grazed for sheep (e.g. Huttoft: see Chapter 9), although here the successful salt industry, which continued to flourish into the sixteenth century, may have been another factor (Owen 1984; Robinson 1970: 64; Rudkin and Owen 1960; Sturman 1984). Extensive areas of unenclosed summer grazing in the backfens of many coastal wetlands also survived, including the Somerset Levels (Musgrove, forthcoming; Rippon 1997*a*; M. Williams 1970), Norfolk marshland (Silvester 1988), the Cambridgeshire and Lincolshire Fens (Darby 1940*a*; H. Hallam 1965), and the Vale of York (J. Sheppard 1966).

It can be seen, therefore, that the decision not to reclaim extensive areas of saltmarsh in Essex, Norfolk, and Lincolnshire, and to use certain embanked marshes simply for sheep pasture, was due to a number of factors. The fragmented pattern of landholding, derived in part from the enclosure of former common marshes, made it difficult for any one landowner to acquire large estates (in marked contrast to areas such as Somerset and Romney Marsh where the great monastic houses controlled huge tracts of ancient demesne land). The embankment of small areas of marshland was relatively non-cost effective as a long stretch of bank had to be built and maintained in order to protect a small area of land. In some areas, like the Thames Estuary, there was even less incentive to carry out such work as the strong maritime links and proximity to London meant that there was a ready market for dairy produce (along with other natural resources such as fish and shellfish). In Lincolnshire there was a successful salt industry. Thus, although the technology to reclaim these marshes certainly existed, and in the thirteenth century population and grain prices were at their highest, the perception of many landowners was that the cost and risk of reclamation was not outweighed by the potential return considering what could be achieved by simply exploiting the rich natural resources of coastal wetlands.

By way of a postscript, the marshes of Canvey Island were finally enclosed in the early seventeenth century. A number of factors appear to have led to this dramatic transformation of the landscape, including the decreased demand for Essex cheeses, increased demand for beef from London (the biggest market for Canvey's produce), and the consolidation of landholding by the Appleton family (Cracknell 1959: 15–19): thus, two of the factors that discouraged reclamation—demand for wetland resources and the nature of landholding—were reversed.

10.5 **Discussion**

During the twelfth and thirteenth centuries, the landscape of North West Europe was coming under increased strain, reflected generally by rising grain prices and the extent of arable cultivation. This is also reflected in the degree to which coastal resources were exploited, which was far more intensely than during the Roman period. Fish formed an increasingly significant part of the diet, and this resulted in two clear phenomena: around the eighth century, there is evidence of increased investment in the construction and maintenance of fixed fishing weirs, while around the tenth century, there was increased exploitation of off-shore waters as freshwater fisheries could no longer meet demand. A similar tendency can also be seen in the consumption of shellfish, with widespread cultivation (particularly of oysters) from around the twelfth century. Salt was essential for the preservation of fish as it travelled far inland and, throughout the twelfth and thirteenth centuries, coastal salt production flourished in North West Europe.

Also, from around the eighth century, water was increasingly regarded as a resource in terms of its ability to power watermills, as at Corbridge, Oxford, Tamworth, and Old Windsor (Blair 1994: 63; Anon 1996: 5; P. Rahtz and Meeson 1992); possible mill leets have also been recorded at Skerne in the Hull Valley (Dent *et al.* 2000: 242) and Wicken Bonhunt in Essex (Wade 1980: 96). Measures were also taken to overcome the obstacles to transport that bodies of water posed. From the eighth century, the service of bridge work is increasingly mentioned as being owed to the Crown (Stenton 1971: 291). At the end of the seventh century a half mile long causeway between Mersea Island and the Essex coast was constructed using 3,000–5,000 oak piles (Crummy *et al.* 1982). Around the ninth/tenth century a causeway and bridge were constructed in the Hull Valley at Skerne (Dent 1984; Dent *et al.* 2000), while a canal was constructed at Glastonbury (C. Hollinrake and N. Hollinrake 1991). In the mid-eleventh century, the men of Oxford requested that the monks of Abingdon cut a navigation canal between Abingdon and Culham (Blair 1994: 123). The management and exploitation of water as a resource was on the increase.

From around the tenth century, there was a widespread move towards the embanking of coastal marshes, and most of the areas now protected from tidal flooding were used for mixed agriculture, with a strong arable component. Crop yields and land values show that reclamation was certainly worth the cost and risk, although in certain areas the embanked land was simply used for sheep pastures. This reflects the fact that certain landowners realised that profits could also be made from less intensive forms of landscape utilization, particularly in areas close to large towns that provided a market for dairy produce. As was seen in the Roman period, each individual landscape needs to be seen in its local context.

CHAPTER 11

Taking the initiative:

landscape transformation during the medieval period

11.1 Introduction

Having examined the initial recolonization and reclamation of coastal marshes in North West Europe during the early medieval period (Chapter 8), the subsequent expansion into lower-lying backfens (Chapter 9), and the uses to which both reclaimed and unreclaimed wetlands were then put (Chapter 10), it is time to consider *why* these landscapes were transformed to such an extent. First, the context of the early medieval expansion is examined in terms of possible changes in the natural environment and the wider socio-economic circumstances of that time, followed by a discussion of who was responsible for reclamation, and the tenurial context in which it occurred.

11.2 The processes of reclamation

In Chapter 3 the basic process of embankment was described along with two approaches to reclamation: the *systematic* drainage of most, or all, of the area protected from tidal flooding, and the *unsystematic*, piecemeal, enclosure of land within an embanked marsh when and if new land was required (Figure 13I and J; Figure 18C and D). During the early medieval period the only example of systematic reclamation in North West Europe appears to be the tenth century peat reclamations in North Holland (Figure 62; Chapter 8). It was not until the major expansion into the freshwater backfens, seen throughout the coastal wetlands of North West Europe from around the twelfth century, that systematic drainage and enclosure occurred on a large scale (Chapter 9).

Figure 51(A–G) shows a schematic model for wetland reclamation, initially based upon a detailed examination of the Severn Estuary Levels (Rippon 1996a; 1997a), and modified in the light of fieldwork on the early 'infield' enclosures, which raised the possibility of their being seasonal 'ring-dikes' similar to those used on the continent (Figure 51: 1–4). The relationship between infields and coastal sea walls around the Severn Estuary remains unresolved, but otherwise the basic sequence appears to be one of early settlement on the higher coastal marshes, associated with piecemeal enclosure and drainage leading to a highly irregular landscape, followed by an expansion into the lower-lying backfens associated with long droveways, fen-banks, and the more systematic enclosure of land.

The same is true in many other British coastal wetlands (Chapter 8). For example, in Fenland, recent work has shown that reclamation was preceded by a phase of settlement in a high intertidal environment and, although efforts were made to modify that landscape through the digging of drainage ditches, there were no attempts at even localized embankment. Some of these settlements were located on the naturally raised ground afforded by relict creeks (roddons) but there were no artificially raised mounds. When reclamation was finally undertaken, a sea wall appears to have built along the coast (see Figure 51B) as there is no evidence for 'ring dikes'. Initially, piecemeal enclosure and drainage was then centred on the rodden-based settlements, and proceeded into the lower-lying backfens. The historic landscape that subsequently developed in Norfolk marshland, for example (Figure 60), is broadly similar to those around the Severn Estuary and presumably results from the same basic approach to enclosure and drainage.

On the Continent, the colonization of coastal wetlands appears to have, broadly, followed the model shown in Figure 51 (1–4), with the earliest embankment being of localized areas, whether behind the sand dune barrier of the western Netherlands or on the more open marshes of the northern Netherlands and Germany. Thereafter, reclamation proceeded in a broadly similar fashion to that shown in Figure 51(D–G), as the lower-lying backfens were enclosed and drained in a far more systematic fashion compared to the coastal marshes. The human response to flooding changed from the relatively *passive*—building raised mounds—to the far more *active*—the exclusion of water from the landscape as a whole. So, why was a broadly similar process of landscape transformation seen throughout much of North West Europe during the medieval period?

11.3 The context of reclamation

This process of marshland colonization and reclamation must not be viewed in isolation: it was part of a wider western European phenomena that saw economic growth and settlement expansion into other 'marginal' areas such as forest and heathland. Traditionally, the major period of expansion has been regarded as starting in the twelfth century. For example, Duby (1968: 69) has argued that 'Pioneering activity which had remained timid, discontinuous and locally dispersed throughout two centuries became more intense and co-ordinated around 1150'. This view, that the main period of reclamation and settlement expansion was during the twelfth century, is based upon the available documentary material which, as Duby (1968: 69) also notes, only becomes abundant during the twelfth century. In this respect it is a shame that a more telling observation was reserved for a footnote:

> This [lack of earlier documentary material] encourages us to ask whether reclamations in the ninth and tenth centuries were not more widespread than they

appear in the documents of the period which almost all originate from monasteries of this type. This brings us up against one of the main difficulties of historical research: are not the changes revealed illusory, and do they not merely reflect the provenance of the documentary material rather than reality?

In the light of these doubts, it is unfortunate that Duby (1968: xi) had earlier dismissed archaeology as 'auxiliary research' since, where field survey, excavation, and palaeoenvironmental research has taken place on the early medieval landscape (for example in Fenland), it has proved far more informative than the available documents. In fact, the period of reclamation and settlement expansion that characterized the twelfth and thirteenth centuries simply represented the culmination of a much longer-term process that had its roots several hundred years before.

So, why did human communities leave the relative comfort and safety of dryland areas in order to settle physically marginal environments such as coastal wetlands? In Chapter 1 (Table 1), three sets of factors were identified:

- push factors that make occupation of a specific region less favourable so forcing human communities to consider settling the adjacent areas;
- pull factors that represent positive qualities specific to those destinations that attracted human communities to them;
- contextual factors that encourage an increasing intensity of landscape exploitation in all areas and, as such, would have particularly affected relatively under-exploited landscapes such as coastal wetlands.

During the early medieval period, two simplistic arguments have traditionally dominated all discussion of the expansion and contraction of settlement in coastal areas: environmental change and migrations. For example, Behre (1990*b*: 35) states that 'This first Wurten phase lasted from the first to the fifth century AD when the Wurten were abandoned, probably because their inhabitants emigrated to England together with their neighbours from the Geest areas.' With regard to the embanking in the *terp* region of the northern Netherlands, Lambert (1971: 81) states that,

> By this date [AD 1000] the Viking raids were practically over and a marine regression had set in. Freed from the onslaughts of both man and nature the inhabitants of these regions turned back to the task of protecting their lands not only from the obvious effects of sea floods but also from the more insidious penetration of the salt water inland.

So, were coastal communities simply being bounced around North West Europe by folk movements, barbarian raids, and the sea, or did they take a more pro-active part in the utilization of their environment?

11.3.1 The physical environment

The recent perception of coastal wetlands has been dominated by the view that they are physically marginal environments (see Chapter 1), but, in practice, even tidally inundated marshland could be extremely productive. The excellent opportunities for communication that their coastal location afforded, meant that marshlanders occupied what were often 'core' political-economic regions. For example, when the distribution of early medieval wealth is viewed for the whole of The Netherlands, a number of areas—or 'nuclear regions'—stand out, one of which is the marsh region of the northern Netherlands (e.g. Heidinga 1990: fig. 1; 1997: 21; Lambert 1971: fig. 30). While part of this wealth reflects the success of the Frisians in their trading activities, it was ultimately supported by an agrarian/ subsistence economy revolving around the successful rearing of cattle and sheep. This was landscape exploitation at its most successful, and represents one of the major 'pull' factors that encouraged the colonization of these marshes.

Certain changes in the natural environment may have made coastal wetlands a more attractive place to live (so constituting another set of 'pull' factors). The climatic amelioration at this time would have made marshlands easier to farm: the eighth century was relatively mild and dry and, although the ninth century saw a brief return to colder and wetter conditions, there may then have been a period of drought throughout North West Europe during the tenth century which marked the onset of the medieval climatic optimum (Chapter 2; Heidinga 1984; Lamb 1995: 171–2: figs 30 and 59). At the same time, these same climatic conditions may have pushed certain communities towards the coastal wetlands, as the formation of the 'Younger Dunes' buried fields and settlements along the coast and conditions on the inland sandy areas became increasingly difficult (Besteman 1990: 96; Hallewas 1984: 301).

In Chapter 2 it was shown that there is little lithostratigraphic or palaeoenvironmental evidence for a widespread period of marine regression during the late first millennium AD, and Hofstede (1991) even argues for a rise in sea level between the seventh and thirteenth centuries. However, there were other, more localized, changes in the natural environment that do appear to have made *certain* coastal wetlands a more favourable place to live. In North Holland, for example, breaches to the coastal barrier appear to have improved the natural drainage as the discharge of fresh water was made easier (Besteman 1990: 93), while the diversion of the 'proto-Rother' in Romney Marsh meant that an extensive area of marshland was now relatively flood free. A combination of these 'push' and 'pull' factors meant that, overall, coastal wetlands were increasingly more hospitable despite the lack of a widespread marine regression.

11.3.2 Contextual factors

In addition to changes in the natural environment that often worked at a very localized scale, it is also important to see developments in coastal wetlands, or any individual region, in their wider cultural context. For example, in two instances, events on coastal wetlands appear to form part of what were much wider phenomena affecting much of North West Europe: the mass folk migrations seen around the fifth century (see Chapter 7) and the period of economic expansion at the end of the millennium.

The later first millennium AD saw a general increase in the vigour with which human communities utilized landscapes throughout North West Europe, with an expansion of settlement into many 'wilderness' areas such as forests and heathlands. In coastal wetlands this was usually associated with arable cultivation, but increased agricultural production could be achieved not just through extensification—the creation of new land—but also through intensification—using existing land more effectively. For example, it was not just in Fenland that rural landscapes were reorganized during the late first millennium AD, as a dispersed scatter of settlements was replaced by nucleated villages throughout the adjacent East Midlands (Brown and Foard 1998; D. Hall 1988; D. Hall and P. Martin 1979; C. Lewis et al. 1997). As C. Lewis (1996: 100) has observed, these episodes of village creation coincide with a major transformation of North West Europe and 'a period of widespread economic and social expansion ... which saw increasingly systematic law and government, considerable growth in the market economy, and the spread of institutions such as castles, monasteries or towns by example and emulation'.

This socio-economic dynamism manifests itself in a number of ways. For example, in parts of lowland Britain, including Somerset, the tenth century saw mass-produced pottery reappear on rural settlements for the first time since the Roman period, suggesting an increasingly market-based system of exchange. These pottery industries were closely linked to the emerging network of towns, and the growth of urbanism itself is indicative of an expanding economy (D. Hinton 1990: 82–105). In a number of coastal towns the tenth century saw an expansion in waterfront development, often associated with craft activities, and both the raw materials and food to sustain these urban communities largely came from the countryside. Such conditions would have been favourable to increased agricultural production in all areas, especially coastal wetlands, with their enormous potential for agricultural productivity. The church, a major landowner in coastal areas, was an important player in the tenth century revival, experiencing a period of monastic reform, one aspect of which was a renewed interest in the management of its estates (Stenton 1971: 444–50). Many lands that had been appropriated by the lay nobility were recovered, and on the estates of Glastonbury Abbey, for example, whole landscapes were reorganized as nucleated villages replaced dispersed settlement patterns, being part of what Costen (1992: 25) describes as 'an economic and social revolution which was going on in a rural tenth century Somerset' (and see Aston 1997; Corcos 1983). The expansion of settlement into physically marginal environments, and the investment of considerable resources in reclamation enabling an intensification in how that landscape was utilized, sits very comfortably in this period of expansion and innovation.

In summary, a wide range of factors appears to have contributed to both the initial expansion of settlement into coastal wetlands around the eighth and ninth century, and the subsequent decision to start building embankments around the tenth century. Though there does not appear to have been a general fall in relative sea level, breaches in natural coastal barriers appear to have improved drainage in a number of areas. Climatic changes may have had a fairly positive effect on wetlands, and may have made any adjacent sandy soils increasingly difficult to work. However, it is probably to the more general, contextual, factors that we must look: coastal wetlands appear to have offered enormous opportunities at a time of expanding population and economic growth.

11.4 Cultural landscape change: who was responsible?

Much of the discussion so far, regarding the expansion of settlement into coastal wetlands, has talked very generally of 'human communities' and the decisions that they made in the light of a variety of environmental, social, economic, and political 'push', 'pull', and 'contextual' factors. A key issue that must now be addressed is how those communities were organized, and who took the decisions to modify and transform coastal wetlands. In Chapter 3 (Figure 18), four possible estate structures were identified within which coastal marshes may have been used:

A. Marshland exploited directly from a fen-edge estate centre

B. Marshland exploited by a settlement attached to a fen-edge estate centre

C. Marshland exploited by a wholly marshland, and tenurially independent, community

D. Marshland forming a detached part of a distant estate centre

Those people who settled the coastal areas may have established themselves in a number of ways including:

1. Piecemeal settlement on the initiative of independent farmers, in what was regarded as waste land that was not owned by anyone

2. A tenant population attracted to a lord's estate through incentives (e.g. low rents), as part of that lord's strategy of improving productivity, but still resulting in a piecemeal process of reclamation as there was no overall planning

3. planned colonization on the initiative of an estate owner as part of that lord's strategy of consolidating political control and improving productivity

Model 1 is most likely to have occurred with Estate Structure C, whereas Colonization Models 2 and 3 would have occurred in Estate Structure B or D (Model A not being associated with colonization of the marshland).

The simple exploitation of the natural resources of a saltmarsh required relatively little input of resources. Even the modification of a small area of marsh through the digging of localized ditched drainage systems, or even summer dikes, was not a major undertaking. However, the decision to construct a continuous sea wall along a coast, and its subsequent maintenance, was a major undertaking: so who took that decision?

For the Roman period, we can only guess at the structure of landholding, although the concentration of settlement along many fen-edges, and analogy with the medieval period, suggests that a pattern of 'federative' estates may have existed, whose boundaries straddled several environmental zones and included a range of settlements, some of which may have had a specialized economy (Chapters 5–6). This was certainly the situation in the medieval period with, particularly, the pastoral resources of coastal wetlands forming part of the wider agrarian economy of many great estates (Chapter 10). However, this still leaves the issue of who was responsible for modifying and transforming these landscapes: lords or tenants?

The documentary record for the medieval period leads to a strong impression that the great estate owners were the key players (see Duby 1968: 69 quoted above). In both Britain and on the Continent, charters show that by the twelfth century monastic houses were major landlords in coastal areas, and it has often been assumed that they were directly involved in the reclamation and settlement of their estates. This certainly was the case with religious orders such as the Cistercians who actively improved their estates from the twelfth century (e.g. Duby 1968: 146), but there are problems in assuming that this was necessarily the case as far back as the eighth century (not least because the highly interventionist Cistercian order was not founded until the twelfth century). The estate management policies of a landlord can also change over time, illustrated, for example, by altering preferences for leasing versus direct management of demesne land during the twelfth and thirteenth centuries. It must once again be stressed that throughout the medieval period, and particularly before the twelfth century, our documentary record is very biased towards the achievement of the Crown and the Church. In assessing their role in landscape change we also need to know about the work of lesser lords and the rural population as a whole, yet they have left us few records. Yet another bias is that the records we have tell us much about the maintenance of existing features, but far less about their creation in the first place.

11.4.1 Centralized control

There are examples where the decision to reclaim coastal wetlands appears to have been the result of direct intervention by the estate owners though, in most cases, day-to-day work appears to have been delegated to others. The clearest example is the 'cope' reclamations of South Holland. Around the tenth century, the authority of the Carolingian kings started to collapse as new territorial rulers, such as the Bishops of Utrecht and Counts of Holland, assumed many royal powers and privileges, including regalian rights over wilderness areas (TeBrake 1985: 49, 138–9). This resulted in a cultural environment that was favourable to the more effective utilization of landscape resources. In contrast to the old social order, who were content to keep peasants in the traditional areas of settlement and cultivation, the new landlords actively encouraged the colonization of new land, offering tenants favourable terms such as low rents and complete personal freedom. This led to the 'great reclamation' of the peat bogs of South Holland using the 'cope' system (see Chapter 9).

In thirteenth century Delfland the Counts of Holland used a similar approach of encouraging others to undertake reclamation at a time when increased storm floods were a growing problem (Lambert 1971: 99–102). The Counts of Holland owned the majority of the land, and they attracted wealthy individuals to invest in reclamation in return for privileges such as permission to build moated sites (Bult 1986: 23–4).

A similar situation applied in the coastal marshes of northern Germany. Hövermann (cited in Mayhew 1973: 49) argues that reclamation may have been initiated by local nobles who wanted to regularize the work of local farmers, whereas, Kersting and Mangels, supported by Mayhew (1973: 49), argue that it was only after the introduction of

Dutch settlers by the great territorial landlords, such as the Archbishop of Bremen and Hamburg, that systematic reclamation was undertaken. A process of colonization not dissimilar to the 'cope' reclamations of South Holland appears to have been undertaken, with 'lokators' employed to survey the land and undertake the necessary engineering works, and groups of tenants encouraged to the area with very low rents in order to colonize the newly reclaimed land. There are even agreements whereby Dutch colonists were used to undertake the drainage, for example in AD 1149 when the archbishop granted undrained land on the Lower Weser to two men in order for them to found new settlements and reclaim the land 'according to the rights and duties of the dutch' (Mayhew 1973: 50). In addition to references to the colonists as *Hollandense* (Dutchmen), Dutch technical expressions were used, and the size of holdings in the newly enclosed landscape and form of tax (*census*) paid to the lord, was the same as in the 'cope' reclamations of South Holland: 'the Dutch immigrants ... brought, from home, their whole system of settlement and reclamation to Germany' (Van der Linden 1982: 46–7).

Another area of North West Europe that may have been colonized in a similar way is South West Wales, where English and Flemish colonists were introduced by Henry I during the early twelfth century in order to improve the productivity of what was a previously sparsely populated and under-cultivated landscape. Flemings enjoyed a reputation for being rigorous colonizers and were also planted in parts of Clydesdale and Moray by the Kings of Scotland during the twelfth century (R. Davies 1987: 98–9: 159; Rowlands 1980: 146). This use of colonists was part of a conscious part of the policy employed by the Anglo-Norman lords of increasing productivity and security on their newly-acquired estates, which can also be seen in the foundation of numerous castles, small boroughs, and planned villages (M. Beresford 1967; M. Beresford and Finberg 1973; Kissock 1996; 1997; K. Murphy 1997).

Reclamation on the Gwent Levels, in South East Wales, may have been part of a very similar process. Personal names as well as place-names, field-names show that English colonists were certainly settled on the Gwent Levels during the twelfth century, and the structure of nucleated settlements and open fields is typical of Midland England (Rippon 1996a: 63–5; 1997b; forthcoming, c; Sylvester 1969). There is no documentary evidence that Flemings were also employed here, though there is place-name evidence in the form of 'Cogan-Fleming' on the Wentlooge Level (though the earliest reference is seventeenth century), and the planned village of Whitson, which is morphologically very similar to the examples in South West Wales (Rippon 1996a: 84–7). Flemish involvement in other British coastal wetlands is less clear and references, such as that in AD 1311 to a 'Flemingges Wall' on the Plumstead and Erith marshes in North Kent (Bowler 1968: 151; Spurrell 1885: 302), may simply represent the work of an individual water engineer rather than the settlement of that region with a population of colonists.

11.4.2 Early peatland drainage in North Holland

Bos (1990: 124) has argued that the initial reclamation in North Holland was carried out under some form of aristocratic supervision, but admits that while the Counts of

Holland may have had a role to play in Kennemerland and West Friesland, it was not to the same extent as in South Holland. By contrast, Besteman (1988: 340) argues that the decision to reclaim the backfen peat bogs appears to have been taken by free village communities while Lambert (1971: 98) describes the reclamation as 'spontaneous peasant activity before the Count had much to say about these developments'. Borger (1992: 142) also argues that the irregular layout of the ditched drainage systems indicate that these early wetland reclamations were the result of 'free enterprise, not superintended by the authority of a count, noblemen of the church'.

The possibility of some lordly involvement cannot be ruled out, however. Charters show that the region was already divided into large estates, many of which were granted to the church and local lords who are unlikely to have had no role in deciding how their land was managed. There was royal property in Medemblik, Texel, and Wieringen, some of the rights of which had been acquired by the Bishop of Utrecht. Although there appears to have been a lack of any standard unit of planning used in the reclamation, compared with the far more carefully planned 'cope' system used in twelfth century South Holland, the organization of space within the tenth century drainage of places like Assendelft does indicate a considerable degree of co-ordination (Figure 62). Indeed, as Besteman (1990: 117) points out, a picture of 'free reclaimers who wielded the spade in mutual harmony' is not compatible with our understanding of the hierarchical nature of an early medieval society dominated by inequality and social dependence.

11.4.3 The role of the Church

It is generally assumed that monastic landlords were great improvers of their lands, and the Church was certainly granted extensive estates in marshland areas. In many cases the documentary record gives the impression that monasteries in particular were at the forefront of marshland drainage during the medieval period (e.g. Bowler 1968; M. Williams 1970; 1982). But this evidence warrants further examination with two specific questions in mind: first, what was the role of the church in the initial act of reclamation during the ninth to eleventh centuries and, second, just how significant was their contribution even in the twelfth and thirteenth centuries?

The early medieval period

The relatively abundant charter evidence for Romney Marsh allows the condition of a number of marshland estates before they were granted to the Church to be examined through features described in the boundary clauses (Table 16). These reveal a landscape that was *already* divided up into a series of well-defined estates, with cultivation in some places extending to the very bounds of these estates: the *initial* colonization and reclamation of Romney Marsh cannot have been the work of the Church.

So, were the landowners who granted these estates to the Church responsible for the initial act of reclamation? During the late seventh to late eighth century the recorded grants were made exclusively by the Kings of Kent or Mercia, depending on who ruled the region at the time (Table 16), though from the late eighth and, more especially, the

Table 16. Early medieval landownership on Romney Marsh

Date	Granted by	Received by	Estate	Sawyer 1968
697x700	King Wihtred of Kent	St Mary's Lyminge	Pasture at *Rumening seta*	S.21
724	King Aethelberht of Kent	St Mary's Lyminge	Land and meadow at *Hammespot*	S.1180
741	King Aethelberht II of Kent	St Mary's Lyminge	Properties in Romney	S.24
773	King Aethelberht II of Kent	St Mary's Lyminge	Land for saltworks [Sandtun]	S.23
774	King Offa of Mercia	AB of Canterbury	3 ploughlands [in Lydd]	S.111
798	King Cenwulf of Mercia	Oswulf	*Hafingseota* and *Bobingseata*	S.153
798	Oswulf	St Mary's Lyminge	*Hafingseota* and *Bobingseata*	S.153
805	King Cuthred of Kent	St Mary's Lyminge	Two ploughlands at Hrocing	S.39
811	King Cenwulf of Mercia	AB Canterbury	Land in Romney Marsh	S.168
830	Werhard	Christchurch, Cant.	Land including *Lambahamm*	S.830
845	King Egbert of Kent	Bishop of Winchester	Land at *Flotham*	S.282
<848	Aedbald	Winemund	Land at Burmarsh *Halfsaeta*	S.1193
848	Winemund	St Augustine's, Cant.	Land at Burmarsh	S.1650
848x864	Winemund	St Augustine's, Cant.	Land at Burmarsh and *Wyk*	S.1651
875	Eardulf	Wihelm	Land and marsh at *Hamme*	S.1203
924	AB Canterbury	Byrhtraed	80 acres in *Waering* Marsh	S.1288
946	King Edmund	Ordhelm and Alfwold	10 cornfields at *Gamelanwyrthe*	S.510
1009	Godweald	St Augustine's, Cant.	10 acres at Sturton	S.1656

AB = Archbishop; Cant. = Canterbury

mid-ninth century, there were a number of gifts recorded by the laity. The presence of extensive royal estates is also reflected by the number of references to *terra regis* in the charter bounds, such as near 'Sandtun' (S.23; S.270) and Burmarsh *Halfsaeta* (S.1193). However, while the Crown was clearly a significant landowner on Romney Marsh during the early medieval period, it is unlikely that the Kings of Mercia took a great interest in saltmarsh reclamation on a distant corner of their territory. We are, therefore, left with the paradox that the construction of a sea wall along the line of what later became Yoke Sewer would have been a major undertaking but, once completed, the dispersed settlement pattern and irregular systems of fields and roads that were created suggest a gradual and piecemeal system of reclamation without any overall direction.

During the early medieval period a number of early monastic foundations acquired estates in Fenland e.g. Crowland (Raban 1977), Peterborough, (King 1973), Ramsey (Raftis 1957), and Thorney (Raban 1977). The greatest was that of Ely whose estate included all of the Cambridgeshire coastal marshland along with a number of holdings in Norfolk around Walton (Miller 1951; Silvester 1988: 160, fig. 3.5). In AD 1109 these estates were divided between the bishop and the convent, and later many parcels of land came into the hands of powerful lessees (Pugh 1953), but as the initial colonization of the marshlands around the eighth/ninth centuries, and the decision to embank during the tenth century, pre-dates this fragmentation of the estate, Ely may have had a significant role.

The origins of Ely appear to have lain in the seventh century, although its early history remains obscure until its re-foundation in AD 970 (Miller 1951: 8). By Domesday, it was the dominant landowner in the Cambridgeshire marshes, whereas in Norfolk it was simply one of many landowners who held estates there. It is possible, however, that in earlier centuries Ely may have been the dominant landowner in Norfolk marshland as well. In Wisbech the ancient tradition of administration, based on units known as 'ferdings' or 'leets', shows strong links with the Norfolk marshland villages around West Walton on the other side of the Great Ouse/Nene Estuary, suggesting that they may once have been within the same ancient estate. Indeed, in the thirteenth century organization of the Bishop's estate, Wisbech was associated with the Norfolk marshland bailiwick as opposed to the rest of the Hundred of Ely and 'that association may have had a very venerable origin' (Miller 1951: 33). If Ely had acquired these marshes back in the seventh and eighth centuries, it may have been in this context that they were initially settled during the Middle Saxon period, when the regular arrangement of settlements suggests a planned division of the landscape (Chapter 8: Figure 59).

A second context for Ely's active involvement on the management of their marshland estates was following its re-foundation in AD 970. This led to a period of rapid land accumulation, notably between AD 970 and AD 984 when a contemporary chronicler described how the abbey 'bought many villages from the king and made it very rich' (Miller 1951: 17). Royal endowment was a common feature of this great era of monastic reform and provides a plausible context for the wider reorganization of estate management throughout North West Europe (see above). In Norfolk it is possible that the decision to embank marshland during the tenth century was part of the same drive towards the more efficient utilization of the landscape and, in terms of the possible scenarios for landscape change outlined above, a lord taking the initiative in deciding to improve the productivity of their estate through planned colonization and improvements such as drainage, may have applied in this instance.

The high medieval period

Of the post-Conquest orders, the Cistercians have the greatest reputation of being progressive estate managers with a keen interest in drainage. Unreclaimed marsh or fen is recorded in the foundation grants of several Cistercian houses[48] and, within a few decades, most estates probably had access to some marshland (Donkin 1958; 1978: 116). The site of Meaux in the Hull Valley, for example, was described as dry and fertile though it was surrounded by mere and fen and, during the thirteenth century the abbey was actively draining their lands with a series of granges established at Arnold, Salthaugh, Myton, Sutton, and Tharlethorpe (Donkin 1978: 116). Tintern Abbey in South East Wales held two granges on the Gwent Levels, Lower Grange in Magor and New Grange in Redwick, where the monks were responsible for enclosing and draining the land (Rippon 1996a: 79–81). However, as with Llantarnam Abbey's grange at Pwll-Pan (near Llanwern), these estates lay in the backfen, beyond the higher coastal marshes that had already been protected from tidal inundation through the construction of a sea wall and extensively settled: the Cistercian contribution was in the continued enclosure and drainage of the backfen, not the initial act of reclamation. Similarly, in The Netherlands, a number of monastic houses such as Bloemkamp near Wittewierum, the

---

[48] At Combermere, Hulm Cultram, Kirkstead, Meaux, Revesby, Sawtry, Stanlaw, Stratford Langthorn, Swineshead, and Vaudey.

community of St John the Evangelist at Kloosterburen, and the monastery at Aduard, were also involved in reclaiming the backfens (Lambert 1971: 85).

Other post-Conquest foundations also held areas of marshland, though their contribution towards the initial act of reclamation, as opposed to maintaining and improving the drainage and flood defence systems that they inherited or acquired, is less clear. One example is Lesnes Abbey in North Kent, founded in AD 1178 (Bowler 1968: 61–2; Clapham 1915: 2). By AD 1199 it certainly held an area of marshland, though its condition is not specified; only in AD 1230/40 does it become clear that reclamation had taken place, as the sea walls are recorded as having been breached, and the Abbot spent considerable sums on their restoration. Whether the abbey reclaimed the marshes in the first place is not known. In Fenland there were also a multiplicity of lesser monasteries founded from the late eleventh century,[49] although their role in shaping the landscape was simply as one of many contributors. In Lincolnshire there is very little evidence of ecclesiastical involvement in the enclosure, drainage, and settlement of the coastal marshes, and just one monastic grange lay seaward of the early medieval sea wall: Wykeham, built by Spalding Priory, in the 'newlands' of Spalding in AD 1311 (H. Hallam 1965: 16). Only in the northern Netherlands were monasteries heavily involved in embanking in front of the original sea walls, such as the twelfth century foundation at Anjumand Mariëngarde which reclaimed saltmarshes adjacent to the Oude Bildt polder near Leuwarden (Lambert 1971: 88).

However, in many regions, it was in the improvement of backfen areas, already protected from tidal inundation, that the monastic houses made their greatest contribution. Fenland is a good example. The granting of lands in these areas to various monasteries is evident in Domesday from the entries for Crowland's two holdings in Quadring which were described as 'inland of this manor'. The strong monastic interest in the backfen is also reflected in the distribution of granges, which mostly lay in the backfens. On occasion the monasteries and their granges collaborated with the local communities in the construction of fen-banks, as in AD 1205 when Thomas of Moulton granted Spalding Priory and the villages of Spalding and Weston land in the backfen in order to extend the common bank of Goldyke (H. Hallam 1965: 30). The Priory subsequently acquired, through purchase and exchange, a large block of land in the area now protected from flooding in order to establish, around c. AD 1300, its Goll Grange which, by AD 1330, comprised 292 acres of arable and 195 acres of meadow (ibid.). To the east of Goll Grange, Spalding Priory held another (Gannock Grange), while Crowland Abbey held granges of Aswick and Fenhall, all of which were created during the late thirteenth/early fourteenth century. In AD 1330 it is recorded that 'the manor of Gannock at Sutton . . . can fairly be called newly-tilled lands, since they have only recently been brought into cultivation from the fen' (H. Hallam 1965: 37). Clearly, these monastic houses were directly improving their estates, with arable cultivation being a major goal.

In Norfolk there was also monastic involvement in backfen enclosure and drainage,

[49] Bardney, Barlings, Blackborough, Bury St Edmunds, Castle Acre, Deeping, Frieston, Haverholme, Kirkstead, Norwich, Pentney, Pipewell, Shouldham, Spalding, Stixwould, Swineshead, Walsingham, Waltham, Westacre, and West Dereham (Hallam 1965; Page 1906; Silvester 1988: 22).

such as Ramsey Abbey's demesne farm of Popenhoe in Walsoken, Norfolk (Silvester 1988: 85). Crabhouse Nunnery, founded by AD 1181, lay on the banks of the Ouse in Wiggenhall St Mary Magdalen parish (Silvester 1988: 107–8). The field boundary pattern in this, the southern part of the parish, is markedly different to that in the north (which appears to result from entrepreneurial reclamation by freeholders: see below), and it may have been that the nunnery had a direct part to play.

As we have seen in The Netherlands and Germany, though the Church sometimes took direct responsibility for reclamation, they often delegated this responsibility to others. For example, in the Vale of York, the Bishop of Durham held an extensive area of marshland within the lordship of Howdenshire, which was reclaimed during the twelfth and thirteenth century, after Bishop Hugh de Pudsey granted a series of manors to various individuals who proceeded to embank and drain the land (J. Sheppard 1966: 15). A similar approach was adopted by Christ Church Priory in some of its reclamations in Walland Marsh, illustrated by the grant in AD 1155/67 of lands at Misleham to Baldwin Scadeway 'in so far as he could enclose it against the sea at his own expense' (see Chapter 9).

Another example of tenants being left to their own devices within part of a major estate is the Bishop of Worcester's manor of Henbury, beside the Severn Estuary. A survey of AD 1299 shows that all the arable demesne was located on dryland close to the estate centre, with the reclaimed marshes being the preserve of customary tenants and several sub-infeudated holdings that were created during the 11th and twelfth centuries, such as the five and a half hides held by the Saltmarsh family in Lawrence Weston (Hollings 1950: 438). This suggests that the improvement of the embanked part of the manor, if not the construction of the embankments themselves, was the work of tenants and freeholders and not the Bishop.

11.4.4 Reclamation by the laity

The creation, survival, and subsequent analysis of documentary records, have created a marked bias towards ecclesiastical estates. We must not forget that, although a major land owner, the Church did not dominate all areas of the landscape. Fenland provides an example for while the initial act of settlement colonization and reclamation in the Cambridgeshire and Norfolk marshes may have occurred in the context of a great monastic estate, namely Ely (see above), Lincolnshire presents a far more complex picture. The structure of landholding at Domesday is shown in Table 17.

By AD 1086 land ownership on the Lincolnshire marshes was dominated by Count Alan and Guy of Craon, though both these lordships were post-Conquest creations and before AD 1066 the pattern of land holding was far more fragmented (Platts 1985: 14). Of the 62 manors listed in Table 17 the owner in AD 1066 is listed in 44 cases. There were just 3 lords with more than 3 manors: St Guthlac's (Crowland Abbey) with 8, and Aethelstan and Earl Algar with 7 each. Aethelstan's holdings were scattered, though Earl Algar held much of the eastern part of Elloe wapentake between the Old Whaplode River and the Ouse Estuary. Crowland held a number of scattered manors, though its

Table 17. The structure of 11th century landholding in the Lincolnshire Fenland

Manor	AD 1066	AD 1086
Skirbeck Wapentake		
Wrangle	?	Count Alan
Wrangle	Aethelstan	Guy of Craon
Leake	?	Count Alan
Leverton	?	Count Alan
Butterwick	Wulfweard	Guy of Craon
Frieston	?	Guy de Craon
Fishtoft	?	Count Alan
Fishtoft	Aethelstan	Guy of Craon
Skirkbeck	?	Count Alan
Skirkbeck	?	Eudo, son of Spirewic
Kirton Wapentake		
Wyberton	Aethelric	Count Alan
Wyberton	?	Count Alan
Wyberton	Aethelstan	Guy of Craon
Frampton	?	Count Alan
Frampton	Aethelstan	Guy of Craon
Kirton	Eadric	Count Alan
Kirton	Aelfric	Guy of Craon
Riskenton	?	Count Alan
Algarkirk	St Guthlac's	St Guthlac's [Crowland Abbey]
(Dowdyke)*	St Guthlac's	St Guthlac's [Crowland Abbey]
Burtoft (in Dowdyke)*	St Guthlac's	St Guthlac's [Crowland Abbey]
Riche	?	Count Alan
Drayton	St Guthlac's	St Guthlac's [Crowland Abbey]
Drayton	Bishop Wulfwige	Count Alan
Drayton	Ralph the Constable	Count Alan
Drayton	Aethelstan	Guy of Craon
Stenning	Halfdan	Count Alan
Stenning	Aelfric	Robert Vessey
Bicker	Archbishop ofYork	Archbishop of York
Bicker	?	Count Alan
Bicker	Halfdan	Count Alan
Bicker	?	Countess Judith
Bicker	Aethelstan	Guy of Craon
Bicker	Vitharr	Kolgrimr
Donnington	St Peter's, Peterborough	St Peter's, Peterborough
Donnington	?	Count Alan
Donnington	Ralph	Count Alan
Donnington	Thorketill	Count Alan
Quadring	Thorketill	Count Alan
Quadring	St Guthlac's	St Guthlac's
Quadring	St Guthlac's	St Guthlac's
Gosberton	Asli	Bishop of Lincoln
Cheal	Atsurr and his brothers	St Guthlac's [Crowland Abbey]
Surfleet	Alsige	Heppo the Crossbowman
Elloe Wapentake		
Pinchbeck	?	Ivo Tallboys
Pinchbeck	?	Guy of Craon
Spalding	St Guthlac's	St Guthlac's [Crowland Abbey]
Spalding	Earl Algar	Ivo Tallboys

Table 17. *Continued*

Manor	AD 1066	AD 1086
Spalding	Aethelstan	Guy of Craon
Weston and Moulton	?	Ivo Tallboys
Weston and Moulton	?	Guy of Craon
Whaplode and Holbeach	Count Alan	King
Whaplode and Holbeach	St Guthlac's	St Guthlac's [Crowland Abbey]
Whaplode and Holbeach	Earl Algar	Count Alan
Whaplode and Holbeach	Earl Algar	Count Alan
Whaplode and Holbeach	Aethelstan	Guy of Craon
Fleet	Earl Algar	King
Gedney	Earl Algar	King
Lutton	Earl Algar	King
Long Sutton	King	King
Tydd St Mary	Earl Algar	King
Tydd St Mary	?	Ivo Tallboys
Tydd St Mary	?	Guy of Craon

* Dowdyke, a possession of Crowland Abbey in Sutterton parish, lies seaward of the main line of villages and as such would appear to be a later or secondary foundation. The date when Crowland acquired it is unknown though Hallam (1965, 41–2) suggests the 10th century.

estates around Algarkirk, Dowdyke, and Burtoft, on the northern side of Bicker Haven, were coterminous. However, what Table 17 really shows is the extent to which eleventh century land ownership on the Lincolnshire marshes was firstly, highly fragmented and, secondly, dominated by the laity. This pattern of land holding may go a long way in explaining the strongly communal approach to the *subsequent* enclosure and drainage of the backfens in Lincolnshire, but does not necessarily imply the same for the *initial* construction of sea walls several centuries earlier. Indeed, an analysis of the Domesday estates, and in particular the pattern of manors, berewicks, and sokelands, indicates that the fragmented pattern of holdings in AD 1066 resulted from the systematic division of a larger estate (e.g. between Pinchbeck and Tydd: Roffe 1993*b*). The date when this division occurred is unclear but it may have been at this early period, still shrouded in fenland mist, when the entire wapentake was a single estate, that the decision to embank the marshes was first taken.

The situation is clearer from the twelfth century, when one of the defining characteristics of reclamation in Fenland is that it was primarily a 'small man's enterprise' (H. Hallam 1954: 40; 1965: 16; E. King 1973: 87). While there were a number of powerful lay landlords, only one substantial barony was created, at Friston. Otherwise, the pattern of landholding was relatively fragmented (Platts 1985: 14, fig 7) which resulted in a highly communal approach to reclamation and the creation of common fields. In certain areas, enclosure and drainage appears to have been carried out by individual lords and free holders, sometimes resulting in reclamations that bear the name of the man responsible, though this was most common on the still accreting saltmarshes in front of the original sea walls. The earliest documented example was carried out by AD 1111 when Picot, son of Colswein, granted lands including 'Pigotis Neueland' to Spalding Priory (H. Hallam 1965: 8). References to saltmarsh reclamation continue into the thirteenth century, often being given the name 'Newland'. For example, the AD 1259/60 survey of Spalding Priory's lands in Moulton includes *Neulond, Crosneuland, Estneuland, Westneuland* and *Wormeneulond* (H. Hallam 1965: 14). There is just one reference to a communal saltmarsh reclamation, when Thomas of Holbeach made an agreement with the villages of Holbeach and Whaplode for a common sea-dyke (Hallam 1965: 16).

There appear to be fewer instances of inland reclamations being the work of individuals as opposed to the whole community. One example is Wiggenhall St Mary Magdalen which lies in the backfen of the Norfolk marshland and as a result of its unfavourable environment may have been one of the last communities to be established (in the twelfth century: Owen 1981: 11; Silvester 1988: 105–8). Most of the land in the parish was freehold with the community lying outside any strict manorial organization. Unlike the other marshland parishes, there is little evidence for the communal organization of field systems. The field boundary pattern comprises a series of very long narrow strips, extending from the string of farmsteads that ran along the higher ground afforded by the banks of the River Ouse. These strips appear to have been periodically extended further into the backfen as more land was required, though marked variations in width and length suggests individual owners working on their own. Periodically fen-banks were constructed, indicating some form of communal action, but overall, Wiggenhall St Mary Magdalen appears to have been a small-holders' enterprise.

11.4.5 Communal reclamation in Fenland: the fen-banks

Communal action on a far larger scale is evident in the Lincolnshire backfens. The higher coastal marshes were embanked and settled in the pre-Conquest period, and as the demand for new land increased areas of the lower-lying backfen were also enclosed. In order to prevent freshwaters from the backfens flooding these areas, banks were constructed down the parish boundaries (where they were known as 'Bardikes': Silvester 1988: 164) and then across the entire width of one or more parishes (as 'fen banks') suggesting that these were the work of the whole community, not individual landholders.

In Norfolk a change in the scale of collaboration is evident over time. The early fen-banks must have been constructed by individual communities working on their own, as they are restricted to individual parishes. Each community appears to have worked separately, reclaiming the backfen at their own pace, and it was only as these intakes extended even further inland, that adjacent communities appear to have co-operated in constructing fen-banks that cut across several communities e.g. Castor Dike (Silvester 1988: figs. 58 and 124). This trend towards greater co-operation culminated, sometime before AD 1207, in the construction of the Chancellor Dike and Smeeth Bank which marked the limit of the remaining unenclosed backfen known as 'West Fen' (Silvester 1988: 32, 160–9; 1993: 29). The way that droveways, created to link the coastal settlements with the remaining areas of common pasture, sliced through the landscape suggests that they too were communal work. The strong sense of community probably results from the highly fragmented nature of land-holding in the Norfolk marshland villages. For example, nine monasteries held lands in Clenchwarton,[50] a list 'which reads like a catalogue of religious establishments in West Norfolk' (Silvester 1988: 22).

Whereas, in Norfolk, it appears that individual communities sometimes worked on their own, in Cambridgeshire the presence of a single landowner (the cathedral at Ely) meant that one system of fen-banks was constructed for all five communities, probably in the twelfth century (D. Hall 1981: 43; 1996: fig. 99). In Lincolnshire there was a third variant, with enclosure and drainage largely carried out at the initiative of the community, though once again the level of collaboration appears to have increased over time. Various religious houses played an important part, but only as partners in what were major collaborative ventures: 'the method of consultation and division, the primacy of the townships over the manors, is exactly as we have found in the documents examined. Whatever the men of Elloe enclosed [in] the fen they divided it into portions held in severalty, which they used as each man saw fit. This combination of a strong communal sense with extreme individuality is one of the greatest paradoxes of Fenland history' (H. Hallam 1965: 35; and see Raban 1977: 52–3).

11.4.6 Walland Marsh: reclamation by entrepreneurs

Walland Marsh illustrates a similar range of communal and individual initiative in marshland drainage, notably in Broomhill (M. Gardiner 1988). The earliest phase of reclamation appears to have been undertaken by wealthy local tenants, followed by a period of considerable monastic involvement alongside the community as a whole. An example of the early entrepreneurial reclamation is recorded in AD 1208. John de Gestling granted four groups of partners half the marsh in the east of Broomhill between the land of the 'men of Broomhill' (see below), the marsh called 'Grikes' which Elias had enclosed (see below), and the Battle Abbey demesne land (see below: CRR 5: 20–4; M. Gardiner 1988: 115; Salzman 1937: 149). In return, the partners enclosed the marsh and undertook to maintain the sea wall. If further land was reclaimed, and another sea wall built in front of the first, then half the old wall belonged to the partners while the other half belonged to John de Gestling; neither party could destroy the wall without the others consent. In c. AD 1220 John de Gestling granted Robert Flot and others half of Gestling's land 'which they had enclosed with the help of the Abbot of Robertsbridge and the men of Promhell (Broomhill) . . . in return they have enclosed the other half and will defend it with walls and ditches' (Kingsford 1925: 75). Clearly, reclamation was a major undertaking and the shrewd Gestling shared out the risk.

The example also shows that some of the reclaimers worked in collaboration with monastic houses. For example, c. AD 1220 Robert, son of Thomas Niger, transferred to Robertsbridge Abbey all his share in the marsh called 'Spikespich' on condition that

---

[50] Blackborough, Bury St Edmunds, Castle Acre, Norwich, Pentney, Shouldham, Walsingham, Westacre, and West Dereham.

when enclosed one third remained his (Kingsford 1925: 74). A similar early thirteenth
century agreement was reached between a group of nine men working in co-operation
with Robertsbridge Abbey and the 'men of Broomhill', to reclaim further areas of
marshland in Broomhill (M. Gardiner 1988: 114). Another of these early thirteenth
century entrepreneurs was one 'Doudeman', who owned land in the south and north-east
of Broomhill, as well as in Hope All Saints (M. Gardiner 1988: 114; Kingsford 1925:
69, 80, 89) and, by the early thirteenth century, one of his holdings measured *c.* 600
acres (*CRR* 1: 467; M. Gardiner 1988: 114; Salzman 1937: 149). The descendants of
Doudeman became a loosely-related group of tenants known as 'the men of Broomhill'
whose lands gradually became fragmented through partible inheritance (M. Gardiner
1988: 117–18). A similar group of related tenants were the 'men of Misleham' in
Brookland (see Chapter 9).

During the twelfth century, both Battle and Robertsbridge Abbeys had started to
acquire lands in Broomhill and, by the early thirteenth century, they started to make a
major contribution to reclamation in the area, sometimes working together. For example,
in AD 1222 the two abbeys reclaimed some 1,218 acres between 'la Chene' to the north
and 'Capeness' on the coast (M. Gardiner 1988: 114, fig. 10.1). Another reclamation
undertaken by the monks themselves is described in AD 1234, although this shows that
the small local landholders retained considerable power. Hamo de Crevequer granted
Robertsbridge:

> land in the marsh of Legh from the fleet on the east, part of the house which the
> monks built on the marsh to the water of Rie [Rye] on the west [i.e. the Rother?],
> and on the north from Finchesflet as far as the monks land on the south; the monks
> are to enclose as much of the marsh as they reasonably can in the coming summer;
> after enclosure one third of the arable is to fall to Hamo's share; the residue . . . to
> be the monks property; the monks to maintain walls and waterways at their own
> cost. Any land outside that enclosed in the first year the monks may enclose on the
> same terms within ten years; after ten years it will be at the disposal of Hamo and
> his heirs. (Kingsford 1925: 89).

In AD 1234 Hamo delivered:

> all his land between Finchesflet and Bradesflet, from the head of Finchesflet on the
> east and westwards as far as the water stretching between Rie [Rye] and Morbrigge;
> to be enclosed at the cost of the monks, together with Finchesflet towards the
> enclosure of which Hamo will contribute 12 marks before Accession Day. After
> enclosure Hamo will take 5 acres next to the share of Finchesflet extending in length
> from the east wall to the west wall, and on the other side of the fleet 5 acres in the
> like manner, together with the fleet which he shall retain for his own use. The
> remainder the monks will hold to their own use and profit. Out of any subsequent
> enclosure one third of the arable is to go to Hamo. Towards the cost, Hamo grants
> as much land as the walls would occupy. (Kingsford 1925: 90).

11.4.7 **Communal inertia**

Whilst in many instances the community may have been the driving force behind landscape improvement, in other cases it could have a stifling effect. In Chapter 10 the lack of reclamation on extensive areas of marshland in Essex and Norfolk (Broadland) was discussed, and the fragmented pattern of landownership, partly derived from the enclosure of commonland, may have been a significant factor. Relatively extensive areas of coastal marsh remained as un-enclosed common pasture on the Caldicot level and in Walling Fen at the head of the Humber estuary (Chapter 9).

In other cases, the ability of a landlord to improve his estate could be constrained by the community. For example, in the mid-twelfth century the Knights Templar agreed with the men of Dartford (Kent) that 'neither party would plough or sow in the salt marsh in Dartford unless both intended to bring land into cultivation' (Bowler 1968: 127). In AD 1274 the Abbot of St Augustine's in Canterbury became involved in a dispute over his decision to drain some marshes which formed a detached part of his manors of Stonar and Minster, in the Wantsum Channel west of Thanet in Kent (Neilson 1928: 51). The Abbot had allowed local communities to pasture their sheep for payment of one penny per five sheep, and when he decided to reclaim the marshes the tenants protested, beat the Abbot's men, and drove off his sheep. Whilst illustrating the significant part that local custom could have in preventing change in the countryside, it is interesting to note that the Abbot won the legal case.

11.5 **Discussion**

It can be seen that the contexts within which coastal marshlands were modified and transformed during the medieval period varied enormously. There is no evidence for a marine regression at this time and, indeed, relative sea level may have been rising. Although there was a climatic amelioration, it was a combination of social, political, and economic changes at the end of the first millennium AD that provide the context for this marked phase of settlement expansion and marshland reclamation. This occurred within a very wide range of estate structures and, though biases in the documentary record point to a major ecclesiastical role, in practice it appears to have been local communities that carried out much of the work, either through the active encouragement of their landlords or on their own initiative. Indeed, the physical structure of the landscapes that were created suggests that the early phases of reclamation were mainly piecemeal, resulting in highly irregular patterns of fields and roads. It was only with the push into the lower-lying backfens during the twelfth and thirteenth centuries, when there appears to have been greater intra- and inter-community co-operation, that larger-scale enclosure and drainage started to take place. Once again, however, the context for this expansion appears to lie of socio-economic conditions rather than any changes in the natural landscape: human communities created these landscapes of their own free-will.

CHAPTER 12

Conclusions:

landscapes in their local context

12.1 The utilization of the coastal wetlands

In essence, this study has been about why human communities throughout North West Europe chose to use the same type of landscape—coastal wetlands—in different ways at different times. However, many of the issues addressed here, such as changing regional economies, are not specific to that one type of environment: this has been an examination of the factors affecting the human decision making process, and as such is relevant to all landscapes of all periods.

All too often, scholars have tried to explain variation in landscape utilization in terms of the physical environment: differences in the fertility of soils, climatic fluctuations, and marine transgressions/regressions. There are certainly examples of the environment determining how landscapes were used—for example, a low saltmarsh flooded twice a day is clearly not suitable for agriculture. However, in the majority of areas the physical characteristics of a landscape simply raised a series of *possibilities*, and it was up to the vagaries of human decision making to determine which path was chosen. For example, a saltmarsh only flooded by the highest of spring tides could either be *exploited* for its rich seasonal grazing, *modified* through the construction of summer dikes and drainage ditches allowing its seasonal use for arable cultivation, or *transformed* through reclamation making it suitable for permanent occupation. This study has revealed that all three strategies were adopted in different areas at the same time, and that in seeking to explain why this was the case, a wide variety of local and more general factors were important (see Table 1). Occasionally, these decisions may have been forced upon the communities, for example, through a particularly severe environmental change or period of social, political, or economic unrest. But more often than not, human communities were faced with choices, and it is explaining differences in the decisions they reached that is the central theme of this study.

If the use of coastal wetlands of North West Europe in the early first century AD is compared with that in the thirteenth century, then the major trend was clearly towards increasing landscape productivity through reclamation (though with a brief set-back in the mid-first millennium). The embanking and drainage of wetlands represents two processes: an expansion of the amount of land available for occupation, and then an increase in the intensity with which that land is used. However, reclamation is a high cost, high risk, as well as a high return strategy towards landscape utilization and it was not always adopted, reflecting the perception of human communities as to whether the benefits outweighed the costs and risks.

12.2 **The potential of coastal wetlands**

Traditionally, scholars have sought to understand the expansion and intensification of agriculture in terms of 'marginality' and, though this model has rightly seen much criticism, the concept is still of some use, particularly if re-worked as 'landscape potential' (see Chapter 1 and Table 1). Landscapes have a wide range of physical (topography, soils, drainage etc.), environmental (climate etc.), and cultural facets (tenurial patterns, centres of consumption etc.) all of which can change over time. Some of these facets are particular to an individual area (such as the soils and proximity to markets: push/pull factors), whereas others affect a much wider area (such as changes in population and grain prices: contextual factors). It is also important to appreciate that the potential of an area should not just be thought of in terms of agriculture: landscapes can contain a variety of non-agricultural resources that will affect the human perception of the costs, risks, and benefits of particular utilization strategies.

It has been shown that coastal wetlands are highly dynamic landscapes, particularly prone to environmental changes, but endowed with a wide range of natural resources and potentially productive soils. It is in this context that reclamation must be seen, since it involves an attempt to interfere with these natural processes and substitute the varied ecological mosaic of coastal saltmarshes and freshwater backfens, with a far more uniform and controlled ecology based upon a regulated watertable.

The physical topography of coastal wetlands throughout North West Europe shows certain basic similarities. Towards the coast, areas of alluvium are derived from saltmarshes and mudflats and, being flooded most often (resulting in more sediment deposition), will be higher than areas further inland. In the more substantial areas of coastal wetland a freshwater backfen lies between the tidally inundated marsh and the fen-edge/dry land, in which peat will often form in a variety of environments (notable reed swamps, carr woodland, or raised bog: Figure 5). Both the coastal marshes and fringes of the backfen will be drained by a network of tidal creeks, whose raised banks provide areas of slightly better drained land in an otherwise waterlogged landscape. Another feature of many coastal wetlands is a natural coastal barrier of sand and shingle, whose evolution was often critical to the development of the wider marshland landscape.

The extent of tidal influence in these low-lying landscapes has varied enormously through a series of transgressive and regressive events, which have traditionally been linked to changes in relative sea level. It is now clear that sea level fluctuates due to a series of local, regional, and world-wide processes, and that it is wrong to assume a simplistic and synchronous series of rises and falls. The direct link between relative sea level and marine transgression/regression events is further weakened because the latter could occur without any sudden change in the former, if a coastal barrier was breached, for example (e.g. Figure 9). However, it does appear that in the first and second centuries AD, relative sea level was stable or even falling in much of North West Europe (though this is less apparent around the Severn Estuary: Figure 12 and Chapter 2), and that this did lead to a regressive event that made coastal wetlands a more attractive place to settle. Then, from around the third century relative sea levels appear to have risen and, during the subsequent centuries a thick layer of alluvium was deposited over the earlier Roman landscapes. Since this is observed in wetlands that were reclaimed, protected by natural coastal barriers, and open to direct tidal influence, this flooding must have occurred as a result of a general rise in relative sea level, rather than local events such as the breaching of barriers due to storms. There is less evidence, however, for a fall in relative sea level during the medieval period, and in fact conditions may have been deteriorating from around the eleventh century, just as settlement was expanding.

The Roman period also appears to have had a favourable climate, though a return to cooler and wetter conditions during the early medieval period can only have made coastal wetlands more inhospitable. From around the eighth century there was an amelioration leading to a marked period of drought during the tenth century and the subsequent medieval climatic optimum. Alongside these long-term trends in sea level and climate, there may also have been short-term fluctuations in the weather, and several particularly bad storm surges that smashed through coastal barriers may have had a far more profound affect upon marshland landscapes than a gradual rise in sea level. This was particularly the case from the later thirteenth century, but is beyond the scope of this study.

Just as the opportunities that coastal wetlands have to offer change over time, so they also vary in space (Figure 13). The intertidal zone can be used for fishing, while the coastal marshes offer good grazing (particularly for sheep). Further inland, the freshwater backfen provides a wide range of useful plants and peat for fuel. Salt can be produced either by directly heating sea water, or washing sea water through already salt-impregnated intertidal muds, or peat, and then evaporating the resulting brine. Agriculture is possible on a high intertidal marsh as long as the crop is not inundated at the seedling stage, though productivity is relatively low; if the marsh is embanked, however, crop yields on reclaimed marshland can be higher than on dryland soils.

Coastal wetlands, like any environment, can be utilized within the context of a variety of estate structures. Relatively narrow stretches of marsh could be exploited by communities living on the adjacent dryland, but if the distances between fen-edge and shoreline were too great then subsidiary, initially seasonal, settlements could be established, for example on the higher ground afforded by the banks of tidal creeks. Coastal resources were so highly valued that in certain cases, communities many kilometres away held detached parts of their estate down on the marshes. These seasonal marshland settlements would have been socially and economically dependent on the fen-edge or more distant estate centre, though if agriculture was possible following modification and transformation of the landscape, then independence could be gained with the establishment of permanent communities whose territory was wholly on the marshland.

12.3 **The Roman period**

The modification of coastal marshes began in the late prehistoric period, most notably on the continent, where settlements were often located on artificially raised mounds. In the western Netherlands there is evidence that attempts were made to modify the landscape by controlling the flow of water through the construction of dams and sluices. In Britain, however, the prehistoric use of coastal wetlands appears to have been largely associated with salt production and (presumably) grazing, and it was only during the Roman period that these marshes were first modified and transformed. Throughout the whole of North West Europe the only evidence for a comprehensive transformation of the landscape at this time is around the Severn Estuary, with the systematic reclamation of the Wentlooge Level and more piecemeal enclosure and drainage of parts of the Somerset Levels. Far more common was the localized modification of coastal marshes, as seen in Fenland, around the Humber Estuary, and extensively on the continent.

Natural resources were also exploited more heavily than during the preceding Iron Age, with an expansion of coastal salt production and increased consumption of fish and shellfish. Both travelled long distances inland, for which salt would have been needed for their preservation, and the communities responsible probably occupied the coastal zone on a seasonal basis, supplementing their income through grazing livestock, particularly sheep, on the marshes. In South East Dorset and North Kent the exploitation of these coastal resources may have occurred alongside pottery manufacturing as part of a wider crafts-based economy. The decline of coastal salt production during the later Roman period is curious, as demand cannot have declined in a market-based economy where meat and fish were transported long distances. By the third and fourth centuries, the industry appears to have been largely restricted to South East Dorset, the Central Somerset Levels, and the inland brine springs of the West Midlands, with just a light scatter of sites in the east of the province. The evidence from the coasts of mainland Europe also becomes relatively thin after the Early Roman period. It is difficult to explain this decline of production in terms of environmental change or wetland reclamation. There was a change in the technology of production in the British West Midlands, but this use of lead pans does leave archaeologically-visible traces which are simply not present in the areas where coastal salt production went into decline. There does appear to have been a general decline in prosperity in these areas during the later Roman period, though substantial populations, and hence demand, still remained. It is tempting, therefore, to see some non-market forces at work, particularly as classical texts tell us that salt was regarded as a state monopoly. The imperial authorities certainly took a strong interest in Britain's other mineral resources and, though direct control ended in the Early Roman period, patronage by the procurators office and the military establishment, which had two of its legionary bases in the west of Britain, may have contributed to the continued success of the salt industry in these areas.

It is not just the geography of salt production that shows marked regional variations: the occurrence of reclamation and landscape modification also requires explanation. Reclamation appears to have been restricted to the Severn Estuary, and it may be no coincidence that this area lay next to that part of Roman Britain which saw the greatest level of Late Roman prosperity, reflected for example in the vibrancy of towns and investment in villas. Two of the most extensive areas of marshland by the Severn—the Central and North Somerset Levels—both appear to have seen reclamation associated with individual villas built on the marshes, while further up the estuary in Avonmouth and Gloucestershire, embanking may have been undertaken by villa owners living on the fen-edge or up on the Cotswolds.

Reconstructing the patterns of land ownership in Roman Britain is difficult because of the lack of documentary sources. In particular, there has been much debate over the status of Fenland and though the traditional view, that this was an imperial estate, has seen much criticism, a closer examination of the evidence, including the results of recent excavations of a possible estate centre at Stonea, suggest that this issue is far from resolved. As an area of relatively under-exploited land, the imperial authorities may well have regarded the state as having a legal claim to it. The Sawtry inscription, and possibly the Car Dykes (which cannot have functioned as catchwater drains) are plausible boundary markers, and there certainly was a rapid expansion of settlement in the first half of the second century. The morphology of the resulting settlements, fields, and roads shows very little sign of planning, and there does not appear to have been any planned colonization, but rather a gradual process of settlement expansion, perhaps encouraged by low-rents or other incentives.

On the continent there are signs of military involvement in the coastal wetlands of the western Netherlands south of the *Limes*, notably at Midden-Delfland but, overall, the impact of Roman occupation does not appear to have been so profound as was the case in Britain. This is in keeping with trends in the region as a whole, where there was a strong tendency toward continuity in native traditions, reflected, for example, in a lack of villa building even on the dryland areas.

During the Roman period, environmental changes meant, therefore, that conditions on coastal wetlands appear to have improved, though human communities throughout North West Europe made very different decisions as to how they should take advantage of these circumstances. It is particularly apparent that local factors were often of great importance, notably proximity to centres of resource consumption, such as the Wentlooge Level and the legionary base at Caerleon, the Brue Valley in Central Somerset next to the trade route between South East Dorset and the military establishment in Wales, and the growth of London which may initially have encouraged the flourishing Thames-side pottery and salt industries. The establishment of a possible imperial estate in Fenland, and the military involvement south of the *Limes* in The Netherlands are other possible examples. However, some of the trends observed in coastal wetlands at this time may also have been a response to more general phenomena, such as Roman Britain's westwards shift in economic prosperity that may have been a factor in promoting reclamation on the Severn Estuary Levels.

12.4 **The Late to post-Roman period**

During the Late/Early-Post Roman period there was a widespread desertion of the coastal wetlands of North West Europe, and an equally widespread episode of marine transgression. The two phenomena appear to be related, since in a number of places the date of settlement desertion (based on material culture) is very close to radiocarbon dates for the onset of sediment deposition (though it must be remembered that two different types of dating are being compared here). The cause of this flooding appears to have been a genuine rise in relative sea level as Roman landscapes are buried under later alluvium in areas that had been embanked (e.g. Somerset), were partly protected by sand dunes or shingle ridges (e.g. Romney Marsh, the western Netherlands) and, most critically, in areas that had no coastal barriers (e.g. Fenland, the northern Netherlands, and Germany). Clearly, local explanations such as a failure to maintain flood defences or breaches in a natural barrier caused by a storm surge, cannot account for this widespread inundation.

A deteriorating environment cannot be the whole explanation, however, as human communities clearly had the technology to cope with rising water levels. It seems that, just as life on coastal wetlands was becoming more difficult, there was a period of considerable economic and political instability. For example, when the once reclaimed Roman landscape on the North Somerset Levels was again subject to tidal inundation, there is pollen evidence for woodland regeneration on the nearby uplands (Rippon, forthcoming *a*). In The Netherlands and Germany, the abandonment of coastal wetlands similarly occurred at a time when the adjacent dryland areas were being used less intensively, or were even abandoned. A declining economy, the collapse of the Roman *Limes*, and the onset of migrations all appear to have combined to create enormous instability that made life in the increasingly inhospitable wetlands unsustainable.

12.5 **The Roman and medieval periods compared**

Following the widespread abandonment and flooding of coastal wetlands during the Late/Post-Roman period, most areas reverted to saltmarshes and peat bogs onto which medieval society subsequently grafted another cultural landscape that, in most cases, represents the origins of our present pattern of settlements, roads, and fields. In certain cases, such as the Somerset Levels and the Vale of York, all that we can say is that reclamation had begun by the eleventh century: there is neither the archaeological nor documentary evidence to say when this process began. However, elsewhere, notably in Fenland, The Netherlands, and Germany, the early medieval recolonization of coastal wetlands provides a particularly clear example of the gradual intensification of wetland utilization starting around the seventh or eighth century, with the simple exploitation of natural resources, through modification of the environment via limited flood defences, to large-scale landscape transformation in the form of reclamation.

There are a number of contrasts between the these landscapes and the other 'highwater mark' of cultural intervention in coastal wetlands, during the Roman period. First, although the latter saw a marked increase in natural resource exploitation compared to the Iron Age, the medieval period, in turn, saw an even greater increase. Second, the impression of a landscape under ever increasing strain is confirmed in that reclamation was far more widespread during the medieval period. Third, and at first sight somewhat paradoxically, settlement was more widespread during the Roman period. This is partly because in a number of places, such as the Thames-side marshes, areas that had been settled were now exploited from fen-edge or more distant estate centres, though the main reason is the marked nucleation of settlement in the medieval period. This can be seen most clearly in Fenland where the Romano-British scatter of settlement with an emphasis on the marsh/fen margins was replaced by a series of villages on the higher coastal marshes. Fourth, there is a sense that, in the Roman period, decisions as to how coastal landscapes should be used was very strongly influenced by local factors, such as proximity to centres of consumption (e.g. military establishments) and economic development in the immediate hinterland of individual marshland (e.g. prosperous regions such as the Cotswolds). In the medieval period, there is far greater uniformity in how marshlands were used, with the domination of mixed agriculture in a reclaimed landscape (though local circumstances, such as particularly fragmented patterns of landholding, could inhibit reclamation in certain areas). Once again, this would suggest that, during the medieval period, communities were responding to more general socio-economic conditions that encouraged the extension and intensification of agriculture well beyond where it reached during the Roman period.

12.6 The medieval period

There are signs of embanking and ditching from as early as the eighth century on the North Kent marshes, while two features recorded in charter bounds on Romney Marsh may also indicate artificial modifications to the drainage system from the ninth century. The earliest dike building in North Holland may also date to this time. It was around the tenth century, however, that the first large-scale reclamation took place evidenced in Fenland, northern Holland, and the northern Netherlands. Only in the Gwent Levels, the Pevensey Levels, Belgium, and South Holland do major schemes of reclamation appear to have been first initiated in the late eleventh or twelfth centuries, while in certain areas, notably eastern Essex and the Norfolk Broadland, extensive tracts of marsh were left unenclosed for most of the medieval period.

The vagaries of archaeological dating and the character of early documentary references mean that great care must be taken in order to avoid telescoping a series of

81. Hope All Saints Church, Romney Marsh (see Bennell 1995). The Marsh contains numerous isolated and even ruinous churches in an often sparsely populated area. However, documentary evidence, including the density of 11th century churches, and fieldwalking surveys, have shown that this was once a well-settled landscape.

poorly dated events, over a very wide area, into a closely dated synchronous event. However, even bearing this in mind, the extent of tenth to eleventh century settlement expansion and reclamation all around North West Europe does appear quite remarkable. This must be seen in the context of the whole agrarian economy which was expanding, reflected for example in the replanning of villages and fields, and the growth of urban markets. At a time of great opportunity, coastal wetlands were a resource just waiting to be tapped. In fact, it was not just the use of landed resources that intensified at this time. From at least the eighth century there is increased evidence for the investment of resources in fixed intertidal fishing weirs, while around the tenth and eleventh centuries, greater use of was made of off-shore fish stocks. From around the twelfth century, shellfish start to be cultivated and the consumption of freshwater fish, along with wildfowl, appears to have become restricted to the higher echelons of society. All the signs are that the landscape was coming under increasing strain, and far more so than was the case during the Roman period.

During the twelfth and thirteenth centuries there was a continued increasing intensity with which coastal wetlands, now largely reclaimed, were utilized. The views of later topographical writers, and decline in settlement seen in certain areas during the late and post-medieval periods (e.g. Figure 81) should not obscure the fact that, by the thirteenth century, these were well-populated areas of valuable land. Even areas of the unenclosed common land were carefully regulated, reflecting the pressure under which resources to coming (e.g. Figure 82).

82. Mark Moor, Somerset Levels. This low-lying backfen environment is now relatively unimproved pasture, drained by a network of ditches. However, in the medieval period it was an important common pasture (Thurlemere) that was managed through stringent regulation, and was the subject of numerous disputes reflecting how highly valued this resource.

12.7 **The costs, risks, and benefits of reclamation**

All too often, the colonization coastal wetlands has been seen as the result of 'push' factors, such as over-population and soil exhaustion elsewhere. For example, Waterbolk (1965–6: 43–5) reflected the traditional view that settlement expansion into the marsh region of the northern Netherlands was due to the erosion of arable lands on the adjacent sandy regions, while Roeleveld (1974: 109) argued that soils erosion was simply the symptom of over-population, and that it was this which prompted migration to the marshlands. Gijn and Waterbolk (1984) later added that soil exhaustion diminished the economic potential of the sandy region just at the time that changing environmental conditions meant that the marsh district became available for habitation. But were human communities always shunted about the landscape in this way?

It is true that sometimes relatively dramatic environmental change may have altered the nature of coastal wetlands to such an extent that what had been regularly flooded land did start to dry out: early medieval Romney Marsh provides a good example. It is also true that equally rapid environmental change could force human communities to abandon an area: the destruction of Old Winchelsea in the late thirteenth century is a good case in point (Eddison 1998). However, for the past 2,000 years, human communities in North West Europe have had the technology to control water (the earliest dam and sluice at Vlaardingen dates to the pre-Roman period) and they should not be seen simply as the passive victims of environmental change. As Abbink (1993: 294) has observed:

> The economic use of a particular environment is the result of the strategies and choices made by people within society. These strategies determine what people define and use as resources and how they use them. Time and again wetlands have been chosen for settling all over the world; these choices cannot be explained by geological factors alone, nor by necessity.

In the costs, risks, and benefits equation of how best to utilize this particular type of environment, the perception of human communities was usually that the benefits of reclamation far outweighed the costs and risks.

The issue of risk could to a certain extent be minimized through the incorporation of many coastal marshes into federative estates, which was an efficient and logical way of utilizing varied landscapes such as those around the coastal fringes of North West Europe. However, logical though it was, the adoption of this type of estate structure was still the result of human decision making, based upon the available information and their understanding of the landscape. A. Ward's (1997: 103) comments with regard to upland areas are just as pertinent to the lowland environments that are the focus of this study:

> Relevant characteristics of risk management strategies in the more unpredictable environments ... include a conservatism in approaching decision making. Human judgement is an important feature in adaptation to fluctuating food supplies, a cognitive input which is not obviously accessible via the archaeological record.

Quite simply, one strategy to spread risk is to exploit a range of ecological niches. Over the past 2,000 years, human communities have progressively become more independent of the their natural environment, and the expansion of settlement and drainage that continued into the twelfth and thirteenth centuries may actually have occurred against a background of gradually rising sea level.

By the thirteenth century, most of the coastal marshes around North West Europe were embanked and drained. Certain areas of saltmarsh and more extensive tracts of the lowest-lying backfen survived, often as common pastures, but a clear consensus had been reached that increased agricultural production was more highly valued than the natural resources that these landscapes had to offer. Looking back over both the Roman and medieval periods, a logical progression can be observed as the productivity of marshland landscapes was gradually increased through modification and finally transformation. There are certainly similarities over very large areas in how these landscapes developed, but when the evidence is examined in detail, it is local variations—deviations from the norm—that are perhaps most striking. Individual communities were choosing to utilize broadly similar types of environment in ways that suited their local circumstances, and even when there were general pressures, such as rising population and increased demand for agricultural produce, local initiative led to local solutions.

12.8 **Transformation and control: a study of landscape**

This study has been an attempt to understand landscape, rather than the landscape simply being considered as the background for an otherwise site-based consideration of the past. It has also been the first attempt at an integrated analysis the coastal wetlands of North West Europe during the Roman and medieval periods and, as such, has attempted to distinguish objective synthesis from subjective discussion. No doubt both will become outdated—a perfectly healthy sign that research in these remarkable landscapes is continuing—but it is hoped that the importance of the archaeological, palaeoenvironmental, documentary, and historic-landscape evidence from this period will now be recognized alongside the more familiar prehistoric archaeology of our wetlands.

It is also hoped that this will not simply be regarded as a study of wetlands. A key theme has been the value of studying one type of landscape that occurs particularly widely, in order to examine the socio-economic factors that influence how human communities decide to use their environment, thereby addressing issues of far wider significance than the wetlands themselves. It is clear that even in these 'physically marginal' and environmentally vulnerably landscapes, mankind was rarely forced into a certain course of action. The rich ecological mosaic that wetlands constitute offered a series of pathways ranging from simple natural resource exploitation, through the moderate investment of resources in the form of landscape modification, to the major commitment that is transformation. Indeed, the issues of where, when, and why reclamation occurred, and who was responsible, has been another major theme. The answer is that many local communities came to many local solutions based upon their perception, and knowledge, of landscape potential and the costs, risks, and benefits of each landscape utilization strategy.

Bibliography

Abbink, A. A. (1993). The Midden-Delfland Project: Iron Age occupation. *Helinium* XXXIII/ii, 253–301.

Ackeroyd, A. V. (1972). Archaeological and historical evidence for subsidence in southern Britain. *Phil. Trans. Roy. Soc. London, A* 272: 151–71.

Adam, P. (1990). *Saltmarsh ecology.* Cambridge: Cambridge Univ. Press.

Adams, M. (1993). History of the Demesne Farm at Appledore from contemporary building records. *Archaeologia Cantiana,* 112: 283–98.

Albarella, U. and Davis, S. J. M. (1994*a*). Mammals and birds from Launceston Castle, Cornwall: decline in status and the rise of agriculture. *Circaea,* 12/1: 1–156.

Albarella, U. and Davis, S. J. M. (1994*b*). *Saxon & medieval animals bones excavated 1985–1989 from West Cotton, Northamptonshire.* London: Ancient Monuments Lab. Rep., 17/94.

Allen, J. R. L. (1987). Late Flandrian shoreline oscillations in the Severn Estuary: the Rumney Formation at its typesite. *Phil. Trans. Roy. Soc. London,* B 315: 157–84.

Allen, J. R. L. (1988). Reclamation and sea defence in Rumney Parish, Monmouthshire. *Archaeologia Cambrensis,* CXXXVII: 135–40.

Allen, J. R. L. (1990). The Severn Estuary in South West Britain: its retreat under marine transgression and fine sediment regime. *Sedimentary Geology,* 66: 13–28.

Allen, J. R. L. (1991). Saltmarsh accretion and sea level movement. *J. Geol. Soc. London,* 148: 485–94.

Allen, J. R. L. (1996*a*). The sequence of early land-claims on the Walland and Romney Marshes, southern Britain: a preliminary hypothesis and its implications. *Proc. Geol. Ass.,* 107: 271–80.

Allen, J. R. L. (1996*b*). The seabank on the Wentlooge Level, Gwent: date of set-back from documentary and pottery evidence. *Archaeology in the Severn Estuary,* 7: 67–84.

Allen, J. R. L. (1997*a*). A conceptual model for the archaeology of the English coastal zone, in M. G. Fulford *et al.* (eds.), 50–55.

Allen, J. R. L. (1997*b*). Romano-British and early medieval pottery scatters on the alluvium at Hill and Oldbury, Severn Estuary Levels. *Archaeology in the Severn Estuary,* 8: 67–81.

Allen, J. R. L. (1997*c*). The geoarchaeology of land-claim in coastal wetlands: a sketch from Britain and the north-west European Atlantic—North Sea coasts. *Archaeol. J.,*154: 1–54.

Allen, J. R. L., Bradley, R. J., Fulford, M. G., Mithen, S. J., Rippon, S. J., and Tyson, H. (1997). The archaeological resource: chronological overview, in M. G. Fulford *et al.* (eds.), 103–53.

Allen, J. R. L. and Fulford, M. G. (1986). The Wentlooge Level: a Romano-British saltmarsh reclamation in South East Wales. *Britannia,* 17: 91–117.

Allen, J. R. L. and Fulford, M. G. (1987). Romano-British settlement and industry on the wetlands of the Severn Estuary. *Antiq. J.,* 67/2: 237–89.

Allen, J. R. L. and Fulford, M. G. (1990*a*). Romano-British and later reclamations on the Severn saltmarshes in the Elmore area, Gloucestershire. *Trans. Bristol & Gloucestershire Archaeol. Soc.*, 108: 17–32.

Allen, J. R. L. and Fulford, M. G. (1990*b*). Romano-British wetland reclamations at Longney, Gloucestershire, and evidence for the early settlement of the inner Severn Estuary. *Antiq. J.*, 70/2: 288–326.

Allen, J. R. L. and Fulford, M. G. (1992). Romano-British and later geoarchaeology at Oldbury Flats: reclamation and settlement on the changeable coast of the Severn Estuary, South West Britain. *Archaeol. J.*, 149: 81–123.

Allen, J. R. L. and Fulford, M. G. (1996). The distribution of South East Dorset black burnished Category 1 pottery in South West Britain. *Britannia*, 27: 223–81.

Allen, J. R. L. and Pye, K. 1992*a*). *Saltmarshes. morphodynamics, conservation and engineering significance*. Cambridge: Cambridge Univ. Press.

Allen, J. R. L. and Pye, K. (1992*b*). Coastal saltmarshes: their nature and importance, in J. R. L. Allen and K. Pye (eds.), 1–18.

Allen, J. R. L. and Rae, J. E. (1988). Vertical salt-marsh accretion since the Roman period in the Severn Estuary, Southwest Britain. *Marine Geology,* 83: 225–35.

Allen, J. R. L. and Rippon, S. J. (1997*a*). Iron Age to early modern activity and palaeochannels at Magor Pill, Gwent; an exercise in lowland coastal zone geoarchaeology. *Antiq. J.*, 77: 327–70.

Allen, J. R. L. and Rippon, S. J. (1997*b*). A Romano-British shaft of dressed stone and the settlement at Oldbury-on-Severn, County of Avon. *Trans. Bristol & Gloucestershire Archaeol. Soc.*, 115: 19–27.

Anderson L. M. (1995). Upton Country Park, Creekmoor, Poole. *Proc. Dorset Nat. Hist. Archaeol. Soc.*, 117: 125.

Andrews, D. and Brooks, H. (1989). An Essex Dunwich: the lost church at Little Holland Hall. *Essex Archaeol. Hist.*, 20: 74–83.

Andrews, P. (1995). *Excavations at Redcastle Furze, Thetford, 1988–9*. East Anglian Archaeology, 72.

Anthony, D. W. (1990). Migration in archaeology: the baby and the bathwater. *Amer. Anthropologist*, 92/5: 895–914.

Anthony, D. W. (1992). The bath refilled: migration in archaeology again. *Amer. Anthropologist,* 94/1: 174–6.

Anthony, D. (1997). Prehistoric migration as social process, in J. Chapman and H. Hamerow (eds.), *Migrations and invasions in archaeological explanation*. Oxford: BAR S.664: 21–32.

Anon (1988). The work of the Hereford and Worcester County Museum Archaeology Section, 1986–7. *Trans. Worcestershire Archaeol. Soc.* 3rd Ser., 11: 59–70.

Anon (1996). Anglo-Saxon watermill found in Tyne. *Brit. Archaeol.*, Feb. 1996, 11: 5.

Anon (1997). Bone-tests suggest monks preferred fish. *Brit. Archaeol.*, 25: 5.

Astill, M. and Grant, A. (1988). *The countryside of medieval England*. Oxford: Blackwell.

Aston, M. (1986). Post-Roman central places in Somerset, in E. Grant (ed.) *Central places, archaeology and history*. Sheffield: Dept of Archaeology, Univ. of Sheffield, 49–77.

Aston, M. (1988*a*). *Medieval fish, fisheries and fishponds in England*. Oxford: BAR 182.

Aston, M. (1988*b*). Medieval fish, fisheries and fishponds—forethoughts, in M. Aston (ed.), 1–6.

Aston, M. (1997). The Shapwick project. *Current Archaeol.*, 151: 244–54.

Aston, M. and Iles, R. (1987). *The archaeology of Avon.* Bristol, Avon County Council.

Aston, M. and Lewis, C. (1994). *The medieval landscape of Wessex.* Oxford: Oxbow Monogr., 46.

Aston, M., Austin, D., and Dyer, C. (1989). *The rural settlements of medieval England.* London: Batsford.

Atkin, M. (1985). Excavations on Alms Lane, in M. Atkin *et al.* (eds.), 144–265.

Atkin, M., Carter, A. and Evans, D. H. (1985). *Excavations in Norwich 1971–78 Part II.* East Anglian Archaeology, 26.

Attema, P., Haagsma, B-J., and Delvigne, J. J., forthcoming. Survey and sediments in the *ager* of ancient *Setia* Lazio, central Italy. *Caecvlvs* III. Papers on Mediterranean Archaeology. Groningen: Archaeological Institute, Groningen Univ., 113–21.

Ayers, B. (1987). Excavations at St Martin-at-Palace Plain, Norwich, 1981. *East Anglian Archaeology*, 37.

Ayers, B. S. (1994). Excavations at Fishergate, Norwich, 1985. *East Anglian Archaeology*, 68.

Ayers, B. and Murphy, P. (1983). A waterfront excavation at Whitefriars Street Car Park, Norwich, 1979. *East Anglian Archaeology,* 17: 1–60.

Bailey, C. J. (1962). Early Iron Age 'B' hearth site indicating salt working on the north shore of the Fleet at Wyke Regis. *Proc. Dorset Nat. Hist. Archaeol. Soc.,* 84; 132–6.

Bailey, M. (1989). *A marginal economy?. East Anglian Breckland in the later Middle Ages.* Cambridge: Cambridge Univ. Press.

Bailey, M. (1991). 'Per Imperetum Maris'; natural disaster and economic decline in eastern England, 1275–1350, in B. M. S. Campbell (ed.), *Before the Black Death: Studies in the crisis of the early fourteenth century.* Manchester: Manchester Univ. Press, 184–208.

Baker, F. T. (1960). The Iron Age salt industry in Lincolnshire. *Lincs. Architectural & Archaeol. Soc. Reports and Papers,* 8: 26–34.

Baker, F. T. (1975). Salt making sites on the Lincolnshire coast before the Romans, in K. de Brisay and K. A. Evans (eds.), 31–2.

Bakker, H. de (1982). Soils and their geography, in H. De Bakker and M. W. Van den Berg (eds.), 85–97.

Bakker, H. de and Van den Berg, M. W. (1982). *Proceedings of the symposium on peat lands below sea level.* Wageningen: ILRI publication, 30.

Bakker, H. de and Kooistra, M. J. (1982). Marine polders in The Netherlands. *Polders of the World, Volume 1. Polder projects, land and water management aspects.* Wageningen: The Netherlands, 25–36.

Balaam, N., Bell, M., David, A., Levitan, B. Macphail, R., Robinson M., and Scaife, R. (1988). Prehistoric and Romano-British sites at Westward Ho!, Devon: archaeological and palaeo-environmental surveys 1983 + 1984, in N. D. Balaam, B. Levitan, and V. Straker (eds.), *Studies in palaeoeconomy and environment in South West England.* Oxford: BAR 181, 163–264.

Ballard, A. (1920). *An eleventh century inquisition of St. Augustine's, Canterbury.* London: Brit. Acad.

Barber, K. E. (1982). Peat-bog stratigraphy as a proxy climate record, in A. Harding (ed.), 103–13.

Barber, K. E., Chambers, F. M., Maddy, D., Stoneman, R., and Brew, J. S. (1994). A sensitive high-resolution record of late Holocene climatic change from a raised bog in northern England. *The Holocene,* 4/2: 198–205.

Barber, L. (1998). Medieval rural settlement and economy at Lydd: preliminary results from the excavations at Lydd Quarry, in J. Eddison *et al.* (eds.), 89–108.

Barford, P. M. (1982). A new type of briquetage. *Kent Archaeol. Rev.,* 69: 204–5.

Barford, P. M. (1988). After the red hills. Salt making in Late Roman, Saxon and medieval Essex. *Colchester Archaeol. Group Annual Bull.,* 31: 3–8.

Barford, P. M. (1990*a*). Briquetage finds from inland sites, in A. J. Fawn *et al.* (eds.), 79–80.

Barford, P. M. (1990*b*). Salt production in Essex before the red hills, in A. J. Fawn *et al.* (eds.), 81–4.

Barford, P. M. (1995). Briquetage and chaff-tempered ware, in K. Blockley, M. Blockley, P. Blockley, S. Frere, and S. Stowe, *Excavations in the Marlowe Street Car Park and surrounding areas. Part II The finds.* Canterbury: Canterbury Archaeol. Trust, 672–3.

Barker, F. E. (1947). Sussex Anglo-Saxon charters. *Sussex Archaeol. Coll.,* 86: 42–101.

Barker, F. E. (1949). Sussex Anglo-Saxon charters. Part III. *Sussex Archaeol. Coll.,* 88: 51–113.

Barker, G. (1996). *Farming in the desert: the UNESCO Libyan Valleys archaeological survey. Volume 1. Synthesis.* London: Soc. for Libyan Studies.

Barnett, C., Stanley, P., Trett, R. and Webster, P. V. (1990). Romano-British pottery kilns at Caldicot, Gwent. *Archaeol. J.,*147: 118–47.

Bassett, S. (1989). In Search of the origins of Anglo-Saxon kingdoms, in S. Bassett (ed.) *The origins of Anglo-Saxon kingdoms.* Leicester: Leicester Univ. Press, 3–27.

Bateman, N. and Milne, G. (1983). A Roman harbour in London: excavations and observations near Pudding Lane, City of London, 1079–82. *Britannia,* 14: 207–226.

Bateson, M. (1913). The Borough of Droitwich. *VCH Worcestershire,* 3: 72–89.

Beck, D. (1995). The drainage of Romney Marsh and maintenance of the Dymchurch Wall in the early seventeenth century, in J. Eddison (ed.), 164–8.

Bedwin, O. (1980). Neolithic and Iron Age material from a coastal site at Chidham, West Sussex, 1978. *Sussex Archaeol. Coll.,* 118: 163–70.

Behre, K-E. (1985). Die ursprüngliche Vegetation in den deutschen Marschgebieten und deren Veränderung durch prähistorische Besiedlung und Meeresspiegelbewegungen. *Verhandlungen der Gesellschaft für Ökologie* XIII, 85–96.

Behre, K.-E. (1990*a*). *Environment and settlement history in the N. German coastal region* Wilhelmshaven: Niederchsisches Institut für historische Küstenforschung.

Behre, K.-E. (1990*b*). History of landscape and habitation in the coastal region of Niedersachsen, in K.-E. Behre (ed.), 5–66.

Behre, K.-E. (1990*c*). Wurten and archaeobotany in the Krumhörn, in K.-E. Behre (ed.), 81–3.

Behre, K.-E. (1990*d*). The salt-making site at Diekmannshausen, in K.-E. Behre (ed.), 90–1.

Behre, K-E and Jacomet, S. (1991). The ecological interpretation of archaeobotanical data, in W. Van Zeist, K. Wasylikowa, and K.-E. Behre (eds.), *Progress in Old World palaeoethnobotany.* Rotterdam: Balkema, 81–108.

Behre, K.-E. and Kucan, D. (1990). Pollen diagrams from kettle-hole bogs in the Siedlungskammer Flögeln, in K.-E. Behre (ed.), 108–12.

Behre, K.-E., Menke, B., and Streif, H. (1979). The Quaternary geological development of the German part of the North Sea, in E. Oele *et al.* (eds.), 85–113.

Bell, M. (1977). Excavation at Bishopstone. *Sussex Archaeol. Coll.,* 115: 1–291.

Bell, M. (1990). *Brean Down. Excavations 1983–1987.* London: English Heritage.

Bell, M. (1994). Field survey and excavation at Goldcliff 1994. *Archaeology in the Severn Estuary 1994*: 115–44.

Bell, M. (1997). Environmental archaeology in the coastal zone, in M. G. Fulford *et al.* (eds.) 56–73.

Bell, M. and Neumann, H. (1995). Intertidal peat survey in the Welsh Severn Estuary. *Archaeology in the Severn Estuary 1995*, 6: 29–34.

Bell, M. and Neumann, H. (1997). Prehistoric intertidal archaeology and environments in the Severn Estuary, Wales. *World Archaeol.*, 29/1: 95–113.

Bell, M. and Walker, M. C. (1992). *Late Quaternary environmental change.* London: Longman.

Benham, H. (1993). *Essex gold: the fortunes of the Essex oystermen.* Chelmsford: Essex Records Office.

Bennell, M. (1995). Hope All Saints: a survey and discussion of the ruins and earthworks, in J. Eddison (ed.), 99–106.

Bennett, P. and Williams, J. (1997). Monkton. *Current Archaeol.*, 151: 258–64.

Bennett, S. and Stewart, N. (1993). *An historical atlas of Lincolnshire.* Hull: Univ. of Hull Press.

Berendsen, H. J. A. (1990). River courses in the central Netherlands during the Roman period. *BROB*, 40: 243–9.

Berendsen, H. J. A. and Zagwijn, W. H. (1984). Some conclusions reached at the symposium on geological changes in the western Netherlands during the period 1000–1300 AD. *Geologie en Mijnbouw*, 63: 225–9.

Beresford, G. (1975). *The medieval clayland village: excavations at Goltho and Barton Blount.* London: Society for Med. Archaeol. Monogr., 6.

Beresford, G. (1981). Climatic Change and its effect upon the settlement and desertion of medieval villages in Britain, in C. Smith and M. Parry (eds.), 30–9.

Beresford, M. (1967). *New towns of the Middle Ages: town plantation in England, Wales and Gascony.* London: Lutterworth Press.

Beresford, M. (1986). Inclesmoor, West Riding of Yorkshire circa 1407, in R. A. Skelton and P. D. A. Harvey (eds.). *Local maps and plans from medieval England*, Oxford: Clarendon Press, 147–61.

Beresford, M. and St Joseph, J. (1979). *Medieval England: an aerial survey* (2nd edn). Cambridge: Cambridge Univ. Press.

Beresford, M. W. and Finberg, H. P. R. (1973). *English medieval boroughs: a hand-list.* Newton Abbot: David and Charles.

Bernick, K. (1998). *Hidden dimensions: the cultural significance of wetland archaeology.* Vancouver: Univ. of British Columbia Press.

Berridge, N. G. and Pattison, J. (1994). *Geology of the country around Grimsby and Patrington.* Memoirs of the Geological Survey of Great Britain.

Berry, E. K. (1975). Medieval Droitwich and the salt trade, in K. de Brisay and K. Evans (eds.), 76–80.

Besteman, J. C. (1974). Frisian salt and the problem of salt-making in North Holland in the Carolingian period. *BROB*, 24: 171–4.

Besteman, J. C. (1988). The history of medieval settlement in North Holland and the reclamation of the peat areas in archaeological perspective, in P. Murphy and C. French (eds.), *The exploitation of wetlands.* Oxford: BAR S.186, 327–68.

Besteman, J. C. (1990). North Holland AD 400–1200: turning tide or tide turned?, in J. C. Besteman *et al.* (eds.), 91–120.

Besteman, J. C., Bos, J. M., Gerrets, D. A., Heidinga, H. A., and De Koning, J., (1999). *The excavations at Wijnaldum. Reports on Frisia in Roman and medieval times.* Rotterdam: Balkema.

Besteman, J. C., Bos, J. M., and Heidinga, H. A. (1990). *Medieval archaeology in The Netherlands.* Assen/Maastricht: Van Gorcum.

Besteman, J. C. and Guiran, A. J. (1987). An early peat bog reclamation area in medieval Kennemerland, Assendelver Polders, in R. W. Brandt *et al.* (eds.), 297–332.

Bestwick, J. D. (1975). Romano-British inland salting at Middlewich Salinae, Cheshire, in K. de Brisay and K. Evans (eds.), 66–70.

Beug, H-J. (1982). Vegetational history and climatic changes in central and southern Europe, in A. Harding (ed.), 85–102.

Birley, A. (1997). *Hadrian: the restless Emperor* London: Routledge.

Birley, E. 1953. *Roman Britain and the Roman Army.* Kendal: Titus Wilson and Son.

Blaauw, W. H. (1848). Remarks on the Nonae of 1340, as relating to Sussex. *Sussex Archaeol. Coll.,* 1, 58–46.

Black, E. W. (1987). *The Roman villas of South-East England.* Oxford: BAR 171.

Black, G. (1976). Excavations in the sub-vault of the misericorde of Westminster Abbey. *Trans. London & Middlesex Archaeol. Soc.,* 27, 135–71.

Blagg, T. F. C. (1982). Roman Kent, in P. E. Leach (ed.), *Archaeology in Kent to* AD *1500.* London: CBA Res. Rep. 48, 51–60.

Blair, J. (1991). *Early medieval Surrey: landholding, church and settlement before 1300.* Stroud: Alan Sutton.

Blair, J. (1994). Anglo-Saxon Oxfordshire. Stroud: Alan Sutton.

Blair, J. and Ramsay, N. (1991). *English medieval industries.* London: Hambledon Press.

Bloe, J. W., Ray, J. E., Meads, W. E. and Salzman, P. L. (1937). The Hundred of Bexhill. *VCH Sussex* 9, 115–24.

Bloemers, J. H. F. (1979). *Rijswijk (Z. H.), 'De Bult'. Eien Siedlung der Cananefaten* Amersfoort: ROB Nederlandse Oudheden 8.

Bloemers, J. H. F. (1983). Acculturation in the Rhine/Meuse basin in the Roman period. a preliminary study, in R. W. Brandt and J. Slofstra (eds.), 159–210.

Bloemers, J. H. F. (1988). Periphery in pre- and proto-history. structure and process in the Rhine-Meuse basin between *c.*600 BC and 500 AD, in R. Jones, J. Bloemers, S. Dyson, and M. Biddle (eds.), *First Millennium papers: Western Europe in the First Millennium AD.* Oxford: BAR S.401, 11–35.

Bloemers, J. H. F. (1989). Acculturation in the Rhine/Meuse basin in the Roman period: some demographic considerations, in J. Barrett, A. Fitzpatrick, and L. Macinnes (eds.), *Barbarians and Romans in North-West Europe.* Oxford: BAR S.471, 175–97.

Blumstein, M. (1956). Roman pottery from Hoo. *Archaeologia Cantiana,* 70, 273–7.

Body, D. (1970). Ruckinge. *Archaeologia Cantiana,* 85: 179.

Bond, D. (1988). *Excavations at the North Ring, Mucking, Essex. a Late Bronze Age enclosure.* East Anglian Archaeology, 43.

Bond, J. (1988). Monastic fisheries, in M. Aston (ed.), 69–112.

Bonney, D. (1979). Early boundaries and estates in southern England, in P. Sawyer (ed.), *English medieval settlement.* London: Edward Arnold, 41–51.

Bont, C. de (1994). Reclamation patterns of peat areas in The Netherlands as a mirror of the medieval mind. *Wageningen Studies in Hist. Geography,* 2: 61–8.

Boon, G. C. (1978). Excavations on the site of a Roman quay at Caerleon and its significance, in G. C. Boon (ed.), *Monographs and Collections*, 1. Cardiff: Cambrian Archaeol. Ass., 1–24.

Boon, G. C. 1980. Caerleon and the Gwent Levels in early historic times, in F. H. Thompson (ed.), 24–36.

Boon, G. C. (1987). *The Legionary fortress of Caerleon—Isca*. Cardiff: National Museum of Wales.

Borger, G. J. (1992). Draining—digging—dredging: the creation of a new landscape in the peat areas of the low countries, in J. T. A. Verhoeven (ed.), *Fens, and bogs in The Netherlands*. Dortrecht: Kluwer Academic, 131–71.

Bos, J. M. (1990). The bog area of North Holland after AD 1000: crises and opportunity, in J. C. Besteman *et al.* (eds.), 121–32.

Bottema, S., Hoorn, T. C. Van, Woldring, H., and Gremmen, W. H. E. (1980). An agricultural experiment in the unprotected saltmarsh Part II. *Palaeohistoria* XXII, 127–40.

Bowler, E. E. M. 'The reclamation and land use of the Thames marshes of North West Kent'. Ph.D thesis (London School of Economics and Political Science, 1968).

Bradley, R. (1968). Roman salt-boiling near Eastbourne. *Sussex Notes and Queries,* 17/1: 23–4.

Bradley, R. J. (1975). Salt and settlement in the Hampshire Sussex borderland, in K. de Brisay and K. Evans (eds.), 20–5.

Bradley, R. J. (1992). Roman salt production in Chichester Harbour: rescue excavations at Chidham, West Sussex. *Britannia,* 23: 27–44.

Bradley, R. J., Fulford, M. G. and Tyson, H. J. (1997). The archaeological resource: regional review, in M. G. Fulford *et al.* (eds.), 154–78.

Bradshaw, J. (1970). Ashford area: Ruckinge. *Archaeologia Cantiana,* 85: 1.

Bramwell, D. (1977). The bird bones, in H. Clarke and A. Carter (eds.), *Excavations at King's Lynn 1963–1970*. London: Soc. Med. Archaeol., 399–403.

Brandon, P. F. (1971*a*). Demesne arable farming in coastal Sussex during the later Middle Ages. *Agric. Hist. Rev.,* 19/2: 113–34.

Brandon, P. F. (1971*b*). Agriculture and the effects of floods and weather at Barnhorne, Sussex, during the Late Middle Ages. *Sussex Archaeol. Coll.,* 109: 69–93.

Brandon, P. F. (1971*c*). The origin of Newhaven and the drainage of the Lewes and Laughton Levels. *Sussex Archaeol. Coll.,* 109: 94–106.

Brandon, P. F. (1972). Cereal yields on the Sussex estates of Battle Abbey during the later Middle Ages. *Econ. Hist. Rev.* 2nd Ser., 25/3: 403–20.

Brandon, P. F. (1974). *The Sussex landscape*. London: Hodder and Stoughton.

Brandt, R. (1983). A brief encounter along the northern frontier, in R. Brandt and J. Slofstra (eds.), *Roman and native in the Low Countries: spheres of interaction*. Oxford: BAR S.184, 129–43.

Brandt, R. W., Groenman-Van Waateringe, W., and Leeuw, S. E. Van der (1987). *Assendelver Polder Papers 1*. Amsterdam: Albert Egges Van Giffen Instituut voor Prae- en Protohistorie.

Brandt, R. W. and Van der Leeuw, S. E. (1987). Conclusions: Assendelver Polders, in R. W. Brandt *et al.* (eds.), 339–52.

Branigan, K. (1976). *The Roman villa in South-West England*. Bradford-on-Avon: Moonraker Press.

Branigan, K. (1989). Specialisation in villa economies, in K. Branigan and D. Miles (eds.), *The economies of Romano-British villas*. Sheffield; Dept of Archaeology and Prehistory, Univ. of Sheffield: 42–50.

Bray, S. (1994). Excavations of Romano-British cropmarks at Throckenholt Farm, Parson Drove. *Fenland Res.*, 1994: 60–3.

Bridbury, A. R. (1955). *England and the salt trade in the later Middle Ages*. Oxford: Clarendon Press.

Briffa, K. and Atkinson, T. (1997). Reconstructing Late-Glacial and Holocene climates, in M. Hulme and E. Barrow (eds.), 84–111.

Brigham, T. (1990). The Late Roman waterfront in London. *Britannia,* 21: 99–183.

Brigham, T. and Watson, B. (1998). Regis House: the Romans erect their port. *Current Archaeology,* 158: 44–7.

Brinkhuizen, D. C. (1979). Preliminary notes on fish remains from archaeological sites in The Netherlands. *Palaeohistoria* XXI; 83–90.

Brinkhuizen, D. C. (1983). Some notes on recent and pre- and proto-historic fishing gear from Northwestern Europe. *Palaeohistoria* XXV: 7–53.

Brinkkemper, O. (1962). *Wetland farming in the area to the south of the Meuse Estuary during the Iron Age and Roman period: an environmental and palaeo-economic reconstruction.* Leiden: Proefschrift Rijksuniversiteit te Leiden.

Brinkkemper, O., Duistermaat, H., Hallewas, D. P., and Kooistra, L. I. (1995). A native settlement from the Roman period near Rockanje. *BROB* 41: 123–71.

Brisay, K. de (1979). The excavation of a red hill at Peldon, Essex, with notes on some other sites. *Antiq. J., LVIII:* 31–60.

Brisay, K. de and Evans, K. (1975). *Salt: the study of an ancient industry.* Colchester: Colchester Archaeological Group.

Britnell, R. H. (1986). *Growth and decline in Colchester, 1300–1525.* Cambridge: Cambridge Univ. Press.

Broeke, P. W. Van den (1993). A crowded peat area: observations in Vlaardingen-West and the Iron Age habitation of southern Midden-Delfland. *Analecta Praehistorica Leidensia,* 26: 59–82.

Broeke, P. W. Van den (1995). Iron Age sea salt trade in the Lower Rhine area, in J. D. Hill and C. G. Cumberpatch (eds.), *Different Iron Ages: studies on the Iron Age in temperate Europe.* Oxford: BAR S.602, 149–62.

Broeke, P. W. Van den (1996). Southern sea salt in the Low Countries: a reconnaissance into the land of the Morini. *Acta Archaeologica Lovaniensia Monographiae,* 8: 193–205.

Broeke, P. W. Van den and Londen, H. Van (1995). *5000 jaar wonen op veen en klei. Archeologisch onderzoek in het reconstructiegebied Midden-Delfland.* Utrecht: Dienst Landinrichting en Beheer Landouwgronden.

Bromwich, J. (1970). Freshwater flooding along the Fen margins south of the Isle of Ely during the Roman period, in C. W. Phillips (ed.), 114–26.

Brongers, J. A. and Woltering, P. J. (1973). Prehistory in The Netherlands: an economic–technological approach. *BROB,* 23: 7–47.

Brooks, H. (1992). Two rural medieval sites in Chignall St James: excavations 1989. *Essex Archaeol. Hist.,* 23: 39–50.

Brooks, N. (1988). Romney Marsh in the Early Middle Ages, in J. Eddison and C. Green (eds.), 90–104.

Broughton, T. R. S. (1938). Roman Asia, in T. Frank (ed.), *An economic survey of Ancient Rome* IV. Baltimore: John Hopkins Press, 499–916.

Brown, L., Corney, M., and Woodward, P. J. (1995). An Iron Age and Romano-British settlement on Oakley Down, Wimborne St Giles, Dorset. *Proc. Dorset Nat. Hist. Archaeol. Soc.,* 117: 67–79.

Brown, T. and Foard, G. (1998). The Saxon landscape: a regional perspective, in P. Everson and T. Williamson (eds.), *The archaeology of landscape.* Manchester: Manchester Univ. Press, 67–94.

Brugge, J. P. ter (1995). Vlaardingen: Hoogstad. *Holland,* 27/6: 383–6.

Buckland, P. C., Magilton, J. R., and Hayfield, C. (1989). *The archaeology of Doncaster 2. The medieval and late town.* Oxford: BAR 202.

Buckland, P. C. and Sadler, J. (1985). The nature of the Late Flandrian alluviation in the Humberhead Levels. *East Midland Geogr.,* 8/8: 239–51.

Buckley, D. G. and Hedges, J. D. (1987). *Excavations at Woodham Walter and an assessment of Essex enclosures.* East Anglian Archaeology, 33.

Bulleid, A. (1914). Romano-British potteries in Mid-Somerset. *Proc. Soc. Antiq.,* 26: 137–54.

Bult, E. J. (1983). *Midden-Delfland, een archeologische kartering, inventairisatie, waardering end bewoningsgeschiedensis tekst.* Amersfoort; Rijksdienst voor het Oudheidkundig Bodemonderzoek.

Bult, E. J. (1986). Moated sites in their economical and social context in Delfland. *Chateau Gaillard,* XIII: 20–39.

Bult, E. J. and Hallewas, D. O. (1990). Archaeological evidence for the early-medieval settlement around the Meuse and Rhine deltas up to *c.*AD 1000, in J. C. Besteman *et al.* (eds.), 71–90.

Burleigh, G. R. (1973). An introduction to deserted medieval villages in East Sussex. *Sussex Archaeol. Coll.,* 111: 45–83.

Burnham, B. C. and Wacher, J. (1990). *The 'Small Towns' of Roman Britain.* London: Batsford.

Burrin, P. J. (1988). The Holocene floodplain and alluvial fill deposits of the Rother Valley and the bearing on the evolution of Romney Marsh, in J. Eddison and C. Green (eds.), 30–52.

Burrows, J. W. (1909). *Southend on Sea and district: historical notes.* (Reprinted 1970). Wakefield: S. R. Publishers.

Butcher, A. F. (1974). The origins of Romney Freemen, 1433–1523. *Econ. Hist. Rev.* 2nd Ser., 27/I: 16–27.

Camden, W. (1637). *Britannia.* (Translated by P. Holland). London.

Campbell, A. (1973). *Charters of Rochester.* London: British Academy.

Campbell, E. M. J. (1962). Kent, in H. C. Darby and E. M. J. Campbell (eds.), 483–562.

Canti, M., Heal, V., Jennings, S. McDonnell, R., and Straker, V. (1995). Archaeological and palaeoenvironmental evaluation of Porlock Bay and Marsh. *Archaeology in the Severn Estuary 1995,* 6: 49–69.

Cappers, R. T. J. (1993–4). Botanical macro-remains of vascular plants of the Heveskesklooster *terp* (The Netherlands) as tools to characterise the past environment. *Palaeohistoria,* 35/36: 107–67.

Carr, A. P. and Baker, R. E. (1968). Orford, Suffolk: evidence for the evolution of the area. *Trans. Inst. Brit. Geogr.,* 45: 107–23.

Carter, G. A. (1998). *Excavations at the Orsett 'Cock' enclosure, Essex, 1976.* East Anglian Archaeology, 86.

Casey, P. J. and Hoffmann, B. (1995). Excavations at Alstone Cottage, Caerleon, 1990. *Britannia,* XXVI: 63–106.

Catherall, P. D. (1983). A Romano-British pottery manufacturing site at Oakleigh Farm, Higham, Kent. *Britannia,* 14: 103–41.

Ceunynck, R. de and Thoen, H. (1981). The Iron Age settlement at De Panne-Westhoek; ecological and geological context. *Helinium,* 21: 21–42.

Challis, A. J. and Harding, D. W. (1975). *Later prehistory from the Trent to the Tyne.* Oxford; BAR 20.

Chaplin, R. E. and Coy, J. P. (1961). Cliffe, 1961. *Archaeologia Cantiana,* 76: 205–6.

Chapman, J. and Dolukhaov, P. M. (1992). The baby and the bathwater: pulling the plug on migrations. *Amer. Anthropology.,* 94/1: 169–74.

Chapman, J. and Hamerow, H. (1997). On the move again—migrations and invasions in archaeological explanation, in J. Chapman and H. Hamerow (eds.), *Migrations and invasions in archaeological explanation.* Oxford: BAR S.664: 1–10.

Christy, M. (1906). A history of salt-making in Essex. *Essex Nat.,* 14: 193–204.

Christy, M. (1907*a*). The gathering of shell-fish. *VCH Essex,* 2: 439.

Christy, M. (1907*b*). Salt making. *VCH Essex,* 2: 445.

Christy, M. (1920). On Roman roads in Essex. *Trans. Essex Archaeol. Soc.,* New Ser. 15: 190–229.

Christy, M. (1925). The Battle of Assandon. Where was it fought? *J. Brit. Archaeol. Ass.,* New Ser. 31: 168–90.

Christy, M. and Dalton, W. H. (1925). On two large groups of marsh mounds on the Essex coast. *Trans. Essex Archaeol. Soc.,* 18: 27–56.

Churchill, D. M. 1970. Post-Neolithic to Romano-British sedimentation in the southern Fenlands of Cambridgeshire and Norfolk, in C. W. Phillips (ed.), 132–46.

Churchill, I. J., Griffen, R., and Hardman, F. W. (1956). *Calendar of Kent Feet of Fines.* Canterbury: Kent Archaeol. Soc.

Clapham, A. W. (1915). *Lesnes Abbey, in the parish of Erith, Kent.* London: Cassio Press.

Clark, J. G. D. (1949). Report on excavations on the Cambridgeshire Car Dyke 1947. *Antiq. J.,* 29: 145–63.

Clark, J. G. D. (1954). *Excavations at Star Carr.* Cambridge: Cambridge Univ. Press.

Clarke, C. P. (1988*a*). Late Iron Age enclosures at Kelvedon: excavations at the Dousecroft site 1985–86. *Essex Archaeol. Hist.,* 19: 15–39.

Clarke, C. P. (1988*b*). Roman Coggeshall: excavations 1984–85. *Essex Archaeol. Hist.,* 19: 47–90.

Clarke, C. P. (1993). Collins Creek, in P. J. Gilman (ed.). Archaeology in Essex 1992. *Essex Archaeol. Hist.,* 24: 195–210.

Clarke, H. and Carter, A. (1977). *Excavations in King's Lynn, 1963–70.* London: Society for Medieval Archaeology.

Clarke, P. (1998). *Excavations south of Chignall Roman villa Essex, 1977-91.* East Anglian Archaeology, 83.

Clarke, R. R. (1960). *East Anglia.* London: Frederick A. Praeger.

Clason, A. T. (1967). Animals and man in Holland's past. *Palaeohistoria* XIII: 1–247.

Clevedon-Brown, J. (1965). A Romano-British site at St Marys Lane, Portishead, Somerset. *Proc. Univ. Bristol Speleol. Soc.,* 8: 119–23.

Clutton-Brock, J. (1976). The animal resources, in D. M. Wilson (ed.), 373–92.

Coles, B. (1992). *The wetland revolution in prehistory.* Exeter: WARP Occ. Pap., 6.

Coles, B. and Coles, J. (1986). *Sweet Track to Glastonbury: the Somerset Levels in prehistory.* London: Thames and Hudson.

Coles, B. and Coles, J. (1989). *People of the wetlands: bogs, bodies and lake dwellings.* London: Thames and Hudson.

Coles, B., Coles, J., and Jørgensen, M. S. (1999). *Bog bodies, sacred sites and wetland archaeology.* Exeter: WARP Occ. Pap., 12.

Coles, B. P. L. 'The Holocene Foraminifera and Palaeogeography of Central Broadland'. Ph.D. (East Anglia, 1977).

Coles, B. P. L. and Funnell, B. M. (1981). Holocene palaeoenvironments of Broadland, in S.-D. Nio *et al.* (eds.), 123–131.

Coles, J. (1984). *The archaeology of wetlands.* Edinburgh: Edinburgh Univ. Press.

Coles, J. (1998). Prologue: wetland worlds and the past preserved, in K. Bernick (ed.), 3–23.

Coles, J. and Coles, B. (1996). *Enlarging the past: the contribution of wetland archaeology.* Edinburgh: Soc. Antiq. Scotland Monogr., Series 11.

Coles, J. and Hall, D. (1997). The Fenland Project: from survey to management and beyond, *Antiquity,* 71: 831–44.

Coles, J. and Lawson, A. (1987). *European wetlands in prehistory.* Oxford: Clarendon Press.

Coles, J. and Minnitt, S. (1995). *Industrious and fairly civilised: the Glastonbury Lake Village.* Taunton: Somerset Levels Project/Somerset County Museum Service.

Colley, S. (1983). Interpreting prehistoric fishing strategies: an Orkney case study, in C. Grigson and J Clutton-Brock (eds.) *Animals and Archaeology. 2. Shell Middens, Fishes and Birds.* Oxford; BAR S.183, 157–71.

Collingwood, R. G. and Myres, J. N. L. (1937). *Roman Britain and the English settlements.* Oxford: Clarendon Press.

Collingwood, R. G. and Wright, R. P. (1965). *The Roman inscriptions of Britain.* Oxford: Clarendon Press.

Coney, A. (1992). Fish, fowl and fen: landscape and economy on seventeenth-century Martin Mere. *Landscape Hist.,* 14: 51–64.

Cook, H. (1994). Field-scale water management in southern England to A.D. 1900. *Landscape Hist.,* 16: 53–66.

Cook, H. (1999). Soil and water management: principles and purposes, in H. Cook and T. Williamson (eds.), 15–27.

Cook, H. and Williamson, T. (1999) *Water management in the English landscape: field, marsh and meadow.* Edinburgh: Edinburgh Univ. Press.

Corcos, N. (1983). Early estates on the Poldens and the origins of settlements at Shapwick. *Somerset Archaeol. Nat. Hist.,* 127: 47–53.

Costen, M. (1992). Dunstan, Glastonbury and the economy of Somerset in the tenth century, in N. Ramsay, M. Sparks, and T. Tatton-Brown (eds.), *St Dunstan: his life, times and cult.* Woodbridge: Boydell Press, 25–4.

Courtney, P. (1981). The Early Saxon Fenland; a reconsideration, in D. Brown, J. Campbell, and S. C. Hawkes (eds.), *Anglo-Saxon studies in archaeology and hist.* Oxford: BAR 92, 91–102.

Cox, M., Straker, V. and Taylor, D. (1995). *Wetlands: archaeology and nature conservation.* London: HMSO.

Cox, P. W. (1988). Excavation and survey on Furzey Island, Poole Harbour, Dorset, 1985. *Proc. Dorset Nat. Hist. Archaeol. Soc.,* 110: 49–72.

Cox, P. W. and Hearne, C. W. (1991). *Redeemed from the heath: the archaeology of the Wytch Farm oilfield 1987–90.* Dorchester: Dorset Natural Hist. & Archaeol. Soc. Monogr., 9.

Crabtree, P. J. (1989). *West Stow, Suffolk: Early Anglo-Saxon animal husbandry.* East Anglian Archaeology, 47.

Cracknell, B. E. (1959). *Canvey Island: the history of a marshland community.* Leicester: Univ. of Leicester Dept of English Local Hist. Occ. Pap., 12.

Crawford, D. J. (1976). Imperial estates, in M. Finley (ed.), *Studies in Roman Property.* Cambridge: Cambridge Univ. Press, 35–70.

Cross, R. (1997). Archaeology at West Hythe: excavations in October 1996. *The Romney Marsh Irregular.* Newsletter of the Romney Marsh Res. Trust, 12; 6–7.

Crossley, D. W. (1981). *Medieval industry.* London: CBA Res. Rep., 40.

Crouchman, C. (1977). Work of the Essex County Council Archaeology Section 1977. *Essex Archaeol. Hist.,* 9; 60–94.

Crowson, A. (1994). Excavations on the Fen Causeway at Straw Hill Farm, Downham West. *Fenland Res.,* 9: 24–5.

Crowson, A., forthcoming. Excavation of a late Roman saltern at Blackborough End, Middleton, in T. Lane (ed.), *A millennium of saltmaking. prehistoric and Romano-British salt production in the Fenland.* Lincoln; Lincolnshire Archaeol. & Heritage Rep.

Crowson, A., Lane, T., and Reeve, J., (2000). *Fenland Management Project excavations 1991–1995.* Lincolnshire Archaeol. & Heritage Rep., 3.

Crowther, D. and Didsbury, P. (1988). Redcliff and the Humber, in J. Price and P. R. Wilson (eds.), 3–20.

Crummy, P. (1992). *Excavations at Culver Street, the Gilbert School, and other sites in Colchester 1971–85.* Colchester: Colchester Archaeol. Rep., 6.

Crummy, P., Hillam, J., and Crossan, C. (1982). Mersea Island: the Anglo-Saxon causeway. *Essex Archaeol. & Hist.,* 14: 71–6.

Crump, B. (1991). Foulness Island—the evolution of its buildings. *Essex J.,* 26/1: 14–18.

Crump, B. and Wallis, S. (1992). Kiddles and the Foulness fishing industry. *Essex J.,* 27/2: 38–42.

Crump, R. W. (1981). Excavation of a buried wooden structure at Foulness. *Essex Archaeol. Hist..* 13: 69–71.

Cunliffe, B. (1966). The Somerset Levels in the Roman period, in C. Thomas (ed.), *Rural settlement in Roman Britain.* London: CBA Res. Rep., 7: 68–73.

Cunliffe, B. (1980). Excavations at the Roman fort at Lympne, Kent 1976–78. *Britannia,* 11: 227–88.

Cunliffe, B. (1984). *Danebury: an Iron Age hill fort in Hampshire, Vol. 2.* London: CBA Res. Rep., 52.

Cunliffe, B. (1987). *Hengistbury Head Dorset, Vol. 1. the prehistoric and Roman settlement, 3500 BC–AD 500.* Oxford: Oxford Univ. Comm. for Archaeol.

Cunliffe, B. (1988). Romney Marsh in the Roman period, in J. Eddison and C. Green (eds.), 83–7.

Cunliffe, B. and Poole, C. 1991. *Danebury: an Iron Age hillfort in Hampshire. Vol. 5. The excavations 1979–1988: the finds.* London; CBA Res. Rep., 73.

Cunliffe, B. (1995). *Danebury: an Iron Age hillfort in Hampshire. Vol. 6. A hillfort in perspective.* York: CBA Res. Rep., 102.

Daniels, R. 1997. The church, the manor and the settlement: the evidence from the Tees Valley, England, in J. Fridrich *et al.* (eds.), 102–14.

Darby, H. C. (1940a). *Medieval Fenland.* Cambridge: Cambridge Univ. Press.

Darby, H. C. (1940*b*). *The draining of the Fens.* Cambridge: Cambridge Univ. Press.

Darby, H. C. (1962). The south-eastern counties, in H. C. Darby and E. M. J. Campbell (eds.), 563–610.

Darby, H. C. (1977). *Domesday England.* Cambridge: Cambridge Univ. Press.

Darby, H. C. (1983). *The changing Fenland.* Cambridge: Cambridge Univ. Press.

Darby, H. C. and Campbell, E. M. J. (1962). *The Domesday geography of South-East England.* Cambridge: Cambridge Univ. Press.

Darby, H. C., Glasscock, R. E., Sheail, J., and Versey, G. R. (1979). The changing geographical distribution of wealth in England: 1086–1334–1525. *J. Hist. Geogr.,* 5/3: 247–62.

Darling, M. J. and Gurney, D. (1993). *Caistor-on-Sea, excavations by Charles Green 1951–55.* East Anglian Archaeology, 60.

Dark, K. and Day, P. (1997). *The landscape of Roman Britain.* Stroud: Sutton Publishing.

Davies, J. (1996). Where eagles dare: the Iron Age of Norfolk. *Proc. Prehist. Soc.,* 62: 63–92.

Davies, R. (1987). *Conquest, coexistence and change in Wales 1063–1415.* Cardiff: University of Wales Press.

Davies, R. R. (1991). *The age of conquest: Wales 1063-1414.* Oxford: Oxford Univ. Press.

Davies, W. (1979*a*). *The Llandaff Charters.* Aberystwyth: National Library of Wales.

Davies, W. (1979*b*). Roman settlement and Post-Roman estates in South East Wales, in P. J. Casey (ed.), *The end of Roman Britain.* Oxford: BAR 71, 153–73.

Davis, S. (1992). *Saxon & medieval animals bones from Burystead and Langham Road, Northants, 1984–1987 Excavations.* London: Ancient Monuments Laboratory Rep., 71/92.

Dell, R. F. (1962). *The records of Rye Corporation: a catalogue.* Lewes: East Sussex County Council.

Dell, R. F. (1963). *Winchelsea Corporation records.* Lewes: East Sussex County Council.

Dell, R. F. 1965/6. *Rye shipping records 1566–1590.* Lewes; Sussex Rec. Soc., LXIV.

Dent, J. (1984). Skerne. *Current Archaeol.,* 91: 251–3.

Dent, J. (1990). The upper Hull Valley: archaeology under threat, in S. Ellis and D. R. Crowther (eds.), 102–8.

Dent, J., Loveluck, C., Fletcher, W., and East, K. (2000) The Early Medieval Site at Skerne. In R. Van de Noort and S. Ellis (eds.) *Wetland Heritage of the Hull Valley,* Hull, 217–42.

Denys, L. and Baetman, C. (1995). Holocene evolution of relative sea level and local mean high water spring tides in Belgium—a first assessment. *Marine Geol.,* 124: 1–19.

Desfossés, Y. (1998). L'occupation protohistorique de la vallée de la Canche France: l'apport des fouilles de l'autoroute A16. *Lunula Archaeologia Protohistorica,* 6: 19–29.

Detsicas, A. (1983). *The Cantiaci.* Gloucester: Alan Sutton.

Devoy, R. J. N. (1979). Flandrian sea level changes and vegetational history of the lower Thames Estuary. *Phil. Trans. Roy. Soc. London,* B 285: 355–407.

Devoy, R. J. N. (1980). Post-glacial environmental change and man in the Thames Estuary: a synopsis, in F. H. Thompson (ed.), 134–48.

Devoy, R. J. N. (1982). Analysis of the geological evidence for Holocene sea level movements in South East England. *Proc. Geol. Ass.,* 93: 65–90.

Devoy, R. J. N. (1990). Controls on coastal and sea level changes and the application of archaeological–historical records to understanding recent patterns of sea-level movement, in S. McGrail (ed.), *Maritime Celts, Frisians and Saxons.* London, CBA Res. Rep. 71: 17–26.

Dewilde, M., Ervynck, A., Strobbe, M., and Verhaeghe, F. (1995). Lampernisse: protecting a landscape of major archaeological and environmental value, in M. Cox *et al.* (eds.), 218–28.

Didsbury, P. (1988). Evidence for Romano-British settlement in Hull and the lower Hull Valley, in J. Price and P. R. Wilson (eds.), 21–35.

Didsbury, P. (1989). Recent discoveries in Hull and district, in P. Halkon (ed.), *New light on the Parisi*. Hull, East Riding Archaeol. Soc., 23–6.

Didsbury, P. (1990). Exploitation of the alluvium of the lower Hull Valley in the Roman period, in S. Ellis and D. R. Crowther (eds.), 199–212.

Dinnin, M. and Van de Noort R. (1999). Wetland habitats, their resource potential and exploitation: a case study from the Humber wetlands, in B. Coles *et al* (eds.), 69–78.

Dobney, K., Jacques, D., and Irving, B. (1995). *Of butchers and breeds: report on vertebrate remains from various sites in the City of Lincoln*. Lincoln: Lincoln Archaeol. Studies, 5.

Dobson, M. (1998*a*). *Contours of death and disease in Early Modern England*. Cambridge: Cambridge Univ. Press.

Dobson, M. (1998*b*). Death and disease in the Romney Marsh area in the 17th and 18th centuries, in J. Eddison *et al.* (eds.), 166–81.

Donkin, R. A. (1958). The marshland holdings of the English Cistercians before *c.*1350. *Citeaux in de Nederlanden,* 9: 262–75.

Donkin, R. A. (1978). *The Cistercians: studies in the geography of medieval England and Wales*. Toronto: Pontifical Institute of Medieval Studies.

Douglas, C. C. (1944). *The Domesday Monachorum of Christ Church Canterbury*. London.

Dowker, G. (1900). Deal and its environs. *Archaeologia Cantiana,* 24: 108–21.

Drury, P. J. (1976). Braintree: excavations and research 1971–76. *Essex Archaeol. & Hist.,* 8: 1–143.

Drury, P. J. (1978). *Excavations at Little Waltham 1970–71*. London: CBA Res. Rep., 26.

Drury, P. J. (1988). *The mansio and other sites in the south-eastern sector of Caesaromagus*. London: CBA Res. Rep., 66.

Drury, P. J., Rodwell, W. J., and Wickenden, N. P. (1981). Finds from the probable site of a Roman villa at Dawes Heath, Thundersley, Essex. *Essex Archaeol. Hist.,* 13: 66–8.

Duby, G. (1968). *Rural economy and country life in the medieval west*. London: Edward Arnold.

Dugdale, W. (1662). *The history of imbanking and draining ... ,* (1777, 2nd edn). (ed.) C. N. Cole. London: Bowyer and Nichols.

Dugdale, W. (1693). *Monasticon Anglicanum, or the history of ancient abbeys ... ,* abridged and translated by James Wright. London: Sam Keble.

Dulley, A. J. F. (1966). The Level and Port of Pevensey in the Middle Ages. *Sussex Archaeol. Coll.,* 104: 26–45.

Dunning, G. C., Hurst, J. G., Myres, J. N. L., and Tischler, F. (1959). Anglo-Saxon pottery: a symposium. *Med. Archaeol.,* 3: 1–78.

Dunning, R. W. and Siraut, M. C. (1992). Cannington. *VCH Somerset,* 6: 73–91.

Dyer, C. (1985). Power and conflict in the medieval village, in D. Hooke (ed.) *Medieval villages: a review of current work*. Oxford: Oxford Univ. Comm. for Archaeol. Monogr., 5: 27–32.

Dyer, C. (1988). The consumption of freshwater fish in medieval England, in M. Aston (ed.), 27–38.

Dyer, C. (1989). *Standards of living in the later Middle Ages: social change in England c.1200–1520*. Cambridge: Cambridge Univ. Press.

Dyer, C. (1990). The past, present and future in medieval rural history. *Rural Hist.,* 1/1: 37–50.

Dyer, C. (1996). Seasonal settlement in medieval Gloucestershire: sheepcotes, in H. Fox (ed.), 1996*a*: 25–33.

Dyer, C. (1997). Medieval settlement in Wales, in N. Edwards (ed.) *Landscape and settlement in medieval Wales*. Oxford: Oxbow Monogr., 81: 165–8.

Dyson, A. G. (1981). The terms 'quay' and 'wharf' and the early medieval London waterfront, in G. Milne and B. Hobley (eds.), 37–8.

Dyson, T. (1986). *The Roman riverside wall and monumental arch in London: excavations at Baynard's Castle, Upper Thames Street, London 1974–76*. London: London & Middlesex Archaeol. Soc. Special Pap., 3.

Eagles, B. N. (1979). *The Anglo-Saxon settlement of Humberside*. Oxford: BAR 68.

Eddison, J. (1983a). The evolution of barrier beaches between Fairlight and Hythe. *Geogr. J.,* 149: 39–75.

Eddison, J. (1983b). The reclamation of Romney Marsh: some aspects re-considered. *Archaeologia Cantiana,* 99: 47–58.

Eddison, J. (1985). Developments in the lower Rother Valleys up to 1600. *Archaeologia Cantiana,* 102: 95–110.

Eddison, J. (1988). 'Drowned Lands': changes in the course of the Rother and its estuary and associated drainage problems, 1635–1737, in J. Eddison and C. Green (eds.), 142–161.

Eddison, J. (1995a). *Romney Marsh: the debatable ground*. Oxford: Oxford Univ. Comm. Archaeol. Monogr., 41.

Eddison, J. (1995b). Attempts to clear the Rother Channel, 1613–24, in J. Eddison (ed.), 148–63.

Eddison, J. (1998). Catastrophic changes: a multidisciplinary study of the evolution of the barrier beaches of Rye Bay, in J. Eddison *et al.* (eds.), 65–87.

Eddison, J., Carr, A. P., and Jolliffe, L. P. (1983). Endangered coastlines of geomorphological importance. *Geogr. J.,* 149/1: 39–75.

Eddison, J. and Draper, G. (1997). A landscape of medieval reclamation: Walland Marsh, Kent. *Landscape Hist.,* 19: 75–88.

Eddison, J., Gardiner, M., and Long, A. (1998). *Romney Marsh: environmental change and human occupation in a coastal lowland*. Oxford, Oxford Univ. Comm. Archaeol. Monogr., 46.

Eddison, J. and Green, C. (1988). *Romney Marsh: evolution, occupation, reclamation*. Oxford: Oxford Univ. Comm. Archaeol. Monogr., 24.

Eddy, M. R. (1980). Work of the Essex County Council Archaeology Section, 1979. *Essex Archaeol. & Hist.,* 12: 51–85.

Eddy, M. R. (1982). *Kelvedon: the origins and development of a Roman small town*. Chelmsford: Essex County Council Archaeol. Occ. Pap., 3.

Eddy, M. R. (1984/5). Excavations in medieval Rochford. *Essex Archaeol. & Hist.,* 16: 7–22.

Edelman, C. H. (1950). *Soils of The Netherlands*. Amsterdam; N. Holland Publishing Company.

Edwards, N. (1997a). *Landscape and settlement in medieval Wales*. Oxford: Oxbow Monogr., 81.

Edwards, N. (1997b). Landscape and settlement in Wales: an introduction, in N. Edwards (ed.), 1–11.

Eigler, F. (1983). Regular settlements in Franconia founded by the Franks in the early middle ages, in B. K. Roberts and R. E. Glasscock (eds.), *Villages, fields and frontiers*. Oxford: BAR S.185: 83–91.

Elkington, H. D. H. (1976). The Mendip lead industry, in K. Branigan and P. J. Fowler (eds.) *The Roman West Country*. Newton Abbot: David and Charles, 183–97.

Ellis, S. (1990). Soils, in S. Ellis and D. Crowther (eds,), 29–42.

Ellis, S. and Crowther, D. R. (1990). *Humber perspectives: a region through the ages.* Hull: Hull Univ. Press.

Elliston-Erwood, F. C. (1916). The earthworks at Charlton, London. *J. Brit. Archaeol. Ass.*, New Ser., 22: 125–91.

Elliston-Erwood, F. C. (1951). Further excavations on the site of the earthworks at Charlton. *Archaeologia Cantiana,* 64: 158–60.

Ervynck, A. (1997). Following the rule? Fish and meat consumption in monastic communities in Flanders Belgium, in G. de Boe and F. Verhaeghe (eds.), *Environment and subsistence in medieval Europe.* Zellik: I. A. P. Rapporten 6: 67–81.

Es, W. A. Van 1965/6. Friesland in Roman times. *BROB,* 15–16: 37–68.

Es, W. A. Van (1968). Paddepoel: excavations of frustrated terps, 200 BC–250 AD. *Palaeohistoria* XIV: 187–352.

Es, W. A. Van (1973*a*). Early medieval settlements. *BROB,* 23: 149–58.

Es, W. A. Van (1973*b*). Terp research, with particular reference to a medieval terp at Den Helder, Province of North Holland. *BROB,* 23: 337–45.

Es, W. A. Van and Miedema, M. (1970/71). Leeuwarden: small terp under Oldehave cemetery. *BROB,* 20–21: 89–117.

Evans, A. (1941). Battle Abbey at the Dissolution. *Huntingdon Library Q.,* 4: 393–442.

Evans, A. (1942). Battle Abbey at the Dissolution: expenses. *Huntingdon Library Q.,* 6/I: 53–102.

Evans, C. (1994). Langwood Farm West and environs. *Fenland Res.,* 9: 3–11.

Evans, D. H. (1993). *Excavations on Hull 1975–76.* East Riding Archaeol. Soc.

Evans, D. H. and Carter, A. (1985). Excavations on 31–51 Pottergate, in M. Atkin *et al.* (eds.), 9–86.

Evans, D. H. and Steedman, K. (1997). Recent archaeological work in the East Riding. *East Riding Archaeol.,* 9: 116–71.

Evans, D. H and Steedman, K. (2000). Archaeology in the modern city of Kingston upon Hull, and recent research at Kingswood. In R. Van de Noort and S. Ellis (eds.) *The Wetland Heritage of the Hull Valley,* Hull, 193–216.

Evans, D. R. and Metcalf, V. M. (1992). *Roman gates, Caerleon.* Oxford: Oxbow Monogr., 15.

Evans, J. G. (1893). *The Book of Llan Dav.* Reprinted 1979, (ed.), D. Jenkins. Aberystwyth: National Library of Wales.

Evans, J. H. (1950). Roman remains from Upchurch Marshes. *Archaeologia Cantiana* 62: 146–7.

Evans, J. H. (1951*a*). Roman pottery from Cliffe Marshes. *Archaeologia Cantiana,* 64: 156.

Evans, J. H. (1951*b*). Earthwork near Hoo St Werburgh. *Archaeologia Cantiana,* 64: 156–8.

Evans, J. H. (1951*c*). Roman vase from the Isle of Grain. *Archaeologia Cantiana,* 64: 158.

Evans, J. H. (1953). Archaeological horizons in the North Kent Marshes. *Archaeologia Cantiana,* 66: 103–46.

Everard, C. E. (1980). On sea-level changes, in F. H. Thompson (ed.), 1–23.

Everitt, A. 1986. *Continuity and colonization: the evolution of Kentish settlement.* Leicester: Leicester Univ. Press.

Everson, P. and Hayes, T. (1984). Lincolnshire from the air, in N. Field and A. White (eds.), 33–41.

Ey, J. (1990). The excavation of the Wurt Oldorf/Wangerland, in K.-E. Behre (ed.), 89.

Ey, J. (1997). Early diking and early settlement in Lower Saxony, in C. U. Larsen (ed.), 24.

Farrar, R. A. H. (1962a). Miscellaneous discoveries and accessions. *Proc. Dorset Nat. Hist. Archaeol. Soc.,* 84: 111–16.

Farrar, R. A. H. (1962b). A note on the prehistoric and Roman salt industry in relation to the Wyke Regis site, Dorset. *Proc. Dorset Nat. Hist. Archaeol., Soc.* 84: 137–44.

Farrar, R. A. H. 1973. The techniques and sources of Romano-British black-burnished ware, in A. Detsicas (ed.) *Current Research in Romano-British Coarse Pottery.* London: CBA Res. Rep., 10: 67–103.

Farrar, R. A. H. (1975). Prehistoric and Roman saltworks in Dorset, in K. de Brisay and K. Evans (eds.), 14–20.

Farrar, R. A. H. (1976). Interim report on excavations at the Romano-British potteries at Redcliff near Wareham. *Proc. Dorset Nat. Hist. Archaeol. Soc.,* 97: 49–51.

Farrar, R. A. H. (1977). A Romano-British black burnished ware industry at Ower in the Isle of Purbeck, Dorset, in J. Dore and K. Greene (eds.), *Roman pottery studies in Britain and beyond.* Oxford: BAR S.30, 199–228.

Farrar, R. A. H. (1982). Black burnished ware factory at Redcliff, Arne. *Proc. Dorset Nat. Hist. Archaeol. Soc.,* 104: 186–7.

Fasham, P. J., Farwell, D. E., and Whinney, R. J. B. (1980). *The archaeological site at Easton Lane, Winchester.* Winchester: Hampshire Field Club and Archaeol. Soc. Monogr., 6.

Faulkner, N. (1993a). Summary of earlier work at Leigh Beck and other Canvey sites. *Trans. Rochford Hundred Field Archaeol. Group,* 1: 2–14.

Faulkner, N. (1993b). Interim report on fieldwork at Leigh Beck. *Trans. Rochford Hundred Field Archaeol. Group,* 1: 15–27.

Faulkner, C. and Faulkner, N. (1993). Shellfish. *Trans. Rochford Hundred Field Archaeol. Group,* 1: 47–50.

Fawn, A. J., Davies, G. M. R., Evans, K. A., and McMaster, I. (1990). *The red hills of Essex: salt making in antiquity.* Colchester: Colchester Archaeol. Group.

Fenwick, V. (1972). Recent work on the Graveney Boat, in B. Greenhill (ed.) *Three major boat finds in Britain.* London: National Maritime Museum Monogr, 6: 9–17.

Fenwick, V. (1978). *The Graveney Boat.* Oxford: BAR 53.

Fenwick, V. (1984). Insula de burgh: excavations at Burrow Hill, Butley, Suffolk, 1978–81, in S. C. Hawkes, J. Campbell and D. Brown (eds.), *Anglo-Saxon Studies in Archaeol. & Hist.,* 3: 35–54.

Field, N. and White, A. (1984). *A prospect of Lincolnshire.* Lincoln: F. N. Field and A. J. White.

Finberg, H. P. R. (1955). *Roman and Saxon Withington: a study in continuity.* Leicester: Leicester Univ. Dept of English Local Hist.

Fleming, A. (1988). *The Dartmoor reaves.* London: Batsford

Foard, G. (1978). Systematic fieldwalking and the investigation of Saxon settlement in Northamptonshire. *World Archaeol.,* 9/3: 357–74.

Först, E. (1988). 'Briquetage' funde im Weser-Ems-Gebiet. *Archäologisches Korrespondenzblatt,* 18: 357–64.

Fowler, G. (1949). A Romano-British village near Littleport, Cambs, with some observations on the distribution of early occupation, and on the drainage of the fens. *Proc. Cambridge Antiq. Soc.,* 48: 7–20.

Fowler, P. J. (1975). Continuity in the landscape: some local archaeology in Wiltshire, Somerset and Gloucestershire, in P. J. Fowler (ed.), *Recent work in rural archaeology.* Bradford-on-Avon: Moonraker Press, 121–33.

Fowler, R. C. (1907). Religious houses. *VCH Essex*, 2: 84–203.

Fox, C. F. (1937). Salt works at Hook, Warsash, Hants. *Papers and Proc. Hampshire Field Club and Archaeol. Soc.*, 13: 105–9.

Fox, H. (1989). The people of the Wolds in English settlement history, in M. Aston *et al.* (eds.), 77–101.

Fox, H. (1996*a*). *Seasonal settlement.* Leicester: Univ. of Leicester Vaughan Papers, 39.

Fox, H. (1996*b*). Introduction. transhumance and seasonal settlement, in H. Fox (ed.), 1–23.

Frances, A. G. (1930). On a causeway at the prehistoric settlement of Southchurch, Essex. *Trans. Southend-on-Sea & District Antiq. Soc.*, 2: 49–75.

Frances, A. G. (1932). On subsidence of the Thames Estuary since the Roman period, at Southchurch, Essex. *Essex Naturalist*, 23: 151–70.

Frank, T. (1927). *An economic history of Rome.* London: Jonathan Cape.

French, C. A. I. (1992). Excavation at Parson Drove Site 15, Cambridgeshire. *Fenland Res.*, 7: 62–6.

French, C. (1996). Molluscan analysis, in R. Jackson and T. Potter (ed.) 639–64.

Frere, S. (1987). *Britannia: a history of Roman Britain* (3rd edn). London: Routledge.

Fridrich, J., Klápste, J., Smetánka, Z., and Sommer, P. (1997). *Ruralia I. Conference Ruralia— Prague, 8th–14th September 1995.* Prague: Institute of Archaeology.

Fulford, M. G. (1989). The economy of Roman Britain, in M. Todd (ed.), *Research on Roman Britain 1960–89.* London: Britannia Monograph.

Fulford, M. G. (1996). *The second Augustan legion in the west of Britain.* Cardiff: National Museum of Wales.

Fulford, M. G. and Allen, J. R. L. (1992). Iron-making at the Chesters Villa, Woolaston, Gloucestershire: survey and excavation 1987-91. *Britannia*, 23: 159–216.

Fulford, M. G., Allen, J. R. L., and Rippon, S. J. (1994). The settlement and drainage of the Wentlooge Level, Gwent: excavation and survey at Rumney Great Wharf 1992. *Britannia*, 25: 175–211.

Fulford, M. G. and Champion, T. (1997). Potential and priorities, in M. G. Fulford *et al.* (eds.), 215–34.

Fulford, M. G., Champion, T., and Long, A. (1997). *England's coastal heritage: a survey for English Heritage and the RCHME.* London: English Heritage.

Funnell, B. M. (1979). History and prognosis of subsidence and sea-level change in the lower Yare Valley, Norfolk. *Bull. Geol. Soc. Norfolk*, 31: 35–44.

Funnell, B. (1997). The climates of past ages, in M. Hulme and E. Barrow (eds.), 65–83.

Furley, R. (1874). *A history of the Weald of Kent.* Vol. 2/ii. Ashford and London.

Furley, R. (1880). An outline of the history of Romney Marsh. *Archaeologia Cantiana*, 13; 178–200.

Gardiner, J. (1993). *Flatlands and wetlands: current themes in East Anglian archaeology.* East Anglian Archaeol., 50.

Gardiner, M. (1988). Medieval settlement and society in the Broomhill area and excavations at Broomhill Church, in J. Eddison and C. Green (eds.), 112–27.

Gardiner, M. (1989). Broomhill Church project: 1988 season. *Archaeologia Cantiana*, 107: 377–9.

Gardiner, M. (1994). Old Romney: an examination of the evidence for a lost Saxo-Norman port. *Archaeologia Cantiana*, 114: 329–45.

Gardiner, M. (1995). Medieval farming and flooding in the Brede Valley, in J. Eddison (ed.), 127–37.

Gardiner, M. (1998). A seasonal fisherman's settlement at Dungeness, Kent. *The Romney Marsh Irregular,* Newsletter of the Romney Marsh Res. Trust, 13: 2–6.

Gardiner, M., Stewart, J., and Priestley-Bell, G. (1998). Anglo-Saxon whale exploitation: some evidence from Dengemarsh, Lydd, Kent. *Med. Archaeol., XLII*: 96–101.

Garrod, J. R. (1940). A Romano-British site at Sawtry, Huntingdonshire. *Antiq. J.,* 20: 504–6.

Garwood, A. (1995). Tollesbury, Tollesbury Wick Marsh. *Med. Settlement Res. Group Ann. Rep.,* 10: 29.

Gaunt, G. D. and Tooley, M. J. (1974). Evidence for Flandrian sea level changes in the Humber Estuary. *Bull. Geol. Surv. Great Britain,* 48: 25–41.

Geel, B. Van, Bos, J. M., and Pals, J. P. (1983). Archaeological and palaeoecological aspects of a medieval house terp in a reclaimed raised bog area in North Holland. *BROB,* 23: 417–44.

Geel, B. Van, Hallewas, D. P., and Pals, J. P. (1982/3). A late Holocene deposit under the Westfriese Zeedijk near Enkhuizen (Prov. of Noord-Holland, The Netherlands): palaeoecological and archaeological aspects. *Rev. Palaeobot. Palynol.,* 38: 269–335.

Gelder-Ottway, S. M. Van (1988). Animal bones from a pre-Roman Iron Age coastal marsh site near Middelstrum Province of Groningen, The Netherlands. *Palaeohistoria,* 30: 125–44.

Gelling, M. (1984). *Place-names in the landscape.* London: Dent.

Gelling, M. (1988). *Signposts to the past* (2nd edn). Chichester: Phillimore.

Gerrets, D. (1996). Continuity and change in house construction and the lay-out of rural settlements during the early Middle Ages in The Netherlands, in J. Fridrich (ed.), 33–46.

Gerrets, D. (1999). Evidence of political centralization in Westergo: the excavations at Wijnaldum in a supra- regional perspective. *Studies in Anglo-Norman England,* 10: 119–26

George, M. (1992). *The land use, ecology and conservation of Broadland.* Chichester: Pickard Publishing.

Gibson, J. M. (1993). The 1566 survey of the Kent coast. *Archaeologia Cantiana,* 112: 341–53.

Giffen, A. E. Van (1936). Der Warf in Ezinge, Provinze Groningen, Holland, und seine west-germanischen Häuser. *Germania,* 20: 40–7.

Gijn, A. L. Van (1987). Site N, Assendelver Polders, in R. W. Brandt *et al.* (eds.), 99–113.

Gijn, A. L. Van and Waterbolk, H. T. (1984). The colonisation of the salt marshes of Friesland and Groningen: the possibility of a transhumant prelude. *Palaeohistoria,* 26: 101–122.

Glasscock, R. E. (1973). England *circa* 1334, in H. C. Darby (ed.), *A new historical geography of England.* Cambridge: Cambridge Univ. Press, 136–85.

Glenny, W. W. (1907). Sea fisheries. *VCH Essex,* 2: 439–45.

Glover, J. (1976). *The place-names of Kent.* London: Batsford.

Godbold, S. and Turner, R. (1994). Medieval fishtraps in the Severn Estuary. *Med. Archaeol.,* 38: 19–34.

Godwin, H. (1943). Coastal peat beds of the British Isles and North Sea. *J. Ecol.,* 31: 199–246.

Godwin, H. (1978). *Fenland: its ancient past and uncertain future.* Cambridge: Cambridge Univ. Press.

Godwin, H., Suggate, R. P., and Willis, E. H. (1958). Radiocarbon dating of the eustatic rise in ocean level. *Nature,* 181: 1518–19.

Going, C. (1987). *The mansio and other sites in the south-eastern sector of Caesaromagus: the Roman pottery.* London: CBA Res. Rep., 62.

Going, C. (1996). The Roman countryside, in O. Bedwin (ed.), *The archaeology of Essex. Proc. Writtle Conference.* Chelmsford: Essex County Council, 95–107.

Good, G. L., Jones, R. H., and Ponsford, M. W. (1991). *Waterfront Archaeology* London: CBA Res. Rep., 74.

Goodier, A. (1984). The formation of boundaries in Anglo-Saxon England: a statistical study. *Med. Archaeol.*, 28: 1–21.

Goodsall, R. H. (1965). Oyster fisheries on the North Kent coast. *Archaeologia Cantiana,* 80: 118–51.

Grady, D. M. (1998). Medieval and post-medieval salt extraction in North-east Lincolnshire, in R. H. Bewley (ed.), *Lincolnshire's archaeology from the air.* Lincoln: Occ. Pap. Lincolnshire Hist. & Archaeol., 11.

Gramolt, D. W., 'The coastal marshland of East Essex between the seventeenth and mid-nineteenth centuries'. MA dissertation (London, 1960).

Grant, A. (1988). Animal resources, in G. Astill and A. Grant (eds.), 149–87.

Grant, A. (1989). Animals in Roman Britain, in M. Todd (ed.), *Research in Roman Britain 1960–89.* London: Britannia Monogr., 135–46.

Green, C. [Christopher] (1988). Palaeogeography of marine inlets in the Romney Marsh area, in J. Eddison and C. Green (eds.), 167–74.

Green, C. [Colin] (1992). The Severn fisheries. *Severn Estuary Levels Res. Comm. Ann. Rep. 1992*: 69–73.

Green, R. D. (1968). *Soils of Romney Marsh.* Harpenden: Soil Survey of Great Britain.

Greensmith, J. T. and Tucker, E. V. (1971). Overconsolidation in some fine grained sediments: its nature, genesis, and value in interpreting the history of certain English Quaternary deposits. *Geologie en Mijnbouw,* 50/vi: 743–8.

Greensmith, J. T. and Tucker, E. V. (1973). Holocene transgressions and regressions on the Essex Coast, outer Thames Estuary. *Geologie en Mijnbouw,* 52/iv: 193–202.

Greensmith, J. T. and Tucker, E. V. (1980). Evidence for differential subsidence on the Essex Coast. *Proc. Geol. Ass.,* 91: 169–75.

Gregory, A. (1982). The Romano-British settlement in West Norfolk and on the Norfolk fen-edge, in D. Miles (ed.), 351–76.

Gregson, N. (1985). The multiple estate model: some critical questions. *J. Hist. Geogr.,* 11/4: 39–351.

Greig, J. (1988). Plant resources, in G. Astill and A. Grant (eds.), 108–27.

Grieve, H. (1959). *The Great Tide: the story of the 1953 flood disaster in Essex.* Chelmsford, Essex County Council.

Grieve, H. E. P. (1978). Wennington. *VCH Essex,* 7: 180–90.

Groenman-Van Waateringe, W. (1983). The disastrous effect of the Roman occupation, in R. Brandt and J. Slofstra (ed.), *Roman and native in the Low Countries: spheres of interaction.* Oxford: BAR S.184: 147–57.

Groenman-Van Waateringe, W. (1989). Food for soldiers, food for thought, in J. C. Barrett, A. P. Fitzpatrick and L. Macinnes (eds.), *Barbarians and Romans in North-west Europe.* Oxford: BAR S.471: 96–107.

Groenman-Van Waateringe, W. and Troostheide, C. D. (1987). Palynology of the settlements on the levee: Sites B–F, in R. Brandt *et al.* (eds.), 49–82.

Groot, Th. A. M. de, Westerhoff, W. E., and Bosch, J. H. A. (1996). Sea-level rise during the last 2,000 years as recorded on the Frisian Islands, The Netherlands. *Mededelingen-Rijks Geologische Dienst,* 57: 69–78.

Gross, A. and Butcher, A. (1995). Adaptation and investment in the age of the Great Storms:

agricultural policy on the manors of the principal Lords of Romney Marshes and the marshland fringe *c*.1250-1320, in J. Eddison (ed.), 107–17.

Grozdanova, E. (1995). La production de la roumelie et la vie economique de la ville d'Istanbul aux XVI et XVII siècles, in D. Panzac (ed.) *Histoire economique et sociale de l'Empire ottoman et de la Turquie*. Paris: Peeters, 195–207.

Gurney, D. (1980*a*) Evidence of Bronze Age salt production at Northey, Peterborough. *Northants. Archaeol.*, 15: 1–11.

Gurney, D. (1980*b*). Red hills of the Dengie Peninsula. *Essex Archaeol. & Hist.*, 12: 107–9.

Gurney, D. (1986. *Settlement, religion and industry on the fen-edge*. East Anglian Archaeol., 31.

Gurney, F. G. (1920). Yttingaford and the tenth-century bounds of Chalgrave and Linslade. *Bedfordshire Hist. Rec. Soc.* V, 163–80.

Guthrie, G. L. (1985). Characterising and classifying wetland soils in relation to food production, in D. J. Greenland, G. N. Alcasid, and H. Eswaran (eds.) *Wetland soils: characterization, classification and utilization*. International Rice Res. Institute, 11–20.

Hakbijl, T. (1989). Insect remains from Site Q, an early Iron Age farmstead of the Assendelver Polders Project. *Helinium*, 28/I: 77–102.

Halkon, P. (1989). Iron Age and Romano-British settlement and industry around Holme-on-Spalding Moor, in P. Halkon (ed.) *New light on the Parisi*. Hull: East Riding Archaeol. Soc., 15–22.

Halkon, P. (1990). The archaeology of the Holme-on-Spalding Moor, in S. Ellis and D. R. Crowther (eds.), 147–57.

Hall, A. R. and Kenward, H. K. (1990). *The environmental evidence from the Colonia*. Archaeology of York: the environment, 14/6. York: York Archaeol. Trust/CBA.

Hall, D. (1981). The changing landscape of the Cambridgeshire silt fens. *Landscape Hist.*, 3: 37–49.

Hall, D. (1982). The countryside of the south-east Midlands and Cambridgeshire, in D. Miles (ed.) *The Romano-British countryside*. Oxford: BAR 103/ii: 337–50.

Hall, D. (1987). *The Fenland Project, Number 2: Fenland landscapes and settlement between Peterborough and March*. East Anglian Archaeol., 35.

Hall, D. (1988). The Late Saxon countryside: villages and their fields, in D. Hooke (ed.) *Anglo-Saxon settlements*. Oxford: Blackwell, 99–122.

Hall, D. (1992). *The Fenland Project, Number 6: the South-western Cambridgeshire Fenlands*. East Anglian Archaeol., 56.

Hall, D. (1996). *The Fenland Project, Number 10: the Isle of Ely and Wisbech*. East Anglian Archaeol., 79.

Hall, D. and Coles, J. (1994). *Fenland survey: an essay in landscape and persistence*. London: English Heritage.

Hall, D. and Martin, P. (1979). Brixworth, Northamptonshire—an intensive field survey. *J. Brit. Archaeol. Ass.*, 132: 1–6.

Hallam, H. E. (1954). *The new lands of Elloe: a study of early reclamation in Lincolnshire*. Leicester: Leicester Univ. Dept of English Local Hist. Occ. Pap., 6.

Hallam, H. E. (1960). Salt making in the Lincolnshire Fenland during the Middle Ages. *Lincolnshire Architectural & Archaeol. Soc. Rep. & Pap.*, 8: 85–112.

Hallam, H. E. (1965). *Settlement and society: a study of the early agrarian history of South Lincolnshire*. Cambridge: Cambridge Univ. Press.

Hallam, H. E. (1981). *Rural England 1066–1348*. Glasgow: Fontana.

Hallam, S. (1960). Romano-British salt industry in South Lincolnshire. *Lincs. Architect. Archaeol. Soc. Rep. & Pap.*, 8: 35–75.

Hallam, S. J. (1970). Settlement round The Wash, in C. W. Phillips (ed.), 22–113.

Hallewas, D. P. (1984). The interaction between man and his physical environment in the county of Holland between circa 1000 and 1300 AD: a dynamic relationship. *Geologie en Mijnbouw,* 64: 299–307.

Hallewas, D. P. (1987). The geology in relation to the record of occupation and settlement, in R. W. Brandt *et al.* (eds.), 23–38.

Hamilton-Dyer, S., forthcoming. The animal bones, in S. Rippon, forthcoming *a.*

Harding, A. (1982*a*). *Climatic change in later prehistory.* Edinburgh: Edinburgh Univ. Press.

Harding, A, (1982*b*). Introduction: climatic change and archaeology, in A. Harding (ed.), 1–10.

Harding, N. D. (1930). *Bristol Charters 1155–1373.* Bristol Records Society, I.

Hardman, F. W. and Stebbing, W. P. D. (1940). Stonar and the Wantsum Channel: Part 1— Physiographic. *Archaeologia Cantiana,* 53: 62–80.

Hardman, F. W. and Stebbing, W. P. D. (1941). Stonar and the Wantsum Channel: Part 2— Historical. *Archaeologia Cantiana,* 54: 41–55.

Hare, J. N. (1985). *Battle Abbey. The eastern range and the excavations of 1978–80.* London: HBMC.

Harmer, F. E. (1914). *Select English historical documents of the ninth and tenth centuries.* Cambridge: Cambridge Univ. Press.

Harrison, E. (1949). Report for the year ending 31st Dec. 1948. *Archaeologia Cantiana,* 62: xli–xlvi.

Harrison, J. D., 'The composite manor of Brent: a study of a large wetland-edge estate up to 1350'. Ph.D thesis (Leicester, 1997).

Hart, C. (1957*a*). *The early charters of Essex: the Saxon period.* Leicester: Leicester Dept of English Local Hist. Occ. Pap., 10.

Hart, C. (1957*b*). *The early charters of Essex: the Norman period.* Leicester: Leicester Dept of English Local Hist. Occ. Pap., 11.

Hart, C. R. (1966). *The early charters of Eastern England.* Leicester: Leicester Univ. Press.

Hartley, B. R. (1970). The dating of the Cambridgeshire Car Dyke, in C. W. Phillips (ed.), 126.

Hartley, K. F. and Hartley, B. R. (1970). Pottery in the Romano-British Fenland, in C. W. Phillips (ed.), 165–9.

Harvey, B. (1977). *Westminster Abbey and its estates in the Middle Ages.* Oxford: Clarendon Press.

Harvey, P. D. A. (1989). Initiative and authority in settlement change, in M. Aston *et al.* (eds.), 31–43.

Haselgrove, C. (1987). *Iron Age coinage in South East England: the archaeological context.* Oxford: BAR 174.

Haslett, S. K., Davies, P., Curr, R. H. F. Davies, C. F. C., Kennington, K., King, C. P., and Margetts, A. J. (1998). Evaluating Late Holocene relative sea-level change in the Somerset Levels, Southwest Britain. *Holocene,* 8/ii: 197–207.

Haslett, S. K., Davies, P., and Strawbridge, F. (1997). Reconstructing Holocene sea-level change in the Severn Estuary and Somerset Levels: the foraminifera connection. *Archaeology in the Severn Estuary 1997,* 8: 29–40.

Hasted, E. (1797/1801). *The history and topographical survey of the County of Kent.* Reprinted 1972. Wakefield: E. P. Publishing.

Haverfield, F. J., Taylor, M. V., and Wheeler, R. E. M. (1932). Romano-British remains. *VCH Kent*, 3: 1–176.

Havis, R. (1993). Roman Braintree: excavations 1984–90. *Essex Archaeol. & Hist.*, 24: 22–68.

Hawkins, A. B. (1967). The geology of the Portbury area. *Proc. Bristol. Nat. Soc.*, 31/iv: 421–8.

Hawkins, A. B. (1973). Sea level changes around South West England, in D. J. Blackman (ed.) *Marine archaeology.* Colston Pap., 23: 67–87.

Hayes, P. P. (1988). Roman to Saxon in the south Lincolnshire Fens. *Antiquity*, 62: 321–6.

Hayes, P. P. and Lane, T. W. (1992). *The Fenland Project Number 5: Lincolnshire Survey, the South-west Fens.* East Anglian Archaeol., 55.

Hayes, P. and Lane, T. (1993). Moving boundaries in the Fens of South Lincolnshire, in J. Gardiner (ed.), 58–70.

Healey, R. H. (1975). A medieval salt-making site in Bicker Haven, Lincolnshire, in K. de Brisay and K. Evans (eds.), 36.

Healey, R. H. (1979). Recent Saxon finds from South Lincolnshire. *Lincolnshire Hist. & Archaeol.*,14: 80–1.

Healey, R. H. (1993). Salt making II: Saxon and medieval, in S. Bennett and N. Bennett (eds.), 28–9.

Hearne, C. M., Perkins, D. R. J. and Andrews, P. (1995). The Sandwich Bay Wastewater Treatment Scheme Archaeological Project, 1992–1994. *Archaeologia Cantiana*, 115: 239–354.

Hearne, C. M. and Smith, R. J. C. (1991). A Late Iron Age settlement and black-burnished ware BB1 production site at Wogret, near Wareham, Dorset 1986–7. *Proc. Dorset Nat. Hist. & Archaeol. Soc.*, 113: 53–105.

Heeringen, R. M. Van (1987). The Iron Age in the western Netherlands II: site catalogue and pottery description, Map Sheet 1. *BROB*, 37: 39–122.

Heeringen, R. M. Van (1988). Iron Age occupation of the dunes near Haamstede on the island of Schouwen-Duiveland, Province of Zeeland, The Netherlands. *Helinium*, 28/2: 63–80.

Heeringen, R. M. Van (1989*a*). The Iron Age in the Western Netherlands III: site catalogue and pottery description, Map Sheet 2. *BROB*, 39: 7–68.

Heeringen, R. M. Van (1989*b*). The Iron Age in the Western Netherlands IV: site catalogue and pottery description, Map Sheet 3. *BROB*, 39; 69–156.

Heeringen, R. M. Van (1989*c*). The Iron Age in the Western Netherlands V: synthesis. *BROB*, 39: 157–255.

Heeringen, R. M. Van and Trierum, M. C. Van (1981). The Iron Age in the Western Netherlands I: introduction and method of pottery description. *BROB*, 31: 347–53.

Heidinga, H. A. (1984). Indications of severe drought during the 10th century from an inland dune area in the Central Netherlands. *Geologie en Mijnbouw*, 63: 241–8.

Heidinga, H. A. (1990). From Kootwijk to Rhenen: in search of the elite in the Central Netherlands in the Early Middle Ages, in J. C. Besteman *et al.* (eds.), 9–40.

Heidinga, A. (1997). *Frisia in the first millennium.* Utrecht: Stichting Matrijs.

Heighway, C. (1983). *The East and North Gates of Gloucester and associated sites: excavations.* Bristol: Western Archaeological Trust Excavation Monogr., 4.

Heinrich, D. (1983). Temporal changes in fishing and fish consumption between early medieval Haithabu and its successor Schleswig, in C. Grigson and J. Clutton-Brock (eds.) *Animals and archaeology: 2, shell middens, fishes and birds.* Oxford: BAR S.183: 151–6.

Henderikx, P. A. (1986). The lower delta of the Rhine and the Maas: landscape and habitation from the Roman period to *c*.1000. *BROB*, 36: 445–599.

Herring, P. (1996). Transhumance in medieval Cornwall, in H. Fox (ed.), 35–44.

Hewitt, H. J. (1929). *Medieval Cheshire*. Manchester: Manchester Univ. Press.

Heyworth, A. and Kidson, C. (1982). Sea level changes in South West England and Wales. *Proc. Geol. Ass.*, 93/I: 91–111.

Hill, D. (1981). *An atlas of Anglo-Saxon England*. Oxford: Blackwell.

Hinton, D. (1990). *Archaeology, economy and society: England from the fifth to the fifteenth century*. London: Seaby.

Hinton, P. (1988). *Excavations in Southwark 1973–76, Lambeth 1973–79*. London: Museum of London/London & Middlesex Archaeol. Soc./Surrey Archaeol. Soc.

Hobley, B. and Milne, C. (1981). *Waterfront archaeology in Britain and Northern Europe*. London: CBA Res. Rep., 41.

Hofstede, J. L. A. (1991). Sea level rise in the Inner German Bight (Germany) since AD 600 and its implications upon tidal flats geomorphology, in H. Brückner and U. Radtke (eds.) *Von der Nordsee bis zum Indischen Ozean*. Stuttgart: Franz Steiner Verlag, 11–28.

Hogestijn, J. W. H. (1989). Palaeobotanical analysis of Monnickendam and salination of the Zuiderzee, in H. A. Heidinga and H. H. Van Regteren Altena (eds.), *Medemblik and Monnickendam: aspects of medieval urbanization in northern Holland*. Amsterdam: Cingula, 11: 115–24.

Holden, E. W. (1962*a*). Deserted medieval villages. *Sussex Notes & Queries*, 15/9: 312–5.

Holden, E. W. (1962*b*). Manxey, Pevensey. *Sussex Notes & Queries*, 15/9: 319–20.

Holden, E. W. (1965). Slate roofing in medieval Sussex. *Sussex Archaeol. Coll.*, 103: 67–78.

Hollings, M. (1937). *The Red Book of Worcester I*. Worcestershire Hist. Soc.

Hollings, M. (1950). *The Red Book of Worcester IV*. Worcestershire Hist. Soc.

Hollinrake, C. and Hollinrake, N. (1991). A Late Saxon monastic enclosure ditch and canal, Glastonbury, Somerset. *Antiquity*, 65: 117–8.

Hollinrake, C. and Hollinrake, N. *An archaeological evaluation at the Crooked Chimney, Pawlett* . Unpublished report in Somerset County Council Sites and Monuments Record 10976 (1997).

Holloway, W. (1849). *The history of Romney Marsh*. London: John Russell Smith.

Homan, W. M. (1938). The marshes between Hythe and Pett. *Sussex Archaeol. Coll.*, 79: 197–223.

Homan, W. M. (1949). The founding of New Winchelsea. *Sussex Archaeol. Coll.*, 88; 22–41.

Hook, D. D., McKee, W. H., Smith, H. K., Gregory, J., Burrell, V. G., DeVoe, M. R., Sojka, R. E., Gilbert, S., Banks, R., Stolzy, L. H., Brooks, C., Matthews, T. D., and Shaer, T. H. (1988). *The ecology and management of wetlands*. London: Croom Helm.

Hooke, D. (1981). The Droitwich salt industry, in D. Brown, J. Campbell, and S. C. Hawkes (eds.) *Anglo-Saxon studies in archaeology and history*, 2. Oxford: BAR 92: 123–69.

Hooke, D. (1988). Regional variation in southern and central England in the Anglo-Saxon period and its relationship to land units and settlement, in D. Hooke (ed.), *Anglo-Saxon Settlements*. Oxford: Blackwell, 123–51.

Hooke, D. (1989). Early medieval estate and settlement patterns: the documentary evidence, in M. Aston *et al.* (eds.), 9–30.

Hooke, D. (1994). The administrative and settlement framework of early medieval Wessex, in M. Aston and C. Lewis (eds.), 83–95.

Hooke, D. (1997). Place-names and vegetational history a key to understanding settlement in the Conwy Valley, in N. Edwards (ed.), 79–96.

Horn, D. (1987). Tiddy Mun's Curse and the ecological consequences of land reclamation. *Folklore,* 98.i: 11–15.

Horsey, I. P. and Winder, J. M. (1991). Late Saxon and Conquest-period oyster middens at Poole, Dorset, in G. L. Good *et al.* (eds.), 76–87.

Hoskins, W. G. (1955). *The making of the English landscape.* London: Hodder and Stoughton.

Housley, R. (1988). The environment of Glastonbury Lake Village. *Somerset Levels Pap.,* 14; 63–83.

Howard-Davis, C., Stocks, C., and Innes, J. (1988). *Peat and the past: a survey and assessment of the prehistory of lowland wetlands in North-west England.* London: English Heritage.

Hudson, W. (1892). On a sixteenth century rate book of the corporation of Pevensey. *Sussex Archaeol. Coll.,* 45: 149–79.

Hull, M. R. (1963). Roman gazetteer. *VCH Essex,* 3: 35–204.

Hulme, M. and Barrow, E. (1997). *Climates of the British Isles: present past and future.* London: Routledge.

Hulst, R. S. and Lehmann, L. Th. (1974). The Roman barge of Druten. *BROB,* 24; 7–24.

Hume, I. N. (1954). Romano-British potteries on the Upchurch Marshes. *Archaeologia Cantiana,* 68: 72–90.

Hume, I. N. and Hume, A. (1951). Roman pottery from Upchurch Marshes. *Archaeologia Cantiana,* 64: 168–71.

Hurst, H. R. (1985). *Kingsholm.* Gloucester: Gloucester Archaeol. Rep., 1.

Hurst, H. R. (1986). *Gloucester: the Roman and later defences.* Gloucester: Gloucester Archaeol. Rep., 2.

Hurst, J. D. (1991). Major Saxon discoveries at Droitwich—excavations at the Upwich brine pit. *Current Archaeol.,* 126: 252–5.

Hurst, J. D. (1992). *Savouring the past: the Droitwich salt industry.* Hereford & Worcester County Council.

Hurst, J. D. (1997). *A multi-period salt production site at Droitwich: excavations at Upwich.* London: CBA Res. Rep., 107.

Hurst, J. G. (1976). The pottery, in D. M. Wilson (ed.), 283–392.

Hutchings, R. (1966). Cliffe. *Archaeologia Cantiana,* 81: liv–lv.

Hutchings, R. (1987). Peats and archaeological sites in John's Hope Marshland, Cliffe. *Archaeologia Cantiana,* 104: 374–7.

Hutchings, R. (1988). Some pre-Roman sites at Cliffe. *Archaeologia Cantiana,* 105: 287–90.

Hutchinson, J. N., Poole, C., Lambert, N., and Bromhead, E. N. (1985). Combined archaeological and geotechnical investigations of the Roman Fort at Lympne, Kent. *Britannia,* 16: 209–36.

Insole, P. (1996). An investigation of a medieval and post-medieval field-boundary complex at British Gas Seabank, on the North Avon Levels. *Archaeology in the Severn Estuary,* 7: 95–105.

Isaacson, S. I. (1846). The discovery of roman urns and other ancient remains, at Dymchurch in Romney Marsh. *Archaeologia,* 31: 487–8.

Isserlin, R. M. J. (1995). Roman Coggeshall II; excavations at 'The Lawns', 1989–93. *Essex Archaeol. & Hist.,* 26: 82–104.

Jackson, R. P. J. and Potter, T. W. (1996). *Excavations at Stonea, Cambridgeshire 1980–85.* London: British Museum.

Jansma, M. J. (1981). Diatom analysis from coastal sites in The Netherlands, in D. Brothwell and G. Dimbleby (eds.) *Environmental aspects of coasts and islands.* Oxford; BAR S.94: 145–62.

Jarvis, K. S. (1985*a*). Coastal sites and observations at Hamworthy. *Proc. Dorset Nat. Hist. Archaeol. Soc.,* 107: 159.

Jarvis, K. S. (1985*b*). Boat-house Clump, Upton—A Romano-British saltworking site. *Proc. Dorset Nat. Hist. & Archaeol. Soc.,* 107: 159–62.

Jarvis, K. (1992*a*). *Excavations in Poole 1973–1983.* Dorchester: Dorset Natural Hist. & Archaeol. Soc. Monogr., 14.

Jarvis, K. (1992*b*). An intertidal zone Romano-British site on Brownsea Island. *Proc. Dorset Nat. Hist. & Archaeol. Soc.,* 114: 89–95.

Jefferies, R. S. and Barford, P. M. (1990). Gazetteer 3: pottery from Essex red hills, in A. J. Fawn *et al.* (eds.), 73–8.

Jelgersma, S., de Jong, J., Zagwijn, W. H., and Regteren Altena, J. F. Van (1970). The coastal dunes of western Netherlands; geology, vegetational history and archaeology. *Med. Rijks Geol. Dienst,* New Ser. 21: 93–167.

Jelgersma, S., Oele, E., and Wiggers, A. J. (1979). Depositional history and coastal development in The Netherlands and the adjacent North Sea since the Eemian, in E. Oele *et al.* (eds.), 115–142.

Jenkins, R. C. (1859). *The chartulary of the monastery of Lyminge.* Folkestone: R. Goulden.

Jennings, S., Orford, J. D., Canti, M., Devoy, R. J. N., and Straker, V. (1998). The role of relative sea-level rise and changing sediment supply on Holocene gravel barrier development: the example of Porlock, Somerset, UK. *Holocene,* 8/ii: 165–81.

Jennings, S. and Smyth, C. (1987). Coastal sedimentation in East Sussex during the Holocene. *Progress in Oceanogr.,* 18: 205–41.

Jensen, J., Hofstede, J. L. A., Kunz, H., Ronde, J. de, Heinen, P. F., and Siefert, W. (1993). Long term water level observations and variation, in R. Hillen and H. J. Verhagen (eds.), *Coastlines of the southern North Sea.* Amer. Soc. Engineers, 110–30.

Jerram-Burrows, L. E. (1980). *The history of the Rochford Hundred: smaller islands.* Southend: Rochford Hundred Hist. Soc.

Jessup, R. F. (1942). Notes on a Saxon charter of Higham. *Archaeologia Cantiana.* 55: 12–15.

Jollife, J. E. A. (1933). The origin of the hundred in Kent, in J. G. Edwards, V. H. Galbraith, and E. J. Jacob (eds.) *Historical essays in honour of James Tait.* Manchester.

Jones, A. G. J. (1982). Bulk-sieving and the recovery of fish remains from urban archaeological sites, in A. R. Hall and H. K. Kenward (eds.) *Environmental archaeology in the urban context.* London, CBA Res. Rep., 43: 79–85.

Jones, A. H. M. (1964). *The Later Roman Empire 284–602.* Oxford: Blackwell.

Jones, A. K. G. (1978). A note on the fish bones, in J. Bird (ed.), *Southwark Excavations 1972–74, vol. II.* London: London & Middlesex Archaeol. Soc./Surrey Archaeol. Soc.

Jones, B. and Mattingly, D. (1990). *An atlas of Roman Britain.* Oxford: Blackwell.

Jones, D. M. (1980). *Excavations at Billingsgate Buildings, Lower Thames Street, London, 1974.* London: London & Middlesex Archaeol. Soc.

Jones, G. R. J. (1979). Multiple estates and early settlement, in P. H. Sawyer (ed.) *English medieval settlement.* London: Edward Arnold, 9–34.

Jones, G. R. J. (1985). Multiple estates perceived. *J. Hist. Geogr.,* 11/4: 352–63.

Jones, I. (1953). Roman remains on the Lydd Rype. *Archaeologia Cantiana,* 66: 160–1.

Jones, M. (1981). The development of crop husbandry, in M. Jones and G. Dimbleby (eds.), 95–128.

Jones, M. (1982). Crop production in Roman-Britain, in D. Miles (ed.), 97–108.

Jones, M. (1989). Agriculture in Roman Britain: the dynamics of change, in M. Todd (ed.), 127–34.

Jones, M. and Dimbleby, G. (1981). *The environment of man: Iron Age to the Anglo-Saxon periods.* Oxford: BAR 87.

Jong, J. de (1970/1). Pollen and C14 analysis of Holocene deposits in Zijderveld and environs. *BROB,* 20–21, 75–88.

Keen, L. (1987). Medieval salt working in Poole. *Proc. Dorset Nat. Hist. & Archaeol. Soc.,* 109: 25–8.

Keen, L. (1989). Coastal salt production in Norman England. *Anglo-Norman Studies,* XI: 133–79.

Keil, I. J. E, 'The estates of Glastonbury Abbey in the Later Middle Ages'. Ph.D thesis (Bristol, 1964).

Kelly, D. B. (1968). Snargate. *Archaeologia Cantiana,* 83: 265–6.

Kelly, D. B. (1987). Archaeological notes from Maidstone Museum. *Archaeologia Cantiana,* 104: 33–86.

Kelly, D. B. (1990). Archaeological notes from Maidstone Museum. *Archaeologia Cantiana,* 108: 231–94.

Kelly, D. B. (1991). Archaeological notes from Maidstone Museum. *Archaeologia Cantiana,* 109: 331–52.

Kelly, S. E. (1995). *Charters of St Augustine's Abbey Canterbury, and Minster-in-Thanet.* London: British Academy.

Kelting, E. L. (1967/8). The rivers and sea walls of Somerset. *Proc. Somerset Archeol. & Nat. Hist. Soc.,* 112: 12–20.

Kendrick, J. (1865). Notes on leaden salt pans discovered in August, 1864, at Northwich Cheshire. *Trans. Hist. Soc. Lancs. & Cheshire,* New Ser. VI: 9.

Kenny, E. J. A. (1933). A Roman bridge in the Fens. *Geogr. J.,* 82: 434–41,

Kiden, P. (1995). Holocene relative sea-level change and crustal movement in the southwestern Netherlands. *Marine Geol.,*124: 21–41.

Kidson, C. and Heyworth, A. (1973). The Flandrian sea level rise in the Bristol Channel. *Proc. Ussher Soc.,* 2: 565–84.

King, E. (1973). *Peterborough Abbey 1086–1310: a study in the land market.* Cambridge: Cambridge Univ. Press.

King, H. (1979). Late Pleistocene and Holocene shorelines in western Denmark, in E. Oele *et al.* (eds.), 75–83.

King, H. S. (1962). Sussex, in H. C. Darby and E. M. J. Campbell (eds.), 407–482.

Kingsford, C. L. (1925). *Report on the manuscripts of Lord de l'Isle and Dudley preserved at Penshurst Place, vol. 1.* London: Historic Manuscripts Commission.

Kirk, R. E. G. (1899/1910). *Feet of Fines for Essex: volume I* AD *1182–1272.* Colchester: Essex Archaeol. Soc.

Kirk, R. E. G. (1913/28). *Feet of Fines for Essex: volume II* AD *1272–1326.* Colchester: Essex Archaeol. Soc.

Kirk, R. E. G. (1929/49). *Feet of Fines for Essex: volume III* AD *1372–1422.* Colchester: Essex Archaeol. Soc.

Kirkham, B. (1975). Salt making sites found in North East Lincolnshire since 1960, in K. W. de Brisay and K. A. Evans (eds.), 41–2.

Kissock, J. (1996). The historic settlements of South Pembrokeshire, in J. Fridrich *et al.* (eds.), 15–18.

Kissock, J. (1997). God Made nature and Men Made Towns: post-Conquest and pre-Conquest villages in Pembrokeshire, in N. Edwards (ed.), *Landscape and settlement in medieval Wales.* Oxford: Oxbow Monogr., 81: 123–37.

Knol, E. (1983). Farming on the banks of the river Aa. The faunal remains and bone objects of Paddepoel 200 BC–250 AD. *Palaeohistoria,* 25: 145–82.

Knol, E. (1993). *De Noordnederlandse kustlanden in de Vroege Middeleeuwen.* Amsterdam: Academisch Proefschrift, Vrije Universiteit te Amsterdam.

Knol, E., Prummel, W., Hytterschaut, H. T., Hoogland, M. L. P., Casparie, W. A., de Langen, G. J., Kramer, E., and Scheluis, J. (1995/96). The early medieval cemetery of Oosterbeintum Friesland. *Palaeohistoria,* 37/38: 245–416.

Kooistra, L. (1996). *Borderland farming: possibilities and limitations of farming in the Roman period and Early Middle Ages between the Rhine and Meuse.* Assen: Van Gorcum.

Körber-Grohne, U. (1981). Crop husbandry and environmental change in the Feddersen Wierde, near Bremerhaven, North Germany, in M. Jones and G. Dimbleby (eds.), 287–307.

Kowaleski, M. (1995). *Local markets and regional trade in medieval Exeter.* Cambridge: Cambridge Univ. Press.

Kramer, E. (1984). Finds from the pre-Roman Iron Age near Kimswerd municipality Wonseradeel. *Helinium,* 24: 221–39.

Krog, H. (1979). Late Pleistocene and Holocene shorelines in Western Denmark, in Oele, E. *et al.* (eds.), 75–83.

Lamb, H. H. (1995). *Climate, history and the modern world* (2nd edn). London: Routledge.

Lambert, A. M. (1971). *The making of the Dutch landscape.* London: Seminar Press.

Lambert, J. M. and Jennings, J. N. (1960). Stratigraphic and associated evidence, in J. M. Lambert, J. N. Jennings, C. T. Smith, C. Green and J. N. Hutchison (eds.), *The making of the Broads.* London: Royal Geogr. Soc. Res. Ser., 5: 1–61.

Lane, T. (1992). Excavation and evaluation of an Iron Age and Romano-British waterlogged site at Market Deeping, Lincolnshire. *Fenland Res.,* 7: 43–7.

Lane, T. W. (1993*a*). *The Fenland Project 8: Lincolnshire Survey, the northern fen-edge* East Anglian Archaeol., 66.

Lane, T. W. (1993*b*). The Fenland Project in Lincolnshire: recent evaluations. *Fenland Res.,* 8: 40–2.

Lane, T. W. (1993*c*). Salt making. Iron Age and Roman, in S. Bennett and N. Bennett (eds.), 26–7.

Lane, T. (1994). Leaves Lake Drove, Pinchbeck. *Fenland Res.,* 9: 15.

Langdon, J. (1993). Inland water transport in medieval England. *J. Hist. Geogr.,* 19: 1–11.

Larking, L. B. (1851). The Custumal of Pevensey. *Sussex Archaeol. Coll.,* 4; 205–18.

Larsen, C. U. (1997). Opening speech: aims and perspectives of the workshop, in C. U. Larsen (ed.), *Workshop on the cultural heritage in the Waffen Sea region.* Copenhagen: National Forest and Nature Agency, 1–4 .

Lavender, N. J. (1993). The 'principia' at Boreham: excavations 1990. *Essex Archaeol. & Hist.,* 24: 1–21.

Leah, M. (1992). The Fenland Management Project, Norfolk. *Fenland Res.* 7: 49–59.

Leah, M. and Crowson, A. (1993). Norfolk Archaeological Unit, The Fenland Management Project. *Fenland Res.,* 8; 43–50.

Leah, M., Wells, C. E., Appleby, C., and Huckerby, E. (1997). *North West Wetlands Survey 4: the wetlands of Cheshire.* Lancaster; Lancaster Univ. Archaeol. Unit, Imprint 5.

Leech, R. H. (1977*a*). 'Romano-British rural settlement in South Somerset and North Dorset'. Ph.D thesis (Bristol).

Leech, R. H. (1977*b*). Late Iron Age and Romano-British briquetage sites at Quarryland Lane, Badgworth. *Somerset Archaeol. & Nat. Hist.*, 121: 89–96.

Leech, R. H. (1981). The Somerset Levels in the Romano-British Period, in T. Rowley (ed.), *The evolution of marshland landscapes*. Oxford: Oxford Univ. Comm. for Archaeol., 20–43.

Leech, R. H. (1982). The Roman interlude in the South West; the dynamics of economic and social change in Romano-British South Somerset and North Dorset, in D. Miles (ed.), 209–267.

Leech, R. H., Bell, M. and Evans, J. (1983). The sectioning of a Romano-British saltmaking mound at East Huntspill. *Somerset Levels Pap.*, 9: 74–8.

Levitan, B. (1984). The vertebrate remains, in S. Rahtz and T. Rowley (ed.) *Middleton Stoney*. Oxford.

Lewin, G. (1993). Animal bones. *Trans. Rochford Hundred Field Archaeol. Group*, 1: 44–6.

Lewin, T. (1862). *The invasion of Britain by Julius Caesar with replies to the Astronomer-Royal and of the late Camden Professor of Ancient History at Oxford* (2nd edn). London; Longman, Green, & Roberts.

Lewis, C. (1996). Medieval rural settlement in the East Midlands, in J. Fridrich *et al.* (eds.), 90–101.

Lewis, C., Mitchell-Fox, P., and Dyer, C. (1997). *Village, hamlet and field: changing medieval settlements in central England*. Manchester: Manchester Univ. Press.

Lewis, W. V. (1932). The formation of the Dungeness Foreland. *Geogr. J.*, 80: 309–24.

Lilly, D. (1966). A Romano-British pottery kiln site at Venus Street, Congresbury. *Somerset Archaeol. & Nat. Hist.*, 108: 172–4.

Lilly, D. and Usher, G. (1972). Romano-British sites on the North Somerset Levels. *Proc. Univ. of Bristol Speleol. Soc.*, 13/1: 37–40.

Linder, E. (1939). The 'Red Hills' of Canvey Island. *Essex Naturalist*, 26/3: 136–60.

Linder, E. (1941). The 'Red Hills' of Canvey Island. *Essex Naturalist*, 27/2; 48–63.

Linden, H. Van der (1982). History of the reclamation of the western fenlands and of the organisation of keeping them drained, in H. de Bakker and M. W. Van den Berg (eds.), 42–73.

Locker, A. (1992). Fish bones, in P. Crummy (ed.), *Excavations at Culver Street, the Gilbert School, and other sites in Colchester 1971–85*. Colchester: Colchester Archaeol Rep., 6: 37–50.

Locker, A. (1997). *The Saxon, medieval and post-medieval fish bones from excavations at Castle Mall, Norwich, Norfolk*. Ancient Monuments Lab. Rep., 85/97. London: English Heritage.

Locock, M. (1996). Hill Farm, Goldcliff. A field evaluation on the proposed Gwent Levels Nature Reserve. *Archaeology in the Severn Estuary*, 7: 59–66.

Locock, M. (1997*a*). Gwent Levels Nature Reserve, Hill Farm, Goldcliff: excavations 1997. *Archaeology in the Severn Estuary*, 8: 55–65.

Locock, M. (1997*b*). Rockingham Farm, Avonmouth, 1993–1997: moated enclosures on the North Avon Levels. *Archaeology in the Severn Estuary*, 8: 83–8.

Locock, M., Robinson, S., and Yates, A. (1998). Late Romano-British Sites at Cabot Park, Avonmouth. *Archaeology in the Severn Estuary*, 9: 31–6.

Locock, M. and Walker, M. (1998). Hill Farm, Goldcliff: Middle Iron Age drainage on the Caldicot Level. *Archaeology in the Severn Estuary*, 9; 37–44.

Londen, H. Van (1997). A small Roman terp at Schipluiden, in L. P. Louwe Kooijmans (ed.), *Prehistoric Society overseas study tour to The Netherlands: excursion guide.* Leiden: 18–19.

Londen, H. Van, and Rijn, P. Van (1999). The Midden-Delfland Project: an example of co-operation between planners and archaeologists in The Netherlands, in B. Coles *et al.* (eds.), 133–8.

Long, A. J. (1993). Coastal responses to changes in sea-level in the East Kent Fens and South East England, UK over the last 7500 years. *Proc. Geol. Ass.,* 103: 187–99.

Long, A. and Hughes, P. D. M. (1995). Mid- and Late Holocene evolution of the Dungeness Foreland, UK. *Marine Geol.,* 124: 253–71.

Long, A. J. and Innes, J. B. (1993). Holocene sea-level changes and coastal sedimentation in Romney Marsh, Southeast England, UK. *Proc. Geol. Ass.,* 104: 223–37.

Long, A. and Innes, J. (1995). A palaeoenvironmental investigation of the 'Midley Sand' and associated deposits at the Midley Church Bank, Romney Marsh, in J. Eddison (ed.), 37–50.

Long, A. J., Innes, J. B., Kirby, J. R., Lloyd, J. M., Rutherford, M. M., Shennan, I., and Tooley, M. J. (1998). Holocene sea-level change and coastal evolution in the Humber Estuary, eastern England; as assessment of rapid coastal change. *Holocene,* 8.2: 229–47.

Long, A. and Roberts, D. H. (1997). Sea-level change, in M. G. Fulford *et al.* (eds.), 25–49.

Long, A., Waller, M., Hughes, P., and Spencer, C. (1998). The Holocene depositional history of Romney Marsh proper, in J. Eddison *et al.* (eds.), 45–63.

Long, A., Scaife, R., and Edwards, R., forthcoming. Stratigraphic architecture, relative sea level, and models of estuary development in southern England: new data from Southampton Water, in K. Pye and J. R. L. Allen (eds.), *Coastal and estuarine environments. sedimentology, geomorphology and geoarchaeology.* London: Geol. Soc.

Louwe Kooijmans, L. P. (1974). *The Rhine/Meuse Delta, four studies on its prehistoric occupation and Holocene geology.* Leiden: Analecta Praehistorica Leidensia, 7.

Louwe Kooijmans, L. P. (1993). Wetland exploitation and upland relations of prehistoric communities in The Netherlands, in J. Gardiner (ed.), 71–115.

Lovegrove, H. (1994). *The official guide to the ancient town of Winchelsea.* Winchelsea Corporation.

Loveluck, C. (1997). Uncovering an Anglo-Saxon 'royal' manor. *Brit. Archaeol.,* 28: 8–9.

Luff, R. (1993). *Animal bones from excavations in Colchester, 1971–85.* Colchester Archaeol. Rep., 12.

Lythe, S. G. E. (1938). The Court of Sewers for the east parts of East Riding. *Yorks. Archaeol. J.,* 33: 11–24.

Lythe, S. G. E. (1939). The organisation of drainage and embankment in medieval Holderness. *Yorks. Archaeol. J.,* 34; 282–95.

Macaulay, S. and Reynolds, T. (1993). Excavations and site management at Cambridgeshire Car Dyke, Waterbeach. *Fenland Res.,* 8: 63–9.

McAvoy, F. (1983/4). The marine salt extraction industry in the late medieval period at Wainfleet, Lincolnshire. *Fenland Res.,* 1: 32–9.

McAvoy, F. (1994). Marine salt extraction: the excavation of salterns at Wainfleet St Mary, Lincolnshire. *Medieval Archaeol.,* 38: 19–54.

McAvoy, M., Morris, E. and Smith, G. H. (1980). The excavation of a multi-period site at Carngoon Bank, Lizard, Cornwall, 1979. *Cornish Archaeol.,* 19: 31–62.

McDonnell, R. (1980). Tidal fish weirs, West Somerset. *Proc. Somerset Archaeol. & Nat. Hist. Soc.,* 123: 75–82.

McGrail, S. (1981). *The Brigg 'raft' and her prehistoric environment*. Oxford: BAR 89.

McIntosh, M. K. (1986). *Autonomy and community: the Royal Manor of Havering, 1200–1500*. Cambridge: Cambridge Univ. Press.

McIntosh, M. K. (1991). *A community transformed: the Manor and Liberty of Havering, 1500–1620*. Cambridge: Cambridge Univ. Press.

Mackreath, D. F. (1996). *Orton Hall Farm: a Roman and Early Anglo-Saxon farmstead*. East Anglian Archaeol., 76.

Macpherson-Grant, N., and Gardiner, M. (1998). Pottery from Sandtun, West Hythe, Kent. *Medieval Archaeol. Newsl.*, 18: 7.

Malim, T. (1992). Excavation and site management at Stonea Camp. *Fenland Res.*, 7: 27–34.

Maltby, M. (1979). *The animal bones from Exeter 1971–1975*. Sheffield: Dept of Prehistory & Archaeol., Univ. of Sheffield.

Manning, W. H. (1979). The native and Roman contribution to the development of metal industries in Britain, in *Invasion and Response: the case of Roman Britain*. Oxford: BAR 73: 111–21.

Markham, G. (1636). *The enrichment of the Weald of Kent*.

Marschalleck, K.H. (1973). Die Salzgewinnung and der friesischen Nordseeküste. *Probleme der Kustenforschung Im Sudlichen Nordseegebiet*, 127–44.

Martin, J. J. (1975). Collected notes on the salt industry of the Cumbrian Solway coast, in K. de Brisay and K. Evans (eds.), 71–6.

Mason, C. (1994). Archaeological notes from Maidstone Museum. *Archaeologia Cantiana*, 114: 439–54.

Mason, D. P. J. (1988). *Prata Legionis* in Britain. *Britannia*, 19: 163–90.

Mawer, A. and Stenton, F. M. (1927). *The place-names of Worcestershire*. English Place-names Soc., IV.

Mawer, A. and Stenton, F. (1930). *The place-names of Sussex*. English Place-names Soc., VII.

Mawer, A. and Stenton, F. (1969). *The place-names of Sussex*. English Place-names Soc., VII.

May, J. (1976). *Prehistoric Lincolnshire*. Lincoln: History of Lincolnshire Committee.

May, J. (1984). Major settlements of the later Iron Age in Lincolnshire, in N. Field and A. White (eds.), 18–22.

May, J. (1996). *Dragonby: report on excavations at an Iron Age and Romano-British settlement in North Lincolnshire*. Oxford: Oxbow Monogr., 61.

May, V. J. (1969). Reclamation and shoreline change in Poole Harbour, Dorset. *Proc. Dorset Nat. Hist. and Archaeol. Soc.*, 90: 141–54.

Mayhew, A. (1973). *Rural settlement and farming in Germany*. London; Batsford.

Meddens, F. (1996). Sites from the Thames Estuary wetlands, England, and their Bronze Age use. *Antiquity*, 70: 325–34.

Meddens, F. and Beasley, M. (1990). Wetland use in Rainham, Essex. *London Archaeol.*, 6/9: 244–6.

Medlycott, M. (1994). The othona community site, Bradwell-on-Sea, Essex: the extra mural settlement. *Essex Archaeol. & Hist.*, 25: 60–71.

Medlycott, M. (1996). A medieval farm and its landscape; excavations at Stebbingford, Felsted 1993. *Essex Archaeol. & Hist.*, 27:102–81.

Meiggs, R. (1973). *Roman Ostia*. Oxford: Clarendon Press.

Mellor, J. E. and Pearce, T. (1981). *The Austin Friars, Leicester*. London: CBA Res. Rep., 35.

Miedema, M. (1983). *Vijfentwintig eeuwen bewoning in het terpenland ten Noordwesten van Groningen*. Amsterdam: Academisch Proefschrift, Vrije Universiteit te Amsterdam.

Miles, A. (1965). Funton Marsh, Romano-British salt panning site. *Archaeologia Cantiana*, 80: 260–5.

Miles, A. (1975). Salt panning in Romano-British Kent, in K. W. de Brisay and K. A. Evans (eds.), 26–31.

Miles, D. (1982). *The Romano-British countryside*. Oxford: BAR 103.

Miller, E. (1951). *The Abbey and Bishopric of Ely*. Cambridge: Cambridge Univ. Press.

Millett, M. (1990). *The Romanization of Britain*. Cambridge: Cambridge Univ. Press.

Millett, M. and Halkon, P. (1988). Landscape and economy: recent fieldwork and excavation around Holme-on-Spalding Moor, in J. Price and P. R. Wilson (eds.), 37–47.

Mills, A. D. (1991). *A dictionary of English place names*. Oxford: Oxford Univ. Press.

Milne, G. (1981). Medieval waterfront reclamation in London, in G. Milne and B. Hobley (eds.) 1981: 32–6.

Milne, G. (1985). *The port of Roman London*. London: Batsford.

Milne, G. (1987). Waterfront archaeology in British towns, in J. Schofield and R. Leech (ed.), *Urban Archaeology in Britain*. London: CBA Res. Rep., 61: 192–200.

Milne, G. and Hobley, B. (1981). *Waterfront archaeology in Britain and Northern Europe*. London: CBA Res. Rep. 41.

Milojkovic, J. and Brinkhuizen, D. C. (1984). Bones from a terp remnant near Kimswerd. *Helinium*, 24: 221–39.

Modderman, P. J. R. (1973). A native farmstead from the Roman period near Kethel, Municipality of Schiedam, Province of South Holland. *BROB*, 23: 149–58.

Moffat, B. (1986). The environment of Battle Abbey estates East Sussex in medieval times; a re-evaluation using analysis of pollen and sediments. *Landscape Hist.*, 8: 77–93.

Molen, W. H. Van der (1982). Water management in the western Netherlands, in H. de Bakker and M. W. Van den Berg (eds.), 106–21.

Monaghan, J. (1982). An investigation of the Romano-British pottery industry on the Upchurch Marshes. *Archaeologia Cantiana*, 98: 27–50.

Monaghan, J. (1987). *Upchurch and Thameside Roman pottery*. Oxford: BAR 173.

Moore, J. S. (1982). *Domesday Book: Gloucestershire*. Chichester: Phillimore.

Moore, N. (1918). *The history of St. Bartholomew's Hospital*. London: C. Arthur Pearson.

Moorhouse, S. (1988). Medieval fishponds; some thoughts, in M. Aston (ed.), 475–84.

Morant, P. (1763/8). *The history and antiquities of the County of Essex*. Reprinted 1978. Chelmsford: Essex County Libraries.

Morgan, P. (1983). *Domesday Book: Kent*. Chichester: Phillimore.

Morris, E. (1985). Prehistoric salt distribution: two case studies from western Britain. *Bull. Board Celtic Stud.*, 32: 336–79.

Morris, E. (1994). The organisation of salt production and distribution in Iron Age Wessex, in A. P. Fitzpatrick and E. L. Morris (eds.) *The Iron Age in Wessex: recent work*. Salisbury: Trust for Wessex Archaeol., 14–16.

Morris, E., forthcoming. The briquetage; a comparative summary and discussion, in T. Lane (ed.), *A millennium of saltmaking: prehistoric and Romano-British salt production in the Fenland*. Lincoln: Lincolnshire Archaeol. & Heritage Rep.

Morris, J. (1976). *Domesday Book: Sussex*. Chichester: Phillimore.

Morris, P. (1979). *Agricultural buildings in Roman Britain*. Oxford: BAR 70.

Morzadec-Kerfourn, M.T. (1974). Variations de la ligne de rivage Armoricaine au Quaternaire. *Mém. Soc. géol. mineral. Bretagne*, 17: 1–208.

Motterhead, J. (1986). *Suetonius Claudius*. Bristol: Bristol Classical Press.

Muhlfeld, H. E. (1933). *A survey of the Manor of Wye*. New York: Columbia Univ. Press.

Multhauf, R. P. (1978). *Neptune's Gift: a history of common salt*. Baltimore: Johns Hopkins Univ. Press.

Murphy, K. (1997). Small boroughs in South-west Wales; their planning, early development and defences, in N. Edwards (ed.), *Landscape and settlement in medieval Wales*. Oxford: Oxbow Monogr., 81: 139–56.

Murphy, P. (1992). Environmental archaeology: a review of progress. *Fenland Res.*, 7: 35–9.

Murphy, P. (1993*a*). Environmental archaeology: second progress report. *Fenland Res.*, 8: 35–9.

Murphy, P. (1993*b*). Anglo-Saxon arable farming on the silt fens—preliminary results. *Fenland Res.*, 8: 75–9.

Murphy, P. (1994). Environmental archaeology: third progress report. *Fenland Res.*, 9: 26–9.

Musgrove, D. (1997). The medieval exploitation and reclamation of the inland peat moors in the Somerset Levels. *Archaeology in the Severn Estuary*, 8: 89–97.

Musgrove, D., forthcoming. Modelling landscape development in a wetland environment: the medieval peat moors of the Somerset Levels, in B. Raftery (ed.), *Recent developments in wetland research*. Dublin: Univ. College Dublin.

Nash, S. (1972/3). A deep water inlet at Highbridge: a précis of a paper. *Proc. Somerset Archaeol. & Nat. Hist. Soc.*, 117: 97–101.

Nayling, N. (1996). Further fieldwork and post-excavation: Magor Pill, Gwent Levels intertidal zone. *Archaeology in the Severn Estuary*, 7: 85–93.

Nayling, N. (1998). *The Magor Pill medieval wreck*. York: CBA Res. Rep., 108

Nayling, N., Maynard, D., and McGrail, S. (1994). Barland's Farm, Magor Gwent: a Romano-Celtic boat. *Antiquity*, 68: 596–603.

Neal, D. S., Wardle, A., and Hunn, J. (1990). *Excavation of the Iron Age, Roman and medieval settlement at Gorhambury, St Albans*. London: English Heritage.

Neilson, N. (1928). *The Cartulary and Terrier of the Priory of Bilsington, Kent*. London: British Academy.

Neilson, N. (1932). The Domesday Monachorum. *VCH Kent*, 3: 253–69.

Nenquin, J. (1961). *Salt: a study in economic prehistory*. Brugge: Dissertationes Archaeologicae Gandenses, IV.

Neumann, H. and Bell, M. (1996). Intertidal peat survey in the Welsh Severn Estuary. *Archaeology in the Severn Estuary*, 7: 3–20.

Nicholas, D. (1992). *Medieval Flanders*. London: Longman.

Nichols, J. F. (1925). New light on the history of Milton hamlet. *Trans. Southend-on-Sea Antiq. & Hist. Soc.*, 1: 172–81.

Nichols, J. F. (1926/8). Milton Hall: the extent of 1309 and an inventory of 1278. *Trans. Southend-on-Sea Antiq. & Hist. Soc.*, 2: 7–33, 39–40.

Nichols, J. F. (1930). Milton Hall: farming operations in the fourteenth century. *Trans. Southend-on-Sea Antiq. & Hist. Soc.*, 2: 25–8.

Nichols, J. F. (1932). Milton Hall: the compotus of 1299. *Trans. Southend-on-Sea Antiq. & Hist. Soc.*, 2: 113–67.

Nio, S.-D., Shuttenhelm, R. T. E., and Van Weering, Tj. C. E. (1981). *Holocene marine sedimentation in the North Sea basin*. Oxford: Blackwell.

Nitz, H-J (1983). Feudal woodland colonisation as a strategy of the Carolingian empire in the conquest of Saxony: reconstruction of the spatial patterns of expansion and colonist settlement morphology in the Leine-Weser region, in B. K. Roberts and R. E. Glasscock (eds.), *Villages, fields and frontiers*. Oxford: BAR S.185: 171–84.

Noort, R. Van de and Davies, P. (1993). *Wetland heritage: an archaeological assessment of the Humber wetlands*. Hull: Humber Wetlands Project.

Noort, R. Van de and Ellis, S. 1995. *Wetland heritage of Holderness: an archaeological survey*. Hull: Humber Wetlands Project.

Noort, R. Van de and Ellis, S. (1997). *Wetland heritage of the Humberhead Levels: an archaeological survey*. Hull: Humber Wetlands Project.

Noort, R. Van de and Ellis, S. (1998). *Wetland heritage of the Ancholme and lower Trent Valleys: an archaeological survey*. Hull: Humber Wetlands Project.

Noort, R. Van de and Ellis, S. (1999). *Wetland heritage of the Vale of York: an archaeological survey*. Hull: Humber Wetlands Project.

Norden, J. (1594). *Speculi britanniae pars: an historical and chorographical description of the County of Essex*. Reprinted 1840. London: Camden Soc.

Ocock, M. A. (1969). A Romano-British site near Decoy Farm, High Halstow. *Archaeologia Cantiana*, 84: 255–7.

O'Connell, M. (1990). Spolsener Moor, Friesland: vegetation and land-use history from mid-Holocene to recent time, in K.-E. Behre (ed.), 75–8.

O'Connor, T. (1982). *Animal bones from Flaxengate, Lincoln c.870–1500*. Lincoln: Archaeology in Lincoln, 18/1.

O'Connor, T. (1994). 8th–11th century economy and environment in York, in J. Rackham (ed.), *Environment and economy in Anglo-Saxon England*. York: CBA Res. Rep., 89: 136–47.

Oele, E., Schuttenham, R. T. E., and Wiggers, A. J. (1979). *The Quaternary history of the North Sea*. Uppsala: Acta Universitatis Upsaliensis Annum Quingentesimum Celebrantis, 2.

Ogilvie, A. and Farmer, G. (1997). Documenting the medieval climate, in M. Hume and E. Barrow (eds.), 112–33.

O'Leary, J. G. (1966). Dagenham. *VCH Essex*, 5: 267–302.

Oppenheim, M. (1907). Maritime history. *VCH Essex*, 2; 259–312.

Ordnance Survey (1978). *The Ordnance Survey map of Roman Britain* (4th edn). Southampton.

Oschinsky, D. (1971). *Walter of Henley and other treatise on estate management and accounting*. Oxford: Clarendon Press.

O'Sullivan, A., McErlean, T., McConkey, R., and McCooet, P. (1997). Medieval fishtraps in Strangford Lough, Co. Down. *Archaeology Ireland*, 11/I: 36–8.

O'Sullivan, A. and Daly, A. (1999). Prehistoric and medieval coastal settlement and wetland exploitation in the Shannon Estuary, Ireland, in B. Coles *et al* (eds.), 177–84.

Owen, A. E. B. (1952). Coastal erosion in East Lincolnshire. *Lincolnshire Historian*, 9: 330–41.

Owen, A. E. B. (1975). Medieval salting and the coastline in Cambridgeshire and North-west Norfolk, in K. de Brisay and K. Evans (eds.), 42–4.

Owen, A. E. B. (1981). *The Records of a Commission of Sewers for Wiggenhall 1319–1324*. Norwich: Norfolk Rec. Soc., 48.

Owen, A. E. B. (1984). Salt, sea banks and medieval settlement on the Lindsey coast, in N. Field and A. White (eds.), 1984: 46–49.

Owen, A. E. B. (1986). Mablethorpe St Peter's and the Sea. *Lincolnshire Hist. & Archaeol.*, 21: 61–2.

Owen, A. E. B. (1993). Beyond the sea bank: sheep on the Huttoft Outmarsh in the early thirteenth century. *Lincolnshire Hist. & Archaeol.*, 28: 39–41.

Owen, A. E. B. (1996). *The medieval Lindsey Marsh: selected documents.* Lincoln: Lincoln Rec. Soc., 85.

Oxley, J. E. (1966). Barking and Ilford. *VCH Essex,* 5: 184–266.

Paepe, R. and Baetman, C. (1979). The Belgian coastal plain during the Quaternary, in E. Oele *et al.* (eds.), 143–6.

Page, W. (1906). *The Victoria County History of the County of Lincoln, vol. 2.* London: Inst. of Hist. Res.

Page, W. (1937*a*). The Borough of Rye. *VCH Kent,* 9: 39–62.

Page, W. (1937*b*). Winchelsea. *VCH Kent,* 9: 62–75.

Palmer, R. (1994). Air photo interpretation over the Lincolnshire Fenlands: a second interim note. *Fenland Res.,* 9: 30–6.

Palmer, R. (1996*a*). Appendix 1. The aerial evidence, in D. Hall, *The Fenland Project, Number 10. Cambridgeshire Survey, Isle of Ely and Wisbech.* East Anglian Archaeol., 79: 192–8.

Palmer, R. (1996*b*). Air photo interpretation and the Lincolnshire Fenland. *Landscape Hist.,* 18: 5–16.

Pals, J. P. (1987). Environment and economy as revealed by macroscopic plant remains, in R. W. Brandt *et al.* (eds.), 83–90.

Pals, J. P. and Van Dierendonck, M. C. (1988). Between flax and fabric: cultivation and processing of flax in a medieval peat reclamation settlement near Midwoud Prov. Noord Holland. *J. Archaeol. Sci.,* 15: 237–51.

Parkinson, M. (1980). Salt marshes of the Exe Estuary. *Rep. & Trans. Devonshire Ass.,* 112: 17–42.

Parkinson, M. (1985). The Axe Estuary and its marshes. *Rep. & Trans. Devonshire Ass.,* 117: 19–62.

Parry, M. L. (1975). Secular climatic change and marginal agriculture. *Trans. Inst. Brit. Geogr.,* 64: 1–14.

Parry, M. L. (1981). Evaluating the impact of climate change, in C. Smith and M. Parry (eds.), 3–16.

Payne, G. (1895). Researches and discoveries in Kent. *Archaeologia Cantiana,* 21: xlvii–lvi.

Payne, G. (1897). Researches and discoveries in Kent. *Archaeologia Cantiana,* 22: xlix–lxii.

Payne, G. (1900). Researches and discoveries in Kent. *Archaeologia Cantiana,* 24: li–lx.

Payne, G. (1902). Researches and discoveries in Kent, 1900–1901. *Archaeologia Cantiana,* 25: lix–lxxii.

Payne, G. (1905). Researches and discoveries in Kent, 1902–1904, *Archaeologia Cantiana,* 27: lxv–lxxx.

Payne, G. (1909). Researches and discoveries in Kent, 1905–1907. *Archaeologia Cantiana,* 28: lxxxviii–xcvii.

Payne, G. (1915). Researches and discoveries in Kent, 1912–15. *Archaeologia Cantiana,* 31: 275–86.

Peacock, D. P. S. (1969). A Romano-British salt-working site at Trebarveth, St. Keverne. *Cornish Archaeol.,* 8: 47–65.

Peacock, D. P. S. (1973). The black-burnished pottery industry in Dorset, in A. Detsicas (ed.), *Current research in Romano-British coarse pottery.* London: CBA Res. Rep., 10: 63–5.

Pearson, T. (1996). Tollesbury, Tollesbury Wick Marsh, in A. Bennett and P. J. Gilman (eds.) Archaeology in Essex 1995. *Essex Archaeol. & Hist.,* 27; 261–76.

Pelham, R. A. (1930). Some further aspects of Sussex trade during the fourteenth century. *Sussex Archaeol. Coll.*, 71: 171–204.

Penney, S. and Shotter, D. C. A. (1996). An inscribed Roman salt-pan from Shavington, Cheshire. *Britannia*, 27: 360–5.

Percival, J. (1902). *Agricultural botany* (2nd edn). London.

Petch, D. F. (1987). The Roman period. *VCH Cheshire*, 1: 115–236.

Petchey, W. J. (1991). *A prospect of Maldon 1500–1689*. Chelmsford: Essex Records Office.

Pethick, J. (1984). *An introduction to coastal geomorphology*. London: Edward Arnold.

Pethick, J. S. (1990). The Humber Estuary, in S. Ellis and D. R. Crowther (eds.), 54–67.

Petrie, W. M. F. (1880). Notes on Kentish earthworks. *Archaeologia Cantiana*, 64: 8–17.

Philp, B. J. (1963). Romano-British West Kent AD 43–100. *Archaeologia Cantiana*, 78: 74–82.

Philp, B. J. and Willson, J. (1984). Roman site at Scotney Court, Lydd. *Kent Archaeol. Rev.*, 68: 156–61.

Phillips, C. W. (1970). *The Fenland in Roman Times*. London: Royal Geogr. Soc. Res. Ser., 5.

Plassche, O. Van de (1982). Sea-level change and water-level movements in The Netherlands during the Holocene. *Mededelingen rijks geologische dienst*, 36/1: 1–93.

Plater, A. J. (1992). The Late Holocene evolution of Denge Marsh, Southeast England: a stratigraphic, sedimentological and micropalaeontological approach. *Holocene*, 2/1: 63–70.

Plater, A. and Long, A. (1995). The morphology and evolution of Denge Beach and Denge Marsh, in J. Eddison (ed.), 8–36.

Platts, G. (1985). *Land and people in medieval Lincolnshire*. Lincoln: History of Lincolnshire Committee.

Pollard, R. J. (1982). Roman pottery in Kent: a summary of production and marketing trends, in P. E. Leach (ed.), *Archaeology in Kent to AD 1500*. London: CBA Res. Rep., 48: 61–63.

Pollard, R. J. (1988). *The Roman pottery of Kent*. Canterbury: Kent Archaeol. Soc. Monogr., V.

Pollitt, W. (1953). *Southend before the Norman Conquest*. Southend Museum Handbook, 7.

Pons, L. J. and Zonneveld, I. S. (1965). *Soil ripening and soil classification: initial soil formation of alluvial deposits with a classification of the resulting soils*. Int. Inst. Land Reclamation and Improvement, 13.

Poole, C. (1987). Saltworking, in B. Cunliffe (ed.), 178–80.

Poole, C. (1991). Briquetage, in N. Sharples (ed.), *Maiden Castle: excavations and field survey 1985–6*. London: English Heritage.

Postan, M. M. (1972). *The medieval economy and society*. London: Penguin.

Potter, T. W. J. (1976). Excavations at Stonea, Cambs.: sites of the Neolithic, Bronze Age and Roman periods. *Proc. Cambridge Antiq. Soc.*, 66: 23–54.

Potter, T. W. (1981). The Roman occupation of the central Fenland. *Britannia*, XII: 79–133.

Potter, T. W. (1989). The Roman Fenland: a review of recent work, in M. Todd (ed.), *Research on Roman Britain 1969–89*. London: Britannia Monogr., 11: 147–73.

Powell, W. R. (1973a). East Ham. *VCH Essex*, 6: 1–42.

Powell, W. R. (1973b). West Ham. *VCH Essex*, 6: 43–163.

Powell, W. R. (1978). Hornchurch. *VCH Essex*, 7: 25–56.

Powell, W. R. and Knight, N. (1983a). Aveley. *VCH Essex*, 8: 1–17.

Powell, W. R. and Knight, N. (1983b). West Thurrock. *VCH Essex*, 8: 57–74.

Powell-Cotton, P. H. G. and Pinfold, G. F. (1939). The Beck find: prehistoric and Roman Site on the foreshore at Minnis Bay. *Archaeologia Cantiana*, 51: 191–203.

Pratt, S. (1997). A249 *Iwade Bypass to Queenborough improvement environmental statement, volume 2, part 2. Cultural Heritage.* London: Heighways Agency/Mott MacDonald.

Price, J. and Wilson, P. R. (1988). *Recent research in Roman Yorkshire.* Oxford: BAR 193.

Priestley, H. E. (1984). *A history of Benfleet. Book Two—Modern Times.* Benfleet: Castle Point District Council.

Prummel, W. (1989). Iron Age animal husbandry, hunting, fowling and fishing on Voorne-Putten, The Netherlands. *Palaeohistoria,* 31: 235–65.

Pryor, A. (1978). The Car Dyke. *Durobrivae,* 6: 24–5.

Pryor, F. (1980). *Excavations at Fengate, Peterborough: the third report.* Northants. Archaeol Soc. Monogr., 1.

Pugh, R. B. (1953). *Victoria County History of Cambridge IV.* London: Inst. of Hist. Res.

Purcell, N. (1981). Rome and the management of water: environment, culture and power, in G. Shipley and J. Salmon (eds.) *Human landscapes in classical antiquity.* London: Routledge, 180–212.

Purcell, N. 1995. Eating fish: the paradoxes of sea food, in J. Wilkins, D. Harvey, and M. Dobson (eds.) *Food in antiquity.* Exeter: Exeter Univ. Press, 132–49.

Raban, S. (1977). *The estates of Thorney and Crowland: study in medieval monastic land tenure.* Cambridge: Univ. of Cambridge Dept of Land Economics Occ. Pap.,7.

Rackham, O. (1986a). *A history of the countryside.* London: Dent.

Rackham, O. (1986b). *The ancient woodland of England: the woods of South-east Essex.* Southend: Rochford District Council.

Raftis, J. A. (1957). *The estates of Ramsey Abbey.* Toronto: Pontifical Inst. of Med. Studies.

Rahtz, P. and Meeson, R. (1992). *An Anglo-Saxon watermill at Tamworth.* York: CBA Res. Rep., 83.

Rahtz, S. and Rowley, T. (1984). *Middleton Stoney: excavations and survey in a North Oxfordshire Parish 1970–1982.* Oxford: Oxford Univ. Dept for External Studies.

Rahtz, P., Woodward, A., Burrow, I., Everton, A., Watts, L., Leach, P., Hirst, S., Fowler, P., and Gardner, K. (1992). *Cadbury Congresbury: a Late/post-Roman Hilltop.* Oxford: BAR 223.

Ransome, D. R. (1978). Rainham. *VCH Essex,* 7: 126–43.

Ranwell, D. S. (1972). *Ecology of salt marshes and sand dunes.* London: Chapman and Hall.

RCHME (1970). *An inventory of historical monuments in the County of Dorset, Volume 2. South-East, part 3.* London: HMSO.

Reade, R. C. (1885). The Roman villa at Great Wemberham. *Proc. Somerset Archaeol. Nat. Hist. Soc.,* 31/2; 64–73.

Reader, F. W. (1908). Report of the Red Hills Exploration Committee, 1906–7. *Proc. Soc. Antiq London.,* 22: 164–214.

Reader, F. W. (1910). Report of the Red Hills Excavation Committee 1908–9. *Proc. Soc. Antiq London,* 23: 66–96.

Reader, F. W. (1911). A Neolithic floor in the head of the Crouch River and other discoveries near Rayleigh, Essex. *Essex Naturalist,* 16: 249–64.

Reaney, P. H. (1935). *The place-names of Essex.* English Place-name Soc., XII.

Reaney, P. H. (1959). A survey of Kent place-names. *Archaeologia Cantiana,* 63: 62–74.

Reaney, P. H. and Fitch, M. (1964). *Feet of Fines for Essex IV* AD *1423–1547.* Colchester: Essex Archaeol. Soc.

Reed, D. J. (1990). The impact of sea level rise on coastal salt marshes. *Progress in Phy. Geogr.,* 14/iv: 465–81.

Rees, H. (1986). Ceramic salt working debris from Droitwich. *Trans. Worcestershire Archaeol. Soc.,* 3rd Ser. 10: 47–54.

Rees, S. E. (1979). *Agricultural implements in prehistoric and Roman Britain.* Oxford: BAR 69.

Reeves, A. (1995*a*). Romney Marsh: the fieldwalking evidence, in J. Eddison (ed.), 78–91.

Reeves, A. (1995*b*). Romney Marsh earthworks. *The Romney Marsh Irregular.* Newsletter of the Romney Marsh Res. Trust, 10: 2–3.

Rendel, W. V. (1880). Changes in the course of the Rother. *Archaeologia Cantiana,* 13: 63–76.

Reynolds, J., Beard, M., and Roueche, C. (1986). Roman inscriptions. *J. Roman Studies,* 76: 124–47.

Reynolds, T. (1994). An Iron Age/Romano-British settlement at Milton. *Fenland Res.,* 9: 50–5.

Rhoades, J. D., Kandiah, A., and Mashali, A. M. (1992). *The use of saline waters for crop production.* F.A.O. Irrigation and Drainage Papers, 48.

Richards, M. P., Molleson, T. I., Vogel, J. C., and Hodges, R. E. M., forthcoming. Stable Isotope analysis reveals variations in human diet at the Poundbury Camp Cemetery Site. *J. Archaeol. Sci.,* 25: 1247–52.

Richmond, I. A. (1963). *Roman Britain* (2nd edn). Harmondsworth: Pelican.

Ridder, T. de (1997). Inheems-Romeidse Deltawerken op Bedrijvenpark Hoogstad. *Terra Negra. Mededelingen-en contactblad van afdeling 8 van de Archeologische Werkgemeenschap voor Nederland,* 140: 28–48.

Ridder, T. de (1998). Nederlandse boeren waren de vroegste waterstaatkundige ingenieurs, in K. d'Angremond *et al.* (eds.) *Watertovenaars: Delftse indeeën voor nog 200 jaar Rijkswaterstaat.* beta imaginations publishers, 17–23.

Riehm, K. (1961). Prehistoric salt-boiling. *Antiquity,* 35: 181–91.

Rigold, S. E. (1969). The Roman haven at Dover. *Archaeol. J.,* 126: 78–100.

Rijn, P. Van (1993). Wooden remains, in R. M. Van Dierendonck, D. P. Hallewas, and K. E. Waugh (eds.) *The Valkenburg excavations 1985–1988: introduction and detailed studies.* Amersfoort: ROB Nederlandse Oudheden, 15: 146–216.

Rijniersce, K. (1982). A simulation for physical soil-ripening in the Ijsselmeer polders, in *Polders of the world, Volume 1. Polder projects, land and water management aspects.* Wageningen, 407–17.

Riley, D. (1980). *Early landscapes from the air.* Sheffield, Dept of Prehistory & Archaeol., Univ. of Sheffield.

Riley, D. N., Buckland, P. C. and Wade, J. S. (1995). Aerial reconnaissance and excavation at Littleborough-on-Trent, Notts. *Britannia,* 26: 253–84.

Riley, H. T. (1874*a*). Register of St. Catherine's College, Cambridge. *Hist. Man. Comm.* 4th Rep., pt. 1: 426–8.

Riley, H. T. (1874*b*). Manuscripts of the Corporation of Hythe, Kent. *Hist. Man. Comm.* 4th Rep., pt. 1: 429–39.

Riley, H. T. (1874*c*). Manuscripts of the Corporation of New Romney. *Hist. Man. Comm.* 4th Rep., pt. 1: 439–42.

Riley, H. T. (1876*a*). Manuscripts of the Corporation of Rye. *Hist. Man. Comm.* 5th Rep., pt. 1: 488–516.

Riley, H. T. (1876*b*). The Corporation of Lydd, Kent. *Hist. Man. Comm.* 5th Rep., pt. 1: 516–33.

Riley, H. T. (1876*c*). Manuscripts of the Corporation of New Romney Second Notice. *Hist. Man. Comm.* 5th Rep., pt. 1: 533–54.

Rippon, S. (1991). Early planned landscapes in South East Essex. *Essex Archaeol. Hist.,* 22: 46–60.

Rippon, S. (1994*a*). Medieval wetland reclamation in Somerset, in M. Aston and C. Lewis (eds.), 239–53.

Rippon, S. (1994*b*). The Roman settlement and landscape at Kenn Moor, North Somerset: report on survey and excavation 1993/4. *Archaeology in the Severn Estuary 1994,* 21–34.

Rippon, S. (1995*a*). Human–environment relations in the Gwent Levels. Ecology and the historic landscape in a Coastal Wetland, in M. Cox *et al.*, 62–74.

Rippon, S. (1995*b*). The Roman settlement and landscape at Kenn Moor, North Somerset: interim report on survey and excavation 1994/5. *Archaeology in the Severn Estuary 1995,* 35–47.

Rippon, S. (1995*c*). Roman settlement and salt production on the Somerset coast: the work of Samuel Nash—a Somerset archaeologist and historian 1913–1985. *Somerset Archaeol. Nat. Hist.,* 139: 99–17.

Rippon, S. (1996*a*). *The Gwent Levels: the exploitation of a wetland landscape.* York: CBA Res. Rep., 105.

Rippon, S. (1996*b*). Essex *c.*700–1066, in O. Bedwin (ed.), *The archaeology of Essex. Proc. Writtle Conference.* Chelmsford: Essex County Council, 117–28.

Rippon, S. (1996*c*). Roman and medieval settlement on the North Somerset Levels. Survey and excavation at Banwell and Puxton, 1996. *Archaeology in the Severn Estuary 1996,* 39–52.

Rippon, S. (1997*a*). *The Severn Estuary: landscape evolution and wetland reclamation.* London: Leicester Univ. Press.

Rippon, S. (1997*b*). Wetland reclamation on the Gwent Levels. Dissecting an historic landscape, in N. Edwards (ed.) *Landscape and settlement in Medieval Wales.* Oxford: Oxbow Monogr., 81: 13–31.

Rippon, S. (1997*c*). Roman and medieval settlement on the North Somerset Levels. The second season of survey and excavation at Banwell and Puxton, 1997. *Archaeology in the Severn Estuary 1997,* 41–54.

Rippon, S. (1998). Roman and medieval settlement on the North Somerset Levels. The third season of survey and excavation at Banwell and Puxton, 1998. *Archaeology in the Severn Estuary 1998,* 69–78.

Rippon, S. (1999). Romano-British reclamation of coastal wetlands, in H. Cook and T. Williamson (eds.), 101–21.

Rippon, S., forthcoming *a*. The Romano-British exploitation of coastal wetlands. Survey and excavation in the North Somerset Levels, 1993–7. *Britannia,* 31 (for the year 2000).

Rippon, S., forthcoming *b*. The Rayleigh Hills in South East Essex. patterns in the exploitation of rural resources in a 'woodland' landscape, in S. Green (ed.), *The Essex landscape: in search of its history.* Chelmsford: Essex County Council, 20–8.

Rippon, S., forthcoming *c*. Reclamation and regional economies of medieval marshland in Britain, in B. Raftery (ed.), *Recent developments in wetland research.* Dublin: Univ. College Dublin.

Rippon, S., forthcoming *d*. 'Fields of beans and flocks of sheep': the perception of wetland landscapes during the medieval period, in M. G. Bell and A. Boardman (eds.), *Geoarchaeology: landscape change over archaeological timescales.* Oxford: Oxbow.

Roberts, B. K. (1996). 'The great plough': a hypothesis concerning village genesis and land reclamation in Cumberland and Westmoreland. *Landscape Hist.,* 18: 17–30.

Robertson, A. J. (1939). *Anglo-Saxon charters.* Cambridge: Cambridge Univ. Press.

Robertson, W. A. S. (1880*a*). Destroyed churches of New Romney. *Archaeologia Cantiana,* 13: 237–49.

Robertson, W. A. S. (1880*b*). The Cinque Port Liberty of Romney. *Archaeologia Cantiana,* 13: 261–80.

Robertson, W. A. S. (1880*c*). Romney, old and new. The Saxon ville of St. Martin. *Archaeologia Cantiana,* 13: 349–73.

Robertson, W. A. S. (1880*d*). Churches in Romney Marsh. *Archaeologia Cantiana,* 13: 408–87.

Robinson, D. N. (1970). Coastal evolution in North East Lincolnshire. *East Midland Geogr.,* 5: 62–70.

Robinson, D. N. (1984). The buried forest of Lincolnshire, in N. Field and A. White (eds.), 6–10.

Robinson, G. (1988). Sea defence and land drainage of Romney Marsh, in J. Eddison and C. Green, C. (eds.), 162–6.

Rodwell, K. A. (1983). The excavation of a Romano-British pottery kiln at Palmer's School, Grays, Essex, *Essex Archaeol. & Hist.,*15: 11–35.

Rodwell, K. A. (1988). *The prehistoric and Roman settlement at Kelvedon, Essex.* London: CBA Res. Rep., 63.

Rodwell, W. (1965*a*). Canvey Island. *Trans. Essex Archaeol. Soc.,* 1 3rd Ser.: 265.

Rodwell, W. (1965*b*). Canvey Island, in D. M. Wilson and D. G. Hurst (eds.), Medieval Britain in 1964, *Medieval Archaeol.,* 9: 170–220.

Rodwell, W. (1966). The excavations of a 'Red Hill' on Canvey Island. *Trans. Essex Archaeol. Soc.,* 3rd Ser. 2/I: 14–33.

Rodwell, W. (1968*a*). Canvey Island, *Trans. Essex Archaeol. Soc.,* 3rd Ser. 2/ii: 158.

Rodwell, W. (1968*b*). Canvey Island, *Trans. Essex Archaeol. Soc.,* 3rd Ser. 2/iii: 329.

Rodwell, W. (1971). *South East Essex in Roman times.* Southend: Southend Museum publication.

Rodwell, W. (1974). Canvey Island. *Essex Archaeol. News* 48: 3.

Rodwell, W. (1976*a*). Roman and medieval finds from South Benfleet. *Essex Archaeol. & Hist.,* 8: 259–63.

Rodwell, W. J. (1976*b*). Early Anglo-Saxon Pottery from Canvey Island. *Essex Archaeol. & Hist.,* 8: 265–7.

Rodwell, W. J. (1978*a*). Rivenhall and the emergence of first century villas in Northern Essex, in M. Todd (ed.), *Studies in the Romano-British villa.* Leicester: Leicester Univ. Press, 11–32.

Rodwell, W. J. (1978*b*). Relict landscapes in Essex, in H. C. Bowen and P. J. Fowler (eds.) *Early land allotment.* Oxford: BAR 48: 89–98.

Rodwell, W. (1979). Iron Age and Roman salt-winning on the Essex Coast, in B. C. Burnham and H. B. Johnson (eds.) *Invasion and response—the case of Roman Britain.* Oxford: BAR 73: 133–74.

Rodwell, W. (1982). The production and distribution of pottery and tiles in the territory of the Trinovantes. *Essex Archaeol. & Hist.,* 14: 15–86.

Rodwell, W. J. and Rodwell, K. A. (1993). *Rivenhall: investigations of a villa, church and village, 1950–1977. Volume 2—specialist studies.* London: CBA Res. Rep., 80.

Roeleveld, W. (1974). *The Holocene evolution of the Groningen marine clay district.* Amersfoort: Berichten Van de Rijksdienst voor het Oudheidkundig Bodemonderzoek Supplement Jaargang, 24.

Roffe, D. (1993*a*). *On Middan Gyrwan Fenne.* Intercommoning around the Island of Crowland. *Fenland Res.,* 8: 80–6.

Roffe, D. (1993*b*). Domesday settlement, in S. Bennett and N. Bennett (eds.), 34–5.

Rogerson, A. (1976). Excavations on Fuller's Hill, Great Yarmouth. *East Anglian Archaeol.*, 2: 131–245.

Rostovtzeff, M. (1957). *The social and economic history of the Roman Empire* (2nd edn). Oxford: Clarendon Press.

Round, H. (1903). The Domesday Book, *VCH Essex,* 1: 333–578.

Rowlands, I. W. (1980). The making of the March: aspects of the Norman settlement in Dyfed. *Proc. Battle Conference on Anglo-Norman Studies,* III: 142–57.

Rowley, T. (1974). *Anglo-Saxon settlement and landscape.* Oxford: BAR 6.

Roymans, N. (1996). The Sword or the plough. Regional dynamics in the Romanisation of Belgic Gaul and the Rhineland area, in N. Roymans (ed.), *From the sword to the plough. Three studies in the earliest Romanisation of Northern Gaul.* Amsterdam: Amsterdam Univ. Press, 9–126.

Rudkin, E. H. (1975). Medieval salt making in Lincolnshire, in K. de Brisay and K. Evans (eds.), 37–40.

Rudkin, E. H. and Owen, D. M. (1960). The medieval salt-industry in the Lindsey marshland. *Lincolnshire Architectural & Archaeol. Soc. Rep. & Pap.,* 8: 76–84.

Rudling, D. R. (1990). Late Iron Age and Roman Billericay. *Essex Archaeol. & Hist.,* 21: 19–47.

Rycroft, D. W. and Amer, M. H. (1995). *Prospects for the drainage of clay soils.* F.A.O. Irrigation and Drainage Pap., 51.

Sabin, A. (1960). *Some manorial accounts of St Augustine's, Bristol.* Bristol Records Society, XXII.

Salisbury, C. (1991). Primitive British fishweirs, in G. L. Good *et al.* (eds.), 76–87.

Salisbury, C. (1992). The archaeological evidence for palaeochannels in the Trent Valley, in S. Needham and M. G. Macklin (eds.) *Alluvial archaeology in Britain.* Oxford: Oxbow Monogr., 27: 155–62.

Salway, P. (1967). Excavations at Hockwold-cum-Wilton, Norfolk, 1961–2. *Proc. Cambridge Antiq. Soc.,* 60: 39–80.

Salway, P. (1970). The Roman Fenland, in C. W. Phillips (ed.), 1970: 1-21.

Salway, P. (1980). The Lincolnshire Car Dyke. Navigation or drainage? *Britannia,* 11: 337–8.

Salway, P. (1981). *Roman Britain.* Oxford: Clarendon Press.

Salzman, L. F. (1910). The inning of Pevensey Level. *Sussex Archaeol. Coll.,* 53: 32–60.

Salzman, L. F. (1937). Broomhill. *VCH Kent,* 9: 148–50.

Samuels, J. and Buckland, P. C. (1978). A Romano-British settlement at Sandtoft, South Humberside. *Yorks. Archaeol. J.,* 50: 65–75.

Sawyer, P. H. (1968). *Anglo-Saxon charters: an annotated list and bibliography.* London: Roy. Hist. Soc.

Scargill-Bird, S. R. (1887). *Custumals of Battle Abbey.* London: Camden Society, New Ser. 41.

Schmid, P. (1990*a*). Habitation and diking in Land Wursten, in K.-E. Behre (ed.), 95–6.

Schmid, P. (1990*b*). The Wurt Feddersen wierde, in K.-E. Behre (ed.), 97–9.

Schofield, J. A. (1981). Medieval waterfront buildings in the City of London, in G. Milne and B. Hobley (eds.), 24–31.

Schoute, J. F. TH. (1984). *Vegetation horizons and related phenomena. A palaeoecological–micromorphological study in the younger coastal Holocene of the northern Netherlands Schilmeer area.* Hirschberg: Strauss and Gramner.

Schoorl, M. (1997). Diking and settlement in The Netherlands up till the building of the

Afsluitdijk, in C. U. Larsen (ed.) *Workshop on the cultural heritage in the Waffen Sea region.* Copenhagen: The National Forest and Nature Agency, 2–36

Scott, J. R. (1876). Charters of the monks of Horton Priory. *Archaeologia Cantiana,* 10: 269–81.

Sealey, P. R. (1995). New light on the salt industry and red hills of prehistoric and Roman Essex. *Essex Archaeol. & Hist.,* 26: 65–81.

Searle, E. (1974). *Lordship and community. Battle Abbey and its banlieu 1066–1538.* Toronto: Pontifical Inst. of Med. Studies.

Searle, E. (1980). *The Chronicle of Battle Abbey.* Oxford: Clarendon Press.

Searle, E. and Ros, B. (1967). *Accounts of the Cellarers of Battle Abbey, 1275–1513.* Sydney: Sydney Univ. Press.

Seeman, M. (1987). Faunal remains of excavations during 1978 and 1979, in R. W. Brandt *et al.* (eds.), 91–7.

Shennan, I. (1982*a*). Problems of correlating Flandrian sea-level changes and climate, in A. Harding (ed.), 52–67.

Shennan, I. (1982*b*). Interpretation of Flandrian sea-level data from Fenland, England. *Proc. Geol. Ass.,* 93: 53–63.

Shennan, I. (1986*a*). Flandrian sea-level changes in the Fenland I: the geographical setting and evidence of relative sea level changes. *J. Quaternary Sci.,* 1: 119–54.

Shennan, I. (1986*b*). Flandrian sea-level changes in the Fenland II: tendencies of sea level movement, altitudinal changes, and local and regional factors. *J. Quaternary Sci.,* 1: 155–79.

Shennan, I. (1994). Hypothesis testing, in M. Waller (ed.), 81–4.

Shenstone, J. C. (1907). Oyster fisheries. *VCH Essex,* 2: 425–39.

Sheppard, J. (1957). The medieval meres of Holderness. *Inst. Brit. Geogr. Trans & Pap.,* 23: 75–86.

Sheppard, J. (1958). *The draining of the Hull Valley.* York: East Yorkshire Local Hist. Soc.

Sheppard, J. (1966). *The drainage of the marshlands of South Holderness and the Vale of York.* York: East Yorkshire Local Hist. Soc.

Sheppard, J. B. (1876). The manuscripts of Canterbury Cathedral. *Hist. Man. Comm.* 5th Rep., pt. 1: 126–62.

Sheppard, J. B. (1877). *Christchurch Letters. A volume of medieval letters relating to the affairs of the Priory of Christ Church, Canterbury.* London: Camden Society New Ser., 19.

Sheppard, J. B. (1881). Second report on historical MSS. Belonging to the Dean and Chapter of Canterbury. *Hist. Man. Comm.* 8th Rep., pt. 1: 315–55.

Sheppard, J. B. (1883). Third report on historical MSS. Belonging to the Dean and Chapter of Canterbury. *Hist. Man. Comm.* 9th Rep., pt. 1: 73–129.

Sherley-Price, L. (1969). *Bede. A history of the English Church and people.* London: Penguin.

Silvester, R. J. (1988). *The Fenland Survey, Number 3. Norfolk Survey Marshland & Nar Valley.* East Anglian Archaeol., 45.

Silvester, R. J. (1991). *The Fenland Project, Number 4. Norfolk Survey, The Wissey Embayment & Fen Causeway.* East Anglian Archaeol., 35.

Silvester, R. J. (1993). 'The addition of more-or-less undifferentiated dots to a distribution map'? The Fenland Project in retrospect, in J. Gardiner (ed.), 24–39.

Simmons, B. B. (1975). Salt making in the silt fens of Lincolnshire in the Iron Age and Roman periods, in K. de Brisay and K. Evans (eds.), 33–6.

Simmons, B. B. (1979). The Lincolnshire Car Dyke. Navigation or drainage? *Britannia,* 10: 183–96.

Simmons, B. B. (1980). Iron Age and Roman coasts around The Wash, in F. H. Thompson (ed.), 56–73.

Simmons, B. (1993*a*). Iron Age and Roman coasts around The Wash. I: The background, in S. Bennett and N. Bennett (eds.), 18–19.

Simmons, B. (1993*b*). Iron Age and Roman coasts around The Wash. I: Archaeology, in S. Bennett and N. Bennett (eds.), 20–21.

Sitch, P. (1989). A small Roman port at Faxfleet, near Broomfleet, in P. Halkon (ed.) *New light on the Parisi*. Hull: East Riding Archaeol. Soc., 10–14.

Sitch, P. (1990). Faxfleet 'B', a Romano-British site near Broomfleet, in S. Ellis, S. and D. R. Crowther (eds.), 158–71.

Smit, E. M. A. and Janssen, C. R. (1983). Late Holocene vegetational diversity in an oxbow of the Dommel River, The Netherlands. *BROB*, 33: 95–106.

Smith, A. (1963). Regional differences in crop production in medieval Kent. *Archaeologia Cantiana*, 78: 147–60.

Smith, A. H. (1964). *The place-names of Gloucestershire, Part 1*. English Place-names Soc., 38.

Smith, C. and Parry, M. (1981). *Consequences of climatic change*. Nottingham: Dept. of Geography, Univ. of Nottingham.

Smith, C. D. (1996). Where was the 'wilderness' in Roman times?, in G. Shipley and J. Salmon (eds.) *Human landscapes in classical antiquity*. London: Routledge, 154–79.

Smith, C. R. (1880). The Shorne, Higham, and Cliffe Marshes. *Archaeologia Cantiana*, 13: 494–99.

Smith, J. R. (1970). *Foulness. A history of an Essex island parish*. Chelmsford: Essex Records Office.

Smith, P. D. E., Allan, J. P., Hamlin, A., Orme, B., and Wootton, R. (1983). The investigation of a medieval shell midden in Braunton Burrows. *Proc. Devon Archaeol. Soc.*, 41: 75–86.

Smith, R. A. (1917/18). The Essex red hills as salt-works. *Proc. Soc. Antiq. London*, 2nd Ser. 30: 36–53.

Smith, R. A. L. (1940). Marsh embankment and sea defence in medieval Kent. *Econ. Hist. Rev.*, 10/I: 29–37.

Smith, R. A. L. (1943). *Canterbury Cathedral Priory. A study in monastic administration*. Cambridge: Cambridge Univ. Press.

Smith, R. E. F. and Christian, D. (1984). *Bread and salt. A social and economic history of food and drink in Russia*. Cambridge: Cambridge Univ. Press.

Smoothy, M. D. (1989). A Roman rural site at Rayne, Essex: excavations 1987. *Essex Archaeol. & Hist.*, 20: 1–29.

Smyth, C. and Jennings, S. (1988). Mid- to late-Holocene forest composition and the effects of clearances in the Combe Haven Valley, East Sussex. *Sussex Archaeol. Coll.*, 126: 1–20.

Somerville, E. (1997). The oysters, in M. G. Fulford, S. J. Rippon, S. Ford, J. Timby, and B. Williams, 'Silchester. Excavations at the North Gate, on the North Walls, and in the Northern Suburbs 1988 and 1991–3'. *Britannia*, 28: 135–9.

Somerville, E., forthcoming. The shellfish, in M. G. Fulford and S. J. Rippon (eds.), Excavations at Pevensey Castle, Sussex, 1993–95. *Archaeol. J.*

Sommé, J. 1979. Quaternary coastlines in northern France, in E. Oele *et al.* (eds.), 147–58.

Spencer, C. D., 'The Holocene evolution of Romney Marsh: a record of sea-level change in a back-barrier environment'. Ph.D. thesis (Liverpool, 1996).

Spencer, C. D., Plater, A. and Long, A. (1998*a*). Holocene barrier estuary evolution. The sedimentary record of the Walland Marsh region, in J. Eddison *et al.* (eds.), 13–29.

Spencer, C. D., Plater, A. J. and Long, A. J. (1998*b*). Rapid coastal change during the mid- to Late Holocene. the record of barrier estuary sedimentation in the Romney Marsh region, Southeast England. *Holocene,* 8.2: 143–63.

Spencer, P. J. (1993). Fish remains from Mytongate, in D. H. Evans, *Excavations in Hull 1975–76.* York: East Riding Archaeol. Soc.

Spurrell, F. C. J. (1885). Early sites and embankments on the margins of the Thames Estuary. *Archaeol. J.,* 42: 269–302.

Spurrell, F. C. J. (1889/90). On the estuary of the Thames and its alluvium. *Proc. Geol. Ass. London,* 11: 210–30.

Stacey, N. R., 'The estates of Glastonbury Abbey *c*1050–1200'. Ph.D thesis (Leeds, 1972).

Stallibrass, S. (1996). The animal bones, in R. P. J. Jackson and T. W. Potter, *Excavations at Stonea, Cambridgeshire 1980–85.* London: British Museum.

Start, D. (1993). *Lincolnshire from the air.* Lincoln: Heritage Trust of Lincolnshire.

Stead, I. M. (1976). *Excavations at Winterton Roman villa and other Roman sites in North Lincolnshire.* London: HMSO.

Stead, I. M. (1991). The Snettisham Treasure: excavation in 1990. *Antiquity,* 248: 447–464.

Steane, J. M. and Foreman, M. (1988). Medieval fishing tackle, in M. Aston (ed.), 137–86.

Steers, J. A, (1969). *The coastline of England and Wales.* Cambridge: Cambridge Univ. Press.

Stenton, F. M. (1971). *Anglo-Saxon England* (3rd edn). Oxford: Clarendon Press.

Strachan, D. (1996). Aerial survey 1995, in A. Bennett (ed.), 'Work of the Essex County Council Archaeology Section, 1995'. *Essex Archaeol. & Hist.,* 27: 247–60.

Strachan, D. (1998*a*). *Essex from the air.* Chelmsford: Essex County Council.

Strachan, D. (1998*b*). Inter-tidal stationary fishing structures in Essex: some C14 dates. *Essex Archaeol. & Hist.,* 29: 274–82.

Stradling, W. (1850). Turbaries. *Proc. Somerset Archaeol. & Nat. Hist. Soc.,* 1: 48–62.

Straw, A. (1955). The Ancholme Levels north of Brigg. *East Midlands Geogr.,* 3: 34–42.

Streif, H. (1982). The occurrence and significance of peat in the Holocene deposits of the German North Sea coast, in H. de Bakker and M. W. Van den Berg (eds.), 31–41.

Streurman, H. J. and Taayke, E. (1989). Vegetation horizons and 'frustrated terps'. new radiocarbon ages from the Paddepoel area near Groningen. *BROB,* 39: 345–56.

Stringer, H. (1880). Lydd Records. *Archaeologia Cantiana,* 13: 250–5.

Sturman, C. J. (1984). Salt making on the Lindsey Coast in the 16th and early 17th centuries, in N. Field and A. White (eds.), 50–56.

Sunter, N. (1987). Excavations at Norden, Corfe Castle, Dorset, 1968–69, in N. Sunter and P. J. Woodward (eds.), 9–43.

Sunter, N. and Woodward, P. J. (1987). *Romano-British industries in Purbeck.* Dorchester: Dorset Nat. Hist. & Archaeol. Soc. Monogr., 6.

Swanton, M. (1996). *The Anglo-Saxon Chronicle.* London: J. M. Dent.

Swift, E. (1937). The Obedientiary Rolls of Battle Abbey. *Sussex Archaeol. Coll.* 78, 37–62.

Swinnerton, H. H. (1932). The prehistoric pottery sites of the Lincolnshire Coast. *Antiq. J.,* 12: 239–53.

Swinnerton, H. H. (1936). The physical history of east Lincolnshire. *Trans. Lincs. Naturalists Union,* 9: 91–100.

Sykes, J. B. (1976). *The concise Oxford dictionary of current English.* Oxford: Clarendon Press.

Sylvester, D. (1969). *The rural landscape of the Welsh Borderland.* London: Macmillan.

Tatton-Brown, T. (1984). The towns of Kent, in J. Haslam (ed.), *Anglo-Saxon towns in southern England.* Chichester: Phillimore, 1–36.

Tatton-Brown, T. (1987). St Nicholas's Church, New Romney. *Archaeologia Cantiana,* 104: 344–6.

Tatton-Brown, T. (1988). The topography of the Walland Marsh area between the eleventh and thirteenth centuries, in J. Eddison and C. Green (eds.), 105–11.

Tatton-Brown, T. (1989). Church building on Romney Marsh in the later Middle Ages. *Archaeologia Cantiana,* 107: 253–65.

TeBrake, W. H. (1985). *Medieval frontier: culture and ecology in Rijnland.* Texas: A&M Univ. Press.

Teichman Derville, M. (1936). *The Level and Liberty of Romney Marsh in the County of Kent.* Ashford and London: Headley Brothers.

Tent, W. J. Van and Woltering, P. J. (1973). The distribution of archaeological finds on the Island of Texel, Province of North Holland. *BROB,* 23: 49–64.

Ters, M. (1973). Les variations du niveau marin depuis 10,000 ans le long du littoral atlantique français, in *La Quaternaire. géodynamique, stratigraphique et environnement.* Christchurch, N.Z.: Congress International de l'Inqua, 114–35 .

Teunissen, D. (1986). Palynological investigations of some residual gullies in the Upper Betuwe, The Netherlands. *BROB,* 36: 7–24.

Therkorn, L. L. and Abbink, A. A. (1987). Seven levee sites: B, C, D, G, H, F and P, in R. W. Brandt *et al.* (eds.), 115–67.

Therkorn, l. L., Besselsen E. A., and Oversteegen, J. F. S. (1998). *Assendelver Polders Revisited: excavations 1997.* Faculty of Environmental Sciences, University of Amsterdam.

Thirsk, J. (1967). *The agrarian history of England and Wales IV, 1500–1640.* Cambridge: Cambridge Univ. Press.

Thoen, H. (1975). Iron Age and Roman salt-making sites on the Belgian Coast, in K. de Brisay and K. Evans (eds.), 56–60.

Thoen, H. (1978). *De Belgische Kustvlakte in de Romeinse Tijd.* Brussels: Paleis der Academiën.

Thoen, H. (1981). The third century Roman occupation in Belgium: the evidence of the coastal plain, in A. King and M. Henig (eds.), *The Roman West in the third century: contributions from archaeology and history.* Oxford: BAR S.109: 245–57.

Thompson, F. H. (1965). *Roman Cheshire.* Chester: Cheshire Community Council.

Thompson, F. H. (1980). *Archaeology and coastal change.* London: Soc. of Antiquaries.

Thompson, M. W. (1956). A group of mounds on Seasalter Level, near Whitstable, and the medieval imbanking in this area. *Archaeologia Cantiana,* 70: 44–67.

Thorpe, R. and Zeffertt, T. (1988/)9. Excavation of the Lincolnshire Car Dyke, Baston. *Fenland Res.,* 6: 10–15.

Tiggesbäumber, G. (1983). Regular settlement in 19th-century Transcaucasia as a characteristic feature of German colonisation, in B. K Roberts and R. E. Glasscock (eds.), *Villages, fields and frontiers.* Oxford: BAR S.185: 71–81.

Timby, J. and Williams, D. F. (2000). The briquetage, in M. Fulford and J. Timby *Late Iron Age and Roman Silchester.* London: Britannia, 15, 287–91.

Titow, J. (1960). Evidence of weather in the Account Rolls of the Bishopric of Winchester 1209–1350. *Econ. Hist. Rev.,* 12/3: 360–407.

Todd, M. (1977). *Famosa Pestis* and Britain in the fifth century. *Britannia,* 8: 319–25.

Todd, M. (1989). Villa and fundus, in K. Branigan and D. Miles (eds.) *The economies of Romano-British villas.* Sheffield: Dept of Archaeol. & Prehistory, Univ. of Sheffield, 14–20.

Todd, M. (1991). *The Coritani.* Stroud: Allan Sutton.

Toft, L. A. (1992). Roman quays and tide levels. *Britannia,* 22: 249–54.

Tomlin, R. S. O. (1996). A five-acre wood in Roman Kent, in J. Bird, M. Hassall, and H. Sheldon (eds.), *Interpreting Roman London.* Oxford: Oxbow Monogr., 58: 209–15.

Tooley, M. (1990). Sea level and coastline changes during the last 5000 years, in S. McGrail (ed.) *Maritime Celts, Frisians and Saxons.* London: CBA Res. Rep., 71: 1–16.

Tooley, M. (1995). Romney Marsh: the debatable ground, in J. Eddison (ed.), 1–7.

Törnqvist, T. E. (1990). Fluvial activity, human activity and vegetation 2300–600 yr BP near a residual channel in the Tieterwaard Central Netherlands. *BROB,* 40: 223–41.

Trimpe Burger, J. A. (1973). The islands of Zeeland and South Holland in Roman times. *BROB,* 23: 135–48.

Trimpe Burger, J. A. (1975). The geometrical fortress of Oost-Souburg Zeeland. *Chateau Gaillard,* 7: 215–19.

Turner, A. G. C. (1953). Some Old English passages relating to the episcopal manor of Taunton. *Proc. Somerset Archaeol. & Nat. Hist. Soc.,* 98: 118–26.

Turner, E. (1867). The lost towns of Northeye and Hydneye. *Sussex Archaeol. Coll.,* XIX: 1–35.

Turner, G. J. and Salter, H. E. (1915). *The Register of St Augustine's Abbey, Canterbury, commonly called the Black Book.* London: British Academy.

Tyers, P. (1984). An assemblage of Roman ceramics from London. *London Archaeol.,* 4.14: 367–74.

Tys, D. (1997). Landscape and settlement the development of a medieval village along the Flemish Coast, in G. de Boe and F. Verhaeghe (eds.), *Rural settlements in medieval Europe.* Zellik: I.A.P. Rapporten 6, 157–67.

Vaughan, R. (1993). *The illustrated chronicles of Matthew Paris.* Gloucester: Alan Sutton.

Veale, E. W. W. (1937). *The Great Red Book of Bristol: text part II.* Bristol Rec. Soc., VIII.

Verhaeghe, F. (1981). Moated sites in Flanders: features and significance, in T. J. Hoekstra, H. L. Janssen, and I. W. L. Moerman (eds.), *Liber Castellorum: 40 variaties op het thema kasteel.* Zutphen: De Walburg Pers, 98–121.

Vernimmen, A. P. and Heijligers, J. P. (1982). Protecting the North-Holland polder area against flooding. *Polders of the world, vol. 1. Polder projects, land and water management aspects.* Wageningen, Netherlands: 15–24 .

Vince, A. (1993). Lincolnshire in the Anglo-Saxon period, *c.*450–1066, in S. Bennett and N. Stewart (eds.), 22–3.

Vollans, E. (1988). New Romney and the 'river of Newenden' in the later Middle Ages, in J. Eddison and C. Green (eds.), 128–41.

Vollans, E. (1995). Medieval salt-making and inning of the tidal marshes at Belgar, Lydd, in J. Eddison (ed.), 118–26.

Vos, P. C., (1999). The sub-Atlantic evolution of the coastal area around the Wijnaldum-Tjitsma terp, in J. C. Besteman *et al.* (eds.), 33–72.

Vos, P. C. and Heeringen, R. M. Van (1997). Holocene geology and occupation history of the Province of Zeeland, SW Netherlands. *Mededelingen Nederlands Instituut voor Toegepaste Geowetenschappen TNO,* 59: 5–109.

Vos, P. C. and Wolf, H. de (1997). Palaeo-environmental diatom study of the Holocene deposits of the Province of Zeeland, SW Netherlands. *Mededelingen Nederlands Instituut voor Toegepaste Geowetenschappen TNO,* 59: 111–41.

Wacher, J. 1995. *The towns of Roman Britain* (2nd edn). London: Batsford.

Wade, K. (1980). A settlement site at Bonhunt Farm, Wicken Bonhunt, Essex. In Buckley, D. (ed.), *Archaeology in Essex to AD 1500.* London: 96–102.

Waddelove, A. C. and Waddelove, E. (1990). Archaeology and research into sea-level during the Roman era: towards a methodology based on Highest Astronomical Tide. *Britannia,* 21: 253–64.

Wade-Martins, P. (1980). *Excavations in North Elmham Park 1967–72.* East Anglian Archaeol., 9.

Walker, D. (1998). *The cartulary of St. Augustine's Abbey, Bristol.* Bristol: Bristol & Gloucester Archaeol. Soc.

Walker, E. B. (1880). The town and port of New Romney. *Archaeologia Cantiana,* 13: 201–215.

Walker, G. P. (1927). The lost Wantsum Channel: its importance to Richborough Castle. *Archaeologia Cantiana,* 39: 91–112.

Walker, H. (1996). Tollesbury, Old Hall Marshes, in A. Bennett (ed.), 'Work of the Essex County Council Archaeology Section, 1995', *Essex Archaeol. & Hist.* 27, 247–60.

Walker, K. (1955). The battle of the Clacton Peninsula: man versus the sea. *Essex Rev.,* 14: 103–11.

Walkins, D. R. (1994). *The Foundry: Excavations on Poole waterfront, 1986/7.* Dorchester: Dorset Nat. Hist. & Archaeol. Soc. Monogr., 14.

Wallenberg, J. K. (1931). *Kentish place-names. A topographical and etymological study of the place-name material in Kentish charters dated before the Conquest.* Uppsala: Appelbergs Boktryckeriaktiebolag.

Wallenberg, J. K. (1934). *The place-names of Kent.* Uppsala: Appelbergs Boktryckeriaktiebolag.

Waller, M. P. (1993). Flandrian vegetational history of south-eastern England. Pollen data from Pannel Bridge, East Sussex. *New Phytol.,* 124: 345–69.

Waller, M. P. (1994*a*). *The Fenland Project, Number 9. Flandrian environmental change in Fenland.* East Anglian Archaeol., 70.

Waller, M. P. (1994*b*). Flandrian vegetational history of south-eastern England. Stratigraphy of the Brede Valley and pollen data from Brede Bridge. *New Phytol.,* 126: 369–92.

Waller, M., Burrin, P., and Marlow, A. (1988). Flandrian sedimentation and palaeoenvironments in Pett Level, the Brede and lower Rother Valleys and Walland Marsh, in J. Eddison and C. Green (ed.), 3–29.

Wallis, S. (1993). Aerial survey of the Essex coast, in A. Bennett (ed.), 'Work of the Essex County Council Archaeology Section, 1992'. *Essex Archaeol. & Hist.,* 24: 185–94.

Wallis, S. and Waughman, M. (1998). *Archaeology and the landscape in the lower Blackwater Valley.* East Anglian Archaeol., 82.

Ward, A. (1997). Transhumance and settlement on the Welsh uplands: a view from the Black Mountain, in N. Edwards (ed.), 97–111.

Ward, E. M. (1920). The evolution of the Hastings coastline. *Geogr. J.,* 56: 107–123.

Ward, G. (1931). Saxon Lydd. *Archaeologia Cantiana,* 45: 29–37.

Ward, G. (1933*a*). Sand Tunes Boc. *Archaeologia Cantiana,* 45: 39–47.

Ward, G. (1933*b*). The list of Saxon churches in the Domesday Monachorum, and White Book of St. Augustine. *Archaeologia Cantiana.* 45: 60–77.

Ward, G. (1933*c*). The River Limen at Ruckinge. *Archaeologia Cantiana,* 45: 129–32.

Ward, G. (1933*d*). The Saxon charters of Burmarsh. *Archaeologia Cantiana.* 45: 133–141.

Ward, G. (1935). The forgotten Saxon nunnery at Saint Werburgh at Hoo. *Archaeologia Cantiana*, 47: 117–25.

Ward, G. (1936). The Wilmington Charter of AD 700. *Archaeologia Cantiana*, 48: 11–28.

Ward, G. (1940). The Wi-wara-wics. *Archaeologia Cantiana*. 53: 24–8.

Ward, G. (1944). The origins of Whitstable. *Archaeologia Cantiana*, 57: 51–5.

Ward, G. (1953). The Saxon history of the town and port of Romney. *Archaeologia Cantiana*, 65; 12–25.

Ward, J. (1987). 'Richer in land than in inhabitants'. South Essex in the Middle Ages, *c*.1066–*c*.1340', in K. Neale (ed.), *An Essex tribute: essays presented to Frederick Emmison*. London: Leopard's Head Press, 97–108.

Warren, S. H. (1932). Prehistoric timber structures associated with briquetage sites in Lincolnshire. *Antiq. J.*, XII: 254–6.

Wass, M. (1995). Proposed northern course of the Rother. A sedimentological and microfaunal investigation, in J. Eddison (ed.), 51–77.

Waterbolk, H. T. (1965/6). The occupation of Friesland in the prehistoric period. *BROB*, 15–16: 13–35.

Waterbolk, H. T. (1997). The cultural heritage of the Wadden landscape, in C. U. Larsen (ed.), *Workshop on the cultural heritage in the Waffen Sea region*. Copenhagen: The National Forest and Nature Agency, 5–22.

Welch, M. (1992). *Anglo-Saxon England*. London: Batsford/English Heritage.

Welldon Finn, R. (1962). Hampshire, in H. C. Darby and E. M. J. Campbell (eds.), 287–363.

Whitaker, W. (1889). *The geology of London and of part of the Thames Valley, vol. 1*. London: Memoirs of the Geological Survey of England and Wales.

White, D. A. (1967). Excavations on a Romano-British settlement on the fen-edge at Earith, Hunts., 1963–66. *Proc. Cambridge Antiq. Soc.*, LX: 7–18.

White, K. D. (1984). *Greek and Roman technology*. London: Thames and Hudson.

Whittle, A. (1982). Climate, grazing and man: notes towards the definition of a relationship, in A. Harding (ed.), 192–203.

Whitwell, B. (1988). Late Roman settlement on the Humber and Anglian beginnings, in J. Price and P. R. Wilson (eds.), 49–78.

Whitwell, J. B. (1982). *The Coritani. Some aspects of the Iron Age tribe and the Roman civitas*. Oxford: BAR 99.

Wickenden, N. P. (1986). Prehistoric settlement and the Romano-British small town of Heybridge, Essex. *Essex Archaeol. & Hist.*, 17: 7–68.

Wickenden, N. P. (1988). *Excavations at Great Dunmow, Essex*. E. Anglian Archaeol., 41.

Wickenden, N. P. (1992). *The temple and other sites in the north-eastern sector of Caesaromagus*. London: CBA Res. Rep., 75.

Wickenden, N. P. (1996). The Roman towns of Essex, in O. Bedwin (ed.), *The archaeology of Essex. Proc. Writtle Conference*. Chelmsford: Essex County Council, 76–94.

Wickham, H. (1876). On Roman pottery from Hoo. *Archaeologia Cantiana*, 10: 75–6.

Wilkinson, T. J. (1988). *Archaeology and environment in South Essex*. E. Anglian Archaeol., 42.

Wilkinson, T. J. and Murphy, P. L. (1995). *The archaeology of the Essex Coast, Vol. 1. The Hullbridge Survey*. E. Anglian Archaeol., 71.

Willems, W. J. H. (1981). Romans and Batavians, a regional study in the Dutch eastern Rivers Area I. *BROB*, 31: 7–218.

Willems, W. J. H. (1984). Romans and Batavians, a regional study in the Dutch eastern Rivers Area II. *BROB*, 34: 39–331.

Williams, D. F. (1977). The Romano-British Black-Burnished industry: an essay on characterisation by heavy metal analysis, in D. P. S. Peacock (ed.), *Pottery and early commerce*. London: Academic Press, 163–220.

Williams, J. H. (1979). *St Peters Street, Northampton. Excavations 1973–1976*. Northampton: Northampton Development Corporation Archaeological Monogr., 2.

Williams, J. H., Shaw, M., and Denham, V. (1985). *Middle Saxon palaces at Northampton*. Northampton: Northampton Development Corporation Archaeological Monogr., 4.

Williams, M. (1970). *The draining of the Somerset Levels*. Cambridge: Cambridge Univ. Press.

Williams, M. (1982). Marshland and waste, in L. Cantor (ed.), *The English medieval Landscape*. London: Croom Helm, 86–125.

Williams, M. (1990). Understanding wetlands, in M. Williams (ed.), *Wetlands: a threatened landscape*. Oxford: Blackwell, 1–41.

Williamson, T. (1987). Early coaxial field systems on the East Anglian boulder clay. *Proc. Prehist. Soc.*, 53: 419–31.

Williamson, T. (1988). Explaining regional landscapes: woodland and champion in southern and eastern England. *Landscape Hist.*, 10: 5–13.

Williamson, T. (1997a). *The Norfolk Broads. A landscape history*. Manchester: Manchester Univ. Press.

Williamson, T. (1997b). Fish, fur and feather. Man and nature in the post-medieval landscape, in K. Barker and T. Darvill (eds.), *Making English landscapes*. Oxford: Oxbow Monogr., 93: 92–17.

Wilson, D. G. (1975). Plant remains from the Graveney Boat and the early history of *Humulus lupulus. New Phytol.*, 75; 627–48.

Wilson, D. M. (1976a). *The archaeology of Anglo-Saxon England*. Cambridge: Cambridge Univ. Press.

Wilson, D. M. (1976b). Craft and industry, in D. M. Wilson (ed.), 253–81.

Wilson, E. M. C. (1933). The overseas trade of Bristol, in E. Power and M. M. Postan (eds.), *Studies in English trade in the fifteenth century*. London: Routledge, 183–246.

Winder, J., 'A study of the variation in oyster shells from archaeological sites and a discussion of oyster exploitation'. Ph.D. thesis (Southampton, 1993).

Wise, P. J. (1990). The archaeology of the Grimsby–Cleethorpes area, in S. Ellis and D. R. Crowther (eds.), 213–26.

Witney, K. P. (1989). The development of the Kentish marshes in the aftermath of the Norman Conquest. *Archaeologia Cantiana*, 107: 29–50.

Witney, K. P. (1991). Kentish land measurements of the thirteenth century. *Archaeologia Cantiana*, 109: 29–39.

Woltering, P. J. (1975). Occupation history of Texel, I: the excavations at Den Burg. *BROB*, 25: 7–36.

Woltering, P. J. (1979). Occupation history of Texel, II: archaeological survey, preliminary results. *BROB*, 29: 7–114.

Wood, H. (1883). Roman urns found near Rainham Creek, on the Medway. *Archaeologia Cantiana*, 15: 108–10.

Woodcock, A. (1988). Gazetteer of prehistoric, Roman and Saxon Sites in Romney Marsh and the surrounding area, in J. Eddison and C. Green (eds.), 177–85.

Woodcock, A. (1995). A Late Bronze Age waterlogged site at Shinewater Park near Eastbourne, East Sussex, England. *NewsWARP*, 18: 7–9.

Woodruff, C. E. (1917). Some early Visitation Rolls preserved at Canterbury. *Archaeologia Cantiana*, 32: 143–80.

Woodruff, C. E. (1934). Some early Kentish wills. *Archaeologia Cantiana*, 46: 27–35.

Woodward, A. and Leach, P. (1993). *The Uley Shrines. Excavation of a ritual complex on West Hill, Uley, Gloucestershire, 1977–9*. London: English Heritage.

Woodward, P. J. (1987a). The excavations of a Late Iron Age settlement and Romano-British industrial site at Ower, Dorset, in N. Sunter and P. J. Woodward (eds.), 44–124.

Woodward, P. J. (1987b). The excavations of an Late Iron Age and Romano-British settlement at Rope Lake Hole, Corfe Castle, Dorset, in N. Sunter and P. J. Woodward (eds.), 125–180.

Woodward, P. J., Davies, S. M., and Graham, A. H. 1993. *Excavations at the Old Methodist Chapel and Greyhound Yard, Dorchester, 1981–1984*. Dorchester: Dorset Nat. Hist. & Arch. Soc. Monogr., 12.

Woodwiss, S. (1992). *Iron Age and Roman salt production and the medieval town of Droitwich*. London: CBA Res. Rep., 81.

Wright, E. (1990). *The Ferriby Boats. Seacraft of the Bronze Age*. London: Routledge.

Wright, S. (1976). Barton Blount. Climatic or economic change? *Med. Archaeol.*, 20: 148–52.

Wymer, J. J. and Brown, N. R. (1995). *Excavations at North Shoebury: settlement and economy in South East Essex 1500* BC–AD *1500*. E. Anglian Archaeol., 75.

Young, A., *Locking Castle Business Park, West Wick, North Somerset. Archaeological watching brief*. Unpublished report (Avon Archaeological Unit, 1998).

Young, R. and Simmonds, T. (1995). Marginality and the nature of later prehistoric upland settlement in the north of England. *Landscape Hist.*, 17; 5–15.

Zagwijn, W. H. (1986). *Nederland in het Holoceen*. Haarlem: Rijks Geologische Dienst.

Zeist, W. Van. (1968). Prehistoric and early historic food plants in The Netherlands. *Palaeohistoria*, 14: 41–173.

Zeist, W. Van (1973). The environment of 'Het Torp' in its early phases. *BROB*, 23: 347–53.

Zeist, W. Van (1974). Palaeobotanical studies of settlement sites in the coastal area of The Netherlands. *Palaeohistoria*, 16: 223–371.

Zeist, W. Van (1989). Plant remains from a Middle Iron Age coastal-marsh site near Middelstrum: an intriguing cereal grain find. *Helinium*, 28/I: 103–16.

Zeist, W. Van, Van Hoorn, T. C., Bottema, S, and Woldring, H. (1976). An agricultural experiment in the unprotected saltmarsh. *Palaeohistoria*, 18: 111–53.

Zienkiewicz, J. D. (1986). *The legionary fortress baths at Caerleon I: the buildings*. Cardiff: Cadw.

Zienkiewicz, J. D. (1993). Excavations in the *Scamnum tribunorum* at Caerleon. The Legionary Museum Site 1983–5. *Britannia*, XXIV: 27–140.

Zimmermann, W. H. (1990). The archaeological investigations in the siedlungskammer Flögeln, in K.-E. Behre (ed.), 103–5.

Zimmermann, W. H. (1995). Mittelterliche und frühneuzeitliche Siedlungsspuren und Funde in Dorum, Samtgde. Land Wursten, Ldkr. Cuxhaven, Niedersachen. *Probleme der Küstenforschung im südlichen Nordseegebiet*, 23: 339–52.

Zimmermann, W. H. (1996). Die Besiedlung im Stadtgebiet von Wilhelmshaven in ur- und frühgeschlicher Zeit und ihre Erforschung, in F. W. Wulf (ed.), *Archäologische Denkmale in der Kreisfreien Stadt Wilhelmshaven* (Hannover), 9–44.

Index